ITALIAN POLITICS

The Istituto Cattaneo, founded in 1965, is a private, non-profit organization. It aims to promote, finance, and conduct research, studies, and other activities that contribute to the knowledge of contemporary Italian society and, especially, of the Italian political system.

This publication of the Istituto Cattaneo enjoys the support of the Italian foundation:

COMPAGNIA
di San Paolo

www.compagnia.torino.it

Recently published:

The Second Berlusconi Government, edited by Jean Blondel and Paolo Segatti, Volume 18

Italy between Europeanization and Domestic Politics, edited by Sergio Fabbrini and Vincent Della Sala, Volume 19

Quo Vadis? edited by Carlo Guarnieri and James L. Newell, Volume 20

ITALIAN POLITICS
The End of the Berlusconi Era?

EDITED BY

GRANT AMYOT

AND

LUCA VERZICHELLI

A Publication of the Istituto Cattaneo

Berghahn Books
NEW YORK • OXFORD

Italian Politics: A Review, Volume 21

First published in 2006 by
Berghahn Books
www.berghahnbooks.com

Editorial Offices:
150 Broadway, Suite 812, New York, NY 10038
3, Newtec Place, Magdalen Road, Oxford OX4 1RE, UK

©2006 Berghahn Books

ISBN 1-84545-266-6 (paperback)
ISSN 1086-4946

CONTENTS

THE ISTITUTO CATTANEO'S INTERNET SITE

http://www.cattaneo.org

The Istituto Cattaneo's Internet site, which contains much useful information, may be found at the address given above. The Archives section deserves special attention, as the Istituto Cattaneo provides free access to documentary archives regarding various characteristics of the Italian social and political systems, including a chronology of the main political and social events since 1990; book reviews of studies and empirical research published over the last three years; background data on Italian society; election results; party membership (since 1945); and holders of government and institutional posts in the republican era.

The Archives section allows citizens and the academic community to access data that reflect the Istituto Cattaneo's statutory pledge to promote empirical knowledge about Italian society. Of particular interest to readers of this volume are the data located in two distinct archives that are periodically updated: the first contains detailed Italian election results (ADELE: *Archivio dati elettorali*); the second offers sample survey data (DICA: *Dati inchieste campionarie*).

The *Archivio dati elettorali* (ADELE) contains data concerning the national elections for the Chamber of Deputies from 1948 to 2001; the data are organized at the municipal level (over 8,000 ecological units). For each national election (1948, 1953, 1958, 1963, 1968, 1972, 1976, 1979, 1983, 1987, 1992, 1994, 1996, and 2001), one may access the number of those having the right to vote, actual voters, valid votes, and party list votes. The archive also contains the results of the elections held on 2 June 1946, which gave birth to the Italian Republic (institutional referendum and election of the Constituent Assembly).

The *Dati inchieste campionarie* (DICA) archive currently offers data regarding three major research programs: ITANES (Italian National Election Studies, 1990–2001), Political Participation and the Social Situation in Bologna (1984–1994), and Electoral Abstentionism (1985–1995). The user who accesses this archive can engage in interactive statistical analysis of the results of any survey, generating, for example, frequency distributions, contingency tables, and selected statistics.

ABBREVIATIONS

ACGM	Autorità Garante della Concorrenza e del Mercato (Guarantor Authority for Competition and the Market)
AN	Alleanza Nazionale (National Alliance)
ANCI	Associazione Nazionale dei Comuni Italiani (National Association of Italian Communes [municipalities])
BAV	Banca Antonveneta
BBVA	Banca Bilbao Viscaya Argentaria
BdI	Banca d'Italia (Bank of Italy)
BNL	Banca Nazionale del Lavoro
BPER	Banca Popolare dell'Emilia Romagna
BPI	Banca Popolare Italiana, formerly Banca Popolare di Lodi (BPL)
BPL	Banca Popolare di Lodi, former name of Banca Popolare Italiana (BPI)
CARIGE	Cassa di Risparmio di Genova (Genoa Savings Bank)
CCD	Centro Cristiano-Democratico (Christian Democratic Center)
CdL	Casa delle Libertà (House of Freedoms)
CDU	Cristiani Democratici Uniti (Christian Democratic Union)
CEI	Conferenza Episcopale Italiana (Italian Bishops' Conference)
CGIL	Confederazione Generale Italiana del Lavoro (Italian General Confederation of Labor)
CICR	Comitato Interministeriale per il Credito ed il Risparmio (Interministerial Committee for Credit and Savings)
CISL	Confederazione Italiana Sindacati Lavoratori (Italian Confederation of Workers' Unions)
CL	Comunione e Liberazione (Communion and Liberation)
CONSOB	Commissione Nazionale per le Società e la Borsa (National Commission for Companies and the Stock Exchange)

CRUI	Conferenza dei Rettori delle Università Italiane (Conference of Italian University Rectors)
CSFB	Credit Suisse First Boston
CSM	Consiglio Superiore della Magistratura (Superior Council of the Judiciary)
DB	Deutsche Bank
DC	Democrazia Cristiana (Christian Democratic Party)
DPEF	Documento di Programmazione Economico-Finanziaria (Economic and Financial Planning Document)
DS	Democratici di Sinistra (Left Democrats)
ECB	European Central Bank
ECOFIN	Economic and Financial Affairs Council (European Union)
EMU	Economic and Monetary Union
EU	European Union
Fed	Federazione dell'Ulivo (Olive Tree Federation: federation of center-left parties)
FI	Forza Italia
GAD	Grande Alleanza Democratica (Great Democratic Alliance)
GDP	Gross Domestic Product
IMF	International Monetary Fund
IMI-SIR	Istituto Mobiliare Italiano-Società Italiane Resine (Italian Credit Institute-Italian Resins Company)
IRAP	Imposta Regionale sulle Attività Produttive (Regional Tax on Business Activities)
ISTAT	Istituto Nazionale di Statistica (National Statistical Institute)
ISVAP	Istituto per la Vigilanza sulle Assicurazione Private e di Interesse Collettivo (Institute for the Supervision of Private and Public Interest Insurance)
LN	Lega Nord (Northern League)
MAR	Medically assisted reproduction
MIUR	Ministero dell'Istruzione, dell'Università, e della Ricerca (Ministry of Education, Universities, and Research)
OECD	Organisation for Economic Co-operation and Development
PACS	Patto civile di solidarietà (civil union)
PdCI	Partito dei Comunisti Italiani (Party of Italian Communists)
PDS	Partito Democratico della Sinistra (Democratic Party of the Left), former name of the Democratici di Sinistra (DS)
PEO	Public exchange offer
PETO	Public exchange and tender offer
PPI	Partito Popolare Italiano (Italian People's Party)
PRC	Partito della Rifondazione Comunista (Communist Refoundation Party, often shortened to RC, for Communist Refoundation)

PRI	Partito Repubblicano Italiano (Italian Republican Party)
PSI	Partito Socialista Italiano (Italian Socialist Party)
PTO	Public tender offer
RAI	Radio Televisione Italiana (Italian Radio and Television)
RC	Rifondazione Comunista (Communist Refoundation, short title of the PRC, the Communist Refoundation Party)
RCS	Rizzoli-Corriere della Sera
RI	Rinnovamento Italiano (Italian Renewal party)
SDI	Socialisti Democratici Italiani (Italian Democratic Socialists)
SGP	Stability and Growth Pact
SISMI	Servizio per le Informazioni e la Sicurezza Militare (Military Intelligence and Security Service)
SVP	Südtiroler Volkspartei (South Tyrolese People's Party)
TAV/TGV	Treno Alta Velocità/Train Grande Vitesse (high-speed train)
TFR	Trattamento di fine rapporto (retirement/severance bonus)
TUB	Testo Unico Bancario (Consolidated Banking Act)
TUF	Testo Unico sulla Finanza (Consolidated Financial Sector Act)
UDC	Unione dei Democratici Cristiani e di Centro (Union of Christian Democrats and Center Democrats)
UDEUR	Unione Democratici per l'Europa (Union of Democrats for Europe), officially Popolari-UDEUR
UPI	Unione delle Province Italiane (Union of Italian Provinces)

Chronology of Italian Political Events, 2005

January

1 Broad consensus among the political forces in favor of the year-end message of the president of the Republic, Carlo Azeglio Ciampi. Criticism from the Lega Nord (LN) and Rifondazione Comunista (RC).

3 Data on public expenditure are published: at the end of 2004, the borrowing requirement showed a fall of 1.2 billion euros compared to 2003. For the Ministry of the Economy and Finance, the improvement is a result of the economic recovery and "a series of measures agreed on by Italy and the European Union."

4 Ciampi visits the Neapolitan quarter of Scampia, where numerous homicides attributable to the *camorra* have recently occurred.

After some days of tension within the center-left, Romano Prodi says that he follows "with detachment" what occurs in Rome.

5 The government intervenes against the five referendum questions on artificial insemination in the review proceedings before the Constitutional Court.

6 Protests from secularist members of the center-right against the government's decision to line up against the referenda on artificial insemination.

7 Prodi asks those politicians who intend to challenge him for the leadership of the center-left to "come out into the open." He demands that the primaries be held by the end of May and that there be single lists of the center-left for the next regional elections.

10 The law against smoking comes into force.

Edited by Debora Mantovani

Umberto Bossi, the leader of the LN, threatens to run Roberto Maroni against the outgoing president, Roberto Formigoni, in the regional election in Lombardy.

11 Prime Minister Silvio Berlusconi rejects the idea of "governors' lists" for the regional elections.

At the inauguration of the judicial year, the prosecutor general, Francesco Favara, announces that in Italy 81 percent of crimes remained unpunished.

12 The Casa delle Libertà (CdL) decides that only the "governors" (presidents) of Lazio and Liguria, Francesco Storace and Sandro Biasotti, respectively, may present personal lists at the coming regional elections. Criticism from President Formigoni of Lombardy.

13 The Constitutional Court admits four referenda on artificial insemination, while rejecting the question that requested total abrogation of the law.

14 Berlusconi announces that Forza Italia (FI) will allow its electorate freedom of conscience in the referendum on artificial insemination. Prodi hopes that an agreement will be reached in Parliament prior to the referendum.

Berlusconi meets the governor of the Bank of Italy, Antonio Fazio, to talk about the reform of the law on savings. They agree on the life term of the governor and on the defense of the Italian character of the banks.

15 At the inauguration of the new judicial year, a clash occurs in Palermo between Prosecutor Piero Grasso and Minister of Justice Roberto Castelli on the reform of the judiciary.

16 Nichi Vendola, the representative of RC, defeats Francesco Boccia, the candidate of the moderate forces of the center-left, in the primary elections in Puglia to choose a candidate for president of the region.

17 Cardinal Camillo Ruini, president of the Italian Bishops' Conference (CEI), invites Catholics to abstain from voting in the referendum on artificial insemination.

18 The center-left decides to hold leadership primary elections by the end of May.

19 Yet again, Parliament fails to fill two vacancies on the Constitutional Court. Berlusconi rejects the candidacy of Luciano Violante of the DS (Democratici di Sinistra or Left Democrats).

20 The government is defeated twice in a parliamentary committee on the reform of the savings law: the committee approves both a term limit for the governor of the Bank of Italy and the transfer of supervision of bank competition to the Anti-trust Authority.

21 An Italian soldier is killed in Nassiriya. Berlusconi and the minister of foreign affairs, Gianfranco Fini, rule out the possibility of withdrawing the Italian contingent from Iraq.

24 The center-left wins Senate by-elections in the constituencies of Bari and Rovigo.

25 The Chamber of Deputies approves the European Constitution. The bill goes to the Senate.

27 Negotiations within the center-right to choose a candidate for president of the Campania region fail.

28 The sentences of 18 years in jail for the three found guilty of setting the Primavalle fire in 1973, in which two sons of a neo-fascist perished, are cancelled by the statute of limitations.

The International Monetary Fund (IMF) sounds the alarm over Italy's public finances: in 2005 the deficit will be 3.1–3.2 percent of the gross domestic product (GDP), rather than 2.7 percent as forecast by the Italian government.

29 Alleanza Nazionale (AN) attacks Castelli for not intervening to avoid the cancellation of the sentences for the Primavalle massacre.

31 The center-left remains split on the significance of the Iraqi elections.

February

1 The center-left reaches a common position on Iraq, favoring the withdrawal of Italian troops within the framework of greater involvement by the United Nations.

2 Fiat and General Motors (GM) fail to reach an agreement in negotiations on Fiat's option to sell Fiat Auto to GM.

3 The congress of the Left Democrats (DS) begins in Rome.

4 In Baghdad, the journalist of *Il Manifesto*, Giuliana Sgrena, is kidnapped.

During the DS congress, Romano Prodi is acclaimed as leader of the Ulivo (Olive Tree coalition). Massimo D'Alema relaunches the idea of a single center-left party.

5 Meeting at Palazzo Chigi on the abduction of Giuliana Sgrena. Fini appeals for her liberation on the Arabic television station Al Jazeera.

6 The government decides to include the opposition in the initiatives for the liberation of Sgrena.

8 The minister of the economy and finance, Domenico Siniscalco, announces that the privatization of Radio Televisione Italiana (RAI) will take place this year. The minister of communications,

Maurizio Gasparri, declares that the new board of directors will be nominated by the end of June.

The European Commission asks Fazio for clarification on the degree of openness of the Italian banking system to European banks.

9 The Union of Christian Democrats and Center Democrats (UDC) rejects once and for all the possibility of an alliance between the center-right and the Radicals for the coming regional elections.

10 The center-left decides to vote against refinancing the Italian mission in Iraq.

Strike in the air transport sector.

11 Strike in the railway sector.

12 In response to European Union (EU) criticism, Fazio defends the Italian banking system, saying that "it is the most open system in Europe."

13 Fiat and GM sign an agreement according to which GM will pay Fiat 1.55 billion euros to dissolve the alliance established in 2000 and cancel Fiat's right to sell 90 percent of its automobile sector to GM.

14 The president of the Superior Council of the Judiciary (CSM), Virginio Rognoni, supports the prosecutor of Verona, Guido Papalia, against the harsh criticism directed at him during an LN demonstration.

15 The Unione (the coalition of parties of the center-left) decides to vote against refinancing the Italian military in Iraq, but the reformists of the Margherita come out in favor of abstention.

According to the National Statistical Institute (ISTAT), in 2004 the Italian economy grew by only 1.1 percent. Siniscalco calls this a "negative surprise."

The CSM approves a strongly worded document in which it condemns the declarations of the minister of institutional reforms and devolution, Roberto Calderoli, during the LN demonstration in Verona criticizing the prosecutor, Papalia.

16 Parliament approves (with the Unione voting against) the refinancing of the Italian military mission in Iraq.

17 The Senate fails to reach a quorum four times in the debate on devolution. Calderoli threatens to resign and the LN threatens to leave the government.

The advocate general of the European Court of Justice declares that the IRAP (Regional Tax on Business Activities) is illegitimate.

19 The committee for abstention in the referendum on artificial insemination is formed.

20 EU finance ministers reach an agreement on the reform of the Stability and Growth Pact.

Prodi announces the position of the center-left toward the US: friendship, but "equal dignity." Criticism from the radical wing of the center-left.

The congress of the Union of Democrats for Europe (UDEUR) ends in Naples. It approves a political line that promises loyalty to the center-left, but not unconditionally.

21 Siniscalco announces that the government will see that the Bank of Italy maintains control over competition in the banking sector. He furthermore states that it will not intervene to limit the governor's term of office.

22 Berlusconi meets with the US president, George W. Bush, in Brussels and declares that only at the end of 2005 will Italy consider its eventual withdrawal from Iraq.

23 With a resolution approved by a wide majority, the CSM censures the law to amend the statute of limitations to reduce the time limits for certain crimes (the "save Previti" law), which is still being debated in Parliament.

Ciampi rebukes the CSM on the delays in appointments to senior positions in the judiciary.

24 The Radicals ask Prodi to enter into an agreement with them for the regional elections and the 2006 general election. The leader of the Unione rebuffs the offer.

25 Ciampi issues a warning about the state of the Italian economy, asserting that the economy is suffering from "weak productivity growth, the foreign trade situation is unsatisfactory, and we are losing competitiveness, even in the Eurozone."

The minister of education, universities, and research, Letizia Moratti, announces that 200,000 contract teachers and staff will be taken on permanently within the next five years.

26 Berlusconi invites Ciampi not to "listen to the center-left's deceptive arguments" on the state of the Italian economy.

In Rome, the leaders of the DS, the Margherita, the Italian Democratic Socialists (SDI), and the European Republicans found the Federation of center-left parties, the Fed.

27 The president's office responds to Berlusconi's criticisms: "It is not the habit of President Ciampi to pay attention to promptings, suggestions, or gratuitous criticism from whatever source they may come."

28 Ciampi declares that he will "always be vigilant and strict in protecting the autonomy and independence of the judiciary," and that he does not like to talk of economic decline, as he is "convinced that Italy has the capacity and strength to grow and to maintain a leading position."

March

1 According to ISTAT, in 2004 the public debt decreased, but the deficit remained at exactly 3 percent of the GDP.

As a result of the difficulties they have encountered in their meetings with the two poles, the Radicals decide not to participate in the regional elections.

2 The Chamber amends the law on savings to delete both the introduction of a limited term for the governor of the Bank of Italy and the transfer of supervision of banking competition from the Bank to the Anti-trust Authority.

3 A decision by the Communications Authority rules that the duopoly of RAI and Mediaset in the radio-television market impedes pluralism and competition.

The congress of RC begins in Venice. Fausto Bertinotti announces that it will be his last congress as party secretary.

The Chamber gives first reading to the law on savings.

4 Nicola Calipari, an official of the Military Intelligence and Security Service (SISMI), is killed in Iraq by American soldiers during the liberation of the Italian journalist Giuliana Sgrena. Italy protests to the United States.

5 Ciampi asks for a rigorous American investigation into the death of Nicola Calipari.

6 The RC congress ends with the approval of the political line proposed by Bertinotti.

8 The LN threatens to vote against the decree on competitiveness if the government does not impose duties to protect domestic production.

The Communications Authority fines RAI and Mediaset 2 percent of their advertising income for 2003 because they have exceeded the limits on shares of advertising revenue.

9 Berlusconi reports to the Senate on the liberation of Giuliana Sgrena and the death of Nicola Calipari, claiming credit for the firm attitude of the Italian government and recognizing the opposition's "responsible" behavior.

10 The LN threatens to vote against the decree on competitiveness if a high commissioner is not appointed to combat counterfeit products and if the government does not suspend relations with the European Commission for its failure to protect Italian products.

11 The Council of Ministers launches a package of measures to increase Italian competitiveness. The LN votes against some of the measures because the package does not contain duties against imports from Asia.

12 The electoral commission of the Rome Court of Appeal excludes the Social Alternative list, led by Alessandra Mussolini, from the ballot for the regional election in Lazio.

The LN announces that it is against financing the construction of the bridge over the Strait of Messina and asks that the government not exceed the funding included in the 2005 budget for the renewal of the public sector labor contract.

13 Calderoli proposes the reintroduction of the death penalty "for those who commit very serious crimes against minors, as well as for pedophiles."

Alessandra Mussolini announces a hunger strike in anticipation of the Regional Administrative Court of Lazio's decision on the exclusion of her list from the Lazio regional election.

14 Investigations of false signatures among the presenters of electoral lists in the regional elections spread to various regions.

The government decides to open negotiations for the renewal of the government employees' contracts, offering to use only the resources allocated in the 2005 budget.

15 Berlusconi announces that in agreement with British Premier Tony Blair, the progressive withdrawal of Italian soldiers from Iraq will begin in September. The Chamber approves the refinancing of the Italian mission in Iraq.

16 Blair and Bush correct Berlusconi: they say that no definite date has been chosen for the Italian withdrawal from Iraq. Berlusconi declares: "It was only a hope."

17 Calderoli announces his resignation after the Senate fails four times to reach the quorum in the debate on the reform of the Constitution (devolution).

18 Eurostat does not confirm Italy's public accounts for 2003 and 2004 and announces that "clarification" of the data "could lead to an upward revision of the government deficit."

19 At Confindustria's assembly of small enterprises, Berlusconi announces the abolition of the IRAP in the next budget and states that Italy will demand the reform of the Stability and Growth Pact. Critical remarks from the president of Confindustria, Luca Cordero di Montezemolo.

20 Berlusconi applauds the agreement reached at ECOFIN (the Economic and Financial Affairs Council of the European Union) that loosens the restrictions imposed by the Stability Pact.

21 Prodi describes the reform of the Stability Pact as "modest"; the European Central Bank (ECB) threatens to raise interest rates.

22 The Council of State upholds the appeal against the exclusion of Alessandra Mussolini's list from the regional election in Lazio.

Berlusconi under investigation in Milan for corrupting a witness in the inquiry into Mediaset's film rights.

23 The reform of the second part of the Constitution passes the Senate, with only the majority voting in favor. The center-left leaves the Chamber when the vote is taken.

24 The decrees on education are approved. Education is made mandatory until the age of 18, and the possibility of alternating between education and work is introduced.

25 Marco Follini, secretary of the UDC, says that collaboration on institutional reforms with the center-left (as well as within the majority itself) would have led to better results.

26 Montezemolo asks that entrepreneurs who occupy positions in Confindustria resign if they express themselves in favor of a particular political position.

28 The Bank of Bilbao decides to launch a public exchange offer for 100 percent of the Banca Nazionale del Lavoro (BNL).

29 The majority is divided over the renewal of the government employees' contracts. AN and UDC propose to increase salaries by a hundred euros a month, but Berlusconi is not supportive.

30 The Dutch bank ABN AMRO announces a public exchange offer for 100 percent of the Banca Antonveneta.

31 Berlusconi says he is in favor of the initiatives of foreign banks in Italy.

April

1 The reinstatement of an excluded electoral list leads to the postponement by two weeks of the regional election in Basilicata.

2 Pope John Paul II dies in Rome. The government announces three days of national mourning.

3 On the first voting day in the regional elections, the minister of the interior, Giuseppe Pisanu, orders the removal of party posters with the image of the Pope.

4 The center-left wins the elections in 11 regions, against the 2 (Veneto and Lombardia) won by the center-right. The turnout is only 71.5 percent.

According to the EU, the Italian deficit is heading toward 3.6 percent in 2005.

5 Berlusconi recognizes the center-left's victory in the regional elections and denounces a "parallel state of the Left."

Following the regional election results, Prodi announces that the primaries are no longer necessary.

6   AN and UDC ask Berlusconi to call the election early and to lessen the LN's role in the government. Prodi offers the majority the center-left's collaboration in the renewal of the Italian economy.
    The Senate ratifies the European Constitution.

7   Berlusconi announces that "in the Pole we are talking about an October election."
    Rumors of the probable resignation of Follini and Fini as vice-premiers.

8   Berlusconi is willing to consider Fini's requests. "Let's reflect upon devolution," he says, promising "a clear signal of disconti-nuity in the action of the government."
    Roberto Maroni, the minister of welfare, rejects any possibility of reconsidering the constitutional reform.

9   Berlusconi is working on the possibility of limited changes in the composition of the government and proposes more attention to the South and family incomes.

10 Follini says that the results of the regional elections should be considered as "a vote against a certain way of governing" and proposes calling an early election.

11 The LN opposes the idea of calling an early election. Berlusconi says he is ready to go through a parliamentary vote to resolve the crisis. The leader of the Margherita, Francesco Rutelli, asks the center-right moderates to support the center-left's project.

12 Montezemolo pressures the government, saying that it is better to have an early election than paralysis.

13 The European Commissioner Joaquín Almunia announces that by the end of June, he will commence an infraction procedure against Italy for its excessive deficit.
    Parliament gives final approval to the European arrest warrant.

14 Berlusconi's family holding company puts 17 percent of Mediaset up for sale on the market.
    Follini asks for the opening of a "piloted" governmental crisis. Berlusconi favors only a cabinet reshuffle.

15 Vice-Premier Follini and the three UDC ministers resign. Berlusconi threatens an early election unless the UDC returns to the govern-ment. Ciampi asks for the opening of a formal crisis.

16 Follini refuses to sign Berlusconi's proposed agreement to change the government and its program under the same leader.

17 Berlusconi says he "does not want give in to the First Republic-style games of a party that in 2001 took only 3 percent," the UDC.

18 After a meeting with the president of the Republic, Berlusconi announces that he is not resigning and that he wants to bring the crisis before Parliament. Follini and Fini, with whom the premier

had agreed to form a new government under his own leadership, are caught unprepared.

The center-left wins the regional election in Basilicata.

19 With letters of resignation from the AN ministers in his pocket, Fini criticizes Berlusconi for not resigning.

The new Pope, Joseph Ratzinger, is elected, taking the name of Benedict XVI.

20 Prime Minister Berlusconi resigns.

21 Ciampi initiates consultations for the formation of a new government. Follini announces that he will not be part of it.

22 Berlusconi is commissioned to form a new government.

23 The crisis ends. The new government takes the oath of office before President Ciampi.

24 Prodi accuses Berlusconi of "wrecking the Constitution with senseless reform projects."

25 During the celebrations of Liberation Day, Ciampi declares that "the Resistance lives in the Constitution ... which is the basis of the civil association of the entire nation."

26 Berlusconi presents the government in the Chamber (24 ministers, 9 vice-ministers, and 63 undersecretaries) and proposes a single party of the center-right.

Tension with the UDC.

The Milan prosecutor's office asks that Berlusconi be indicted for Mediaset's purchases of film rights.

27 The Chamber votes confidence in the new Berlusconi government. The UDC's support is "neither aloof nor with any illusions."

Two EU commissioners write to Fazio asking for "clarification" on the delays in authorizing the Dutch group, ABN AMRO, to acquire more than 20 percent of Banca Antonveneta's capital.

28 The new government obtains the Senate's confidence as well. In his speech, Berlusconi raises once again the idea of a single center-right party and attacks the ECB, which he holds responsible for making the euro too strong vis-à-vis the dollar.

29 Italy and the United States confirm their failure to agree on the conclusions of the report regarding the circumstances of Calipari's death.

The Ministry of the Economy and Finance revises its growth estimates downwards: in 2005, the Italian economy will grow by 1.2 percent instead of 2.1 percent, as forecast by the government.

30 Berlusconi announces that he could leave politics when a single center-right party is created.

May

1 Labor unions celebrate May Day in the Neapolitan district of Scampia, where in the past few months the war between gang bosses has claimed many victims.

2 Italy publishes its conclusions on the death of Calipari. They are very different from those of the American commission of inquiry.

3 In discussions with US Secretary of State Condoleezza Rice, Fini reaffirms that Italy's alliance with the US is not in question in spite of their divergence in opinion regarding the death of Calipari.

The European Court of Justice rejects the Milan judges' appeal against the law on falsification of company accounts.

4 The government obtains the confidence of the Senate on the decree on competitiveness and announces it will reintroduce severe penalties for falsification of accounts, even though the decree itself reduces them.

5 In Parliament, Berlusconi declares that there are "evident discrepancies" between the Italian and American versions of Calipari's death. The opposition asks for the withdrawal of Italian troops from Iraq.

The Corte dei Conti (Court of Audit) invites the government not to go further along the path of tax cuts "without specific measures to finance them, which will not be easy."

6 The Bank of Italy allows ABN AMRO to launch a public tender offer for 100 percent of Banca Antonveneta.

The LN's federal council rejects the idea of a single center-right party.

9 The center-left again makes gains in local elections in Sardinia, Trentino-Alto Adige, and Valle d'Aosta, involving about 2 million voters.

10 Fini announces that the withdrawal of Italian troops from Iraq will start in February 2006.

Fini also declares that he will vote "yes" on three of the four referendum questions on artificial insemination. He is criticized from within AN.

11 The Chamber votes confidence in the government on the "urgent measures within the framework of the plan of action for economic, social, and territorial development."

Berlusconi rejects the unions' request to increase government employees' salaries by 111 euros.

12 For the second consecutive semester, ISTAT reports negative growth in Italy.

13 Berlusconi appeals to labor unions and entrepreneurs to revive the nation's economy.

14 At the ECOFIN meeting in Luxembourg, France, Austria, and the Netherlands express preoccupation about the "Italian case." Siniscalco asks for collaboration from the political forces and social partners. Prodi asks Berlusconi to launch an "operation truth" about the public accounts.

15 The minister of agricultural policies and forestry, Giovanni Alemanno, proposes to tax interest income.

16 An Italian volunteer, Clementina Cantoni, is kidnapped in Afghanistan.

In local elections in Catania, Umberto Scapagnini, the center-right candidate, is re-elected mayor. The center-left wins in Enna.

17 Ciampi asks the government to make "credible decisions" in economic policy and not to "weaken the safeguards that ensure stability and provide a guarantee against financial turbulence."

The parliamentary Supervisory Committee appoints seven members to the RAI's new board of directors.

18 Berlusconi rejects the idea of taxing interest income and announces that he wants to reduce the number of government employees.

The Organisation for Economic Co-operation and Development (OECD) comes out against devolution, as it makes it more difficult to control public expenditure, and asks for a pay freeze for public employees.

20 By a large majority, the federal assembly of the Margherita decides to present separate lists for the proportional seats at the next general election.

Berlusconi asks his allies to promote the formation of a single party by the end of the summer. Cool response from Fini and the UDC.

Vittorio Grilli is appointed director general of the Treasury. Mario Canzio becomes accountant general.

22 Prodi asks the center-left to work for "a coalition and a government able to make the decisions necessary to save Italy."

23 Cesare Previti is sentenced to seven years by the appeals court for the IMI-SIR affair and acquitted in the case of the Mondadori judgment.

Eurostat revises Italy's deficit/GDP ratio upwards: in 2003 and 2004, the deficit reached 3.1 percent of GDP.

The center-right wins the communal elections in Bolanzo in the second round, but loses control of many local authorities in Sardinia.

24 According to the OECD, Italy is in a recession. It forecasts that in 2005, the GDP will decrease by 0.6 percent, while the deficit/GDP ratio will reach 4.4 percent.

25 Prodi announces that he wishes to present a list of the Ulivo for the general election, despite the opposition of the Margherita.

26 At the assembly of Confindustria, Montezemolo asks the government and the political class to make decisions even if they are "unpopular" and to "get their heads out of the ballot boxes."

Ciampi appeals to the two poles to act decisively on the economy without waiting for the election.

27 The agreement for the renewal of the government employees' contracts is signed. It provides for a salary increase of 100 euros.

28 The government announces that it wants to revise the mechanisms for negotiating labor contracts. The representatives of Confindustria express concern about the agreement signed with the government employees.

29 Disappointment over France's rejection of the European Constitution. The LN asks for another vote on it in Italy. Bertinotti talks about it as a defeat for the Ulivo.

30 Benedict XVI says he is "close in words and prayers" to the Italian bishops in their call for abstention in the referendum on artificial insemination.

31 The parliamentary Supervisory Committee rejects the Treasury's proposal to appoint Andrea Monorchio as president of RAI.

At the annual assembly of the Bank of Italy, Antonio Fazio declares that Italian firms are characterized by "dwarfism" and have little propensity toward innovation.

Four Italian soldiers die in an accident in Iraq.

June

1 The Netherlands rejects the European Constitution.

Ciampi asks Italy to "shake off the torpor that has spread so widely and avoid the subtle arguments that swallow up our daily life."

2 Siniscalco protests to the European Commission about the document that Brussels is preparing on Italy's public accounts, which will lead to the opening of a procedure for excessive deficit.

Romano Prodi once again proposes primary elections and puts his own leadership on the table.

3   Rutelli announces he will abstain in the referendum; this provokes controversy within the center-left. For Sandro Bondi, coordinator of Forza Italia, the news opens up "new and unprecedented political prospects."

4   Calderoli severely attacks Ciampi, whom he considers one of those "responsible" for Italy's adoption of the euro.

5   In an official note, Berlusconi dissociates himself from the LN's criticism of Ciampi and reminds ministers to "respect their own official position and those of the highest offices of the Republic."

6   The LN announces that it intends to ask for a referendum to put the lira back into circulation alongside the euro. Critical comments by foreign governments and others.

7   The European Commission starts a procedure against Italy for its excessive deficit.

8   Fini says he considers the invitation to abstain in the referendum on artificial insemination "misguided," provoking a bitter controversy within AN and the center-right.

9   After being held hostage for 24 days, the Italian volunteer Clementina Cantoni is released in Kabul.

Prodi criticizes the proponents of abstention in the referendum on artificial insemination.

10   ISTAT confirms the second consecutive fall in the GDP: Italy is technically in a recession.

12   On the first day of voting in the referendum, 18.7 percent of those eligible voted. The Church expresses its satisfaction.

The fourth-largest bank in the Eurozone is created by the Italian bank UniCredit and the German financial institution HypoVereinsbank.

13   The number of voters in the referendum on artificial insemination reaches only 25.9 percent. Giovanni Alemanno and Alfredo Mantovano resign from their positions in AN in protest against Fini's position on the referendum.

Ciampi appeals to the Constitutional Court to rule on who has the power to grant pardons. The appeal follows yet another refusal by Justice Minister Castelli to approve pardons for Adriano Sofri and Ovidio Bompressi.

14   Berlusconi invites the Margherita to build with FI a "common house of the moderates." The idea is rejected out of hand by Rutelli, but within the Margherita the risk of a split by the supporters of Prodi grows.

15   The government's decision to postpone the reduction of the IRAP provokes reactions from the social partners. Berlusconi is whistled at the assembly of Confartigianato.

16 Agreement in the center-left: Prodi gives up the idea of presenting the Ulivo symbol on the proportional lists in the next election in return for primary elections to choose the center-left's leader.

19 Bossi says that he is opposed to the idea of a single center-right party.

20 The center-left parties decide to hold primary elections on 8 and 9 October to choose their candidate for premier. The secretaries of the center-left parties will sign an agreement that will last the whole term of the legislature.

21 During the inauguration of the Food Agency of Parma, Berlusconi defends the euro and reins in the LN.

22 Berlusconi denies any links between the real estate financier Stefano Ricucci and Mediaset in the takeover of Rizzoli-Corriere della Sera (RCS).

24 During the Pope's visit to the Quirinal Palace, Ciampi asserts the secular character of the state.

25 Berlusconi announces that at the end of July, the constituent committee to decide on the timing and procedure for the creation of the unified party of the center-right will begin its work.

26 Siniscalco and Almunia agree on a "re-entry path" for Italy's public accounts deficit: it will have until 2007 to bring the deficit down to the 3 percent ceiling.

28 The Senate approves the reform of the judiciary over the opposition's protests.

29 Following a meeting with Pierferdinando Casini, Gianfranco Fini, and Marco Follini, Berlusconi announces that he will be the center-right candidate for prime minister in the 2006 general election.

30 The government is defeated five times in the Chamber over the decree on competitiveness.

July

1 During the UDC congress, Follini rejects the idea of a single party of the center-right, questions Berlusconi's leadership, and criticizes the government's record.

2 During the national assembly of AN, Fini calls the factions within the party "a creeping disease," attacks Follini, and defends Berlusconi's leadership.

3 Casini ends the UDC congress proposing the creation of a "party of moderates." Follini is re-elected as secretary.

Fini concludes AN's assembly by patching up the internal rift.

4 Siniscalco outlines in advance the main points of the Economic and Financial Planning Document (Documento di Programmazione

Economico-Finanziaria, or DPEF): there will be no increase in the value-added tax, and he will fight against tax evasion.

5   The LN harshly attacks Ciampi during his speech to the European Parliament.

The government is defeated twice in the Chamber on the competitiveness package.

7   Four suicide bombers blow themselves up in London, leading to more than 50 deaths. Fears of terrorism grow in Italy as well.

8   Berlusconi announces that in September a gradual withdrawal of Italian soldiers from Iraq will begin.

Castelli announces that he will report those magistrates who strike on 14 July against the reform of the judiciary.

9   The government is working on a package of measures against terrorism. The LN proposes to declare a state of war in Italy.

11 Prodi expresses his opposition to special measures against terrorism and to the Italian mission in Iraq.

12 Pisanu presents the measures against terrorism in the Chamber. The LN criticizes them; the center-left is open to discussing them.

13 The government is divided on France's initiative to suspend the Schengen Treaty, following the recent terrorist attacks in London.

14 Fourth strike by magistrates against the reform of the judiciary.

Berlusconi announces that Italy will not suspend the Schengen Treaty.

15 Fini asks for the resignations of Ignazio La Russa and Altero Matteoli for some critical remarks against the AN leader in some newspapers. The two party chiefs apologize.

The cabinet gives the DPEF its approval.

16 Pisanu reiterates his decision to approve the anti-terrorism measures, challenging the LN and contradicting Berlusconi, who had downplayed their urgency in order to attenuate the conflict within the majority.

17 Unipol's board of directors gives the go-ahead for the acquisition of a majority share of the BNL.

18 Fini begins a reshuffle of the positions within AN by declaring them all vacant.

19 Meeting between Ciampi and Berlusconi to discuss some technical aspects and deadlines arising from the impending end of the legislature.

20 Parliament gives final approval to the reform of the judiciary, which the government had made a question of confidence.

According to ISTAT, the Italian balance of trade has reached the worst level since 1992.

21 In his first annual report, the chairman of the Communications Authority (Autorità per le Garanzie nelle Comunicazioni), Corrado Calabrò, characterizes the Gasparri law, passed in 2004, as backward.

22 Approval of the government's anti-terrorism plan; the Unione also supports it.

25 The Milan prosecutor's office orders the seizure of the shares of Banca Antonveneta (about 40 percent of the total capital) held by a group of shareholders who, it alleges, acted in concert to block ABN AMRO's public tender offer. Magistrates accuse Governor Fazio of having favored the president of the Banca Popolare Italiana (BPI), Gianpiero Fiorani.

26 Ciampi signs the reform of the judiciary.

27 In the face of strong opposition criticism, the Senate approves the "save Previti" law, which shortens the time limits for the prosecution of crimes.

CONSOB (the securities and exchange commission) suspends BPI's two takeover bids for Banca Antonveneta.

28 The leaders of the majority meet and discuss the Fazio issue. Only the LN openly lines up with the governor.

29 The Rome prosecutor's office opens an investigation of Unipol's takeover bid for BNL.

31 Casini says in an interview with *Corriere della Sera*: "Either the CdL changes or we lose our battle with Prodi."

August

1 The government is considering introducing a limited term for the governor of the Bank of Italy. For the DS, Fazio's resignation would be "opportune."

Follini reaffirms the necessity of changing the leadership of the center-right.

2 The judge for preliminary investigations (GIP) of Milan decides to suspend the BPI's president, Fiorani, for two months.

Claudio Petruccioli is appointed chairman of RAI.

3 The cabinet assesses the situation surrounding the Bank of Italy. Siniscalco stresses that the ongoing events create "a problem of credibility for the country."

5 As a result of a majority vote of the board of directors, Alfredo Meocci becomes general manager of RAI.

Prodi says Fazio should resign.

6 Berlusconi calls the publication of telephone wiretaps that are part of the inquiries into the takeovers of RCS and Banca Antonveneta

"a scandal," and announces a government bill to punish the publication of wiretaps.

8   Standard & Poor's lowers its outlook for Italy from "stable" to "negative," criticizing both the majority and the opposition because neither has shown it has the strength to make the unavoidable choices.

     The banker Ubaldo Livolsi, who is close to Berlusconi, speaks in an interview with *Corriere della Sera* about an agreement with the real estate financier Ricucci to take over RCS.

9   Berlusconi denies he is involved in the takeover of RCS.

10 Documents of the Banca Antonveneta investigation accuse Fazio of having personally intervened in favor of the BPI, despite the fact that the Bank of Italy's technical offices had pointed out problems with its balance sheet.

     Prodi proposes an economic and financial code of conduct for candidates, elected representatives, and leaders of the Ulivo.

11 In the second semester of 2005, the GDP grew by 0.7 percent—the best result since the beginning of 2001.

12 The speaker of the Chamber, Pierferdinando Casini, writes to the president of the Milan Court, Vittorio Cardaci, to ask whether deputies have been wiretapped in the course of the Unipol-BNL investigation. He reminds him of the provisions of Article 68 of the Constitution.

16 Clash between Berlusconi and Casini on the leadership of the center-right for the next election.

17 Montezemolo declares that Fazio should have resigned as governor of the Bank of Italy. Positive reactions from the Unione; caution on the part of FI.

18 Prodi announces that one of the Unione's priorities, in case of electoral success, will be the reduction of payroll taxes.

     Berlusconi puts a damper on the question of Fazio's resignation.

20 Prodi asks the parties of the Unione to end the controversy on political morality over the support given by the DS to Unipol in its bid for BNL.

21 During the festival of Comunione e Liberazione, Marcello Pera warns against the risk of multiculturalism and of a "half-breed society" (*meticciato*) that Europe faces.

22 Fazio requests an internal investigation of the actions of the two senior officials of the supervisory branch of the Bank who wrote the negative opinion on the BPI's takeover of Banca Antonveneta.

23 Casini asks Berlusconi to create a party of moderates. Otherwise, he threatens, the creation of a party of the center could become a real possibility.

24 At the Comunione e Liberazione festival, Rutelli and Formigoni propose a pact among the reformists in the two poles to write common proposals on specific questions.

26 Fazio defends his actions in the affair of the banking takeovers before the Interministerial Committee for Credit and Savings (CICR).

27 The LN defends Fazio, whom it considers the guarantor of a "strong financial presence of a *padano* character." The center-left is also divided: the Margherita asks that Parliament pronounce on Fazio's resignation, while the DS are for taking more time.

28 FI Vice-Chairman and former Economy Minister Giulio Tremonti says that Fazio is "not irremovable."

The UDC declares that its position on devolution and the budget "cannot be taken for granted."

30 The minister for European Community policies, Giorgio La Malfa, asks Fazio to resign.

Follini asks Berlusconi once again for a signal of discontinuity in the government's action.

September

1 The governor of the ECB, Jean-Claude Trichet, initiates the assessment of the Fazio case.

2 The government approves the reform of the Bank of Italy: a limited term of seven years is introduced for the governor, with no age limit.

3 Casini asks the center-right for a signal of change; otherwise, the UDC will run alone in the next election.

4 Siniscalco asks for Fazio's resignation. The LN lines up with the governor.

5 Berlusconi says that Siniscalco's request for Fazio's resignation is "legitimate."

6 Fazio says he will not resign.

7 Meeting between Ciampi and Berlusconi on the Fazio case. For Fini, the governor has an "institutional duty to resign."

8 Fazio decides not to attend the ECOFIN meeting in Manchester.

The ECB voices its preoccupation about Italy's public finances.

9 Berlusconi says that only the ECB can intervene to request Fazio's resignation. The ECB responds that the Italian government has its responsibilities.

Ciampi blocks the government's proposal to use a decree law to change the legislation governing telephone wiretaps.

11 Prodi proposes civil pacts of solidarity (PACS) to regulate the status of de facto couples.

12 Fini lines up with Prodi on the question of PACS. The center-left is divided.
13 The CdL submits a proposal in the Chamber for an electoral reform based on proportional representation.
14 The Pole is divided on the electoral reform. For Fini, Parliament must first approve the constitutional reform and find a way of preserving bipolarism, as well as retaining the 4 percent barrier.
15 Ciampi admonishes the political forces on the issue of reforms: "We must not return to the past." On the Fazio case, he adds that "moral rectitude and ethical behavior are at the basis of our institutions."

    For the first time, the ECB looks specifically at the Banca Antonveneta case.
16 Prodi rejects Berlusconi's proposal of a dialogue on the electoral law. Ciampi invites the parties to focus on the most urgent problems of Italian society.
17 The LN and the UDC reject the proportional electoral reform because there is neither agreement in the majority nor dialogue with the opposition.
18 Prodi closes the Festa dell'Unità attacking the Pole on the electoral law.
19 Cardinal Ruini announces that the Italian bishops are opposed to the legal recognition of de facto couples.
21 The UDC criticizes Siniscalco's budget bill.

    Health Minister Storace issues an order suspending the experimental trials of the "abortion pill," RU486, under way in a hospital in Turin.
22 Siniscalco resigns. Tremonti returns to the Ministry of the Economy and Finance.
23 Tremonti and Fazio run into each other during the G7 summit in Washington, DC, but do not exchange a word.
25 Tremonti withdraws Fazio's mandate to represent Italy at the meeting of the IMF's Development Committee in Washington, DC.
26 Berlusconi is acquitted by the Milan Court in the All Iberian case because "the act is no longer defined as a crime."
27 Berlusconi defends the government's economic policy in Parliament.
28 The first trial concerning the collapse of Parmalat starts in Milan.
29 The cabinet approves the 2006 budget law.

    The Superior Council of the Bank of Italy reaffirms its confidence in Fazio on the same day that the magistrates announce that the governor is being investigated for abuse of authority.

    The Senate votes confidence in the government on the "Dispositions Regarding University Professors and Researchers."

October

3   Casini asks Castelli for the official data on the effects of the implementation of the "save Previti" law and suggests to the government a postponement of the discussion on the floor of the Chamber.

4   Berlusconi threatens a government crisis if the proportional electoral reform is not approved.

Ciampi asks the political forces "not to wreck the Constitution."

5   The reform of retirement bonuses (*trattamento di fine rapporto*, or TFR) is postponed. Welfare Minister Maroni denounces pressures from the business sector.

The Chamber votes confidence in the government on the "Measures to Counteract Violent Incidents during Sports Events."

According to ISTAT, during the first six months of 2005, Italy's government deficit reached 5.1 percent of GDP and the primary surplus fell to 0.1 percent.

6   The president's technical staff express their doubts regarding the constitutionality of some points of the new electoral law.

The Senate approves a term limit for the governor of the Bank of Italy.

8   Montezemolo criticizes the existing single-member system because it does not guarantee governability.

9   Demonstration by the Unione in Rome against the budget and the electoral reform.

10 Fazio is interrogated for six hours by magistrates of the Rome prosecutor's office on the Banca Antonveneta takeover bid.

12 Some center-right deputies disobey the whips to defeat the proposed "pink [i.e., female] quotas" for candidate lists in the new electoral law. Berlusconi invites the UDEUR and parts of the Margherita to enter the CdL.

The CSM appoints Piero Grasso as the national anti-Mafia prosecutor.

13 The Chamber approves the electoral reform, which now goes to the Senate.

14 The DS announce that they are willing to contribute to improving the electoral reform. Berlusconi rejects the offer.

The government launches a maneuver of 2 billion euros to correct the 2005 budget.

15 Follini resigns as secretary of the UDC as a result of conflict with the party line vis-à-vis Berlusconi and the center-right.

16 More than 4 million people participate in the primary election to choose the leader of the Unione. Romano Prodi gets 74.6 percent of the votes, against Bertinotti's 14.6 percent and Mastella's 4.4 percent.

The deputy speaker of the Regional Council of Calabria, Francesco Fortugno, is assassinated in Locri.

17 Prodi once again proposes Ulivo lists for the coming election. Rutelli is open to such a suggestion as long as it leads to the formation of the "Democratic Party."

18 The DS and the Margherita announce that they will present common lists for the Chamber at the next election.

19 Culture Minister Rocco Buttiglione threatens to resign in protest against the cuts in the field of culture contained in the budget bill.

Berlusconi begins to discuss once again the reform of the *par condicio* law on equal access to the means of communication during election campaigns.

20 The Chamber gives a third reading to the constitutional reforms.

Berlusconi moves ahead on the *par condicio*, but Casini reins him in.

22 Prodi says that the "political apportionment" (*lottizzazione*) of RAI's networks must be ended by choosing managers on the basis of "professionalism and autonomy." On the proportional electoral reform, Prodi confirms that he has "doubts regarding the constitutionality of the law."

23 The Nuovo PSI is close to a split. At the end of the congress, two secretaries, Bobo Craxi and Gianni De Michelis, are elected.

25 The Chamber approves the reform of the universities.

26 Ciampi pushes the government to "start from the real problems Italy is facing," now that the economy is showing signs of recovery.

27 At the European Council in London, Berlusconi asks that countries be allowed to engage in deficit spending.

Lorenzo Cesa becomes the new secretary of the UDC.

The Chamber votes confidence in the government on the "Urgent Measures in Agriculture and in Favor of Public Organizations in the Sector, and to Counteract Anomalous Price Movements in Agro-food Products."

28 The government launches a third corrective measure for 2005.

The Margherita approves joint lists with the DS for the upcoming election.

29 Berlusconi announces that he tried to dissuade Bush and Blair from intervening in Iraq.

30 Creation of a new alliance between the SDI and the Radicals, with the symbol of a fist holding a rose.

31 Berlusconi meets with Bush in Washington, DC. At the end of the talks, the premier declares that "the US fears a change of government in Italy." The US government clarifies that it has no intention of intervening in the Italian election.

November

2 Tehran summons the Italian ambassador twice to object to a demonstration in defense of Israel. The demonstration is in response to the declarations of President Ahmadinejad, who seeks the elimination of the Jewish state.

3 Thousands of people participate in the demonstration in defense of Israel in Rome.

The ECB closes the Fazio case, inviting the Italian government to modify the bill on savings and leaving doubt as to whether Fazio's behavior in the Banca Antonveneta affair was in conformity with the principles of the EU.

Berlusconi proposes to raise the age of retirement to 68.

4 In a meeting with Berlusconi, Ciampi manifests his doubts regarding the electoral law, the "save Previti" law, and modifications to the *par condicio*.

Sabino Cassese, Giuseppe Tesauro, and Maria Rita Sulle are appointed judges of the Constitutional Court by Ciampi.

5 Berlusconi denies there has been any conflict with Ciampi on the "save Previti" law, but tension is on the rise in the Pole. There is also unrest concerning the age of retirement: Fini argues that it cannot be increased.

6 The UDC presents an amendment to exclude defendants whose cases have already reached the Court of Appeal or the Court of Cassation from the benefits of the "save Previti" law. FI and AN disagree.

7 The center-left wins the communal election in Bolzano in the first round.

9 The Chamber approves the "save Previti" law but withholds its benefits from defendants whose trials are currently under way. The bill passes to the Senate.

The Senate votes confidence in the government on the proposals to combat tax evasion and on its urgent taxation and financial measures.

10 Ciampi asks the government for structural intervention in the economy, predicting a rise in international interest rates.

Conflict within the executive over measures to support the family.

11 The Senate votes confidence in the government on the 2006 budget bill.

12 Storace suggests that pro-life volunteers from the Movement for Life be present in clinics.

13 Defense Minister Antonio Martino declares that the withdrawal of Italian soldiers from Iraq should be gradual and be completed by the end of 2006.

14 The Constitutional Court declares that the decree law of July 2004, which mandated certain cuts in expenditure for the regions and local authorities, is illegitimate.

15 According to ISTAT, the Italian economy grew by 0.3 percent in the third quarter of 2005, and will grow by 0.1 percent over the whole year.

16 The Senate gives final approval to the reform package that modifies 50 articles in the Constitution; only the senators of the majority support it.

17 The Italian bishops criticize the federalist constitutional reforms. Criticisms also emerge within the CdL.

Criticism from Brussels on the state of Italy's public finances.

18 Cardinal Ruini expresses support for allowing Catholic volunteers from the Movement for Life to give advice in clinics.

19 Fini proposes that Ciampi remain as president for a second seven-year term. While expressing their support, many parties maintain that the discussion is premature.

20 The UDC proposes the establishment of a parliamentary committee on the implementation of law no. 194 (the law on abortion).

21 The *Osservatore Romano* attacks law no. 194, expressing its opposition to abortion.

22 Martino announces that the American nuclear submarines will leave the base at La Maddalena in Sardinia "according to a timetable and in conditions that will be determined later."

Berlusconi announces the withdrawal of Italian troops from Iraq by the end of 2006.

23 Ciampi responds to Fini's suggestion that he be re-elected in 2006: "I want to finish my term with dignity."

24 The cabinet approves the reform of retirement bonuses (the TFR).

The Chamber votes confidence in the government on the proposals to combat tax evasion and its urgent taxation and financial measures.

25 General strike against the budget law, called by the trade-union confederations.

26 According to Berlusconi, in 2005, 200 international terrorists were arrested in Italy.

27 Casini presents himself as a candidate to lead the next center-right government and attacks Berlusconi: "Italians are fed up with illusions and illusionism."

Prodi announces that the single-member electoral system will be restored if the center-left wins.

28 Casini denies having attacked Berlusconi.

The first round of the communal election in Messina ends with the candidates of the center-right and center-left in the run-off.

29   The Senate gives final approval to the ex-Cirielli law, which cuts the time limits for prosecution of those with clean records and increases the penalties for repeat offenders.

The Ulivo decides that Prodi will not be at the top of the center-left's list of candidates in all electoral districts in the next election. In Parliament, however, the center-left will form a single group.

30   In response to demonstrations in Val di Susa, where European transportation corridor no. 5 is to pass, Ciampi defends high-speed trains (TAV).

The Ulivo presents an amendment to the budget bill to introduce an allowance for economically disadvantaged women and thus limit the number of abortions.

December

1   The ECB decides to increase interest rates to 2.25 percent. Disagreement expressed by national governments, including Italy.

2   In front of a DS audience, Prodi proposes to return to the single-member system if the center-left wins the next election.

In Rome, tens of thousands of metal workers demonstrate for the renewal of their contract, which has been held up for 11 months.

3   The DS policy conference in Florence ends with an appeal by Fassino to relaunch the idea of the "Democratic Party."

4   Casini authorizes a parliamentary investigation into the implementation of the law on abortion.

Rita Borsellino wins the primary elections of the Unione in Sicily.

5   The Unione reaches agreement on including the legal regulation of de facto couples and a "rapid" withdrawal from Iraq in its program.

6   The police intervene in Val di Susa to remove anti-TAV barricades, provoking a sharp clash between majority and opposition.

The chairman and CEO of Unipol, Giovanni Consorte, is investigated by the Milan prosecutor's office for stock manipulation in BPI's takeover bid for Banca Antonveneta.

7   The government talks about extremists infiltrating the protests against high-speed trains in Val di Susa. In a meeting of leaders of the majority, Gianni Letta is given the responsibility of coordinating the assessment of its impact on health and the environment.

8   New clashes in Val di Susa between protesters and the police; the construction sites are occupied again.

10   Meeting between the government and the local authorities of the Val di Susa. An agreement is reached that provides for the suspension of construction and the opening of discussions.

12 The center-left candidate, Francantonio Genovese, wins the second round of the communal election in Messina.

13 The European Commission launches the infraction procedure against Italy for the Bank of Italy's behavior in the takeover bids for BNL and Banca Antonveneta. The banker Fiorani is arrested on the charge of conspiracy in the second bid.

Once again, Castelli refuses to grant Sofri a pardon. The president's office announces that it will refer the conflict of jurisdiction over pardons to the Constitutional Court.

14 With only the majority voting in favor, the Senate gives final approval to the proportional electoral reform.

Standard & Poor's threaten to lower Italy's rating again.

15 The Milan prosecutor's office investigates Fazio to ascertain whether he divulged confidential information to Fiorani. The Rome prosecutors open an investigation of the chairman of Unipol, Consorte, whom they suspect of stock price manipulation and distortion of the market.

The Chamber votes confidence in the government on the 2006 budget bill.

16 Tremonti asks for Fazio's resignation.

17 The Rome prosecutor's office asks the Bank of Italy to provide the records of the governor's meetings on the Unipol-BNL affair, thus opening a second line of investigation against Fazio. The government, with the exception of the LN, hurries to approve the law on savings and thus force Fazio's resignation.

19 Fazio resigns from his position as governor of the Bank of Italy "to restore tranquillity, in the higher interest of the country."

20 The government reaches agreement on three amendments to the law on savings. One fixes the length of the term of office of the governor of the Bank of Italy at six years. A second amendment gives the power to appoint the governor to the government with the agreement of the president of the Republic, and a third divides responsibility for supervising bank mergers between the Bank of Italy and the Anti-trust Authority.

Ciampi admonishes holders of high office to respect "not only the law but also ethical and societal norms."

21 A government amendment to the law on savings assigns responsibility for bank mergers to the Anti-trust Authority.

The Greens and the Party of Italian Communists (PdCI) decide to create joint lists for the Senate for the upcoming election.

22 Ciampi signs the new electoral law.

The Anti-trust Authority launches a preliminary investigation of Berlusconi for possible violation of the law on conflict of interest because of the allocations in the budget to subsidize the purchase of decoder boxes for digital cable television.

23   The Senate approves, on a question of confidence, the bill that reforms legislation on savings and the Bank of Italy. The ECB immediately gives the reforms its approval.

Berlusconi announces that the next general election will take place on 9 April.

25   Demonstration in Rome in favor of an amnesty for prisoners, organized by the Radicals.

27   Special session of the Chamber to discuss an amnesty. Few deputies are present.

28   News of another summons to Berlusconi to appear before a magistrate for corruption of witnesses in the trial for bribery of the revenue police and in the All Iberian case.

The chairman of Unipol, Giovanni Consorte, and his deputy, Ivano Sacchetti, resign as a result of the judicial investigations.

29   Mario Draghi is appointed as the new governor of the Bank of Italy.

31   Ciampi delivers the last speech of his seven-year mandate. He recalls the highlights of his activity as president and appeals to the young.

— Translated by Marie-Eve Rény

INTRODUCTION: END-OF-TERM ANXIETIES AND IMPROVISATION

Grant Amyot and Luca Verzichelli

Any observer of the Italian political situation will likely agree that 2005 was yet another transition year, dominated by mostly predictable facts and events. However, a series of factors reveals the imponderable, and somewhat fortuitous, nature of political change in Italy during a period certainly pervaded by the expectation of impending events but also not altogether lacking in critical situations and noteworthy occurrences.

On the side of "predictable" events, there are many circumstances to note. A positive result for the center-left in the regional elections of 2005, for example, was on the whole easy to forecast, as was the further decline in popularity of Silvio Berlusconi, due to a less than impeccable performance in government and to choices that owed more to nearsighted calculations of political advantage than to clear policy objectives. In addition, the fierce antagonism between the center-left and center-right coalitions did not help to reduce the persistent elements of friction within each of them. It was thus easy to foresee the slow progress through an uncertain political agenda, with a tendency to constantly renegotiate some crucial choices and to postpone others. Yet again, therefore, the provisional quality of a long transition was apparent, and any secure anchorage still seems out of reach.

These opening thoughts suggest a cyclical interpretation of political change: exactly as had occurred in 2000, the final year of this legislature showed that attention had shifted back to the dynamics of

---

Notes for this section begin on page 45.

domestic politics and evinced increasing signs of difficulty for the government and its majority. These difficulties climaxed with a resounding defeat in the round of regional elections that took place only one year before the end of the legislature. As in 2000, these electoral losses ushered in a formal government crisis, which was quickly resolved by the majority but without overcoming all of its internal differences over both leadership and policies. However, again as in 2000, the new government was able to bring some of its policy initiatives to fruition, among them a revision of the Constitution—a far more profound modification than that of constitutional law no. 1/2001[1]—which was subject to a confirmatory referendum to be held in the course of the following "electoral year."

Even some of the "hottest" issues brought back onto the political agenda in 2005 show a parallel with 2000. For example, the action taken in the areas of school and university reform and the proposals for the reform of retirement bonuses (*trattamento di fine rapporto*, or TFR) have touched questions that the Ulivo governments had already addressed during the final phase of the 13th legislature.[2]

However, we can also emphasize a few unpredictable factors, or at least the "disconnected" nature of many of the events that occurred this year. The political agenda was often characterized by variations in rhythm and by changes in direction that some political actors were forced to make. Some real surprises have emerged. For example, the bizarre pace of the parliamentary timetable suffered from constraints placed on it by the political debate (in particular, the long *verifica*, or reckoning, within the majority that preceded the government crisis in April and that in one way or another lasted at least until September). It was then reorganized to further the objectives of a coalition that was once again united, at least around the "package" of reforms approved in the final months of the year.

A particular instance of disconnection and chaos was the process leading to the reform of the electoral system (law no. 270 of 14 December 2005), which, after months of legislative inactivity, was suddenly set in motion again following the governmental crisis. The system that emerged must be considered "highly proportional," since the thresholds of exclusion—in particular, those for parties within coalitions—are not a strong deterrent against the fragmentation of the party spectrum. If it is still technically classifiable as a "mixed" system, therefore, it is only so in the sense that it combines with the principle of pure proportionality the majority premium, an Italian invention practically unknown on the democratic planet. This and the other innovation, whereby the parties that plan to vie for the majority premium must formulate a common platform and present a leader of the coalition as candidate for premier, should constitute a complicated mechanism combining a typically "consensual" rule for allocating seats with the majoritarian and bipolar legacy of recent years. The word "should" is apt here, because the way that the majority premium functions in the two chambers (in the Chamber of Deputies it is assigned on a national basis; in the Senate, on a regional one) could, according to authoritative forecasts,[3] produce different results in the two houses and the risk of a governmental stalemate caused by a not improbable "draw" in the upper chamber.

In addition, although the premier was able to convince all the members of Parliament in his own majority to turn the electoral system upside down with the intent of guaranteeing himself the greatest possible advantage in 2006 (this by exploiting the fragmentation of the opposition coalition and the better results obtained by his party and more generally for the Casa delle Libertà in the proportional vote), in the last months of the legislature he was not able to achieve other reforms. For example, the amendment of the *par condicio* for electoral campaigns[4] had the same purpose but was not supported by all the coalition parties, in particular, by the Union of Christian Democrats and Center Democrats (UDC).

This picture strengthens the impression of a nervous, often confused timing of Italian political events. The year 2005 was therefore a classic pre-electoral year but also a period of great effervescence, due to some by now fairly familiar factors (including the particular manner and tone of Berlusconi's leadership) but also some new, explosive elements. For example, the investigations of the bank takeovers in effect monopolized the attention of the media for the entire second semester. A few of the events in question are already ripe for detailed interpretation and have thus been treated extensively in this edition of *Italian Politics*. For other matters, such as the proportional electoral reform, which will not be implemented until April 2006, it will be advisable to wait for further developments.

However, an analysis as events unfolded at the end of 2005 can help to capture the direction of change of a political system that, although in a fairly uncertain context, continues to evolve. In particular, after reflecting on the events of 2005, we believe we should focus our attention on three elements. In the first place, we will track the evolution of the parties, still absorbed in discussions on how they are to coalesce, choose leaders, and formulate common programs in spite of the substantial stability of the electoral groupings and, especially, the fact that we are seeing a return match of the same electoral duel as 10 years ago. In the second place, the enactment of public policy in the principal sectors has revealed in too many cases an uncertain and illogical process of decision-making, giving the impression of a reduced ability to solve problems and of changes being limited to the form and the instruments of policy without producing significant and lasting results in "social learning." The resulting risk is all the more dangerous because it seems likely, in many decision-making areas, to survive the alternation in government between leaders and blocs. In the third place, it is useful to look at the evolution of the relation between politics and society, which in the course of 2005 has shown several moments of tension and the return of the risk of a bifurcation between the two spheres, due to the declining public perception of an ethical sense in governmental institutions and, more generally, in politics.

Leadership and Strategies in the Two Coalitions: Predictable Outcomes, Difficult Preparation

In 2005, the debates over the leadership within the two poles developed in fairly different ways but along inevitably parallel tracks. The events discussed in the chapter by David Hine and Chris Hanretty—the government crisis and the long battle between Silvio Berlusconi and Marco Follini, which led in autumn to the latter's resignation as secretary of the UDC—constitute the principal stages in the transformation of the center-right coalition. In view of the upcoming 2006 election, the result was in the end a foregone conclusion (Forza Italia's pre-eminence and therefore Berlusconi's expectation of again running for the premiership). However, Berlusconi's path has seemed more difficult than expected, and the strategy chosen at the end of a very hot summer—electoral reform in a proportional direction, strongly urged by the UDC, which re-establishes the parties' autonomy and the logic of internal competition expressed by the soccer metaphor of the "trident" made up of the leaders of the major parties in the coalition—raised the price of cohesion, with Berlusconi himself as well as his party suffering the consequences. The episode of the choice of a candidate (although at year-end there were three) to stand against Walter Veltroni in Rome's 2006 mayoral election is an example of this.

Did this signify an erosion of Berlusconi's leadership, or was it a problem of achieving actual unity around a center-right platform? The defeat and resignation of Follini appear to have slowed (or frozen) the former. The price paid by Berlusconi, as suggested above, has nevertheless allowed him to enter the fray very early and on his preferred ground—in a campaign centered on a personal party and (so long as it is possible) on television presence. On the other hand, the National Alliance (AN) and the UDC of the resurrected (in terms of party politics) Pierferdinando Casini have persisted in refusing any concessions to Forza Italia (FI). They have not supported it, for example, on the reform of the *par condicio*, on the correction of the financial maneuver, and on the ex-Cirielli law, which without the UDC's veto would probably have included clauses that were more helpful to the ex-minister of defense, Cesare Previti, in his trial. This episode constituted a rare example of a failure to approve one of the provisions *ad personam* inspired by Forza Italia, demonstrating that the approach of the appointment with the voters strengthened the UDC, making it less compliant to the demands of the premier. But other events during the year also showed that Berlusconi's personal appeal as a unifier, the "catalyst" of a moderate consensus, was fading. The criticisms he received on several occasions, even from center-right commentators, the polemics surrounding his all too prudent conduct in the handling of the Fazio case, and finally the heated discussion with Vittorio Feltri in the course of an episode of *Porta a Porta* in mid-December are all evidence of his diminishing appeal. But there have also been problems with the solidity of the coalition, with some, even if limited, cases of "desertion" of the parliamentary groups of the majority and the defection of a part of the Nuovo PSI, which merged into the center-left.

On the other hand, Berlusconi was able to respond to the attacks, thanks to a relative harmony with the other partners. Gianfranco Fini's party is still in the final analysis a faithful ally, as its loyalty to the author of its political legitimation, or *sdoganamento*, remains firm. There is still a strong rapport with the Northern League, based on shared views on many issues, ranging from Europe to taxes.

During 2005 we saw the re-emergence on several occasions of the crucial problem of the divergent interests and social groups represented by the majority parties, precisely the problem that makes Berlusconi's unifying role essential. The different geographical distribution of moderate voters—those of AN and the UDC in the South, those of the League and a significant part of FI in the North—has caused inevitable conflicts on a wide range of questions, primarily pension reform and economic measures. The idea of a single party of moderates, again proposed by Berlusconi after the regional elections and yet again early in November, has not accidentally been put to one side in favor of a more consensual solution centered on the return to electoral competition in a proportional framework.

Aside from the faded image of the leader and the imperfect unity of the coalition, the problem faced by the center-right is that of holding together a consensus of moderate opinion on the local level. This is difficult for a party like Forza Italia, which lacks a grassroots organization. In this respect, one of the main novelties of the year was the show of strength in Sicily of Raffaele Lombardo's Movement for Autonomy, which gained its initial success within the coalition in the city council election in Catania but then (in the November-December election round) created the conditions for a dramatic defeat of the center-right candidate in Messina, first by selecting a candidate of its own to run against him and then by not supporting him in the second round.

On the other side of the political spectrum, we have Romano Prodi and his long-standing effort to build a finally united, but also sufficiently reliable, center-left coalition. The narrative of events reconstructed by Jonathan Hopkin in his chapter shows how difficult this undertaking was in the course of the last year of the legislature. Just as Sisyphus must endeavor time and again to push a boulder up the slope that inevitably sends it back down again, so Prodi found in the course of 2005 that he had to repeatedly retrace a path of coalition-building by now familiar to him and to the supporters of the Ulivo scattered among the Margherita and the Left Democrats (DS). The year opened with Prodi's official return to Italian politics and continued with a series of voyages: that of ideas and proposals begun in the "Factory"; the actual road trip (this time on an 18-wheeler) that preceded the primaries; and also a difficult political voyage among the many strategic solutions (and snares) offered by the new electoral system, with the additional problem of Prodi's personal position as a candidate. The difficulties for the center-left do not mirror those of the center-right in the sense that here it was primarily a question of reconciling the demands of different political groups and actors, without the sharp conflicts among electoral, social, and local interests and constituencies felt by the Casa delle Libertà. It is no surprise, however, that unity remained a difficult goal for the center-left as well, and that paradoxically the prospect of victory in 2006 in some measure served to weaken the thrust toward unity.

In any case, other specific factors also contributed to the self-defeating behavior of the center-left: the different histories of the parties that compose the center-left Unione have generated inferiority complexes in some and mutual suspicions in others. The DS are not only the largest party in the coalition, but also the only one with a relatively strong structure, raising concerns among the other actors that it might hegemonize the alliance. And in the background there are also important programmatic differences to be resolved, such as how far the radical left can share the reformist vision—inspired in part by the Blair experience—which is favored by the leaders of the two core parties. The polemics about which center-right laws to abrogate have been an index of these tensions. The reformist wing did not ultimately disagree, for example, with some of the motivations for the Biagi law or

Berlusconi's pension reform; rather, it considered it an advantage to find them already approved, in order to avoid conflicts within its own coalition. On the other hand, abrogating the Biagi law was a major plank of Communist Refoundation's program. Even the question of withdrawing Italian forces from Iraq, for example, required difficult negotiations on the left.[5] Differences about policy later took second place to polemics on the composition of the lists of candidates and on the allocation of resources for the election campaign, but they could obviously regain significance in the future.

Next to the changed prospects for the supporters of the Ulivo, or Democratic Party—a concept back in vogue in 2005—the other factor emerging from a rereading of the evolution of the center-left during the year is the unpredictability of the public's reactions. We are not referring here so much to the electorate's behavior at the polls, although it, too, has been the subject of somewhat inaccurate projections, as Salvatore Vassallo points out in his chapter, but rather to how activists and sympathizers of the Unione have interpreted political events and how they have reacted to them. There is no doubt that beyond any possible celebration and exploitation of this political event, the impact of the primaries held by the Unione in October, in terms of overall participation and relegitimation of Prodi's personal leadership, was strong, as was pointed out even by some members of the opposing coalition. The outcome of the 4 December primaries to choose the Unione's candidate for the presidency of the region of Sicily was also significant, with over 180,000 going to the polls and approximately 65 percent of the votes being cast for Rita Borsellino, clearly showing she garnered support well beyond the electoral bases of the parties backing her.

But the most surprising result, in this year of primaries, was surely the double personal success (including of course the April election results) of Nichi Vendola in Puglia. In this case, besides the inherently politically relevant fact—the credit extended by voters to a representative of Communist Refoundation—there was in addition the strong sign of discontinuity represented by the successful candidacy, in such a difficult competition, of a politician like Vendola, who is openly gay, a poet, and a supporter of the anti-Mafia movements that are often in open confrontation with the establishment. Vendola first won over the majority of the supporters of the Unione and then also garnered widespread support among centrist voters in Puglia, bolstered by his pride in being "different" but also by knowing how to avoid gratuitous conflict with the traditional and religious values of the region. On the terrain of religious values, in fact, the center-left—or rather, its left wing—has not known how to read the public's attitude and foresee its reactions. As Chiara Martini notes in her chapter, the center-left misread the public mood not so much on the question of artificial insemination itself as on the possibility of using the tool of the referendum for such complex issues, thus gratuitously creating a new reason for disunity in the coalition. Perhaps this too can be listed as a factor that was in some ways predictable; nevertheless, its effect was also conditioned by improvisation and nervousness.

The Decision-Making Process: Uncertainty of the Political Agenda and Half-Reforms

In recent years, the tendency for many public policies to depend on the electoral cycle of a given majority has become an established fact, thereby signaling a break with the traditionally consensual nature of Italian policy-making while overcoming the inertia that has always characterized decision-making in some sectors. At the same time, these policies seem to undergo a tortuous formulation and an uncertain implementation because of the conflictual nature of the government coalitions and the often difficult relations with the other forces on the policy scene. Commenting on the results of the government's activity in 2004, Carlo Guarnieri and James L. Newell noted the uncertainty of some legislative initiatives and the prices paid by decision-makers in the "laborious processes of negotiation within the coalition."[6]

The year 2005 certainly has not reversed the trend. On the contrary, some reasons for conflict seem to loom larger, in some cases because of the emergence of new constraints that restrict the win set of solutions available to decision-makers. On the other hand, the government's "decisionist" style and its capacity to impose fast-track timetables and exercise a certain partisan control over parliamentary votes now constitute the rule rather than the exception. Government actually moves forward, as the six-by-six-meter posters put up at the end of the year by Berlusconi's new pre-electoral campaign claimed. The battle of the posters was then transferred to brochures, brandished by the premier and his ministers to boast of alleged record-breaking effectiveness and political results. But what does all this mean in terms of real policy change?

The answer to this question must take into account the fact that many public policies are often considered "in place" when legislative action has remained at the level of pure retooling. Or in many cases, policy change boils down to decisions of limited impact that represent minimal costs for the parties and members of Parliament when compared to the media benefits of a trumpeted achievement. Or again, sometimes it is a question of policies that are destined to receive very limited implementation—or indeed, no implementation at all. Therefore, many decisions, even of substantial legislative importance, may be made "so that nothing changes," or they end up having very little effect in terms of policy output. From this point of view, the year in question also shows an evident gap between "legislative results" and actual "reform." For example, there has been a growing alarm over the economy's loss of competitiveness, a concern voiced by many representatives of the business world, starting with the president of Confindustria, Luca Cordero di Montezemolo.

The decree and the government bill presented in March, analyzed by Grant Amyot and Francesco Marangoni in their chapter, in addition to the Economic and Financial Planning Document (DPEF) of July and the subsequent chaotic maneuver in the fall, introduced a wide range of individual measures to support business, along with some legislative and tax adjustments. However, given the scope of the problems, they have seemed relatively inadequate. For example, one question raised by many economists and by the Organisation for Economic Co-operation and Development (OECD) in its last report has not been addressed[7]—that of the lack of competition in many services and professions, which leads to greater costs for Italian exporters. In spite of frequent free-marketeering statements, the premier and his coalition have not wanted, especially in a pre-electoral year, to make enemies of important constituencies of voters. Other structural problems, such as the sectoral concentration of exports, have not been addressed at all.

Budgetary policy, proceeding by improvisation and in fits and starts, has also been affected by the general political instability. Even in a context of substantial continuity in policy aims, individual decisions have been affected by persistent institutional turbulence (the government crisis in April, the resignation of the economy and finance minister in September while the budget bill was being drafted, and the subsequent conflict between Tremonti and Fazio), as well as the "stop-and-go" effect of Italy's delicate situation of being under "special observation" in the context of the Economic and Monetary Union (see Vincent Della Sala's chapter in this volume). Within this framework of constraints, the passage of the last budgetary maneuver of the legislature became, inevitably, the focus of strong pressure on the part of the members of the coalition. The UDC, with the support of AN, persistently pressed to insert a number of measures to support families, from bonuses for newborns and adopted children to deductions for daycare fees. In the end, Casini's party in large measure won its battle, whereas AN and the Northern League were less successful with theirs.[8] To handle the many demands while working within the

framework imposed by the European Stability Pact, the government
had to introduce a maxi-amendment to the budget bill, protecting its
own proposals from attack by invoking the confidence mechanism.
The coalition parties finally dropped some demands after the premier's promise of a new financial decree (the so-called *mille-proroghe*,
or "thousand extensions," decree), which was presented at the end
of the budget session. In sum, this does not appear to be a rigorous
way of managing public finances or an approach that could provide a
concrete response to the serious problems of the country, although we
must not forget some useful measures introduced by Tremonti—for
example, the reduction of employers' social insurance contributions.

Another crucial turning point during the year was the reform of the
TFR, which was finally passed in December. For the first time, workers have the choice of directing contributions destined for the TFR to
investment funds or other financial vehicles. The reform, which gives
preference to closed investment funds established by union agreements, met with resistance on the part of the insurance companies.
Taking advantage of other pressures as well, they secured a postponement of the implementation of the law until 2008, a fact that
qualifies as yet another element of uncertainty and improvisation,
even in the context of a "done deal." A similar point should be made
about the law "for the protection of savings"—rewritten and adopted
immediately after the resignation of the governor of the Bank of Italy,
Antonio Fazio—which has the appearance of a half-reform or one
with a deferred implementation, due in this case to the interplay of
the various political forces and lobbies. Indeed, this law, in the rush
for "fast-track" adoption by the executive, contained only a few of the
measures that had been proposed to aid investors while lightening
some penalties for fraudulent accounting.

In the school sector, the reform introduced by Minister of Education Letizia Moratti does not clearly address the problem of the quality of education and, as Giancarlo Gasperoni explains in his chapter,
poses implementation problems, stemming in part from the regions'
role in creating new vocational courses of study. To remind us that
the problems of the Italian educational system remain largely unresolved, a year-end OECD report showed that Italy still lags far behind
in the secondary education rankings, including students' knowledge
of mathematics and science, in spite of the high costs of the educational system.[9] With respect to universities, the free-market ideas
often invoked by the premier have in reality not been followed up
in the formulation and implementation of policies: there is almost
no trace in the law reforming the career structure for professors of
any moves toward market discipline and greater competition in the

sector, comparable to those introduced in Great Britain under Margaret Thatcher and later under Tony Blair.

The intensified focus on domestic politics did not cause the government to scale back its ambitions and involvement in European and international politics, but its interventions there have also run into various difficulties and led to some partial failures. On the European front, there has been an attempt to gain room for maneuver within the Stability Pact, exploiting the problems encountered by countries like France and Germany. The revision of the pact, however, was less favorable to Italy than the government had hoped, since it set the level of public debt as the basic criterion in the process of multilateral surveillance. As Vincent Della Sala explains, Italy's high debt, together with the behavior of some representatives of the Berlusconi government, who have criticized the pact and attempted to blame the euro for the ills of the economy, has weakened the Italian position. On this issue, the clear differences in the degree of "Europeanism" within the majority have resurfaced, and its distance from those influential forces (among them big industry and high finance) that have long been convinced that there is no alternative to Europe has been made clear.

On the international front, while the bipolar division between the majority's support of the US action in Iraq and the center-left opposition's determination to "exit" from the Iraqi situation persisted in 2005 (although each position is expressed in a wide variety of ways within each camp), there was perhaps a novelty of some importance to the overall picture of foreign policy behind the events discussed by Marco Clementi. The Sgrena-Calipari case shows how new constraints on Italy's policy emerged from the crisis following the calamitous operation near the Baghdad airport on 4 March 2005, but it also shows how the government tried to adopt a new profile in the uncomfortable post-invasion Iraqi situation. Perhaps new spaces are being created for the bipartisan handling of at least some aspects of the fight against terrorism. And the same outcome can be expected in future for the Italian position on the reform of the United Nations, developed in the course of the year under the cautious management of the minister of foreign affairs, Gianfranco Fini.

But the issue about which the government (and in general the political system) has been most indecisive and incapable of finding solutions is the episode of the bank takeovers. This was connected, in a forced and certainly not very effective way, to the goals of the proposed law on savings. In his chapter, Marcello Messori details the events set in motion by the bids of ABN AMRO (for the Banca Antonveneta) and of the Banca Bilbao Viscaya (for the Banca Nazionale del Lavoro) and the subsequent emergence of a depressing reality of clientelistic relations and low ethical standards in public institutions. From a purely political standpoint, the relevant factors are the support that the leadership of the Bank of Italy has had among elements of the majority—especially, but not only, from the Northern League—and the attempt, long pursued by Berlusconi himself, to justify and sustain a strenuous defense of the "Italianness" of the banks that was clearly in conflict with the country's political position and its responsibilities within the EU. In an echo of these maneuvers, the leaders of the DS "rooted" for Unipol's takeover of the Banca Nazionale del Lavoro, as was revealed by telephone wiretaps heard by the investigating magistrates.

Overall, the government's policies in 2005 betrayed a growing sensitivity to the timetable of domestic politics—shown in particular by electoral preoccupations—and a greater willingness to submit to a multitude of contradictory pressures by lobbies and social forces, without, in some cases, a clear vision of the objective to be pursued. In addition, many policies have remained in an amorphous state. The budgetary maneuvers and the reforms of the educational system, as well as other events only touched upon in this volume's chapters, were indicative of a chaotic and disconnected process of piecing together. Moreover, behind the late and incomplete initiatives there lurked a dangerous drift: the "syndrome of program completion," which leads the chiefs of the executive to make choices often dictated by contingent interests, sometimes in conflict with each other, and to push the envelope with procedural manipulations, such as constant tinkering with the parliamentary agenda and frequent recourse to motions of confidence.[10]

However provisional, the answer to the question whether the events of 2005 represent a reshaping of policy-making in Italy must ultimately be no. The decisions made were at best defensive (as the episode of the reform of the Stability and Growth Pact shows) and reactive. They were almost never timed carefully and almost always required rethinking. The "end-of-season sales" dynamic that characterized the decision-making process in the second semester of 2005 was sharpened by a government-opposition relationship that was certainly not inspired by the concept of fair play; it affected many important matters and produced a plethora of formal results that, however, almost never provided a definitive solution to the problem at hand. Obviously, evaluating whether the glass of effective decision-making is more or less empty, compared to the inability of the system, from the administration to the media, to put the government's choices into practice, is a politically sensitive subject that must be left to Italian opinion-makers (and especially to the voters). Indeed, the new media offensive launched by Berlusconi in fall 2005 with the poster campaign, followed by the self-satisfied tenor of his year-end press conference (which inaugurated an innumerable string of appearances on television and public statements by the premier), was precisely an attempt to convince Italians of the decisiveness of the government's proposals despite pre-existing constraints, the "self-destructive" pessimism of the left, and, "naturally," the hostility of the media toward Berlusconi himself and his party.

The Political System and the National "System": Growing Disquiet

We said at the outset that although 2005 was certainly a transitional year for Italian politics, it did demonstrate the limits of the "new" bipolar system, limits that undoubtedly have an effect on the relationship between public opinion and political institutions. The data marshaled at the end of the year by Ilvo Diamanti are incontrovertible:[11] Italian society is permeated by constant anxieties to which the political system seems slow to respond. The year opened with an event—the railway disaster of Crevalcore—which, although due to human error, reminded the country of the poor quality of its public services (and of the resulting lack of security). Fatally, the end of the year was also darkened by the train collision at Roccasecca, less serious in its consequences but equally liable to prompt negative reactions and critical judgments of the authorities. The transportation sector, indeed, is an unforgiving test case of the actual "modernity" of a country like Italy. It is the "little" events that speak here, from newspaper reports on the plight of commuters in many Northern cities to the reiterated complaints about the execrable sanitary conditions on public transport to the problems immediately produced by the—widely forecast—snowfalls in February and December on the Salerno-Reggio Calabria or the Roma-L'Aquila highways. On a question linked to new infrastructure, a heated polemic emerged toward the end of the year between the citizens of the Val di Susa and the supporters of the European high-speed train project (including the government but also the leaders of many center-left local authorities): the Italian end of the Turin-Lyons line would traverse the area.

Polls show that the Italian public is apprehensive about market reactions and news of economic stagnation and the competitiveness gap: it perceives the extent of the difficulties faced by the politicians in addressing such issues (see on this the chapter by Grant Amyot and Francesco Marangoni). In 2005, consumption grew by barely 1 percent,[12] a sign of uncertainty about the future of the economy that probably has also affected voters' behavior and priorities. In a society that at times seeks to anticipate political action, there have been several clear signs of unease. The peripheries are more "active" at such times, and not only on purely local questions, such as the protest against the high-speed train route. The events of 2005 showed the many faces of a single problem that can be summed up as the total absence of the state, evident at Scampia, in Locri, in the repeated discoveries of cases of corrupt administration (in particular, in the health-care sector), but also, by contrast, in demonstrations of courageous "de-alignment." Particularly striking was the protest by students in the Locri area, with their cry of "kill us all" directed against criminality but implicitly also against representatives of the institutions and the older generations.

Conflicts between the "state" in the wider sense and a segment of society also emerged in Bologna, where the strong line taken by the center-left mayor, Sergio Cofferati, in evacuating some immigrants' illegal encampments sparked protests and led to scuffles between demonstrators and the police in front of Palazzo Accursio, the city hall. A comparison with the very different situation in the French *banlieues*, where acts of criminality and vandalism proliferated in 2005, is obviously untenable. However, given the more recent and limited character of immigration in Italy with respect to France, one cannot help but consider the events in Bologna as the precursor of possible (but not inevitable) further developments.[13]

In the intricate knot of delicate relations between politics and society, two other strands are entwined: the long-standing secular-Catholic battle and the more recent conflict over the autonomy of science with respect to sensitive ethical issues. The death of Pope John Paul II in April cast an immense media glare on expressions of renewed and intense religious feeling (with the cry for immediate sainthood, "Santo subito," raised among the crowd at St. Peter's) that did not much divide public opinion, but the first phase of the papacy of Benedict XVI has seen at times far tougher confrontations over some positions of the Church. Doubts on the direction of the theological and political line of the Church are yet to be resolved: Alberto Melloni states in his chapter that it will take some time to understand the meaning and the consequences of the Church's positions for a now very composite and divided Catholic world. However, one cannot fail to note that the Italian Bishops' Conference (CEI) showed this year that it intends to return to expressing, in a frank and timely fashion, a series of positions based on the traditional view of the individual and the family. This view achieved a symbolic victory in the referendum on artificial insemination, a non-decision made as a result of the non-vote of many citizens, which in reality leaves the legislative questions just as unresolved as it does the moral ones (see on this the chapter by Chiara

Martini). The revival of traditionalist Catholic positions is supported by the politically influential interventions of the UDC (but also Francesco Storace and a large portion of AN) and by a combative faction of Italian-style "theo-cons," who backed an investigation of the results of the emblematic law no. 194/1978 on abortion. Inevitably, tensions on these issues also provoke the re-emergence of secularism. The Radical-Socialist alliance, which came together precisely to defend the secular state, is in the end the only new formation on the political scene in 2005, but it probably generates more problems than potential votes for the center-left coalition.

The sharpened debates on religious morality and scientific ethics also constitute a possible sign of a rift between civil and political society. We know from polls[14] that religious issues are not a source of deep divisions in public opinion: 80 percent of Italians accept the role of the Church, and the majority do not reject the crucifix or religious education in school. But the actual positions of this majority on issues of religious freedom and tolerance are perhaps more flexible than those of the politicians. In the parties, Catholic conservatism is prevalent in the center-right alliance, while the leadership of the opposing coalition, in spite of its secular tendencies, often finds itself "seeking out" the ecclesiastical hierarchy, even if it does so in a variety of ways. It is probably no accident that 2005 was the year in which the secretary of the Left Democrats, Piero Fassino, felt the need to declare his religious faith publicly.[15]

Prospects: A Need for Social Learning and Social Awareness

While it may be almost too easy to catalogue 2005 as another stage in a permanent (or perhaps insubstantial?) transformation of the political system, it is also worthwhile to highlight those elements that may, instead, signal a change in the medium term for Italian politics. Naturally, there are two ways of viewing any type of change. On the one hand, these elements could be considered signs of a new order—more or less welcome, according to one's opinion—that breaks out of the cyclical nature of events and stimulates real growth in certain institutions and policies. On the other hand, we could point to the failure of some impulses toward change and then to a series of negative developments and risks of institutional deterioration, due to political stagnation and the persistence of unresolved structural problems.

Among the first set of elements we must include the conclusion of the long-running legislative itineraries of some measures (including devolution) and the consolidation of a series of rules and "sub-systems" in local politics, which by now are able to ensure a notable level of performance from these institutions. We are not, that is, at the year zero of the second (or third)[16] Republic, if we look at the possibilities that are still open for finally constructing an effective political system. However, the risks of stagnation are many and obvious. The rift we noted in the course of the year between society and the political world is a serious problem for Italian democracy. In particular, the risk caused by the blindness of a political class preoccupied with the balance of power within the coalitions, and increasingly less able to measure the long-term effects of its policies on the "policy-takers," remains high.

Ultimately, the parallel between 2005 and 2000, with which we opened this introduction, can presage a kind of settling of the bipolar political system into a sequence of brief legislative cycles. But this does not eliminate the many factors of instability, starting with the reappearance of an embarrassing divergence between politics and public opinion. On the right, the primacy of Silvio Berlusconi is beginning to wane and the problem of choosing his successor is already coming up, with all the resulting threats to the cohesion of the Casa delle Libertà. On the left, the road toward the Democratic Party seems quite rocky, as is shown by the conflicts between Prodi and the leadership of the parties over the Ulivo's electoral lists for 2006.

Cementing support within the two fronts has sometimes seemed more difficult than it was 10 years ago. This is partly due to the complex composition of the two electoral camps, but also to an inability to stimulate the adoption of potential new "identity" values. The repeated efforts of the premier to return to anti-communism as the ideological cement for the moderate bloc are bound to encounter real limits, while free-market economics has difficulty taking root in a country like Italy, except as an expression of irritation at state supervision and the red tape of regulations or taxation. On the left, on the other hand, there is no longer the climate of national emergency or the external constraint of the Maastricht Treaty that had given momentum and unity to the Prodi government and facilitated its relations with its social partners. Mere opposition to Berlusconi has served as a unifying factor in recent years, but it is certainly not a sufficient one. The primaries have shown, however, that a "base" activated to legitimate the leaders directly can be more unified than the elite itself and can dissociate itself from the logic of competition and force the heads of the parties to patch up their differences.

Another element of potential instability is the dramatic reappearance of the issue of public morality, which came to the top of the political agenda first and foremost in the saga of the bank takeovers. It revealed not only the "amoral familism" (to cite Messori) of some high office-holders, but also the involvement of some representatives of the majority in the affair and, on the part of some opposition leaders, at the very least a lack of awareness of the rules of the market (a fact Berlusconi would exploit for electoral purposes at the beginning of the new year). The reform laws in the field of justice, which were perhaps aimed at helping some accused politicians get off more lightly in their trials, have increased the sense of unease among the public.

If the two coalitions were to continue to prove so fragile and unmanageable, the temptation of a centrist solution, perhaps in the shape of an "institutional" government, could emerge once again. Its policy would probably be inspired by "common sense" and technocratic expertise, but it would mean the inevitable eclipse of the prospect of a decisive transformation of the political system. The fact that 2005 avoided detours in this direction must therefore be considered a half-victory. But it is also difficult, writing on the eve of an important round of legislative elections, to say how and to what extent Italian politics can and should still accomplish such a transformation. It is therefore apparent that, leaving aside party coalitions and electoral outcomes, the first desideratum is a shift toward deeper kinds of change in public policy—to social learning that can finally create a solid legacy of understanding, information, and policy tools for the decision-makers of tomorrow. The second objective that the political and social elites should set for themselves is to regain a sense of public morality, which has been shaken by episodes like those involving the Bank of Italy and the everyday (and often offensive) language of politics. In this respect, the final year of the 14th Legislature has seen, if not a return to the dark period of Tangentopoli, at the very least a series of missed opportunities.

— Translated by Laura Kopp

Notes

We wish to thank the participants in the *Italian Politics/Politica in Italia* workshop in Bologna on 12 November 2005, and in particular those who at that time and later on discussed the first drafts of each chapter: Mario Caciagli, Aldo Di Virgilio, Pietro Manzini, Erik Jones, Piergiorgio Corbetta, Gilberto Capano, and Guido Legnante. Our collaboration on this project was also made possible by two periods of study abroad: Grant Amyot was a CIRCaP Visiting Fellow in Siena, and Luca Verzichelli was a guest of the European Studies Centre at St Antony's College, Oxford. We wish to thank the directors of the two centers, Maurizio Cotta and Timothy Garton Ash, respectively, for their hospitality.

1. See S. Vassallo, "The Constitutional Reforms of the Center-Right," in _Italian Politics: Quo Vadis?_ ed. C. Guarnieri and J. L. Newell (New York and Oxford: Berghahn Books, 2005), 117–135.

2. See M. Caciagli and A. Zuckerman, "Introduction: The Year before the Elections," in _Italian Politics: Emerging Themes and Institutional Responses_, ed. M. Caciagli and A. Zuckerman (New York and Oxford: Berghahn Books, 2001), 25–36.

3. R. D'Alimonte, _Il Sole-24 Ore_, 27 October 2005. This forecast was borne out in the subsequent election of April 2006, in which neither coalition obtained a clear majority in the Senate. As a result, the new government had to rely on the votes of the seven senators-for-life (translator's note).

4. This law regulates television advertising during campaigns, reducing somewhat the advantage Berlusconi derives from the ownership of the three largest private channels (translator's note).

5. Agreement was reached during the programmatic seminar held at the beginning of December: a center-left government would draw up a schedule for withdrawing Italian troops, in conjunction with the Iraqi government. This understanding did not fully satisfy any of the members of the coalition; some minor members were not even present at the seminar.

6. C. Guarnieri and J. L. Newell, "Introduction: 2004—a Year 'On Hold,'" in _Italian Politics: Quo Vadis?_ ed. C. Guarnieri and J. L. Newell (New York and Oxford: Berghahn Books, 2005), 41.

7. OECD, _Economic Surveys_, no. 7 (November 2005).

8. Alleanza Nazionale was not able to obtain a cut in social insurance contributions for agriculture, which would have favored its electoral base in the South, but it did instigate the tax on producers of pornographic material. The Northern League also had to accept both the tax amnesty for the years 2003–4 and the use of the funds destined to top up firms' retirement bonus funds to reduce the deficit, pending the implementation of the reform of the retirement bonus (TFR) system.

9. S. Intravaia, _La Repubblica_, 5 January 2006.

10. Particularly intensive use of this tool was made in the final part of 2005, with repeated votes of confidence forced by the government on various provisions, including the bill on the career structure of university professors, the decree law that accompanied the budgetary maneuver, the "maxi-amendment" to the budget bill itself, and the bill on savings. In all, the year saw fully 15 bills passed in 2005 (and 42 in the entire course of the legislature) after recourse to votes of confidence. This is the highest average since 1948.

11. I. Diamanti, ed., "Italia 2005: Sì, svoltare. Ma dove andare?" _Il Venerdì di Repubblica_, no. 926, 16 December 2005, 29–37.

12. According to the 2006 Eurispes report (R. Amato, _La Repubblica_, 27 January 2006).

13. Note in addition that the participation in the demonstration of representatives of the Green Party, and the fact that the city secretary of Communist Refoundation was injured, illustrate the openness of some political groups, which also form part of the coalition supporting the mayor, to the immigrants' concerns.

14. Diamanti, "Italia 2005."

15. F. Ceccarelli, _La Repubblica_, 27 September 2005.

16. The expression was coined by Mauro Calise, who, even if simply as a provocation, proposes a third model after the "partitocracy" of the past and the "post-partitocratic transition" of the last decade. See M. Calise, _La terza repubblica: Partiti contro presidenti_ (Rome-Bari: Laterza, 2006).

1

THE REGIONAL ELECTIONS: WINNING TOO CONVINCINGLY?

Salvatore Vassallo

On 3 and 4 April 2005, elections were held to elect the councils of 13 of the 15 ordinary regions. In Basilicata the election took place two weeks later, on 17 and 18 April, to allow the Unità Popolare list to take part in the campaign. This list had initially been barred from running because of procedural defects in the presentation of its lists of candidates, but it was later readmitted by the Council of State. In Molise, on the other hand, no election was held because in June 2001 the Council of State had invalidated the regional election of the previous year on the ground that some lists (Democratic Union for Europe, Greens, Italian Democratic Socialists, and Party of Italian Communists) had been allowed to run despite not having satisfied the requirements. This required holding a new election, which took place in November 2001.

In Tuscany, Puglia, Calabria, and Lazio, the elections were held under electoral systems that were different in some respects from those used elsewhere. This was a result of constitutional law no. 1/1999, which granted the regions the power to legislate in this and other areas. In particular, the region of Tuscany took advantage of this opportunity to abolish preference votes and introduce regulations governing primaries, which were to be the method for selecting candidates. However, the primaries held in Tuscany attracted less attention from the public and the parties than those organized in Puglia by the center-left, without the benefit of a legal framework, to choose the presidential candidate for the region. The primaries in Puglia showed for the first time how this method—later used to ratify the choice of Romano Prodi as candidate for prime minister—can stimulate a large number of voters to participate and thus legitimize the choice of candidate.

The elections saw an overwhelming victory for the center-left, which held on to the presidency in six regions and captured an equal number from the Casa delle Libertà (CdL, the center-right coalition). Of the regions that voted in 2005, the CdL retained its majority only in Veneto and Lombardy and did not capture any. Subsequently, the interpretation of the regional election results became a factor in the struggle between the various components of the Ulivo: the supporters of gradual unification, on the one hand, and the advocates of maintaining distinct party identities, on the other. The regional elections showed that given the substantial equality of the electoral strength of the two coalitions, even a small change in electoral behavior, such as the phenomenon of "asymmetric abstention,"[1] can lead to sudden major changes in the distribution of governmental power. The prospect of a victory in the 2006 parliamentary election, which was now considered certain, paradoxically led to an accentuation of the conflict within the Ulivo, while it impelled the center-right to take countermeasures by changing the electoral law.

The Amendments to the Regional Electoral Laws

The constitutional reform, passed with the votes of both poles in 1999, incorporated the direct election of the regional presidents into the Constitution and at the same time gave each region the power to modify both its form of government, so that it could revert back to the system in which the president was chosen by the regional council, and its electoral system. The subsequent reform of 2001, which was passed with the votes of the center-left alone, gave further powers to the regions and in practice required them to modify their statutes in order to adapt them to the constitutional changes.[2] For instance, they now had to assign the power to issue regulations, which had belonged exclusively to the regional councils before the reform, and they were required to create councils of local authorities, which the Constitution defines, after the 2001 reform, as necessary organs for consultation between regions and local governments. The regional councils therefore should have amended their statutes, but not all of them did so. In many cases where they did update the statutes, the councils took the opportunity to introduce superfluous statements of principle or tried to maintain a certain room for maneuver for the council in the face of what the councillors tend to interpret as the increasingly overweening power of the presidents and their *giunte* (cabinets). As a result, while the new statutes tend to assert the councils' traditional political prerogatives and bargaining positions vis-à-vis the *giunte*, they do little to rationalize the legislative process or introduce norms and regulations to reduce the fragmentation of the councils into a large number of micro-groups. This tendency reached an extreme in cases like that of Calabria, whose council was made up, on the eve of the elections, of 43 members divided into 22 groups, of which 17 were formed by a single councillor.[3]

In every case in which the regional statute was amended, with the sole exception of Piedmont, the number of members of the council was increased. Overall, the nine ordinary regions that have approved a new statute (besides Piedmont, they are Emilia-Romagna, Marche, Calabria, Lazio, Liguria, Puglia, Tuscany, and Umbria) have increased the number of councillors by 17 percent. The largest percentage increases are in the statutes drafted but not yet approved by Basilicata (from 30 to 40) and Campania (from 60 to 80). We should note, however, that these changes in the size of the council took effect as of the 2005 elections only in Tuscany (from 50 to 65 seats), Puglia (from 60 to 70), Calabria (from 44 to 50), and Lazio (from 51 to 70), the four regions that also changed their electoral laws.

After amending their statues, the regional councils could also have altered their electoral systems.[4] In doing so, they would have been limited only by the general criteria set out in the framework law no. 165/2004, which requires them to adopt "an electoral system that favors the formation of stable majorities in the regional council and ensures the representation of minorities" (art. 4, para. 2, letter a). In this domain as well, no region introduced significant changes, which goes to show that the political class has internalized the dynamic of "fragmented bipolarism," to which the model introduced in 1995—a proportional formula with voting for party lists and a majority premium, the "Tatarellum"—appears particularly suited.

The regional councils could however have profitably amended some problematic features of the 1995 law that have been the focus of debate among experts and in the councils themselves. The most important of these questionable norms is the often noted paradox that in certain circumstances the system gives a party *more seats* if it wins *fewer votes*. This occurs because the majority premium is awarded either as a whole or not at all, rather than in a graduated manner: if the winning coalition has not won 50 percent of the seats through its proportional quota, it receives the whole premium (equal to 20 percent of the seats), but if it has won 50 percent of the seats, it receives a premium of only 10 percent of the seats. For instance, in Lazio, with

50.8 percent of the votes (for the president), the center-left coalition won 60 percent of the seats (42). In Emilia-Romagna, with 63 percent of the votes it won 64 percent of the seats (32), but would have won more if, for instance, it had run Communist Refoundation (RC), the Party of Italian Communists, and the Greens separately from the coalition: the Unione would have received five more seats as a premium, besides the seats that the three left parties running separately would have taken. A second aspect of the law that has often been criticized is the method for assigning the premium. The bonus seats are in fact awarded to candidates on a regional list (*listino*), according to a fixed order that has been predetermined by the parties (i.e., the lists are "closed"—no preference votes are permitted). The *listino* was initially used to run some "technicians" (experts with few party ties) as candidates, but is now used instead to elect members of the political class who are unlikely to win many preference votes and to guarantee minor coalition partners at least one seat on the council. A third problematic feature is the incongruity between awarding the majority of the seats, always and in every case, to the coalition supporting the winner of the presidential election and allowing vote-splitting (between a presidential candidate and a list that does *not* support him or her). The possibility of vote-splitting, while it has not had any practical effect, could lead to paradoxical situations; for instance, the majority premium could be awarded to a coalition that came second in the vote for the council. Finally, criticism has been directed at the low threshold for obtaining seats, which is set at 3 percent for lists that belong to a coalition that obtains at least 5 percent of the votes, and at the absence of provisions to promote the election of women.

The electoral law enacted by Lazio deals with only the last of these problems by providing that each regional *listino* must be composed half of women and half of men, as well as of residents of all the provinces of the region. Moreover, it requires that the lists of candidates in the constituencies must have no more than two-thirds of their members of the same gender; if a list does not meet this criterion, its state reimbursement of election expenses will be reduced proportionally. The Puglian law addresses the problem of the threshold, but postpones the solution to the next legislature: it states that the threshold will be raised to 4 percent for all parties, even if they are part of a coalition, starting with the election after that of 2005. The same law abolishes the regional *listino* and provides that the bonus seats be assigned to candidates on the constituency lists of the parties supporting the winning presidential candidate. Finally, it also requires that no more than two-thirds of the candidates on each constituency list shall be of the same gender. The Calabrian law, on the other hand, introduces a threshold of 4 percent for all lists (whether or not they are in a coalition), starting immediately with the 2005 election.

The Tuscan electoral law is certainly the most far-reaching in the amendments it introduces to the "Tatarellum." In the first place, it makes the majority premium variable and contingent. If the winning coalition obtains at least 45 percent of the valid votes, it receives at least 60 percent of the seats. The premium is not awarded if the winning coalition has already reached that threshold. If the winning coalition receives less than 45 percent of the valid votes, the premium brings its majority to only 55 percent of the seats. Finally, the opposition is guaranteed at least 35 percent of the seats on the council. Therefore, even if the majority coalition won 80 percent of the votes, it would get no more than 65 percent of the seats. In reality, these provisions still do not resolve the paradox referred to above, and in fact considerations of just the sort we have mentioned deterred the center-left in Tuscany from concluding a pre-electoral agreement with RC.

The Tuscan electoral law makes much more effective changes to the mechanisms that govern competition *within* the parties. It abolishes the *listino* and fills the bonus seats from the provincial lists (in regional elections, each province is a multi-member constituency). These lists are closed, and they may be headed by one or two "regional candidates" who are being run in every constituency and who are elected first. As a result, those who draw up the lists not only decide which candidates will have the best chance of being elected in each province, but also, through the regional candidates' choice of which provincial constituency they will sit for, can in practice choose which of the borderline candidates in the different provinces will enter the council. While on the one hand the electoral law thus eliminates intra-party competition during elections, on the other it establishes a legal framework for those political parties that decide to use primaries to choose their candidates.

It is not surprising that Tuscany was the only region to go over to closed lists. It is a region where voters have always made relatively little use of their preference votes (in 2000 only 27 percent were used, a figure higher only than those of Lombardy and Emilia-Romagna), and it is led by a party, the Left Democrats (DS), that is still characterized by a high degree of organizational cohesion. The complete abolition of the preference vote was possible, we can conclude, only where intra-party competition was more highly regulated, that is, where it was needed least. On the other hand, only the DS took advantage of the opportunity to hold primary elections to choose their own candidates—to use the mechanism that was intended to compensate in a certain way for the abolition of preference votes.

The Primaries in Puglia

As far as candidate selection is concerned, the 2005 regional elections witnessed an overall (re)consolidation of practices established before the transition of the 1990s, in particular, the central role played by the regional leaders of the parties as gatekeepers and mediators.[5] However, this picture of substantial continuity and restoration of older practices and power relations must be qualified by the new dynamic set in motion by the first experiment in selecting a candidate for regional president by primary elections.

The primaries held in Puglia follow on from a series of experiments carried out on a smaller scale.[6] However, the theme returned to the top of the agenda in the internal debate in the center-left on 20 October 2004, when Prodi cut through the hesitation on the subject: he presented "draft rules" to the secretaries of the parties of the Unione[7] for primaries in which he would compete in the run-up to the 2006 general election. The politically significant aspect of Prodi's draft was that the primaries would be totally open both to candidates and to voters. The regulations were drafted in a way that even leaders with relatively small followings could take part, while the party secretaries were not allowed any real chance to "filter" the candidacies. A working group was then set up to flesh out a proposal. Chaired by Arturo Parisi, Prodi's political adviser and leader of the pro-Ulivo faction of the Margherita, and composed of representatives of all the center-left parties, the group soon prepared a set of rules along the lines suggested by Prodi.

There was therefore a "model" at the national level that had been endorsed in substance by an agreement among all the parties, in spite of the fact that the agreement was based on an expectation that the "primaries for Prodi" would never take place. This made the idea of holding some form of primary election to choose candidates for regional president also conceivable. The same kind of calculations, expectations, and short-term constraints that made the experiment acceptable at the national level also made it acceptable in the Puglian case, even for those party leaders who were least willing to yield a share of their power to the electorate.

In the first instance there had been a difference of opinion between the DS and the Margherita over the possible candidacy of Francesco Boccia for president of Puglia. Boccia was a young economics professor at the University of Castellanza (Varese) and close collaborator of the ex-minister, Enrico Letta, who had been serving for the past few years as *assessore* (executive committee member) at the commune of Bari. The DS would have preferred a candidate who had deeper local roots (like the entrepreneur Vincenzo Divella, president of the province of Bari) or who was better known (like the ex-minister of agriculture, Paolo De Castro). During this discussion, the candidates suggested by the "reformist" forces as alternatives to Boccia all fell by the wayside for various reasons. At the same time, the candidacy of Nichi Vendola, a Communist Refoundation deputy with a long record of activism in the Italian Communist Party (PCI) and strong links with the pacifist organizations, was gaining ground.[8]

At the beginning of December, then, the idea of running Boccia was revived, thanks to the return of harmony between the DS and the Margherita and, in particular, between the chairman of the DS, Massimo D'Alema (who has strong ties to the cadres and rank-and-file of his party in Puglia), and Letta. At this point, however, RC had no intention of yielding to a *diktat* from its allies, and asked that the choice between Boccia and Vendola be made in a primary election. Initially, the national secretaries of the parties of the Unione agreed on holding a "convention," the outcome of which would have been fairly predictable. Following a formula that had often been suggested in the preceding months, both for other local elections and for a national assembly of the whole center-left that was called but never held, the "investiture convention" would have been made up in equal proportions by local councillors, representatives of the parties, and representatives of unspecified civil society organizations. This proposal was firmly opposed by the secretary of RC, Fausto Bertinotti, which led to the adoption of the model advanced by Prodi for the choice of the candidate for prime minister.

The decision to hold primary elections can be explained in the first place by the structural conditions created by the internal fragmentation of the center-left. In the Unione there is no strong "dominant" party such as the German Social Democratic Party (SPD) or the French Socialist Party (PS), whose leaders, at the national or local level, are the natural candidates for the highest elected office. Therefore, when negotiations between the parties fail or cannot reach a lasting agreement, it is easy to see primaries as a method that can resolve disagreements (in time for the elections) and give complete legitimacy to the common candidate. Naturally, as we shall see below, primaries have a significant cost for the party secretaries, who lose part of their bargaining power. In the second place, in the cases of both the Puglian primary and the subsequent national one, the party secretaries would in all likelihood not have agreed to give up a portion of their sovereign power over candidacies to the electorate if they had not been convinced that they could predict the results of the vote. The primaries were acceptable insofar as RC's pressure was considered more as a demand for recognition of its rights as a full member of the

Unione than as a real challenge to the "reformist" candidate. In sum, even though they were open, the primaries were acceptable as a rite of investiture. The agreement reached on this solution, which was not without its risks, was also facilitated—and this is a third factor that should not be underestimated—by the exertions of the chairman of the Federal Assembly of the Margherita and adviser to Prodi, Arturo Parisi, who was striving to use his limited agenda-setting power to create and foster any possible "supra-party" institution that was independent of the constraints of inter-party bargaining.

All three factors were at work in the subsequent months when the issue of primaries was once again on the agenda—this time in the run-up to the 2006 general election. And one reason they were again on the agenda was that, contrary to all expectations, the Puglian primaries turned out to be an extraordinary success and could not be described in public or within the center-left as anything else. The turnout was very high, equal to 9.5 percent of the voters who had voted for the parties of the Unione in the 2004 European elections; the result was unexpected, which proved that it was not a prefabricated exercise; the contestants, both the winner and the loser, had the good sense to accept the verdict with the necessary humility; and the winner, in spite of his "radical" political label, went on to win the election for president of Puglia.

On the one hand, the result of the election belied the predictions of those prestigious analysts who maintained that primary elections, by over-representing extremist voters, tend to reduce the chance of victory for coalitions that hold them.[9] On the other hand, it encouraged the leader of RC, Bertinotti, to press for the adoption of the same method at the national level, and in a certain sense obliged him to run in the national primary, lending it the justification that it needed and that it would not have had without his candidacy. Only a competitor of his caliber could create a certain amount of uncertainty about the result of a national primary—if not about the result, then about Prodi's margin of victory—and thereby make it more than a pure and simple coronation of the candidate chosen by the major parties.

The Puglian primaries, however, had already demonstrated the expectations and short-term constraints that can explain the readiness of the leaders of the major parties to accept this method of candidate selection. Primaries can be acceptable for those who hold bargaining power as party leaders only insofar as the result is highly predictable (or thought to be so) and only on condition that the method is not generalized. If it were generalized, this would inevitably mean that the leaders' bargaining power would disappear. Predictably, when the issue came up again at the end of October 2005 in the run-up to the

Sicilian regional election, several leaders of the Margherita argued that it was not a good idea to hold primary elections, since, as a result of agreements with the DS, the choice of the candidate was to be made by their party. This position was made untenable by the extraordinary success of the "primaries for Prodi," which were held on 16 October with a turnout even higher than in the Puglian vote.[10] Therefore, primaries were also held to choose a candidate for president of the region of Sicily. The convincing victory of Rita Borsellino[11] over the Margherita's candidate, Fernando Latteri, ex-rector of the University of Catania, highlighted the consequences that the generalization of the method can have on the party leaders' bargaining power. We can easily see this in the statement made the day after the Sicilian primaries by the organization secretary of the Margherita, Franco Marini: "Behind the beatification of this instrument, I see the devil of anti-party feeling reappearing. But I don't agree with the slogan 'primaries always.' It's a short-cut, it's anti-politics."[12]

A New Political Map? Limited Mobility but Large-Scale Asymmetric Abstention

The decision to hold the "primaries for Prodi," however, was not made immediately after the regional elections or as a result of their positive outcome, but rather because of the paradoxical effects of a victory won by too great a margin. Before we return to this question, it will be worthwhile to give an account and an explanation of this victory. As we stated at the outset, the 2005 regional elections were interpreted as a landslide for the center-left, which won 12 regional governments out of 14, taking 6 from the center-right. Given that the differences in votes, in absolute terms, between 2005 and the previous regional elections were quite large for both coalitions, many observers thought that the center-left's victory was due to vote-switching, that is, the shifting of voters who had previously supported the CdL to the Unione. As we shall see, a careful analysis of even just the aggregate data at the regional level suggests that we should be cautious about jumping to such a conclusion; on the contrary, it would seem to demonstrate that, once again, the outcome was decided above all by the phenomenon of asymmetric abstention. Given the major shift in the balance of political forces, it is also worthwhile to ask if the regional elections of 2005 mark a transformation of the electoral map of the country. The data presented in table 1 are an attempt to answer both questions, starting with the second.

In the first and second columns, we present indicators of the electoral strength of the Unione and of the CdL as they are currently constituted,

TABLE 1 *Indicators of the electoral strength of the center-right and center-left in the regions voting in 2005*

	Average 1995–2004[1]					2005 Regional Election				Regional Government		
	CdL	Unione	Diff.	Vol.[2]	Inv.[3]	C.-l.[4]	C.-r.[4]	Turn.[5]	Diff.[6]	1995	2000	2005
Tuscany	37.4	58.6	21.1	4.2	16.9	12.9	−18.6	−3.3	31.9	c.-l.	c.-l.	c.-l.
Emilia-Romagna	37.4	58.1	20.7	3.8	16.9	9.1	−14.4	−3.0	26.5	c.-l.	c.-l.	c.-l.
Umbria	39.6	56.2	16.6	5.1	11.5	10.8	−10.1	−2.6	27.6	c.-l.	c.-l.	c.-l.
Basilicata	36.8	57.3	20.4	16.0	4.4	0.0	−15.9	−5.5	37.6	c.-l.	c.-l.	c.-l.
Marche	42.3	51.5	9.1	6.0	3.1	14.2	−13.9	−2.9	18.2	c.-l.	c.-l.	c.-l.
Liguria	44.5	49.9	5.5	6.8	−1.4	16.1	−6.9	−0.8	6.7	c.-l.	c.-r.	c.-l.
Abruzzo	46.6	47.2	0.6	2.5	−1.9	18.2	−18.2	−1.9	17.4	c.-l.	c.-r.	c.-l.
Campania	45.9	47.3	1.4	7.1	−5.7	12.5	−23.2	−1.8	27.4	c.-l.	c.-r.	c.-l.
Calabria	47.0	46.6	−0.4	9.4	−9.0	22.8	−19.2	−0.2	20.9	c.-r.	c.-r.	c.-l.
Puglia	48.3	45.3	−2.9	6.1	−3.1	18.9	−5.4	0.3	0.4	c.-r.	c.-r.	c.-l.
Lazio	48.1	45.9	−2.2	3.1	−0.8	13.9	−4.6	1.1	1.4	c.-l.	c.-r.	c.-l.
Piedmont	51.0	41.6	−9.4	6.5	2.9	30.2	−8.0	−0.6	2.5	c.-r.	c.-r.	c.-l.
Veneto	55.7	36.5	−19.2	9.7	9.6	9.0	−9.6	−3.2	−10.5	c.-r.	c.-r.	c.-r.
Lombardy	56.1	36.5	−19.6	9.6	9.9	25.9	−15.6	−2.6	−13.3	c.-r.	c.-r.	c.-r.

[1]Average percentage of the vote in all regional, national, and European elections held during the period in question.
[2]Index of volatility: the average value, for the period 1995–2004, of the change in the absolute value of the difference between the center-left and the center-right (col. 3) between one election and the immediately preceding one.
[3]Index of invulnerability of the majority, equal to the absolute value of the average difference (col. 3) minus the index of volatility (col. 4). A high and positive value therefore can mean that the voters have a stable propensity to support either the center-right (regions at the bottom of the table) or the center-left (regions at the top). A low (or negative) value indicates that neither coalition can count on a stable majority of the electorate.
[4]Percentage change in the total vote received by the center-left and the center-right, respectively, in 2005 compared to 2000.
[5]Percentage change in turnout in 2005 compared to 2000.
[6]Difference between the percentages of the vote received by the center-left and the center-right in 2005.

which is close to the most inclusive possible composition for each coalition. This is, more precisely, the average percentage of valid votes for each coalition in every "first order" (Chamber of Deputies) and "second order" (regional, European) election from the beginning of the bipolar pattern in 1995 to 2004. For those elections where voters cast ballots in both a proportional and a majoritarian contest (Chamber and regional), the average of the two figures was used. The third column lists simply the difference in each region between the average vote for the left and that for the right. Taken by itself, this indicator, even when based on elections over a relatively long period, cannot be considered a good index of the dominance of one coalition over the other, and even less a sign of the invulnerability of the coalition that governs each region at the moment. In fact, we have different rates of voter mobility in the different regions. It is possible that even a relatively large difference between center-right and center-left can be reversed if the electorate is volatile, while a small lead can be insuperable if the electorate is immobile.[13] To measure this, we have presented in the fourth column an "index of volatility" of the electoral balance, calculated as the average variation in the difference between center-left and center-right from one election to the next. From these data we can then calculate a summary measure of the degree of contestability of each region (in the medium term). One coalition's superiority over the other is more difficult to overturn the more its margin of advantage exceeds, in absolute terms, the index of volatility. This is how the index of invulnerability presented in the fifth column has been calculated. It is lowest, and can even take on a negative sign, when one coalition's advantage over the other appears more fragile, given the electoral results of the last 10 years. It can be interpreted, then, as a measure of the degree to which there exists, in each region, a stable propensity on the part of the electorate to support a specific coalition.

On the basis of this analysis, we can conclude that seven of the regions that voted in 2005 could not be considered, given their electoral history, fully contestable. Five were held by the Unione, and only two by the CdL. The fact that the center-left won in all the contestable regions is certainly an indicator of its popularity with the voters at that moment and of the unpopularity of the center-right, but it disproves the idea that the elections marked an incipient change in the political map of Italy. If anything, it supports the hypothesis that the number of contestable regions is increasing. Moreover, the "vote-switching" theory seems to be partially disproved by the data presented in the following columns. The fifth and sixth show the percentage change in the total number of votes received by the center-left and the center-right, respectively, between the regional elections of 2000 and 2005.

As we can see, the CdL lost votes in every region, while the center-left gained everywhere. Overall, the CdL lost almost 1.7 million votes, while the Unione gained 2.2 million. But it is important to note that the decrease in the CdL's support and the gains by the Unione are not systematically correlated.

The election results fit the hypothesis that they reflect a general depression on the part of center-right voters and an unusual euphoria, or in any case a significant degree of mobilization, experienced by the center-left's electorate. Both depression and euphoria are heightened by expectations. It is not accidental that the relative fall in the center-right vote is significantly less than elsewhere in the contestable regions in which the center-right was running incumbents with good chances of re-election (Liguria, Piedmont, Puglia, Lazio). On the other hand, the loss of votes was larger in the regions that were not contestable and in those where the right was handicapped by the relative quality of its candidates. In Abruzzo, the center-right ran the incumbent president, Giovanni Pace, a 72-year-old former National Alliance (AN) deputy. As if to demonstrate that they lacked confidence in his ability to win re-election, in 2004 the center-right passed a regional law on incompatibility with the sole purpose of blocking the candidacy of the mayor of Pescara, Luciano D'Alfonso, who had already been chosen some time before by the center-left to oppose Pace. The center-left then, by common agreement, replaced D'Alfonso with the former national vice-secretary of the Italian General Confederation of Labor (CGIL), Ottaviano Del Turco. In Campania, Bassolino's re-election seemed assured, and in Calabria, the CdL decided not to run the incumbent president, Giuseppe Chiaravallotti, again after one term because the polls suggested that his popularity was extremely low. Although the CdL's performance in Piedmont, Puglia, Lazio, and Liguria was comparatively better, it was nevertheless not enough to completely halt the demobilization of its electorate, and its presidential candidates were defeated there, even if by small margins.

We should note in addition that several candidates for president supported the presentation of "civic lists" of candidates, or of "personal" lists. This happened more often in the center-left than in the center-right because of the stronger opposition from the national party leaders in the latter. In the case of Lombardy, there was a tense struggle before the election between the incumbent president, Roberto Formigoni, and the leader of his own party and of the Northern League (Silvio Berlusconi and Umberto Bossi, respectively). It was finally decided at a national meeting of leaders of the CdL on 12 January that a "president's list" would be presented only in regions where the presidential candidate had the approval of his or her own party. As a result, Formigoni had to yield to the decision of the leader of Forza Italia (FI), who was understandably concerned that if a "Formigoni List" did well, it could make the expected fall in the level of support for the party (an expectation that was subsequently borne out) even more painful. Moreover, both Berlusconi and the Northern League saw the Formigoni List as an attempt by the "governor" to increase his already substantial personal power base. It should be noted, in any case, that judging by the good showings of the few presidents' lists that were actually presented, center-right voters are very receptive to this sort of option. The Sandro Biasotti List took 8.7 percent of the vote in Liguria, the Storace List took 7.0 percent in Lazio, and Puglia Above All won 9.1 percent. With the partial exception of the Marrazzo List (6.7 percent in Lazio), lists of the same type did less well in the center-left.

In conclusion, although the 12 to 2 result has an impressive ring, the 2005 regional elections did not signal a radical change in the political map of the country. The outcome seems to be the result of a limited movement of voters from one pole to the other and a more significant shift due to asymmetric abstention, as well as the greater personal appeal of the center-left candidates for president in the most hotly contested regions.

Better United or Divided?

Besides allowing a trial of the method of primary elections and measuring the relative strength of the left and the right, the 2005 regional elections were a further test of another significant innovation in Italian politics that has been under discussion more or less openly since 1996—that is, the project of gradually integrating the major parties belonging to what was called, at the time of the elections, the Federazione dell'Ulivo (Olive Tree Federation: DS, Margherita, European Republicans, and Italian Democratic Socialists). This project was laid out by Prodi before the 2004 European elections and on that occasion took the form of the list "Uniti nell'Ulivo" (United in the Olive Tree).

For the 2005 regional elections, the center-left parties that belonged to the Federation presented a joint list in some regions (Basilicata, Emilia-Romagna, Lazio, Liguria, Lombardy, Marche, Tuscany, Umbria, and Veneto) and ran as separate parties in the others (Abruzzo, Calabria, Campania, Piedmont, and Puglia). This compromise was the result of a struggle between, on the one hand, the secretary of the Margherita, Francesco Rutelli, backed up by the group of former members of the Italian People's Party (PPI) in the Margherita (Franco Marini, Ciriaco De Mita), and, on the other, the *prodiani*, led by Arturo Parisi and at least ostensibly supported by the secretary of the DS, Piero Fassino. In the aftermath of the elections, it is therefore interesting to ask which of the two electoral strategies—a single list or separate lists—was more advantageous for the center-left as a whole and for the Ulivo in particular.

Comparisons with the past are complicated slightly by the fact that the party system has changed in certain respects during the last few years, and this applies to the center-left parties as well. Some groups in the Ulivo camp have changed their names or fused and split in various ways. Moreover, in both the 2000 and the 2005 regional elections, there were also presidents' lists in the running. For instance, in 2000, Massimo Cacciari and Mino Martinazzoli, the center-left candidates for the presidency in Veneto and Lombardy, had two lists that took the place of those of one or more parties of the coalition. In 2005 in several regions there were presidents' lists in addition to the party lists or those of the Olive Tree Federation. Since we have to count them in some fashion, we can assume that the presidents' lists can be assimilated to the Olive Tree component of the coalition (and therefore their votes can be added to those it received). Moreover, the presidential candidates in question, except for Nichi Vendola in Puglia, all came from that component.

We shall compare the two groups of regions, bearing in mind that those in which the Ulivo ran a joint list in 2005 differ in some important ways from those in which the parties ran separate lists. They ran separately principally in Southern regions where the difference between the votes received in regional and general elections is consistently higher than in the Center-North. The reason for this pattern of behavior on the part of Southern voters is one of the factors that led the leaders of the center-left parties, and especially of the Margherita, not to present joint lists there. It is believed that Southern voters are more easily mobilized when there are many candidates in the running competing for preference votes. The most valid comparison seems to be, therefore, between elections of the same type, that is, between the 2000 and 2005 regional elections.

Tables 2 and 3 present the aggregate voting data by year, arranged into the "macro-components" of each coalition: in table 2 we present the data for the regions where the Ulivo ran a joint list in 2005, and in table 3 are the data for those regions where the parties ran separate lists. Figure 1 illustrates the most significant results of this analysis. It compares the movement over time of three aggregates: (1) the sum total of the percentage shares of the vote received by all the components of

TABLE 2 *Percentages of the vote won by the different components of the center-left and the center-right: Regions where the Olive Tree Federation ran a joint list in the 2005 regional election*

	1999	2000	2001	2004	2005
Center-left					
Olive Tree + presidents' lists	32.8	33.1	32.9	32.8	36.2
Uniti nell'Ulivo (joint lists)	32.8	25.6	32.9	32.8	33.9
Center-left presidents' lists	0.0	7.5	0.0	0.0	2.2
Other center-left groupings	9.1	10.3	12.7	13.6	13.6
UDEUR	0.5	0.7	0.0	0.4	0.8
Leftist parties	8.6	9.6	8.9	11.3	11.6
Di Pietro	0.0	0.0	3.8	1.9	1.2
Center-right					
Lega Nord	6.2	6.7	6.0	7.0	7.6
Alleanza nazionale	10.1	13.2	11.6	10.5	10.5
Forza Italia	24.4	25.9	27.4	21.6	20.3
UDC	3.9	5.3	2.7	4.4	5.2
Other center-right groupings	0.0	0.2	0.8	1.6	0.8
Center-right presidents' lists	0.0	0.0	0.0	0.0	1.7
Others*	13.4	5.3	6.0	8.4	4.2
N (total valid votes)	17,824,347	16,461,364	21,193,520	18,734,522	15,939,723

* Including the Radicals, who did very well in 1999.

Note: The regions include Basilicata, Emilia-Romagna, Lazio, Liguria, Lombardy, Marche, Tuscany, Umbria, and Veneto.

TABLE 3 *Percentages of the vote won by the different components of the center-left and the center-right: Regions where the parties of the Olive Tree Federation ran separate lists in the 2005 regional election*

	1999	2000	2001	2004	2005
Center-left					
Olive Tree + presidents' lists	33.5	34.2	28.7	29.5	37.3
Center-left presidents' lists	0.0	0.0	0.0	0.0	1.6
Olive Tree parties	33.6	34.2	28.7	29.5	35.7
DS	14.4	15.9	15.0	0.0	17.0
Margherita	15.7	14.1	13.7	0.0	13.1
Other center-left groupings	10.5	12.1	14.2	16.4	17.6
UDEUR	2.7	3.9	0.0	2.8	5.7
Leftist parties	7.8	8.3	9.8	11.1	10.2
Di Pietro	0.0	0.0	4.4	2.5	1.7
Center-right					
Lega Nord	2.3	1.8	1.6	2.4	2.0
Alleanza nazionale	10.3	12.4	12.9	13.0	10.7
Forza Italia	26.4	24.6	31.3	19.8	15.9
UDC	5.8	9.5	3.5	7.1	8.2
Other center-right groupings	0.0	0.4	1.3	3.0	2.4
Center-right presidents' lists	0.0	0.0	0.0	0.0	2.5
Others*	11.1	5.3	6.5	8.8	3.4
N (total valid votes)	8,694,409	8,752,335	10,455,656	9,163,724	8,864,559

* Including the Radicals, who did very well in 1999.

Note: The regions include Abruzzo, Calabria, Campania, Piedmont, and Puglia.

the center-left; (2) the sum of the percentage shares of the vote received by the components that are now part of the Olive Tree Federation, plus the votes taken by the presidents' lists; and (3) the sum of the percentage shares of the vote won by the other components of the center-left. For all three aggregates, the movement over time is shown separately for the two groups of regions: those in which the Ulivo ran joint lists in 2005, and those in which the parties ran separately.

We can see clearly that in the regions where the Ulivo ran joint lists in 2005, the voters change their behavior less according to the type of election. Here the line is straighter, compared to what happens in the regions where the parties ran separately. If we factor out this phenomenon, the pay-off from the two strategies is the same. The gain for the Ulivo component as a whole is roughly 3 percent of the votes in each case. In the regions where the parties of the Ulivo ran separately, the other components of the center-left gained slightly more than where there was a joint Ulivo list. The main reason for this was the significant growth of the Union of Democrats for Europe (UDEUR) in the South. Once again, as we had already seen with the European elections, neither of the two strategies (having many symbols and candidates on the ballot, or having one strong symbol) proved itself decisively superior to the other in terms of votes won.

FIGURE 1 *Movement over time of the percentages of the vote received by some macro-components of the center-left*

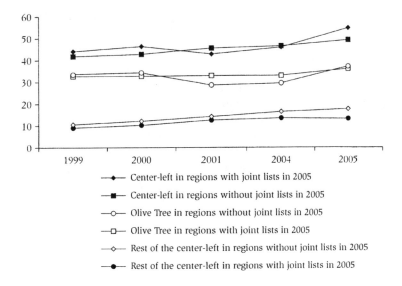

—◆— Center-left in regions with joint lists in 2005

—■— Center-left in regions without joint lists in 2005

—○— Olive Tree in regions without joint lists in 2005

—□— Olive Tree in regions with joint lists in 2005

—◇— Rest of the center-left in regions without joint lists in 2005

—●— Rest of the center-left in regions with joint lists in 2005

Conclusions

Judging by the electoral results, in the aftermath of the regional elections the center-left had the wind in its sails. The coalition had won in every region except Lombardy and Veneto. The performance of the joint lists of the Ulivo parties had proved once again that uniting the reformist components did not have a negative impact on their overall electoral strength. The Puglian experiment had shown that primaries could be a very useful tool for mobilizing a large number of sympathizers and resolving any thorny issues that might arise in leadership selection in a transparent manner.

Each one of these results, however, was marred by a drawback. Above all, the overall shift in electoral fortunes in favor of the Unione was hastily transposed into parliamentary seats by the parties' statisticians and interpreted as a portent of certain victory in the 2006 election. In the meantime, the victory in the regional elections could be interpreted as a functional equivalent of primaries to choose the candidate for premier. Indeed it was Prodi's detractors who had put about this hypothesis in the preceding months, arguing that a result that was below expectations would require Prodi to step down to open the way for a younger candidate, such as his former deputy prime minister, Walter Veltroni, currently mayor of Rome. And Prodi himself announced on the day after the elections that a further test of his own popularity would no longer be necessary.

But at this point the relative "generosity" with which the secretaries of the two principal parties of the Ulivo had promised to give up pieces of the parties' identities and of their own personal sovereignty immediately evaporated. In particular, it became clear to them that that it would be more advantageous to keep their own labels separate in order to increase their own bargaining power before, during, and after the election, with a view to the distribution of governmental positions. The regional elections of 2005, rather than marking a new beginning for the center-left, in the end sparked a (more or less) subterranean war over the coalition's identity and the future balance of power within it, in which different visions and conflicting interests confronted each other. This paradox produced another paradox within itself, as the divisions resulting from these efforts to defend the prerogatives of the parties induced Prodi to once again make a strong plea for primaries. Their result in turn put the idea of unification back on the agenda. On the other hand, the prospect that the Unione would win the general election as well led the center-right and its leaders to envisage a disastrous scenario in which 90 percent of the country—taking communes, provinces, regions, and the national level together—could be governed by the opposing coalition. To avoid such a scenario, any possible expedient could appear legitimate, such as amending the electoral law in a proportional direction so that the winning coalition would have only a narrow majority in the Chamber and an even narrower one in the Senate.

— *Translated by Anna Edwards*

Notes

1. The expression "asymmetric abstention" is used here to describe the movement in votes that occurs when the leadership of one of the coalitions suffers from a generally lower rating by the voters than that of the opposing coalition. The electoral base of the lower-rated leadership reacts chiefly by not turning out to vote, while the turnout of the opposing coalition's base increases.
2. C. Fusaro and M. Rubechi, "Le nuove leggi elettorali e i nuovi statuti," *Le istituzioni del federalismo*, no. 6 (2005).
3. We have to note that a few attempts were made to limit this phenomenon. As we shall see below, the electoral threshold has been increased in some regions, and in Calabria, the new statute of the region provides moreover that groups must have at least three members, unless they represent a political party that has its own national parliamentary groups or a list that received at least 5 percent of the votes in the region as a whole.
4. Abruzzo and Marche also passed reforms of their electoral systems, but these laws were challenged in court by the government, which argued that they should have been passed only *after* the national framework law and the amendments to the regional statute implementing the 1999 constitutional reform had entered into force.
5. On this point, see the research on the selection of regional political representatives coordinated by the author in *Le istituzioni del federalismo*, no. 6 (2005), and in particular the studies by Stefania Profeti, Martino Mazzoleni, Daniela Napoli, Ugo Carlone, and Giuseppe Milella on the cases of Tuscany, Lombardy, Calabria, Umbria, and Puglia, respectively.
6. In 2003, indirect primaries were held to choose the center-left candidate for president of the province of Palermo, while a direct election system had been used to choose the candidates for mayor of several communes in Tuscany.
7. On 19 January 2005, the center-left coalition abandoned the name Great Democratic Alliance, chosen in October 2004, and adopted Union for Democracy, and then, as of 9 February, more simply l'Unione (the Union). To reduce the understandable confusion this could generate for readers, we have decided to use this last title here and elsewhere in this volume; it is the label under which the center-left ran in the 2005 regional elections.
8. G. Milella, "La scommessa vinta delle primarie: La Puglia," *Le istituzioni del federalismo*, no. 6 (2005).

9. For instance, Giovanni Sartori wrote in the *Corriere della Sera* (19 January 2005): "I have always known (from the literature on the issue) that ... those who take part in and win primaries are almost always the militants, the most ideologically motivated, the activists, that is, the 'lefts' of the left and, symmetrically, the 'rights' of the right ... Therefore, for those who understand these things Vendola's victory is not a surprise. The surprise would be if Vendola won the election. In these cases ... the rule is that the winner of the primaries loses the election."

10. On the national primaries, see Jonathan Hopkin's chapter in this volume.

11. Sister of the judge Paolo Borsellino, killed by the Mafia in 1992.

12. *La Repubblica*, 6 December 2005.

13. S. Bartolini, "Collusion, Competition, and Democracy: Part II," *Journal of Theoretical Politics* 12, no. 1 (2000): 53.

2

From Federation to Union, from Parties to Primaries: The Search for Unity in the Center-Left

Jonathan Hopkin

For the parties of the center-left, 2005 was a year of significant progress toward the objective of wresting the government from Berlusconi's center-right coalition. It began with Romano Prodi's initially uncertain return to the Italian political stage after his "exile" in Brussels as president of the European Commission, and familiar divisions—enthusiastically aired in the media—over how the center-left should be organized and structured and over the selection of candidates and alliances for the April regional elections. However, 2005 went on to provide two major boosts to the center-left: a surprisingly decisive victory in the regional elections, and an equally decisive outcome to the primary election held to choose a "premier candidate" for the alliance. Although big questions of organization and coordination remained unresolved, the center-left finished the year in a stronger position than at its beginning. After providing a little background, this chapter will assess the coalition's progress over the year and offer some tentative interpretations of the key turning points.

A Brief History of the Center-Left

Since Italy's electoral reform of 1993, which instituted a system based largely on single-member districts, Italian elections have taken the form of a bipolar competition between an electoral alliance of the left

---

and another of the right, with few parties remaining outside the two coalitions (although the electoral reform passed at the end of 2005 may well undermine this pattern in the future). In 1994, the center and left space of the political spectrum was divided into two alliances: one group with a clearly left-leaning identity took the label of the Progressives (Progressisti) and drew heavily on the Italian Communist tradition, revolving around the Party of the Democratic Left (PDS, later DS) and the Communist Refoundation Party (PRC), plus a collection of small center-left parties such as the Greens and some Socialists. The majority of members of the former Christian Democratic party (DC), stood alone in the 1994 elections as the People's Party (PPI), which failed to match the DC's electoral record and was strongly penalized by the workings of the new electoral law. This division of the center and left was partly responsible for the dramatic victory of Silvio Berlusconi's right-wing Pole of Freedom (Polo delle Libertà) in the first election under the new majoritarian system.

This electoral defeat paved the way to closer cooperation among center and left parties. In 1996, the center-left united around the Olive Tree coalition (Ulivo), which included the PDS, the Greens, some Socialists, and those Christian Democrats who had refused to follow their more conservative colleagues into Berlusconi's Pole of Freedom. The PRC remained outside the coalition, while negotiating a "stand-down" (*desistenza*) arrangement with the Olive Tree whereby the two formations would not stand candidates against each other in the single-member electoral districts. The addition of moderate Christian Democrats and the leadership of Prodi, a former member of the left faction of the DC, gave the electoral coalition a more clearly centrist identity, and the term "center-left"[1] has been used increasingly since then to describe the coalition, particularly since the PRC withdrew its support for the Prodi government in 1998, formally bringing the Olive Tree coalition government to an end.

Despite the apparent instability of the center-left alliance and the frequent changes of label for both the coalition as a whole and its component parties, the broad political space represented by the center-left has remained stable since 1996: the former Communists of the DS, former Socialists who did not sign up to the Berlusconi project, the Christian Democrat left (now named Democrazia e Libertà, abbreviated to Margherita), and the Greens. The center-left in its broadest sense has also included Antonio Di Pietro's various anti-corruption tickets, prominent centrist individuals such as Lamberto Dini, and the radical left groups present in the Italian Parliament. The Communists split in 1998 over their relations with the center-left, with a "loyalist" faction (the Party of Italian Communists, PdCI) leaving the PRC to support the new center-left government under Massimo d'Alema, along with some conservative Christian Democrats (the UDEUR, which has remained in the center-left ever since, despite frequent threats to leave). In 2001, the center-left failed to coordinate as effectively as in 1996, with both PRC and Di Pietro refusing to enter comprehensive stand-down agreements. Given the opprobrium heaped on the PRC after Berlusconi's decisive victory in 2001, there has since been greater pressure for unity, and both the PdCI and the PRC have maintained a close, although often ambiguous, association with the center-left.

What Is the Center-Left? GAD, Fed, or Unitary Party?

In the 2001 election, the center-left parties supporting the government coalition had faced an uphill task in defending a patchy governing record against a cohesive and well-organized center-right coalition led by the powerful and resource-rich figure of Silvio Berlusconi. Berlusconi's convincing victory in that election reflected Italians' disillusionment with the internal wranglings inside the center-left coalition and the lack of clear leadership, which contrasted with the well-packaged and optimistic message of the center-right. By 2005, however, the Berlusconi government was severely debilitated by its own internal divisions on key policy issues, which left it bereft of any coherent discourse about how to address Italy's accelerating economic decline. This presented the center-left opposition with a great opportunity to win back power in the legislative election due in 2006.

That this election victory appeared less than certain in early 2005 reflected the center-left's own disarray as the composition of the center-left coalition, the nature of the coordination between the parties, and the label under which the parties would fight the election all underwent a succession of changes. In the European election of 2004, a first attempt at unifying the center-left had been made, with the Left Democrats (DS), the Margherita, the Italian Democratic Socialists (SDI), and a tiny group of Republicans forming a single unified list—"Uniti nell'Ulivo" (United in the Olive Tree). This unitary list was a qualified success. On the one hand, the co-existence of the key center-left parties in the same electoral list sent a clear message to other potential partners that the core of the coalition was intent on closer and more structured cooperation. On the other, the refusal of parties such as the Greens, Di Pietro's group, and the Communists (PdCI and PRC) to take part, as well as the failure of the list to mobilize many votes beyond the support bases of the parties within it, suggested limits to the unification strategy. Smaller parties, fearful of losing their identity

within a larger formation, were aware that the best-organized parties—
in particular, the DS and Margherita—would dominate decisions about
candidates' positions on the lists. The strategy was also hampered by
its lack of a clear leader. Although Prodi was presented as the leader of
the coalition, he was not standing for election. Moreover, his position
as outgoing president of the European Commission raised legitimate
objections as to the appropriateness of his partisan involvement in a
European election, restricting his role in the campaign itself.

With Prodi's formal return to Italian politics at the end of 2004,
new impetus was given to the push toward unification, but the initial
result was more confusion. First, the label GAD (Grande Alleanza
Democratica, or Great Democratic Alliance) was coined as the identity
around which both the unitary list parties and the other center-left
forces could mobilize. The GAD represented an attempt to design a
broad coalition with the 2004 unitary list parties as its core. It contained 10 parties, ranging from the Communist PRC and PdCI on the
left to the Christian Democratic UDEUR and Antonio Di Pietro's Italy
of Values (Italia dei Valori) on the right. This broad range of ideological positions suggested difficulties in reaching common policy proposals, a difficulty immediately demonstrated by divisions over Italian
policy in Iraq, motivated by a parliamentary vote in November 2004.
The unitary list parties, bound by a tighter relationship, became the
Fed—a "federation" of parties, more formally, the Federation of the
Olive Tree (Federazione dell'Ulivo). At the beginning of December
2004, the "Statute of the Federation of the Olive Tree" was agreed to
by the DS, Margherita, SDI, and European Republicans, establishing
a formal territorial and leadership structure and, perhaps most significantly, committing the federation to primary elections to choose a
prime ministerial candidate for the 2006 election.

However, these bold steps quickly led to the brakes being applied.
A number of center-left leaders expressed discontent at the terms
"GAD" and "Fed,"[2] which were quietly dropped. They were replaced
by the label "Unione" for the center-left as a whole, while the term
"Olive Tree" was revived to describe the core parties. This "stop-go"
pattern of unifying measures being followed by internal dissent and
then steps backward was the defining characteristic of center-left politics throughout 2005.

These events demonstrated clearly the contours of the center-left
dilemma.[3] On the one hand, there was sufficient common ground
between the two biggest components of the center-left—the DS and
Margherita—to move beyond a coalitional model toward closer coordination.[4] On the other, these two parties alone had no chance of winning
a majority of parliamentary seats without including the other, smaller

center-left parties in their electoral coalition. The tension between a narrower and more cohesive formation, as opposed to a broader but inchoate coalition, remained to be resolved. As Giuliano Amato explained in a newspaper interview in early 2005,[5] the center-left contained within it historic divisions between Communists and Socialists (partly resolved by the collapse of the PSI and the creation of the DS in the early 1990s), and between lay forces (Communists, Socialists, and some Republicans and representatives of the business world) and Catholics (former Christian Democrats, mostly in the Margherita). The inevitability of divisions over policy led Amato to propose a "Schengen" of the center-left—a metaphor that reflected the profound distinctiveness of the different traditions present in the coalition.

The nature of the center-left dilemma was comparable to the situation of the center-right. Within the House of Freedoms (Casa delle Libertà) alliance there are similar divisions between lay (sectors of the Northern League and liberals within Forza Italia) and Catholic (the former Christian Democrats in the UDC and Forza Italia, and the conservatives in AN), as well as a clear territorial division between the representatives of the industrial North (Northern League and, to an extent, Forza Italia) and the economically dependent South (UDC, AN, and parts of Forza Italia). The center-right's inability to deal with the most important challenges facing Italy—economic reform, the budget, and the territorial structure of the state—is in large part due to these fundamental divisions. However, the center-right has been very cohesive and disciplined on some issues, in particular, matters concerning Berlusconi personally (broadcasting regulation and judicial issues), but also, for example, the electoral reform pushed through in late 2005. Where the center-left has appeared divided over both policy and electoral strategy, the center-right has appeared much more capable of uniting in the bid to maintain political power. The presence of a dominant leadership figure personally controlling key political resources—money and media influence—seems to make the difference here.

Prodi's participation was therefore crucial to the management of the center-left, and in 2005 he became very directly involved in developing a political and organizational strategy. This met with some resistance, much of which, perhaps unexpectedly, came from within the Margherita, the political party with which Prodi was personally most closely identified. Early in January 2005, the leader of the Margherita, Francesco Rutelli, passed a motion in his party's federal assembly that ruled out moves toward a unitary party and postponed any such development to the distant future.[6] For Rutelli, moves toward closer union would clearly undermine his leadership, given that Prodi was the most obvious reference point for the centrist, Catholic component of the Olive Tree. Moreover, those sectors of the Margherita that were less close to Prodi were wary of moves to turn the Fed into a unitary party, which they feared would marginalize them, given the greater organizational strength of the DS.[7] Despite this, Prodi has refused to force a split in the Margherita to form his own party, preferring instead to stand as a leader *super partes*, while maintaining close relations with the minority faction of the Margherita.[8]

The fact that so many of the organizational difficulties of unifying the Ulivo parties revolved around the relationship between the center-left's leader, Prodi, and the party apparently closest to him ideologically, the Margherita, suggested a battle for power and visibility rather than policy disagreement. To the extent that the leadership and coordination problems were resolved in the course of 2005, it had come down to the nuts and bolts of power politics: who had the votes?

The Electoral Prospects of the Center-Left

The uneasy balance of power in the Italian center-left has also depended heavily on electoral considerations and parties' judgments of their political advantage. The regional elections in April 2005 were the last major popular vote before the forthcoming legislative elections. As such, they constituted a decisive political and electoral test for the most prominent center-left leaders and their preferred strategies, and the detailed results would serve as the benchmark upon which negotiations over candidates for the legislative elections—and indeed the broad political and organizational strategy of the center-left—would be based.

With so much at stake, the preparations for these elections naturally became a further arena for competition and conflict between the components of the center-left alliance. The process got off to a gloomy start with the failure to agree to a unitary list of the Fed, or indeed to any single coordinated mechanism for candidate selection in the 14 regions where elections were taking place.[9] The set of center-left parties in each region would therefore be left to negotiate their lists of council candidates and candidates for the role of regional president (or "governor"). To complicate matters further, the center-left in the region of Puglia decided to use a primary election to choose their candidate for governor, an exercise that led to the unexpected victory of a Communist (from RC) Nichi Vendola, against the Margherita's candidate, Francesco Boccia. The prospect of the alliance being represented by a Communist gay activist in a Southern region governed by the center-right provoked some pessimistic judgments from leading center-left figures and the derision of the incumbent center-right governor.[10] Similarly unpromising was the difficulty of reaching an agreement with the centrist UDEUR, which was determined to maintain its own identity within the alliance. The parties of the Fed presented a united list in only 9 out of the 14 regions where elections were taking place. If one considers that the same parties managed to present a single list throughout the national territory at the European Parliament election of the previous year, this appeared to be a clear step backwards.

In any event, the results of the elections confounded this unpromising backdrop. The performance of the federated parties, at 33.75 percent of the vote, and of the center-left alliance as a whole, 53 percent, both showed unmistakable progress compared with previous elections, marking a clear improvement even on the European election of 2004, also held in a favorable climate for the center-left. In contrast, the center-right could do little but acknowledge a crushing electoral defeat, with just 44.2 percent of the vote for the House of Freedoms coalition, and only 18.5 percent for Berlusconi's own party, Forza Italia. These vote shares corresponded to a near whitewash in terms of the "governorships" of the regions where elections were being held, with the center-right retaining control only of Lombardy and the Veneto. Even in these two regions, where the House of Freedoms won relatively comfortably, the center-left made important inroads into the center-right vote, seriously undermining the Berlusconi government's support base in the prosperous and populous North. Key regions lost by the center-right included Piedmont, Lazio, and Puglia, the last representing an unexpected triumph for the Communist Vendola, the controversial winner of the center-left's primary election in the region. Moreover, the center-left even improved on its dominant position in the "red" regions of Tuscany, Emilia-Romagna, and Umbria.[11]

These results were probably better than anything the leaders of the Unione could have hoped for. They certainly suggested a high level of public disillusionment with the Berlusconi government and with the prime minister himself, whose party's vote share was reduced by around a third compared with the high-water mark of the 2001 legislative election. The results confirmed the center-left's advantage in electoral competitions in which regional and local leadership positions were at stake: mainstream candidates with popular appeal, such as television presenter Alberto Marrazzo in Lazio, proved extremely successful not only in mobilizing the center-left's loyal electorate, but also in reaching out to discontented center-right voters.

The success of the regional elections, of course, had implications for the balance of power within the center-left and hence for the organizational and political strategy that the coalition would follow.

Ironically, the coalition's strong performance had the almost immediate effect of halting the progress toward greater unity: the leader of
the Margherita, Rutelli, opted to commit his party to maintaining its
own list in the 2006 election, overriding the pro-Ulivo faction headed
by Arturo Parisi.[12] At first sight, this appears a paradoxical reaction
to the center-left's strong performance in elections where, in most of
Italy, the parties of the Fed had presented joint candidatures. However,
closer inspection confirms that this was a strategically sensible move
from the point of view of the party's narrow interests. Not only had
the Margherita performed well (13 percent) in those regions where it
presented its own list, the poor showing of the center-right coalition
opened up the possibility of many disillusioned conservative voters
looking for a new political home, which would be likely to benefit the
Margherita in particular, and certainly more than the Left Democrats.
Although this reasoning was based on an optimistic misreading of the
electoral data,[13] it provided the Margherita's leadership with the justification for postponing yet again a full integration of the Fed parties
into a unitary organization, a process that would likely undermine the
leadership positions of Rutelli and others. Rutelli's strategy was also
influenced by developments in the center-right, with the Christian
Democratic UDC threatening to withdraw its support for the Berlusconi government. Alongside the respectable performance of Clemente
Mastella's UDEUR in the regional poll, it became possible for centrist
politicians on either side of the political divide to contemplate a future
role as "kingmaker" after Berlusconi's likely defeat in 2006.

Of course, there were obstacles to center-left unity in the other parties as well. The DS, although strongly committed to supporting Prodi's
leadership and, by extension, the Olive Tree federation, had reasons to
be wary of fuller integration into a broad center-left movement. First,
the party had already undergone the traumatic transformation from
being the largest Communist party in the Western world to becoming
a mainstream party that lacked a clear programmatic identity and was,
organizationally, a shadow of its former self. The formal abandonment
of the party's political autonomy would threaten further decline of its
organizational structure and activist base. More concretely, subsuming
the DS into a federation led by a former Christian Democrat carried
the risk of dramatically reopening the internal divide within the party
between the majority position led by Fassino and the left-leaning *correntone* faction. At worst, leftist sectors of the party could refuse to
participate in the unitary structure, creating an even stronger challenge from the left and defeating the object of the unification process.
At best, a fusion would imply pooling organizational and financial
resources with organizationally weaker parties such as the Margherita

and micro-parties such as the SDI and the European Republicans. Shortly after the primaries, arguments over campaign funds that arose between the DS and the Olive Tree federation leadership gave a taste of the inevitable conflicts that would occur.[14]

The Primary Election of October 2005: Prodi Beats the Parties

The notion of using primary elections among center-left voters to choose a candidate for the leadership of the coalition had been discussed at various points since the 2001 election, building on the pioneering experiences of components of the alliance in some subnational elections (notably the 1999 local election in Bologna). It also came up in academic and intellectual debates[15] on the role of primaries in addressing the increasing detachment of party organizations from the broader electorate. Primaries were of particular interest for the center-left leadership because of the vulnerability of Romano Prodi as a prime ministerial candidate without a party of his own. Prodi's leadership rested on his position at the head of the Olive Tree federation, which itself was undermined by the reluctance of the component parties to commit to closer cooperation.[16]

The parties themselves had chosen Prodi in the absence of obvious alternatives after the failure of D'Alema's social-democratic strategy in 1998–2000 and Rutelli's electoral defeat in 2001. Without being a party leader himself or having control of indispensable political resources for the center-left, Prodi could easily be overturned by the DS or the Margherita if either felt their interests could be better served by another candidate, as was made clear by occasional veiled threats in this direction. A primary election could go some way toward bolstering Prodi's legitimacy as a center-left leader and could protect him from the tactical maneuvers of the supporting parties. Although the experience of the primary held in Puglia before the regional election had suggested a high degree of risk inherent in the process, Prodi had already committed himself to primaries on his return from Brussels in 2004, and could not afford to row back on this commitment. After some delay and a good deal of jockeying for position among center-left leaders, the primary election was held on 16 October 2005.

The principal uncertainty about the primary was whether or not the result would constitute a decisive endorsement of Prodi's bid to lead the Unione into government. A poor level of participation in the poll or, even worse, procedural and organizational problems that called into question the validity of the result would undermine the object of the exercise and leave Prodi just as vulnerable as before. Similar uncertainties surrounded the level of competitiveness of the contest. If a rival candidate such as the PRC leader Fausto Bertinotti were to win a significant vote share and reduce Prodi's margin of victory (increasingly likely with a low turnout), the center-right would be able to portray Prodi as a "Trojan horse" for the radical left. But without a credible challenger, a victory for Prodi would appear meaningless. The months preceding the vote were therefore characterized by debates within the Unione about the appropriateness of a Bertinotti candidacy and the desirability of additional candidates taking part.[17] In the event, not only Bertinotti but other center-left leaders stood, as well as some less prominent figures.

Holding primary elections on a national scale was a major organizational challenge for the center-left, given that the only previous occurrences of similar elections in Italy were local or regional polls, such as those in Bologna and Puglia. The task of preparing for this event was assigned to a committee (Ufficio di Presidenza della Primaria 2005) in which each of the center-left parties had one representative, headed by the DS deputy, Vannino Chiti, a leading figure in the Unione's most organized and territorially articulated party. This committee drew up a short rule book for the poll, agreed to by the representatives of the nine parties and by Prodi as leader of the Unione.[18] Aspiring candidates in the primary election were required to collect 10,000 signatures (a minimum of 1,000 in at least 10 regions) and declare their endorsement of the Unione's program. The organization committed to establishing at least one voting station in each province, plus one station for every 10,000 votes won by the Unione parties in the 2001 election. For their part, the voters in the election were required to present an identity card and polling card (for national elections), to agree to being registered by name and address, and to pay a minimum contribution of one euro. By voting, participants would state their support of the program of the Unione. In practice, this meant that any Italian voter could take part (plus those who would become 18 by the time of the 2006 election), opening up the theoretical possibility of "infiltration" by center-right supporters. These were the basic rules governing the innovative event of a nationwide primary election held by a coalition of parties, the first of its kind in Europe (although the Spanish Socialist Party had held a national primary election that was open only to party members in 1998).

The outcome of the poll could hardly have been more favorable to Prodi or indeed to the electoral prospects of the Unione in general. First of all, not only did Prodi win a clear victory, but that victory was sufficiently overwhelming to counteract the claims of the center-right that the Unione would be a hostage to the radical left: Prodi took 74.1 percent of the vote to only 14.7 percent for Bertinotti, the main challenger—a decisive victory. The Christian Democrat Mastella took 4.6 percent, Di Pietro, 3.3 percent, and the Green leader, Alfonso Pecoraro Scanio, 2.2 percent. In short, Prodi was clearly preferred as the center-left candidate for prime minister, taking three-quarters of the vote in an election with eight candidates. Prodi polled a higher proportion of the center-left vote than that received by the DS and Margherita, the two parties most committed to his candidacy. Prodi had therefore secured a personal legitimation that drastically changed the balance of power between him and the supporting parties.

Perhaps even more overwhelming was the level of participation in the election—well over 4 million voters, which was four times as many as the most optimistic estimates made by external observers and party officials themselves prior to the event.[19] This was first of all a logistical triumph for the Unione. The organizing committee had managed to establish 9,651 polling stations throughout the national territory that were sufficiently staffed to allow for a rapid and apparently trouble-free count of the votes cast. But it also indicated a remarkable degree of mobilization of the center-left electorate: 4,311,149 voters participated in the primary, about one-third of the total vote for the parties of the Unione in the 2004 European election.[20] This eliminated any doubts over the veracity of the result (any infiltrations would be comfortably cancelled out) and augured well for getting out the center-left vote in the 2006 election. This high participation also had a financial payoff. Not only did over 4 million supporters contribute to funding the Unione's activities, but they gave rather more than the one euro minimum, with 40 million euros being raised, according to one estimate—an average of 9.28 euros per voter. But most significantly, these results confirmed and legitimated Prodi's leadership in decisive fashion, conferring the direct measurable support of a large slice of the center-left electorate.[21] This impressive personal mandate upset the existing balance of power in the coalition, sparking an intense debate on how to enhance the unity of the center-left.

The "Party of the Democrats" and the Future of the Center-Left

The result of the primaries provoked a range of comment favorable to further unity among the center-left parties. Prodi's decisive victory and the failure of party leaders such as Bertinotti, Mastella, and Pecoraro Scanio to reach beyond their core voters were interpreted by a number of observers as a clear statement from a center-left electorate

in favor of a unified political movement in which the component parties of the Unione would play a secondary role.[22] This was certainly
the line of argument promoted by circles close to Prodi that for some
time had been pushing for the unification of the center-left around
a single political force, usually referred to as the "Democratic Party"
(Partito Democratico) or "Party of the Democrats" (Partito dei Democratici). Figures such as Michele Salvati, Giuliano Amato, and Arturo
Parisi were prominent in this campaign, alongside Prodi's intellectual
support base in the forum Governareper, a group of center-left intel-
lectuals charged with the elaboration of a program for Prodi to present
to the electorate in 2006. For them, the primaries had been viewed as
a way of forcing unity upon the parties by mitigating the role of party
elites in mediating between the electorate and the Unione leadership
and a means of providing Prodi with a protective coat of democratic
legitimacy to ensure that the center-left parties would commit to supporting his government throughout the legislature.[23]

The success of the primaries therefore provided a clear opportunity
to drive home this unitary strategy, placing the party leaderships on the
back foot (with the exception of the majority faction of the DS, which
provided Prodi with consistent support). The left factions of the Unione
were placed on the defensive, with Bertinotti's high-profile challenge
ending in disappointment and Pecoraro Scanio polling a paltry share
of the primary vote. The Margherita leader Rutelli, whose decision
in May not to join a unitary list for the 2006 election represented the
principal obstacle to Prodi's strategy, initially claimed that the success
of the primary vote changed little, and that the strategy of a coalition
of parties remained intact.[24] But as the scale of Prodi's success became
clear, Rutelli immediately changed tack, accepting that his party could
after all join a unitary list and making enthusiastic protestations of support for the idea of a unitary party.[25] The intuition of the proponents
of a unified Democratic Party—that the use of primaries could play an
important role in overcoming obstacles to cooperation between center-
left parties—appeared vindicated. However, the changes in the balance
of power within the coalition did not eliminate resistance to greater
unity, and indeed the primaries themselves became a target of inter-
party tensions in the period following Prodi's victory.

In early November, further primaries were held in Sicily to select a
center-left candidate for the governorship in the forthcoming regional
elections. While the Margherita and UDEUR supported the centrist
former Christian Democrat Latteri, the DS and left parties supported
Rita Borsellino, sister of a prominent judge murdered by the Mafia
in 1992. After Borsellino's victory in the primary, Rutelli and several
former Christian Democrats in the Margherita protested that an agree-

ment with the DS to choose a centrist candidate had been broken, and that the primaries, by selecting a "radical left" candidate, had condemned the center-left to defeat.[26] This claim rested in part on the center-left's success in the local election in Messina on 12 December, where a Margherita candidate, Genovese, won the mayor's office from the center-right. The continued electoral decline of Berlusconi's House of Freedoms coalition provided the Margherita with opportunities to pick up votes from disgruntled center-right voters who would be unlikely to contemplate supporting other, more left-leaning parties in the Unione. Margherita leaders—in particular, former members of the DC such as Franco Marini and Sergio D'Antoni—therefore argued for the center-left to adopt a moderate Christian Democratic image in areas of the South where the center-right was strongest, a strategy difficult to reconcile with the primary elections, as the Puglian and Sicilian votes demonstrated.[27]

This argument, not entirely backed up by a close analysis of the electoral results,[28] followed a clearly partisan logic. Moreover, in the context of the split within the center-right coalition, with the Christian Democrats of the UDC threatening to leave the Berlusconi government in the summer and autumn of 2005, such moves were interpreted by the Margherita's allies as an attempt to keep all options open and potentially cut deals with the center-right in a future Parliament. Nor was the degree of trust between the parties of the Unione helped by the ramifications of the Unipol scandal and the accusations of DS involvement in that bank's dubious attempted takeover of the Banca Nazionale del Lavoro. Here the Margherita, as well as some representatives of the left parties and even of the DS's own left-wing faction, the *correntone*, raised the "moral question," accusing the DS leadership of connivance with shady business dealings.[29] These tensions followed closely on from disagreements between the DS and Margherita over how to allocate financial resources within the Unione—a thorny issue, particularly given the significant organizational and resource advantages enjoyed by the former. In short, the kind of compact and close cooperation between political forces aspired to by Prodi and the proponents of the Democratic Party remained elusive right to the end of 2005. Although the principle of a unitary list for the 2006 election to the Chamber of Deputies appeared to have been accepted by the end of the year, the nature of this list, the relationship with the other parties of the Unione, and the organization of the center-left in the Senate election still remained to be decided.

There is a clear strategic rationale to the behavior of the various party leaders in the Unione. The difficulties in reaching a stable form of cooperation are in large part the result of a structural problem: unification will produce benefits for the coalition as a whole, and these benefits must then be allocated to the different political forces involved. Given a certain lack of trust and a significant disparity of electoral and organizational strength between them, it is difficult for the parties to agree to pool resources for the collective good in the absence of firm guarantees that this will not leave them individually worse off. Similar problems within the center-right were more easily resolved because of the commanding position of Berlusconi, the coalition leader. Even after the primaries, Prodi did not enjoy such a dominant status, and he certainly lacked the financial and media resources of his opponent. Disunity and instability in the center-left therefore appeared set to continue, particularly in view of the electoral reform passed at the end of the year. The return to proportional representation, albeit with higher thresholds than before 1993, lowered the costs and risks for small parties of failing to negotiate an agreement with larger political forces and provided incentives for parties to maintain their organizational and electoral autonomy. In this new electoral context, the instability suffered by the center-left until the end of December 2005 was unlikely to be resolved easily, in the absence of major initiatives designed to strengthen and institutionalize inter-party cooperation.

Of course, strategic parameters are not the only reason why the center-left has lacked cohesion. As well as having to span a broad range of positions on the left-right scale, from hard-line Communists, left-libertarians, and ecologists on the left to relatively conservative and Christian Democratic groups in the center of the political spectrum, the Unione also straddles the religious divide between lay-secular culture and Catholic culture in the nation that is home to the Holy See. One of the greatest difficulties involved in closer cooperation between the DS and the Margherita is that such an alliance needs to span this social cleavage, which underpinned the tensions in Italian politics during the Cold War era.

One example of these difficulties arose soon after the regional elections in the form of the ill-advised referendum sponsored by the DS and other parties of the left with the aim of overturning the Berlusconi government's relatively restrictive law on artificial insemination passed in February 2004. This controversial law was opposed in Parliament by all the left parties, but the Margherita's parliamentarians voted mostly in favor, neatly illustrating the clear division within the Olive Tree over the role of Catholic values in policy-making.[30] Although this religious cleavage is far less important than in the past, it remains a potential obstacle to cooperation, since the parties on the radical left have often sought to mobilize precisely around the secular-Catholic divide, emphasizing issues, such as the rights of gay couples, that still trouble sectors of the Margherita.[31] The decision of Marco

Pannella's libertarian Radicals to join the Unione in late 2005 further complicated relations over the religious issue. The Radicals formed a joint secularist list with Enrico Boselli's SDI, which had up until then been a core member of the Fed, demonstrating once more how this cleavage continues to offer windows of opportunity to groups looking for an electoral constituency.[32]

Similar difficulties emerged in other policy fields. The Unione's attitude toward the Iraq war, for instance, revealed divisions over how to respond to the involvement of Italian troops in the occupation. The radical left has taken a predictably tough stance, demanding the immediate withdrawal of Italian forces from Iraq, whereas the DS leadership has taken a more cautious position, arguing that the withdrawal should be carried out in consultation with the United States. Divisions over economic policy have been equally evident. The liberalizing measures and fiscal rigor proposed by Prodi and supported by the Margherita and sectors of the DS have drawn predictable criticism from the left parties. Finally, just as in the center-right coalition, there has been a certain tension that derives from the presence in the Unione of parties such as the UDEUR, but also sectors of the Margherita (and even to an extent the DS) in the South, which rely on a clientelistic "vote of exchange" to mobilize electoral support. In short, there are obvious fault lines in the center-left that have not been clearly addressed or resolved in the coalition's programmatic statements thus far.

Conclusion

The year 2005 was a good one for the center-left. Opinion polls suggested a substantial and consistent lead over the center-right, and evidence from elections at the regional and local levels confirmed that the Unione was successful exploiting the difficulties of the Berlusconi government. The primary election to select a prime ministerial candidate—an unprecedented exercise in a European democracy—was an extraordinary success, not only confirming Prodi as undisputed leader of the center-left, but also revealing a level of mobilization of the core center-left vote that the political leadership of the Unione had come nowhere near to anticipating. Indeed, the experience of the primaries provided a neat snapshot of the strengths and weaknesses of the center-left more broadly in this pre-electoral period.

On the one hand, the candidate Prodi proved successful in mobilizing support from large numbers of voters ranging from sectors of the left (witness the weak performance of Bertinotti and Pecoraro Scanio) to the moderate center. The high level of participation and generous financial support of center-left voters augured well for the 2006 election, and the feat of organizing the primary suggested an activist base capable of coordinating a grassroots campaigning effort, a prerequisite for center-left success given Berlusconi's colossal advantage in more capital-intensive forms of campaigning.

On the other hand, the inability of the center-left party leaders to gauge the mood of their own supporters before the primaries, and the continued resistance to closer cooperation even afterwards, demonstrated the key weakness of the coalition: the reluctance of the center-left's political elite to subordinate its own priorities to the collective goal of defeating Berlusconi. Given the unpopularity of the government and the poor state of the Italian economy in 2005, cohesive collective action may not be necessary to achieve that goal. However, even if this were the case, maintaining a stable parliamentary majority in support of a putative Prodi government could prove elusive in the absence of further moves to reorganize the center-left before the 2006 election.

Notes

1. It should be clear that the term "center-left" refers here to the parties of the center-left of the "Second Republic" after 1993, not to the Christian Democrat-Socialist coalitions of the 1960s, which took the same name.
2. E. Alberti, "Prodi: Nessun cambio il nome resta Alleanza," *Corriere della Sera*, 26 November 2004.
3. See, for example, E. Mauro, "Il destino in bilico della sinistra senza nome," *La Repubblica*, 23 December 2004.
4. As has been forcefully and repeatedly argued by Michele Salvati, in *Il partito democratico* (Bologna: Il Mulino, 2003) and various newspaper articles since.
5. Interview with Giuliano Amato and Massimo Giannini in *La Repubblica*, 4 January 2005.
6. F. Rutelli, "Le idee-chiave per l'Alleanza," *La Repubblica*, 3 January 2005.
7. For cogent assessments of these strategic parameters, see N. Dilmore, "Fragili e stabili: Le alleanze nel sistema politico italiano," *Il Mulino*, no. 418 (2005): 239–249; I. Diamanti, "Confusi e infelici: Dal partito dell'Ulivo all'Unione dei partiti," *Il Mulino*, no. 421 (2005): 863–872.
8. I owe this point to Salvatore Vassallo.
9. A depressed Prodi did not hide his disappointment at this failure of coordination. See his communiqué, "Resoconto del Vertice della Federazione dell'Ulivo sulle elezioni regionali del 2005" (http://www.ulivo.it/cms/archive).
10. See R. Fitto (president of the Puglia region), "Questa la mia Puglia coraggiosa,'" *La Gazzetta del Mezzogiorno*, 20 January 2005.

11. On the regional elections, see Salvatore Vassallo's chapter in this volume.

12. F. Monaco, "Margherita: Distinti per unire," *Europa*, 6 July 2005.

13. See S. Vassallo, "Meno voti, più seggi: I conti in tasca a Rutelli," *Il Riformista*, 24 May 2005.

14. M. T. Meli, "Il tesoriere DS contro Rovati: Tutti diano contributi, non solo noi," *Corriere della Sera*, 20 November 2005.

15. See, for example, G. Pasquino, "Le primarie per riformare partiti e politica," *Il Mulino*, no. 370 (1997): 271–277; "Primarie? Sì grazie," *Il Mulino*, no. 402 (2002): 649–657; G. Sartori, "Primarie? Sì ma intelligenti," *Micromega*, no. 3 (June 1999); A. Barbera and S. Ceccanti, "Primarie per l'Ulivo (e non solo)," *Italianieuropei*, no. 5 (2002): 9–18.

16. As Prodi candidly admitted in a newspaper interview. See M. Marozzi, "Prodi: 'Risultato aperto alle primarie; chi vince decide il programma,'" *La Repubblica*, 25 July 2005.

17. M. Salvati, "Primarie non vere: Conviene a Prodi rischiare?" *Corriere della Sera*, 4 February 2005.

18. *Regolamento quadro per le "Primarie 2005,"* 11 July 2005 (http://www.perlulivo.it/2005-primarie/regoleprimarie.html).

19. S. Vassallo, "Analisi dell'Istituto Cattaneo sui risultati delle elezioni primarie nell'Unione di centrosinistra," Istituto Cattaneo, 27 October 2005 (http://www.istcattaneo.org/pubblicazioni/analisi/pdf/Analisi_Cattaneo_Primarie_Unione_2005.pdf).

20. Reaching as high as 41.6 percent in Emilia-Romagna and as much as 20.9 percent even in the lowest turnout, that in Puglia. See Vassallo, "Analisi dell'Istituto Cattaneo sui risultati."

21. I. Diamanti, "Due concezioni dell'Italia," *La Repubblica*, 18 October 2005.

22. E. Mauro, "L'occasione dei riformisti," *La Repubblica*, 18 October 2005; G. Riotta, "Partito democratico e unità dell'Ulivo," *Corriere della Sera*, 18 October 2005; C. Maltese, "Quel pasticcio della sinistra presuntuosa," *Il Venerdì di Repubblica*, 28 October 2005.

23. See, for instance, Governareper-Laboratorio ulivista, "Dall'Ulivo verso il partito dei democratici: Per un governo forte, una democrazia sana" (http://www.governareper.it). See also L. Contu, "Intervista con Walter Veltroni: Un baricentro riformista per dare stabilità ai governi dell'Ulivo," *La Repubblica*, 20 October 2005; M. Salvati, "'Il partito democratico, casa del riformismo," *Corriere della Sera*, 21 October 2005; G. Amato and A. Parisi, "Dalle primarie è nata la più grande forza politica dell'Europa," *La Repubblica*, 26 October 2005.

24. G. Casadio, "Per l'Unione un nuovo bivio. D'Alema: 'Ora serve intelligenza,'" *La Repubblica*, 17 October 2005.

25. U. Rosso, "Listone, ecco la svolta di Rutelli 'Sì, ma poi il partito democratico,'" *La Repubblica*, 18 October 2005; M. Guerzoni, "Rutelli: Via le leggi ad personam. Sbagliato chiudere i centri per immigrati," *Corriere della Sera*, 2 November 2005.

26. M. Ajello, "Ora primarie regolate per legge," interview with Francesco Rutelli, *Il Messaggero*, 13 December 2005.

27. F. Cavallaro, "D'Antoni: Qui tutta la sinistra ha sbagliato. Dietro Rita chi cerca solo visibilità," *Corriere della Sera*, 5 December 2005; G. De Marchis, "Marini: 'Sì all'intesa con Latteri. I voti per vincere sono i nostri,'" *La Repubblica*, 6 December 2005; R. Zuccolini, "Fioroni: 'Lezione per gli alleati. Senza Margherita non si vince,'" *Corriere della Sera*, 13 December 2005.

28. Vassallo, "Meno voti, più seggi."

29. M. Guerzoni, "Rutelli ai DS: Sarà così il nuovo partito democratico," *Corriere della Sera*, 28 October 2005. Rutelli argued that the close cooperation (*collateralismo*) between the DS and financial organizations (apparently implying Unipol and the cooperative movement in general) must end if the Democratic Party was to be established.

30. On this issue, see Chiara Martini's chapter in this volume.

31. An impression of these tensions can be gleaned from Rutelli's cautious tones in his public statements on the issue of unmarried couples. See M. Tarquino, "Rutelli: Alle coppie di fatto riconosciamo alcune facoltà," *Avvenire*, 7 December 2005; F. Fantozzi and R. Rossi, "Forum con Rutelli: La Chiesa può suggerire ma la laicità è intangibile," *L'Unità*, 7 December 2005.

32. See the provocative remarks of Socialist leader Boselli, the principal sponsor of the Radicals' incorporation into the center-left coalition, in M. T. Meli, "Boselli: D'Alema sbaglia, sul concordato vado avanti," *Corriere della Sera*, 7 November 2005.

3

ITALY AND WORLD AFFAIRS:
THE SGRENA-CALIPARI CASE

Marco Clementi

On 4 February 2005, Giuliana Sgrena, the correspondent of *Il Manifesto* in Baghdad, was kidnapped by Islamic Jihad, who asked for the withdrawal of Italian troops within 72 hours. On 4 March, Nicola Calipari, an official of the SISMI (Military Intelligence and Security Service) that ran the operation to liberate the Italian journalist, died under "friendly fire" at an American checkpoint while he was accompanying Sgrena to the Baghdad airport. On 29 April, a joint statement was issued by the Italian Ministry of Foreign Affairs and the American State Department stating that the two countries "have not reached shared final conclusions" as to what happened.[1]

These facts represent the three chapters of the Sgrena-Calipari case, which has dramatically attracted the attention of Italian politicians and the public because of its tragic ending and because it occurred in the course of a long Italian military commitment abroad. This operation took place in the most dangerous crisis zone for the present international system, and over which, moreover, Western and European countries are sharply divided. For these reasons, the Sgrena-Calipari case is one of the recent events with the greatest impact on Italian foreign policy, and it has stirred up debate on the international position of the country—i.e., the Italian presence in Iraq—on the international political alignment of the country—i.e., Italian support for the United States—and on the solidity of relations between the two countries. Consequently, this case has become very

Notes for this chapter begin on page 103.

significant as a reflection of the way in which the country confronts and debates foreign policy issues.

In this chapter we will attempt to determine the characteristics of Italian foreign policy using the Sgrena-Calipari case as our starting point. We will do so in three parts. In the first part we will reconstruct the facts of the three chapters that form the Sgrena-Calipari case, keeping in mind that these facts are the nodal points of this dramatic event and are worth distinguishing for analytical purposes. The second part, based on this reconstruction, discusses the way in which Italy has responded in general to the politics behind the kidnappings and consequently will consider comparatively the issues that have emerged from other kidnappings of Italians in Iraq. The third and final part will discuss the issues that have surfaced as a result of these events to examine to what degree, in the present Italian political system, the limitations and constraints that have traditionally characterized the formulation and implementation of foreign policy still apply.

The Sgrena-Calipari Case

The Kidnapping of Giuliana Sgrena

The news of the kidnapping of Giuliana Sgrena arrived in the middle of a debate that was raging in Italy on the utility and legitimacy of the Iraqi elections, and whether to vote funds to continue the "Antica Babilonia" (Ancient Babylon) mission in Iraq, on which Parliament was expected to make a decision within a few days. The political and emotional impact of the news was extremely strong, and it manifested itself in instantaneous reactions and in statements that continued throughout the duration of the abduction in which both political leaders and the public expressed solidarity, concern, and a desire for dialogue.

The Italian public had mobilized by the following day. Crowds appeared in Rome, Milan, Turin, and other Italian cities to demonstrate for the liberation of the abducted journalist. Meanwhile, Al Jazeera, the principal Arabic television network, quickly became the medium of communication to the Arabic public. On 5 February, the minister of foreign affairs, Gianfranco Fini, launched an appeal to the kidnappers to release Sgrena on the grounds that "she is a woman who loves peace, a friend of Iraq."[2] On the 6th, an appeal by *Il Manifesto* was broadcast that, on the advice of Fini, among others, underlined the pacifist convictions of the journalist and her closeness to the Iraqi people. On the 7th, even the journalists of Al Jazeera took a stand, asking for her liberation. On the 8th, a video produced by *Il Manifesto* was circulated, which was intended to let viewers know who Giuliana Sgrena was, to confirm her activities in Baghdad, reporting the point of view of the Iraqi population, and to explain why she was there—because of her love of peace.

Shortly after, the voices of top religious and political authorities joined those of ordinary people and the representatives of civil society. On 13 February, the Pope asked for the journalist's liberation; on the 19th, 500,000 people demonstrated in Rome for her liberation and the end of the "Antica Babilonia" mission; on the 23rd, the president of the Republic, Carlo Azeglio Ciampi, launched his first appeal; on 1 March, the Beati Costruttori di Pace, the Tavola Valdese, Un Ponte Per, and other groups and personalities promoted an all-out hunger strike for Sgrena's liberation, for the withdrawal of Italian troops, and for the end of the war; on 2 March Ciampi launched a second appeal.

Against this background of wide-ranging and continual activity, the political authorities attempted to control the effects of the kidnapping and to manage events. The news of 4 February met with a prompt reaction from the government, which immediately began negotiations. Gianni Letta, undersecretary to the prime minister, took into his confidence the leaders of the principal parties of the center-left, who in return cooperated in handling the issue. The leadership of the Left Democrats (Democratici di Sinistra, DS) tried to separate the kidnapping from the debate over the refinancing of the mission in Iraq and asked their allies not to discuss the request to withdraw Italian troops at that moment in the name of the principle "no to blackmail." In fact, majority and opposition agreed on the necessity of a one-week postponement of the Senate vote on the mission.

The push for a unified response that would not concede anything to the demands of the terrorists appeared serious and strong. For example, the speaker of the Chamber of Deputies, Pierferdinando Casini, praised the two coalitions for their "remarkable display of national unity" during the long hours of Sgrena's imprisonment.[3] However, it was not enough to close fully the gaps between the two alliances or within each of them. The center-left was divided on the issue of which position to take in Parliament on the mission in Iraq: the Union of Democrats for Europe (UDEUR) was intending to support it; the reformist left was divided between the abstentionism of the Margherita and the opposition of the Left Democrats, which aimed not at the immediate withdrawal of troops from Iraq, but at the redefinition of the mission; the Communist Refoundation (RC) party was determined to vote "no" without qualification. When on 15 February the Unione, the alliance of center-left parties, except for the UDEUR, decided to vote "no" in Parliament, a top representative of the National Alliance (AN), Maurizio Gasparri, declared that "ultimately, anyone who votes 'no' to the refinancing of the Italian mission in Iraq is on the side of the terrorists,"[4] harshly revealing how easy it was for the Italian political class to create a short-circuit between the foreign policy of the country and the kidnapping. A few days before, the cartoonist Vauro, a symbol of the radical left, had followed the same sort of logic from the opposite side. Speaking on the causes of the kidnapping, he underlined the fact that "the situation in Iraq today is terrifying, the war has brought about terrorism, civil society is torn, there are 25,000 mercenaries about, there's Al Qaeda, there's Allawi, there are entities that are controlled by interests that are completely against those of the resistance.... There's the American ambassador, Negroponte, who is an old acquaintance from Honduras, from Nicaragua—there the death squads were prowling around, remember? But maybe this abduction was just a mistake. Let's hope so."[5]

In this climate of imperfect unity, on 16 February the majority in the Senate approved the refinancing of the mission, with 141 votes in favor, including those of the UDEUR. In the meantime, Italian television showed a touching video in which Sgrena begged for help and appealed to the government to withdraw the troops. The timing of its arrival was impeccable. On 26 February, buoyed up by the wave of emotion, the Unione gave its support to the requests of the Sgrena family and *Il Manifesto* to temporarily suspend the military offensive on Ramadi to facilitate negotiations with the terrorists. On 3 March, the negotiators received further proof that Sgrena was alive, and this gave the "green light" to the operation to bring the journalist back to Italy.

The Death of Nicola Calipari

On 5 March, the country received the long-awaited news of the liberation of Giuliana Sgrena. Shortly after, it learned that the head of international operations of the SISMI, Nicola Calipari, had lost his life protecting the journalist of *Il Manifesto* with his own body from the gunfire of an American patrol that was guarding the street to the airport. In a tragic combination of relief and dismay, Italians asked themselves how such an incident, in which one life was lost to save another, was possible. Prime Minister Silvio Berlusconi immediately summoned the American ambassador, Mel Sembler, to demand an explanation and affirmed in clear terms that "someone will have to assume responsibility for their actions."[6] The United States extended its condolences over what had happened and promised a thorough investigation, a promise that was reiterated in talks between the leaders of the two countries: the president of the United States, George W. Bush, repeated it to Berlusconi, and Secretary of State Condoleezza Rice and Defense Secretary Donald H. Rumsfeld confirmed this promise to their opposite numbers, Fini and Antonio Martino, the Minister of Defense.

In the meantime, on 6 March at the Altare della Patria in Rome, thousands of citizens filed past the coffin of Calipari, who was given the military gold medal for heroism by President Ciampi, while thousands more participated in the funeral that took place the following day. The pain of those moments was even more acute because of the tension and confusion generated by the doubts and ambiguities surrounding the particulars of the incident. Although the SISMI agent who was wounded while driving the car affirmed that the American authorities had been informed of the mission and although Sgrena spoke of the event in terms of "a shower of fire,"[7] the first US report of 7 March maintained that the patrol had not been informed of the passage of the car and that it had been driving suspiciously fast.

Italy's official version came the following day, with a report to the Chamber by Fini, who defended the actions of the secret services, affirming that "Dr. Calipari made all the necessary contacts—I repeat— all the necessary contacts with the American military authorities in charge of airport security, not only to notify them of his presence and that of his colleague, but also to obtain permission to move freely in the airport and in the neighboring zones, which they were granted." He also stated that once Calipari had secured the liberation of Sgrena, he made telephone calls "with the aim of announcing in advance to the American military authorities that they would soon be entering the airport zone, in order to obtain every possible facilitation for an easy and direct passage." Fini related that the car "approached at a reduced speed, no faster than 40 km/hr, which allowed it to stop almost immediately."[8] Facing such hugely dissimilar preliminary versions, and in order to maintain their relationship of profound friendship and mutual respect, Italy and the United States arrived at an unprecedented decision on 9 March. To counter any doubt about the seriousness of the investigation, it would be turned over to a joint commission in which two representatives of the Italian government would take part.

While the Rome prosecutor's office proceeded with the inquiry that it had immediately opened for voluntary homicide, and the joint commission began its work in Baghdad, the political climate became ever more animated. Initially, the reaction to the news from Baghdad reflected appreciation for the position of the government and heartfelt admiration for Nicola Calipari and his heroism.[9] At the funeral, Gianni

Letta thanked Calipari for having given Italians back their homeland, and *l'Unità* of that same day ran the headline "Italian Pride."[10] In his speech to the Chamber, Fini used the words of Letta, stating that the tragic death of the official of the secret services had revived in Italians the "sense of belonging to the national community."[11] It did not take long, however, before different themes surfaced in public discussion, producing divisions that tore apart the solemn unity that had been formed around the figure of Calipari. Relations with the United States, the ransom that it was supposed had been paid to obtain Sgrena's liberation, the crisis in Iraq, and the use of force in foreign policy were some of these issues.

In fact, in spite of the immediate exhortation by Sergio Romano, an ex-ambassador and authoritative political commentator, not to "instigate an anti-American campaign and ask for the withdrawal of the troops now," in order to avoid "splitting the country in two factions, exhibiting a quarrelsome and unreliable Italy to the world,"[12] the Italian political class appeared immediately divided in their judgment of the event and its consequences with respect to the international position of the country. On the one hand, different representatives of the center-left assumed a cautious position, attempting to bring the debate back to the establishment of the facts. For example, a representative of the Margherita, Enrico Letta, cautioned not to "follow the anti-American path." The secretary of the Left Democrats, Piero Fassino, asked that "the circumstances and the responsibility for an incident that is as tragic as it is distressing be ascertained." On the other hand, signs of tension and open hostility toward the United States could be seen, and not only from the left. Giovanni Alemanno, the AN minister of agricultural and forest policy, proceeded to state that one must be "allied, not subordinate." Fausto Bertinotti, secretary of RC, criticized the American soldiers' propensity to shoot and urged people not to ignore the interests that might have opposed the liberation of Sgrena, endorsing to a certain degree the theory of an American ambush that came out when the journalist said she had been warned by the kidnappers that the Americans intended to kill her. Senator Gianfranco Pagliaruolo of the Party of Italian Communists (PdCI) immediately announced the distribution of flyers entitled "Shame on Bush."[13]

The position vis-à-vis the United States was further complicated by the hypothesis that the liberation of Sgrena was obtained by ransom. The government repeatedly denied the payment of a ransom, and the secret services spoke of rewards paid to informers, but controversy raged around the question of whether it was right to pay a ransom that would ultimately end up financing terrorist groups. Responses to this question were varied and not based on political alignments. The ex-president of the Republic, Francesco Cossiga, rejected the idea, recalling how Italy had survived the period of domestic terrorism by a policy of intransigence. Emanuele Macaluso, one of the leaders of the moderate current of the Left Democrats, former prime minister Giuliano Amato, and Marco Follini, the secretary of the Union of Christian Democrats and Center Democrats (UDC), were of the same mind. Others, like Rosy Bindi of the Margherita and Bertinotti of RC, accepted paying ransom as a last resort to save a human life. Valentino Parlato, a prominent editorialist of *Il Manifesto*, maintained that if a state is strong, it is not weakened by dealing with terrorists.

Amid arguments of increasing complexity, in which a distinction was made between two types of ransom—those paid during peace-keeping operations (and therefore politically legitimate) and those paid during wartime operations (and therefore illegitimate)—the belief spread that the government, despite Berlusconi's and Fini's resolute denials, had paid a ransom of several million dollars. Naturally, this new political certainty rekindled tensions with the American allies, given their aversion to dealings with terrorist groups. At this point it seems clear that this difference of approach may have been, at least indirectly, at the root of the incident since it could have made communications between the Italian secret services and the American military authorities in Iraq defective and difficult.

In this politically charged and confused climate, the Chamber of Deputies approved the refinancing of "Antica Babilonia" on 15 March. The votes in favor totaled 246, which included those of Clemente Mastella of the Democratic Union for Europe; 180 votes were against the refinancing, including Romano Prodi's Unione (which could not prevent the Party of Italian Communists from presenting their own motion for the immediate withdrawal of the troops); and there were 8 abstentions. The evening of the vote, however, Prime Minister Berlusconi seemed to want to lessen the significance of the refinancing motion and to undercut the opposition's strategy, announcing during a television talk show that Italy would begin withdrawing troops in September. President Ciampi, unaware of the decision, was taken by surprise, as were Italy's allies, Bush and Tony Blair, who the following day stated that no dates had been set for troop withdrawal and urged that the coalition not be undermined. Berlusconi corrected himself, saying that he "hoped" withdrawal would be possible. Prodi commented: "He shouldn't play with the country."[14]

In response to the decision by Parliament, 100,000 people marched in Rome on 19 March against the war in Iraq. In that context, DS Secretary Fassino demonstrated some courage in an interview in which he urged Italian politicians to address the theme of the ends and means of foreign policy, and stated his own opinion: the goal of exporting democracy without compromise, which is part of Bush's doctrine, is acceptable; the use of military means, such as preventive war, the other part of the same doctrine, is not.[15] The reaction from his own party was immediate: Fabio Mussi, a leading representative of the internal left, for example, asked if war was not ultimately the most uncompromising means of exporting democracy.

The Joint Commission of Inquiry and the Joint Declaration of Disagreement

As the weeks passed, public opinion was focused more and more on the ongoing investigation, as it looked for answers to numerous questions regarding the unfolding of the incident: Were the communications between the Italian services and the American authorities sufficient to guarantee the security of the mission? Was the car driving quickly or at reduced speed? Was the checkpoint at an appropriate position on the road? How much time had elapsed between the warning lights and the shots? How many soldiers opened fire on the car? Did the soldiers aim at the engine to stop it or at the passenger seats? The wait for the results of the Italo-American commission became even more tense, however, when on 21 March news arrived that the two Italian experts nominated by the Italian Embassy in Baghdad to examine Calipari's car on behalf of the Rome prosecutor had not received permission from the US command to carry out their assignment, on the grounds of "claimed security requirements."[16] The Italian Foreign Ministry called this "a procedural misunderstanding" and denied that "the United States wants to hinder the investigation."[17]

Doubt concerning the actual willingness of the United States to permit a serious and rigorous inquiry into what happened became the central point of controversy on 14 April, when *Corriere della Sera* published an article headlined "Calipari, the Italians Don't Want to Sign Off." The article held that blatant differences over the reconstruction of the incident brought the representatives from the two countries to a position where they were "distant on the question of responsibility. The representatives of the United States continue to insist on the inclusion of a declaration which in substance absolves the soldiers who shot at the car … but the Italian representatives are opposed and will not sign the conclusions…. [T]he Rome prosecutor's office has formally protested and urged the government to make representations to the United States authorities: 'We want the car for examination' … to overcome the stalemate, the American commissioners are said to have proposed reaching a double conclusion—that of the US and the divergent one of the Italians. The Italian delegates, however, rejected this solution. In any event, the investigation is in fact at an end."[18]

The impression that the United States wanted to relieve itself of any responsibility became even more apparent, given that "none of the rogatory letters signed by the Minister [of Justice, Roberto Castelli], sent as soon as the day after Calipari's death, which requested the names of the United States military personnel ... were ever answered."[19] Ultimately, this resistance on the part of the United States provoked the reaction of the Rome prosecutor's office in the form of a letter sent to Gianni Letta in which it judged the situation as "conflicting with the constitutional rules governing the autonomy of the judicial authorities and the criminal prosecution function"—clear and strong words that refer, among other things, to the accord signed by the two governments that initiated the investigations. The tone of the head of the office, Giovanni Ferrara, did not seem to leave room for doubt about his attitude when he stated: "This office is not aware of either the content of the treaty that established the technical commission, or the contents, or even the existence, of a further treaty regulating or affecting, in this specific case, the relationship between the United States administration and the Italian judicial authorities that purportedly requires a specific rogatory letter to permit the participation of the Italian investigative team in the activities of the commission."[20]

In spite of the fact that it was clear by that point that the joint commission had finished its work, time passed during the search for a political solution that would allow its conclusions to be presented in a way that was acceptable to both the United States and Italy. However, it was quickly becoming clear that it was the latter that was stalling, in an attempt to reach a version that did not put the government in a difficult spot and that did not cause negative repercussions for Italy's commitment in Iraq. On 25 April, the Pentagon leaked some of the contents of the report, which hinted at the complete innocence of the American soldiers, leaks that were not denied by Donald Rumsfeld. In the four days that passed before the two governments issued a joint declaration, there was a lot of finger-pointing, with leaks that were more or less denied, public declarations, and the repeated summoning of Ambassador Sembler. Italy wanted an admission of some sort of error on the part of the American soldiers, while the United States maintained that the facts spoke to the contrary. The commission of inquiry suddenly lost its "joint" character since the Italian members claimed that they had had the documents only at the end of the inquiry and therefore had not genuinely participated in its work; satellite images were circulated that purportedly proved the car was traveling at high speed; and Berlusconi spoke of friction between the State Department and the Pentagon—and was immediately contradicted.

On 29 April, the joint statement was finally issued. The two countries preserved the forms: the work of the joint commission—it said—was carried out in "an atmosphere of great mutual collaboration; it has been intense and productive.... The alliance between Italy and the United States is firm, and there is a strong and solid friendship between the two countries that is based on shared ideals and values—values that commit us to remain at the side of the Iraqi people."[21] The substance, however, was that the positions were irreconcilable. The report published by the United States on 30 April, which preceded the Italian one, attributed responsibility for what had happened to the Italian secret services, albeit admitting the lack of experience of the American patrol. The Italian report was finalized on 2 May and, instead, highlighted the absence of signals at the blockade and its faulty position, the inexperience and stress levels of the American soldiers, and the faulty communication within the American military chain of command.

In these days of intense anticipation, the debate became particularly confused and fragmented, with all of the themes raised by the events becoming inextricably tied up with one another. On 28 April, ex-President Francesco Cossiga had explicitly linked the occurrence to Italy's fundamental foreign policy options and called for the withdrawal of troops from Iraq should there be a failure to agree on the dynamics of the incident; when this became reality, the pacifist left repeated the demand. While representatives of the center-right, such as the Radical Daniele Capezzone and Gustavo Selva of AN, demanded the resignation of the head of the SISMI, Niccolò Pollari, the Green Party deputy, Paolo Cento, defended him. Prodi's Unione spoke of amateurism, referring to the uselessness of the joint commission, and the Party of Italian Communists accused the government of servility toward the Americans. On the other hand, *Il Manifesto* commended the government for its firm resolve in not signing the report, and Ernesto Galli della Loggia, in his editorial of 4 March, called on the United States to play the role of a world leader that has "constant regard for the sentiments of public opinion in its ally, and to begin with its sense of national dignity and of the interests that it represents."[22] Massimo D'Alema, chairman of the Left Democrats, raised the question of the objectives and means of foreign policy again: his claim made at the Italianieuropei Foundation conference that the spread of democracy is an acceptable objective and that force may be a necessary instrument for maintaining international security and order was supported by Francesco Rutelli of the Margherita. Bertinotti, however, did not agree, maintaining that war should be avoided even under the sponsorship of the United Nations, with the exception of cases in which it could prevent genocide. The issue of the politics of ransom-paying came back onto the agenda in full force a few days later with the kidnapping in Afghanistan of Clementina Cantoni, who according to anonymous sources was ransomed for five million dollars.

At the end of these long weeks there still remained the investigation that the Rome prosecutor's office continued to pursue, which offered hope of obtaining justice and preserving national sovereignty. In the meantime, the car involved in the incident had arrived in Italy, and an unusual oversight on the part of the American authorities had divulged the names of the members of the patrol at the checkpoint. Nevertheless, the prosecutor's office could not proceed with unofficial information and had to wait for the Department of Justice in Washington, DC, to formally release the list of names of the soldiers who had fired their weapons. At the end of October, the report of the consultants appointed by the Rome prosecutor arrived. It confirmed, as was maintained in the US report, that only one gun had been fired, but stated that it was fired not for the purpose of stopping the car but rather "to kill." The report also specified that the car had indeed been proceeding at reduced speed. At this point, the Italian judges "could decide to follow the same procedure as their Spanish colleagues, who had signed an international arrest warrant for two US soldiers accused of having killed a cameraman of *Telecinco* at the Hotel Palestine in Baghdad."[23]

Italy and the Policy of Kidnapping

With the Sgrena-Calipari case, Italy had to confront the particular consequences of the crisis in Iraq—a crisis in which terrorist groups continually resort to kidnapping in order to pursue a wide range of objectives, such as financing their operations, keeping international tension high, and "generalizing" the conflict by attracting the attention of public opinion in the countries of the victims and then trying to intervene in their decision-making processes. The policy of kidnapping and blackmail using the lives of abducted civilians should be understood as a particular international challenge—one that directly involves the domestic political sphere of the affected countries.

If the controversial logic of the policy of kidnapping puts every affected country in some difficulty,[24] it can be particularly hazardous in a country like Italy, in which domestic constraints on the formulation and management of foreign policy have been traditionally very significant. In consequence, from this point of view, a consideration of the manner in which the country reacted to the incident under study can be useful in illustrating the way in which Italy defines its foreign policy. This reflection can perhaps be even more useful if the issues that this case raises are viewed comparatively, even if in a preliminary way, with the addition of those elements that can be extracted from the other cases of kidnapping that Italy has had to confront: the kidnapping of the bodyguards Salvatore Stefio, Maurizio Agliana, Umberto Cupertino, and Fabrizio Quattrocchi, the last of whom was killed, in April–June 2004; that of Enzo Baldoni in August 2004; the kidnapping of Simona Pari and Simona Torretta in September 2004; and, finally, that of Clementina Cantoni in May–June 2005.[25]

The point of departure of this reflection is the observation that even in the difficult conditions that we have highlighted above, and notwithstanding the unceasing series of abductions, the Italian government has remained firm in the face of this international challenge. It did not show signs of weakening or of internal fractures; on the contrary, in the course of the Sgrena-Calipari case, it was able to surmount even a delicate parliamentary passage intact when its majority voted solidly in favor of the continuation of the "Antica Babilonia" mission. Moreover, in addition to the solidity of the executive in the face of the internal repercussions of the policy of kidnapping, in several instances and in different ways, majority and opposition were propelled by a sentiment of national unity that led them to manage the events with an approach that was, on some level, bipartisan.

If we follow the three chapters of the Sgrena-Calipari case, we can identify the different forms that this bipartisan tendency took—forms that are also found to some extent in the cases of the other kidnappings. In the first chapter of this case, as we have seen, majority and opposition made a genuine if limited attempt to react in the same way to the incident, since they agreed on the need to give a unified response so as not to surrender to the demands of the terrorists with regard to the withdrawal of troops from Iraq. A similar response was manifest in the course of the kidnapping of the four bodyguards and, even more so, of that of the "two Simonas": in these cases, appeals for national unity had come from both political fronts and the most prominent columnists in the country. To highlight the importance of this climate of unity, moreover, after the liberation of the "two Simonas," similarly to the Sgrena-Calipari case, many comments recognized and appreciated the basically bipartisan approach with which the demand to withdraw the troops was denied.

In the second of the chapters considered, the specific manifestation of bipartisanship occurred for a different reason: thanks to Calipari's heroism, majority and opposition found themselves united in a sense of belonging to the national community. Through the death of the

SISMI officer, concern for the unity of the country rose above the partisan divisions of opinion on the mission in Iraq and on its consequences. But it is necessary to underline not only this accord between the two coalitions, but also the exceptional nature of this form of bipartisanship or, to put it another way, its extreme fragility. In the case of the death of Fabrizio Quattrocchi in 2004, the way in which the bodyguard faced his execution and his words, "This is how an Italian dies," were invoked as evidence of "Italian heroism" by the top office-holders and the majority, but this view lacked the support of a large part of the center-left. On the contrary, the debate on the actual role of the bodyguards in Iraq, and thus the issue of the legitimacy of the stabilization mission, superseded any unity over the death of the kidnapped bodyguard, to the point that the decision to hold a state funeral became a subject of political debate and a part of the coalition of the left in Parliament abandoned the chamber during the parliamentary sitting in which this terrorist victim was commemorated.

In the third chapter of the Sgrena-Calipari case, finally, bipartisan elements were evident in the pursuit of yet another objective: the preservation of national sovereignty with respect to a country that, even though a close ally, had conducted itself in such a way that its actions were formally judged as detrimental to Italy's independence, as well as its political dignity. This form of the bipartisanship was manifested in a manner that was unique with respect to the other chapters since, metaphorically, it took on opposite signs in the government and in the opposition. Unity in this case was achieved not in the sense that majority and opposition united in a strong way; rather, it existed in the sense that both defended and invoked the same fundamental values and principles, either in the form of the demand that the United States fully respect Italian sovereignty (voiced by both the majority and part of the opposition), or in the form of criticism of the government for its inability to obtain this respect (expressed by the other part of the opposition).

In this connection, it should be added that this element was more or less absent in the other kidnappings. In fact, it assumed great importance in the Sgrena-Calipari case because of the dramatic nature of the incident and perhaps also because in this period other events intervened to complicate relations between Italy and the United States. Prominent among these, without doubt, was the abduction—this time carried out by the American Central Intelligence Agency (CIA)—of the Egyptian citizen Abu Omar, who was seized in Milan on 17 February 2003 and transported to, and then incarcerated in, Egypt. In this case, too, the infringement of Italian sovereignty, not to speak of the rights of Abu Omar, provoked a heated and prolonged political polemic and had legal consequences comparable to those of the Sgrena-Calipari case, since the Milan prosecutor's office demanded the extradition of the 22 American citizens accused of having taken part in the operation.

We can perhaps conclude that overall these impulses toward national unity helped produce a certain degree of bipartisanship in the manner in which the country responded to the international challenge of the policy of kidnapping. Notwithstanding the mobilization that often linked solidarity with the victims to the demand for a change in Italian policy in Iraq, which was very intensive in terms of numbers of participants and continuity in time in at least two cases— the "two Simonas" and the Sgrena-Calipari case—a large part of the opposition maintained a constantly calm attitude, refusing to take advantage of the emotional side of the events to press for the immediate withdrawal of the troops. On the contrary, the Left Democrats and the Margherita rejected that demand and opted for a solution that might be labeled one of unitary dialectic, asking for the redefinition of the role of Italy in Iraq. At the same time, another party of the left, RC, albeit reasserting its opposition to the Italian mission, subdued its tone somewhat in the most delicate moments of the kidnapping cases. Further evidence of this tendentially common orientation was the parliamentary vote on the refinancing of the mission in Iraq, in which the government, in the middle of the Sgrena-Calipari case, received the explicit backing of the Union of Democrats for Europe (UDEUR), and the demand to withdraw the troops appeared as an exception in both political coalitions.

Conclusions: The Kidnappings and the Evolution of Italian Foreign Policy

In this chapter we have reconstructed the principal points of the Sgrena-Calipari case in an attempt to illustrate the way in which political elites and the Italian public confronted a situation that was dramatic and complex, given all the questions and problems it raised. We have also tried to set out through a comparative analysis the implications that can be drawn for some aspects of Italian foreign policy from the responses Italy gave to the kidnappings that occurred in the course of its recent international involvement. With this framework in mind, we can now conclude by asking what the principal foundational characteristics of Italian foreign policy and its domestic determinants are, and if these are significantly different from those that have traditionally been invoked to describe it.

In this connection, we should recall that Italy's international action has often been described as volatile and largely ineffective. Sergio

Romano has highlighted the fact that during the First Republic, its military and economic weakness, the great instability of its governments, and the large ideological distances within its party system all contributed to make Italian foreign policy (1) uncertain in the definition of the strategic objectives to follow in order to achieve the interests of the country, (2) incapable of acting in a bipartisan fashion, (3) oscillating between the aspirations of a great power and the capabilities of a small to medium power, (4) concerned to obtain success in terms of image rather than strategic goals, and (5) prepared to cooperate with the big powers but not prepared to support the costs or the consequences when these "threatened to modify ... the equilibrium of domestic politics."[26] Roberto Gaja has underlined the fact that during the same period, Italy displayed a constant tendency "to confront international political issues in legalistic terms instead of in terms of *Realpolitik*," in other words, in dealing with international problems, to pay more attention to their formal aspects and the principles involved than to their substantial and strategic significance.[27]

After 1989, nevertheless, some signals of discontinuity indicated that such an image was no longer an accurate summary of Italian foreign policy and of the coherence of its position in international affairs. The political transition that followed the dissolution of the USSR saw a reduction of the weight of the "anti-system" forces and an electoral reform in a majoritarian direction, increasing, to a certain extent, the unity of the political class with respect to the big issues of international politics and its willingness to address them in a bipartisan manner. The country assumed direct responsibilities outside its own frontiers on several occasions, even participating in a few military operations with high levels of conflict. It proceeded to reform the armed forces, adopting, even if somewhat late with respect to other Western countries, the professional model, which was considered necessary to permit interventions in contemporary crises. The country was notably active in bilateral relations, especially with some of the principal great powers of the system—the United States being first and foremost.

In sum, while the reduction of the distance between the political forces and the logic of majoritarianism could reduce the volatility of foreign policy and the difficulty of conducting it in a bipartisan way, the unique challenges that emerged in the contemporary international system could elicit a quicker and more active response from the country, with regard to both its international alliances and its attempts to meet these challenges. As a result, Italy seemed to present itself in some ways as a country that was capable of making a qualitative leap that would take it if not into the desirable "club" of the great powers, given its continuing military and economic weakness, at least into the group of states that want and are capable of undertaking international responsibilities. But how much of this road has really been traveled? How great are the obstacles along the way, and which are more significant than others? Italy's foreign policy in the matter of the kidnappings seems to offer some elements for formulating some initial answers to these questions.

The way in which Italy has reacted to these instances of kidnapping seems to indicate that the country has a certain capacity to maintain the obligations it has assumed in the international system, even if these imply some costly and divisive decisions. It also seems to suggest that the Italian political class has confronted questions of foreign policy—or at least those connected with the events discussed here—with a more bipartisan spirit. This was because the executive maintained a high degree of cohesion when confronted with the internal repercussions of the kidnappings, because majority and opposition reacted in a relatively unified way to the repeated demands of the terrorist groups for the withdrawal of Italian troops, and because majority and opposition had achieved unity, even if in varying degrees with each kidnapping, in the common values of national pride and the defense of national sovereignty.

Yet certain other factors must also be taken into account. First of all, the impulses toward unity manifested in these incidents were of a particular type: the political class came together predominantly around symbolic and formal issues, such as national pride and sovereignty, rather than strategic and substantial issues of foreign policy. In other words, this unity was attained around the same issues that represented the cohesive element of Italian foreign policy throughout the Cold War. In the second place, those same unitary impulses reached their peak, within the group of kidnappings considered here, in one specific incident: the Sgrena-Calipari case. It is difficult not to look for the reason for this greater unity in one contingent element—the fact that the dramatic death of an officer of the secret services occurred in addition to the kidnapping of a journalist, thus lessening the possible divergences between the political coalitions. In fact, when one of the two elements was missing, the response was much less unified. A case in point is the death of Fabrizio Quattrocchi. The reaction to Quattrocchi's kidnapping was filtered through political judgments on the Iraqi crisis and the role that the Italian bodyguards were playing there, which diminished the support of a large part of the opposition. The same was true in part in the case of Clementina Cantoni, in which the relatively weak mobilization by the pacifist groups was motivated by Cantoni's lack of political affiliation.

In sum, the instances in which Italy's foreign policy displayed a greater bipartisanship in the face of the policy of kidnapping occurred particularly when, by chance, the bases of the traditional internal political divisions were absent, and, even in this case, the unity was of an eminently formal kind. To these considerations, finally, we can add others of a less contingent type if we examine what the Italian reaction to the policy of kidnapping can tell us about the three fundamental problems that must be resolved in order to produce a bipartisan foreign policy that is stable and pro-active in the international system. These problems are (1) the selection of the strategic objectives to follow within the system, (2) the selection of suitable means to carry out these strategic objectives, and (3) the selection of the alliances within which to carry out these objectives—in other words, what to do in the international community, by which means, and with whom.

As far as the first problem—what to do—is concerned, taking as a given the division between majority and opposition on the subject of Iraq, three issues can be highlighted. The first is the serious difficulty that the opposition had in dialoguing pragmatically on exporting democracy, a crucial issue in present-day international politics. In the second place, the government itself several times sent signals that weakened its underlying option to contribute to the stabilization of Iraq, such as the repeated announcements of the withdrawal of Italian troops or the ambiguous statement by the prime minister at the end of October that he never wanted the war in Iraq. In the third place, both the majority and the opposition, or at least some of their components, demonstrated a great readiness to connect the kidnappings to the fundamental issues of foreign policy. It happened more than once that the kidnappings became one more argument either to demand a change in the country's foreign policy positions or to demonstrate their validity. More particularly, especially in the cases of Enzo Baldoni, the "two Simonas," and Giuliana Sgrena, many underlined the pacifist convictions of the victims and their closeness to the Iraqi people, even in some cases to the insurgent groups. In this way, they called for the liberation of the prisoners in a "partisan" manner; that is, they advanced and justified the request for the hostages' freedom in light of a specific understanding of the Iraqi crisis. On both sides, in sum, the kidnappings were exploited in domestic political competition, a sign of the willingness of all segments of the political class, whatever their political position, and of the rest of the country, to make international political goals subordinate to domestic politics—a willingness that can be considered as a clear indicator of the lack of a bipartisan culture with regard to foreign policy issues.

With respect to the second problem—that of means—two issues emerge. In the first place, the reaction to the policy of kidnapping shows

in various ways how there was very little agreement between majority and opposition on the use of force as a legitimate instrument of
foreign policy, apart from very exceptional conditions. In the second
place, even the majority displayed a great deal of fragility on this topic,
as we can see by considering the issue of whether to pay ransom, a
policy that was discussed in all of the cases of kidnapping and that
seems to have been implemented in at least some of them, such as
in the cases of the "two Simonas," of Sgrena, and of Cantoni. The
policy of paying ransom stems from an unwillingness to sustain the
consequential costs of fundamental foreign policy choices, and thus
its repeated adoption indicates a great difficulty in matching foreign
policy instruments with—in this case—the political goal of the struggle against the terrorist groups. From this point of view, it also seems
significant that the majority did not show signs of friction when Italy
lost military lives in Iraq, but that many cracks appeared in it at the
loss of civilian lives—almost, it seems, as a dramatic symbol of the
unbroken osmosis between the domestic arena and the international
activities of the country, or, in other words, the decisive importance of
domestic constraints upon the conduct of Italian foreign policy.[28]

As for the third problem—that of with whom to act—we must note
the ambivalence with which the country views the super-power to
which the government chose to ally itself in Iraq. In this regard, two
points can be highlighted. First of all, in many of the demonstrations
during which Italians expressed their solidarity with the kidnap victims, the United States was the explicit object of political criticism and
was looked on not as an ally in the pursuance of a national foreign
policy objective, but rather as being co-responsible for the situation
that led to the kidnappings. At least, this is what happened when the
participation in the mass mobilizations reached an intense level during the kidnappings of the "two Simonas" and of Sgrena. Secondly,
the critical or openly hostile stance toward the United States was, to a
certain degree, preconceived. This came to light with the Sgrena-Calipari case, in which critical positions were expressed immediately following the death of Nicola Calipari before any explanation founded on
an analysis of the evidence could be formulated. Both observations,
taken together, seem to give the impression that the international alliance with the United States is a choice that is not shared by a large
part of the country and that it is, therefore, potentially unstable.

To conclude, the assessment that Italian foreign policy, when confronted with the kidnappings, demonstrated significant signs of unity
and bipartisanship needs to be qualified by adding, first, that these
signs seem to have been particularly significant in conditions that
were totally unique, and, second, that in these circumstances Italy had

great difficulty in addressing in a unified way the three issues of what to do, how, and with whom in the international community. In consequence, if we look at the evolution of the fundamental features of Italian foreign policy, it seems that the elements of novelty that we can observe are still strongly counterbalanced by the traditional factors that influence it: the decisive weight of the domestic constraints on foreign policy; a fundamentally symbolic and normative orientation; great difficulty in considering the use of force; potential instability in maintaining the fundamental goals of foreign policy and the international alliances that follow from it; and, finally, difficulty in bearing the costs that flow from it.

— Translated by Anna Edwards

Notes

1. Joint statement of the Italian Ministry of Foreign Affairs and the American State Department, 29 April 2005 (http://www.esteri.it).
2. *Corriere della Sera*, 5 February 2005.
3. M. Guerzoni, *Corriere della Sera*, 10 February 2005.
4. *Corriere della Sera*, 16 February 2005.
5. F. Caccia, *Corriere della Sera*, 5 February 2005.
6. *Corriere della Sera*, 5 March 2005.
7. M. Imarisio, *Corriere della Sera*, 6 March 2005.
8. Speech of the minister of foreign affairs, Gianfranco Fini, to the Chamber of Deputies on the liberation of the journalist Giuliana Sgrena, 8 March 2005 (http://www.esteri.it).
9. Of the sentiments expressed by left-wing leaders and journalists such as Fausto Bertinotti, Sandro Curzi, and Rossana Rossanda, one example is more notable than the others: Furio Colombo, the outgoing director of *l'Unità* and a sharp critic of the government and of its leader, praised in the columns of his newspaper Berlusconi's "statesmanlike" behavior.
10. C. Sereni, *l'Unità*, 6 March 2005.
11. Speech of the minister of foreign affairs, Gianfranco Fini, to the Chamber of Deputies on the liberation of the journalist Giuliana Sgrena, 8 March 2005 (http://www.esteri.it).
12. S. Romano, *Corriere della Sera*, 5 March 2005.
13. D. Gorodisky, *Corriere della Sera*, 5 March 2005.
14. P. Di Caro, *Corriere della Sera*, 17 March 2005.
15. G. Fregonara, *Corriere della Sera*, 21 March 2005.
16. F. Sarzanini, *Corriere della Sera*, 23 March 2005.
17. F. Sarzanini, *Corriere della Sera*, 24 March 2005.

18. *Corriere della Sera,* 14 April 2005.
19. F. Sarzanini, *Corriere della Sera,* 14 April 2005.
20. F. Sarzanini, *Corriere della Sera,* 18 April 2005.
21. Joint statement of the Italian Ministry of Foreign Affairs and the American State Department, 29 April 2005 (http://www.esteri.it).
22. E. Galli della Loggia, *Corriere della Sera,* 4 May 2005.
23. F. Sarzanini, *Corriere della Sera,* 26 October 2005.
24. See, for example, the repercussions in France, during the same months when Giuliana Sgrena was in captivity, in response to the kidnapping of Florence Aubenas, a journalist of *Libération.*
25. The bodyguards were kidnapped on 13 April 2004, and the following day news came of the execution of Quattrocchi, whose pictures were circulated worldwide. The kidnapping was ended thanks to the intervention of the American special forces, who liberated the hostages on 8 June. During their long imprisonment, while the kidnappers repeatedly asked the government to withdraw its troops and asked Italians to protest to that end, in Italy there was a heated debate over the actual role of the bodyguards in Iraq: were they security agents or mercenaries? The kidnapping of Baldoni began on 20 August, when the Milanese freelance journalist and collaborator on the weekly *Diario* was captured while he was accompanying a convoy of the Red Cross that was headed to Baghdad from Najaf. Notwithstanding the fact that the journalist was killed almost immediately, the kidnappers, in the following days, demanded that Italian troops be withdrawn from Iraq and released a video of the abducted man, creating a sense of dismay in the public, given his pacifist convictions. On 27 August, Al Jazeera broadcast the news of the death of Baldoni. The "two Simonas," who were pacifists, volunteers of the Un Ponte Per association, and active in aid to children in Baghdad, were abducted on 7 September and released, presumably after the payment of a ransom, on 28 September. Their kidnapping saw not only demands to withdraw the troops but also a vast mobilization on all levels that also included Arabic public opinion. Clementina Cantoni, a volunteer aid worker with women in Afghanistan who worked with the humanitarian organization Care International, was abducted in Kabul on 16 May 2005 and was released on 9 June, presumably after the payment of a ransom and the release of the mother of one of the kidnappers. Her kidnapping did not receive intense media coverage nor was there a strong mobilization in solidarity with her, in spite of the fact that the kidnappers' demands led to the broadcast of a video of her.
26. S. Romano, *Guida alla politica estera italiana* (Milan: Rizzoli, 1993), 41.
27. R. Gaja, *L'Italia nel mondo bipolare: Per una storia della politica estera italiana (1943–1991)* (Bologna: Il Mulino, 1995), 28.
28. On the major influence that these constraints still exercise in the Italian political system and on the particular form that they take, see F. Andreatta and E. Brighi, "The Berlusconi Government's Foreign Policy: The First 18 Months," in *Italian Politics: The Second Berlusconi Government,* ed. J. Blondel and P. Segatti (New York and Oxford: Berghahn Books, 2003): 221–236.

4

GAMES ADVANCED DEMOCRACIES PLAY: THE COALITION CRISIS OF APRIL 2005

David Hine and Chris Hanretty

The coalition crisis of April 2005 was the first and only one in the Parliament elected in 2001. One of Berlusconi's chief political goals had been to survive the entire legislature. He fell short by only a year, and he survived as prime minister for the full five years. The interpretation of this crisis is therefore complex. In one light it can be seen as the inevitable outcome of a series of tensions that had built up over the preceding two years within an increasingly divided and unsuccessful government. In another it can be seen as a temporary hiatus in what was essentially a *governo di legislatura* of a new type. Certainly, even after his formal resignation and a new investiture, Berlusconi's efforts to minimize the significance of the crisis had some justification. Despite being forced to resign and face a formal coalition crisis, neither his leadership nor his government was destroyed, as the crises of 1998 and 1999–2000 destroyed Romano Prodi and Massimo D'Alema.

The government was reassembled under the same prime minister and with rather few fundamental changes to its composition. Perhaps even more remarkable, the aftermath did not appear to leave the prime minister as weak as the initial crisis suggested. There was no collapse into the torpor of inactivity that is characteristic of post-crisis coalitions in the last year of an Italian legislature. On the contrary, the autumn of 2005 was a period of exceptional energy, with major legislation achieved in a number of areas, each linked to the balance of power within the coalition.

This chapter therefore argues that Berlusconi's increasing contingent weakness explains the need for a crisis in the first place, while his underlying strength and uniqueness as a political actor explain its particular outcomes, which are different from the usual outcomes in Italy, even in the "Second Republic." But precisely because this outcome depends on Berlusconi's uniqueness, other aspects of the crisis are not without their significance. The tactics and overall strategy of the minor-party veto players are also important, not least because they emphasize the continuing vulnerability of the center-right coalition (House of Freedoms, or CdL) to its internal contradictions. The most active of these veto players—the Union of Christian Democrats and Center Democrats (UDC)—may be seen as a winner or loser as a result of the crisis, depending on where the emphasis lies. However, it was certainly a player of significance well beyond its modest electoral dimensions in the last two years of the coalition. In a post-Berlusconi world, that significance would probably be greater still.

The chapter is divided into three sections. In the first, we examine the background to the crisis and its formal outcome. We then offer a more detailed analysis of the position of the two chief antagonists: Berlusconi as the hegemonic leader, and the UDC as the key veto player. Finally, we consider what the outcome and its aftermath tell us about the real winners and losers and the implications for coalition theory. The emphasis on the personal confrontation between Berlusconi and the UDC—in particular, the UDC's leader, Marco Follini—is intentional. The other parties, National Alliance (AN) and the Northern League (LN), had their reasons for discontent both before the crisis and during it, but the most profound conflict was between Berlusconi's party, Forza Italia (FI), and the UDC. The strategic location of the UDC in the wider party spectrum, its relatively solid electoral support in a period of generally poor performance by the center-right, and the unsettling possibility of individual or wholesale defection to the opposition appeared to give it enhanced bargaining power in the aftermath of the April elections.

Since 2001, commentary on the center-right has placed much emphasis on the so-called Northern axis created between Berlusconi and the LN, and the latter has been a powerful veto player since the early 1990s. But in the last two years, it is the UDC that has sought to play the role of veto player most actively. How it used that power was interesting and unusual, and is certainly not necessarily best interpreted through a simple hypothesis of seat or policy maximization. The UDC had a range of objectives: (1) curbs on prime ministerial power; (2) budgetary policy and other outcomes; (3) the manipulation of electoral perceptions of responsibility for, or distance from, policies that might be alternatively attractive or repugnant to party electorates; (4) the re-election prospects of parliamentary incumbents; and (5) perhaps the long-term prize of Palazzo Chigi (i.e., the prime ministership). How Berlusconi dealt with the UDC was no less interesting.

The Political Context and the Formal Outcome

The crisis of April 2005 was the result of a long process of negotiation and adjustment inside the government that was part symbolic argument over the style and procedure by which adjustment occurs, and part, but probably the minor part, substantive reworking of government personnel and policy. Above all, the coalition crisis was a clash of cultural interpretations. On the one side stood the hegemons of the coalition, Berlusconi and Forza Italia, intent on preserving the new narrative of "Second Republic" governance—that governments should be elected for the entire duration of a Parliament, under a single prime ministerial candidate, and on the basis of an agreed-upon five-year program. Berlusconi would frequently try to argue that his legitimacy as prime minister should come in some quasi-direct way from the general election, and should be revoked only by a further decision of the electorate. In the Senate confidence debate on his new government in April 2005, he went so far as to refer—erroneously—to European democracies in which prime ministers are directly elected by the people, who enjoy, by virtue of this, a power to make adjustments to a ministerial team without reference to extended crises and parliamentary approval: "Così si fà nelle democrazie più avanzate."[1]

On the other side stood the minor partners, intent on pursuing their own demands and determined to safeguard their distinctive identities and avoid being eclipsed by the prime minister and his party. They were adamant that the spirit of parliamentary democracy in Italy still required policy-making and office-holding under coalition government to be periodically examined, negotiated, and adjusted. This should take place not just at its outset but during the life of a Parliament and might involve, if necessary (and it probably *was* necessary, to remind everyone that it was a serious matter), the formal constitutional processes of government resignation, presidential consultations, a new investiture, and a parliamentary vote of confidence. In formal terms, these minor partners, and not the prime minister, had constitutional right on their side: a basic convention of the Italian version of parliamentary democracy—unaltered since 1948—is that Parliament can, if it wishes, be the arbiter of coalition crises.[2]

However, the crisis of April 2005 was not solely a stubborn battle over style and formal principle. Real issues of policy continued to reverberate throughout the coalition even after the crisis was formally over. The roots of the trouble in fact lay in the demands for a *verifica* (reassessment) of the government's composition, first aired roughly 10 months earlier. Giulio Tremonti's resignation of July 2004, the abortive nomination of Rocco Buttiglione as EU commissioner, and a minor reshuffle of undersecretaries in December 2004 were all signs of parties within the coalition jockeying for position.

Such tension was not unexpected, given the wider economic context. A government that had presided over an economy growing at only 1 percent per annum, and in which a major national debate had developed over a serious and enduring loss of national competitiveness, was, by the latter stages of its parliamentary life, likely to be suffering a serious loss of public support. The first signs of this came in the limited local elections of 2003, when FI strengthened its support in its Sicilian heartland but lost badly in Rome, and lost out more generally to the UDC and the LN. Following this, Berlusconi agreed that formal measures would be introduced to make the government more collegial by adding to the cabinet new inner groups of senior ministers and party leaders, with Gianfranco Fini playing the coordinating role. But the proposal backfired and was never implemented: the UDC objected to the ministerial group, and the LN to Fini.

A year later, the struggle repeated itself. Electoral defeat (in the European Parliament elections) was followed by recriminations, the eruption of arguments within the coalition, and a long, drawn-out battle over the budget. Electoral defeat was this time much clearer, especially for FI. Negotiations over the pre-budget Economic and Financial Planning Document (DPEF) were even more difficult: Italy's sovereign debt rating was downgraded; Finance Minister Tremonti was forced by joint pressure from AN and the UDC to resign, in order to avert what would have otherwise become a full-blown coalition crisis; and the autumn budget cycle proved so difficult that the bills transmitted from the Council of Ministers to Parliament on the 30 September deadline contained large gaps to be filled as and when agreement could be reached.

Against this background it was hardly surprising that when the third iteration arrived, in the spring of 2005, against a background of polls showing a serious decline in confidence in the prime minister's performance, and in the government as a whole, the electoral defeat would be a much bigger one and would bring even more serious repercussions for the government. The center-left won 11 out of 13 regions, leaving the CdL in control only of Lombardy and the Veneto.[3]

By past standards, such a defeat would have been highly likely to provoke a cabinet crisis from dissatisfied elements of the coalition. But if,
as was likely, no one really wanted fresh elections (even the "winners"
of 2005—the LN and the UDC—had performed less well than one year
before), the situation had to be managed carefully, inevitably resulting
in a game of brinkmanship.

In the wake of the regional elections, it appears that leaders of the
UDC and AN would have been content with a relaunch of the existing government, with a new presentation and/or revised policies, but
their demands that the government signal a change of course were
rebuffed by Berlusconi. In the run-up to a meeting of the UDC party
executive on 12 April, Berlusconi first promised a "period of reflection" on the government's plans for devolution and then threatened
early elections, should the UDC withdraw its ministers and support
the government from outside. The UDC's national executive met and
agreed, with one vote against (Minister for Relations with Parliament
Carlo Giovanardi), to withdraw from the Council of Ministers, seeking a new government that would work "for families, business, and
workers, and for the South, starting with the abolition of the IRAP
[Regional Tax on Business Activities] and the gradual adoption of the
'family quotient.'"[4]

Over the next few days, it seemed as if the crisis prompted by
the UDC's withdrawal might be resolved quickly with agreement on
the formation of a Berlusconi III government, but both the UDC and
Berlusconi were hesitant to commit. The Nuovo PSI added to the pressure by withdrawing its undersecretaries from the government, while
ministers from AN gave undated letters of resignation to Fini. On 20
April—five days after the withdrawal of the UDC and two weeks after
the elections—Berlusconi resigned. His speech to the Senate that same
day minimized the decision: while the public had registered its discontent, resignation was both "an act of clarification," which would
allow the "relaunch of the government's program," and an awkward
constitutional impediment to an otherwise humdrum reshuffle. By 23
April, the list of ministers of the new Berlusconi government had been
finalized. The government subsequently won votes of confidence in
the Chamber and the Senate on 27 and 28 April, respectively.

The new government was not substantially different from that
which preceded it. There were nine exits from the government,
including four departmental ministers (Sirchia, Urbani, and Marzano
from FI, and Gasparri from AN) and Vice-Premier Follini from the
UDC. Three ministers were appointed: Francesco Storace (AN), former president of the Lazio region, replaced Sirchia; Giorgio La Malfa
(Italian Republican Party, PRI) became minister for EU affairs; and

Mario Landolfi (AN) replaced Gasparri. The most significant development of the new government was its increased size. No patterns of
partisan advantage are obvious. Table 1 shows the composition of the
Berlusconi II government at the beginning and end of its term and that
of Berlusconi III, following its confirmation.

The increase in the number of posts available, largely through the
appointment of twelve new undersecretaries, made the formation of
Berlusconi III—in appearance at least—a positive-sum game. As Carol
Mershon reports, "published notes from coalition bargaining show that
Italian politicians focus on *both* cabinet shares and the value added
by new posts."[5] Where the number of posts held by a party across all
categories—minister, vice-minister, and undersecretary—has increased,
this may reflect an increased share of power for that party or—as seems
likely in the case of the LN—may reflect the increased size of the government. Where the number of posts held by a party has increased across
some categories but decreased in others—as is the case for FI and the
UDC—any judgment about the party's new weight in government will
depend on the relative importance attributed to particular ministries,
to ministers versus undersecretaries, and so on. Certainly, the simple,

TABLE 1 *Party composition of the Berlusconi II and III governments
over time*

		FI	AN	LN	UDC	Others	Total
Berlusconi II,	PCM	1					1
June 2001	V-P		1				1
	M	9	4	3	2	5	23
	V-M	2	2		1	1	6
	U	24	10	3	5	5	47
Berlusconi II,	PCM	1					1
April 2005	V-P		1		1		2
	M	7	4	3	3	5	22
	V-M	2	2		1	1	6
	U	24	11	5	5	6	51
Berlusconi III,	PCM	1					1
April 2005	V-P		1				1
	M	6	5	3	3	6	23
	V-M	3	2		1	3	9
	U	30	13	7	8	5	63

Key: PCM = President of the Council of Ministers (prime minister); V-P = Vice-
President of the Council of Ministers (vice-premier); M = Ministers; V-M = Vice-
Ministers; U = Undersecretaries.

old-fashioned Cencelli scores for each party[6] have not changed much across time: FI's relative score has decreased somewhat, while the other parties' scores have increased slightly. In general terms, it might be concluded, according to these allocative criteria, that

- *the UDC did not benefit*: it has lost the post of vice-premier and gained three undersecretaries in a general expansion of this latter category;
- *AN's gain was slight*: it gained one new minister (Storace) in the context of a general increase in the size of the cabinet;
- *the minor parties benefited despite playing a minor role in the coalition's collapse*: both the Nuovo PSI and PRI gained a minister (Caldoro and La Malfa, respectively).

If crude measures of party power within the coalition do not suggest that those parties prompting the collapse have gained from it, has the formation of Berlusconi III changed the direction of government policy to their benefit? To answer this question is to make a broader judgment on events spanning the last months of the 2001–2006 legislature, to which we return in the conclusion. In a limited way, the UDC and AN have achieved the demands that they voiced during the coalition crisis. In his speech to the Chamber on 26 April, Berlusconi promised measures "in three precise directions: supporting the family, supporting business, and supporting the South."[7] The at least verbal concession to the demands of the two parties most representative of Southern and state-dependent families—which had been evident in the 2005 budget law the previous autumn—was clear. Though this support was heavily qualified[8] and lacking in specifics, these issues had been raised repeatedly by the UDC and AN, and were to be brought back again in the next budget cycle.

The UDC eventually pronounced itself satisfied with the 2006 budget outcome.[9] By then, of course, with the return to party politics of the real leader of the party, Pierferdinando Casini, and the election of Lorenza Cesa to replace Marco Follini as party secretary, the UDC was itself a party more disposed than six months earlier to work with the rest of the coalition. But this did not prevent perhaps the most serious standoff of the entire 2006 budget cycle, when the UDC appeared to threaten a unilateral withdrawal from the coalition and even to vote against the government in a confidence vote over the funding of family policy.[10] How far the details of budget policy were actually agreed upon in the process of resolving the April crisis is unclear. In advance of the DPEF and the drafting of the budget by the Treasury, it seems that such promises could have been only implicit, but the UDC appeared to have believed that it had won a concession, that its size had been defined, and that the government was committed. Whether it would have followed up on the threat of withdrawal if Tremonti had dug his heels in is unclear, but the available evidence is that on this issue at least, the UDC got its way.

Whether the UDC and AN were able to signal to their Southern voters that they had shifted policy inside the coalition more broadly remains doubtful. The Northern axis to which Berlusconi had attached such importance in the early years of the government was strengthened twice over during the summer: the LN was for many months able to keep Antonio Fazio in his post as governor of the Bank of Italy despite a scandal that eventually engulfed him,[11] and Giulio Tremonti returned to front-line politics. Tremonti's return—first as vice-premier in April, and then as finance minister in September, following Domenico Siniscalco's resignation in protest against Fazio's continuation in office—further complicates any clear interpretation of the outcome of the crisis. It was at the behest of AN and the UDC that Tremonti had resigned the previous summer, and even if he returned in less trenchant style than before, far less critical of the coalition's two Southern partners and their policy demands, it could hardly be scored as a visible public gain for the UDC.

We might therefore conclude that in office- or policy-seeking terms, there were no obvious and immediate winners from the crisis. To understand this counter-intuitive result better, we should explore in more detail the power bases and aspirations of the two chief antagonists in the coalition battle: the prime minister on one side, and the UDC on the other.

The Strengths and Weaknesses of the Key Players

The Berlusconi government of 2001–2005 had, for Italy, a strongly prime ministerial style. It contained a hegemonic party, a large majority in both chambers, and two and sometimes three party leaders inside the cabinet. This was a state of affairs traditionally seen in Italy as an important test of coalition solidarity, frequently proposed but rarely achieved. The government's program was based directly on Berlusconi's "contract with Italians" and seemed more the promise of a leader than a complex coalition platform, like the one produced as a result of long negotiations by the Ulivo in 1996.

In addition to these structural features of the coalition, Berlusconi has benefited from his personal standing and resources. The prime minister's position as a fulcrum between two otherwise incompatible parties, the LN and AN, has been widely commented on.[12] His personal popularity and that of his party clearly bolster his position as a fulcrum, as does his ability to communicate and set the terms of political debate. These last two features were manifestly evident in 2001, when Berlusconi's personal popularity outpolled that of his government, and when FI was two and a half times larger than AN, its nearest rival within the coalition.

In principle, these qualities should have greatly strengthened the position of the prime minister, though quantification is difficult. There was a great deal of media discussion of this theme at the beginning of 2005, sparked by a book by Luca Ricolfi, which highlighted the innovative aspects of the center-right's term but also pointed out the many aspects of the famous "contract with Italians" that had not been fulfilled.[13] The Center for the Study of Political Change (CIRCaP) has recently attempted to compare Berlusconi's position with that of the other arguably quite strong prime minister of the "Second Republic," Romano Prodi.[14] Both governments were successful in reaching agreement within the Council of Ministers and presenting legislation on more than three-fourths of their pre-election promises. While the Berlusconi government's output in numerical terms was higher than Prodi's, this is not surprising since Berlusconi lasted twice as long. The Prodi government passed less legislation, with only 35 percent of government bills approved, compared to 60 percent for Berlusconi II, but it was more energetic and rapid while it lasted, reflecting the performance of a politically fragile government in a hurry. While the Berlusconi government had a more secure parliamentary base, it may have prepared the ground in advance less well and, with a broad territorial spread reflected in differential party strength in different areas, may have contained within it some potentially difficult distributional conflicts. Not surprisingly, therefore, we find a higher level of objective conflict between ministers in the Berlusconi government than in the Prodi government.[15] We also find in the Berlusconi government a falling rate of parliamentary approval of its bills and a comparatively greater use of decree laws (generally attributed to weakness, decisional delays, and hence time constraints), as well as a greater propensity to make the measures it submitted to Parliament questions of confidence.

Naturally, specific sectoral studies will be needed to fully understand the limits and possible failures of the government's policy program. Nevertheless, on the basis of the available analyses, we can say that, on the one hand, the thesis (promoted by the center-left) that the Berlusconi government is totally paralyzed by inaction is not completely supported by the facts. On the other hand, the argument (typical of the center-right and of Berlusconi's followers in particular) that the personal characteristics of the leader and the political nature of the coalition have automatically produced a "strong" government that is decisive in its policy-making seems rather weak in light of the empirical evidence.

How far can it be claimed that these advantages—the hegemony of FI, Berlusconi's dominant role within the coalition, and greater communicative ability—were in decline in the year leading up to the crisis in 2005? First, there is a clear, though limited, loss of electoral dominance. FI's share of the vote in European and regional elections has decreased, while that of its smaller rivals has increased. Consequently, FI's share of the total CdL vote and its electoral dominance within the coalition have declined.

Second, having once been the indispensable leader, Berlusconi is no longer so dominant. Polling conducted shortly after the coalition crisis suggested that Casini would be a more popular candidate as coalition leader,[16] and from both the UDC and AN there are claims that with FI less dominant, a candidate from another party is perfectly feasible. Within the legislature as well, the level of intra-coalition contestation has risen, as judged by both overt clashes and the propensity to amendment.[17] Additionally, poll data show that Berlusconi's personal popularity no longer outpaces the popularity of his government by the margin it once did.[18] We should be wary of inferring too much from these polls: Fini has had personal approval ratings consistently higher than Berlusconi but lacks the latter's fulcrum-like position at the center. Finally, there is ample evidence of decline in the government's popularity and in Berlusconi's own position. The prime minister might take some comfort from the fact that according to longitudinal data accumulated by ISPO, his own personal approval ratings have remained slightly ahead of those of the government as a whole, but the two are closely related. As long as this is so, Berlusconi cannot easily escape responsibility for the decline.[19]

Third, Berlusconi's advantage as a salesman has decreased: ratings for his television appearances have fallen.[20] Whereas during the 2001 election he could strictly limit appearances by himself and other center-right politicians on the "treacherous" programs of RAI, after the 2005 regional elections he was himself forced to appear on "opposition" territory, that is, on RAI's political discussion program, *Ballarò*.[21]

What we see, therefore, is greater weakness on Berlusconi's part, precisely as we would expect from a government that has faced a difficult economic recession and a sustained critique from moderate opinion leaders over a range of governance issues—public finances, devolution, leadership, conflict of interest, judicial issues, etc.—on which the government has appeared vulnerable.[22] But declining popularity is to be expected, and the possibility of a sustained recovery makes it unlikely that the coalition would seek to replace Berlusconi lightly, even without the huge downside, in terms of coalition disunity and repudiation of record, that it would bring. In short, Berlusconi grew politically weaker yet remained in control of his coalition: even after the coalition crises, he retained many cards up his sleeve.

The decrease in Berlusconi's resources matters less if there are no other members of the coalition with alternate bases of power. Certainly, there is little scope for unity among the smaller members of the coalition, divided by tactics, policy, and geography. The LN not only sought a devolution outcome unwanted by AN and the UDC, but its relationship to FI was far more ambiguous. While it was a difficult party for the prime minister to handle, it could also serve as an outlet for sentiments he might want aired but could not say himself. Nor were AN and the UDC—conventionally viewed as united against Berlusconi—always comfortable allies. Gianfranco Fini had patiently established a role for himself that required deep involvement in government. His admittedly fortuitous arrival at the Foreign Ministry in late 2004 was another stage in a long-term strategy to bring AN into the mainstream and to make himself an eventual candidate for the prime ministerial office. Deeply embedded in the coalition, he could criticize gently but could not easily threaten coalition mayhem. AN had nowhere else to go.

The UDC, with no such worry about its democratic credentials, had its estranged former Christian Democrat partners as siren voices on the other side of the government/opposition divide. It could conceive more easily of a different, post-Berlusconi, and perhaps post-bipolar political order. It could take more risks and with some reason. The regional elections signaled not only weaknesses in Berlusconi's leadership but also strength for the UDC—in particular, its stable electoral base and its central position in the political spectrum. Such strengths seemed to depend on several assumptions:

1. *The UDC's vote is stable since its vote share is independent of the vote share of the coalition.* The stability of the UDC's electorate can be inferred from numerous election results. Not only has the UDC's share of the vote increased markedly since the 2001 general election, it has done so in the context of a shrinking vote for the CdL. The share of the "Biancofiore"[23] in the proportional element of the 2001 election to the Chamber of Deputies was 3.2 percent, and the share of the CdL was 49.5 percent. Since then, the UDC increased its vote in the 2004 European Parliament elections (5.9 percent) and held that share in the regional elections of 2005 (5.8 percent). Meanwhile, the vote share of the CdL as a whole has declined to 45.5 percent in the European Parliament

elections and to 44.2 percent in the regional elections. Consequently, from furnishing almost 6.5 percent of the CdL's votes in the 2001 election, the UDC now provides over 13 percent; conversely, FI has moved from being dominant within the coalition, with almost 60 percent of its votes, to providing a little over two-fifths. These figures should be interpreted cautiously, since they come from elections conducted at different levels using different electoral systems. Nonetheless, the contrast between the UDC's sustained performance and FI's lackluster showing suggests that in nationwide elections, decreases in FI's vote share have little or no effect on the vote share of the UDC.

2. *The UDC's vote is stable since it is regionally concentrated.* In the 2001 general election, 48 percent of the UDC's vote came from the South and from the islands. In the 2004 European elections, it was closer to 50 percent. While that figure declined somewhat in the 2005 regional elections, the UDC's vote remains more geographically concentrated than that of any other part of the coalition, apart from the LN. While being less of an advantage in a proportional system with the proportional element applied nationally, this gave the UDC strong negotiating potential under the old electoral system.

3. *The UDC has attempted to engage in dialogue with the left.* Of all the governing parties, the UDC has been the least vituperative toward the left. Indeed, a group, led by Sergio D'Antoni, that had been federated with the UDC split to join the Ulivo in the June 2004 European Parliament elections. Subsequently, the UDC—or more particularly, Marco Follini—made a number of gestures to the left. Follini twice appealed to the Unione to support the government, once by requesting that the Unione abstain on the motion authorizing the continued presence of troops in Iraq (12–13 February), and once by requesting that the Unione work with the government in its battle to remedy the perceived defects of the Stability and Growth Pact (20 March). While these particular requests went unheeded,[24] Follini, alone on the center-right, received some recognition from the left with invitations to both the Left Democrat (DS) and Communist Refoundation (RC) party congresses in February and March, respectively. Follini's view of the left was much more charitable than that of Berlusconi, and indeed, of his own party. He argued in February that the anti-communism rhetoric was a "broken record," and, in the wake of the regional elections, downplayed Berlusconi's depiction of the left, calling it still viciously anti-communist. On one occasion (July 2004), the UDC broke with the government to endorse a left-wing proposal by supporting a Unione motion to require the administrative council of RAI to resign.

4. *The UDC has maintained an ambivalent stance toward the government of which it is part.* The UDC has broken with coalition partners

over issues close to its (Southern electorate's) heart: amendments to the LN's federalizing reform and limits on public expenditure. More importantly, the UDC has squabbled with its partners over the form of the coalition itself. September 2004 brought tension within the coalition, as Fini was reported to be concerned about the impact of Follini's performance as vice-premier. In February 2005, the UDC temporarily blocked the CdL's lists for the regional elections: after 79 of 81 places on the list had been filled, the UDC demanded the remaining two places for itself. Since the coalition break-up, Follini repeatedly raised the possibility that without a change of leader and/or a return to proportional representation, the UDC may present candidates independent of the CdL.

There are of course qualifications to several of these assumptions. First, the UDC's relative friendliness toward the center-left has not been consistent. After his comments of February, members of his party sought to remind Follini that communism was "still the enemy"; in his speech to a party congress some months before, he had to dispel the "fantasy" that the UDC was amicable toward or in any way soft on the left.[25] Second, the UDC's threat to leave the coalition does not mean that it will. Comments about a possible UDC-Radical list in the 2005 regional elections eventually came to naught as Follini declared their differences "insurmountable." Third, and most importantly, although Follini defined much of the UDC's position in these debates, Follini himself became increasingly isolated from the rest of his party throughout 2005, leading to his eventual resignation as party secretary in October. In his resignation speech, he criticized the UDC ministers for being "opaque" and "obsequious."[26] The dispute between Follini and his internal opponents, including Mario Baccini and Carlo Giovanardi, seemed to concern the UDC's positioning within the coalition rather than any questions of policy.

Analysis and Prospects

The coalition crisis presents a paradox. Although the resources available to Berlusconi had decreased and those available to the UDC had increased, this did not lead to favorable developments for the UDC (and AN) in terms of policy or cabinet portfolios. So what benefit, if any, did the UDC derive? The UDC seems to have been attempting to maximize a complex basket of variables, including portfolios, policy, distance from electorally damaging government policy, and re-election prospects. Some of these variables are inversely correlated: parties cannot credibly distance themselves from government policy when at the same time they are taking on an increasing number of cabinet posts.

In the run-up to the coalition crisis, the value of holding a share of government portfolios was decreasing as the end of the legislature, and with it the prospects of enacting significant legislation that the UDC could claim credit for, approached. Conversely, the regional elections showed that the value of distancing the party from the rest of the coalition had increased, given the lackluster performance of other coalition members. Considering the independence of the UDC's vote share from the rest of the coalition, the election results also suggested that such distancing would not bring large negative consequences—if it were controlled. It is thus not surprising that the UDC should have enacted a coalition crisis only to return to government with a lighter load of ministerial portfolios. The UDC needed to signal its distance from the rest of the coalition, although not at the expense of bringing down the government. However, it could not signal distance if it received a greater number of cabinet posts—hence Follini's resignation from the role of vice-premier.

This strategy of signaling distance in order to maximize future re-election prospects initially seemed to pay off. Two polls conducted during the coalition crisis showed the UDC polling between 8 and 11 percent, significantly above trend.[27] However, the UDC's gains have not been as impressive as might have been hoped. Since May–June 2005, Berlusconi has demonstrated that even with his traditional strengths diminished, he is able to coordinate the parties within the coalition by playing fairly acute distributional politics. The autumn of 2005 produced a level of activism and purpose in the coalition that no one expected. For a government in the middle of a budget cycle, still less one in its last year of office, to pass a constitutional reform, an electoral reform, and a judicial reform (each admittedly open to the charge of egregious short-term expediency) was extraordinary, whatever one might think of what was produced. Even the 2006 budget seemed to produce a higher level of broad intra-coalition satisfaction than its two predecessors.

On the institutional front, the reforms of Part II of the Constitution satisfied FI in relation to the *premierato* (strong prime ministership) and the LN with respect to devolution, and yet seemed to leave the UDC comfortable with at least the federalist elements, if not the proposed new relationship between Senate and Chamber.[28] Most importantly, Berlusconi undercut Follini and appeared to buy off the majority in the UDC with the passage of a new electoral reform bill. The return to a closed-list proportional system offers security to notables within the smaller parties, who can expect safe re-election with a high position on their party's list. At the same time, it undercuts the more ambitious plans of those party leaders who would use their regional concentration to extract more from the CdL under a plurality system. This has accentuated tensions in the UDC and Nuovo PSI between ministers and party leaders. When Follini resigned as secretary of the UDC, he was highly critical of the ministers Baccini and Giovanardi.[29] In many ways, in fact, Berlusconi's astuteness in maneuvering Follini into a position where he felt obliged to resign was the master coup of the entire year. Casini was always the real leader of the UDC, even when occupying a neutral role as speaker of the Chamber. Berlusconi ably exploited Casini's ambition to return to front-line politics and, in effect, bought off the UDC with an offer on electoral reform that destroyed any basis for broad cross-party agreement that included the opposition, thereby undercutting a part of Follini's strategic plans. Berlusconi offered something that not only served UDC incumbents but lined them up to support aspects of judicial reform and devolution that otherwise might have been hard to swallow.

The explanation we have given of the coalition crisis—that in light of a decline in the resources available to the prime minister and an increase in the resources available to the UDC, the latter engaged in a partially successful attempt at distancing itself from the government in order to maximize future electoral prospects—is complex and sits ill with the current literature on government termination. Existing game-theoretic literature on government termination views governments as stable allocations of cabinet portfolios.[30] Parties wish to maximize both the percentage of portfolios and the percentage of seats they hold. New information can disturb these equilibria by providing parties with clues as to likely future shares of seats. Given these clues and the expectations of the parties, the allocation of portfolios may remain as it is, may change, or may result in new elections being called.

Lupia and Strøm's model suggests correctly that absent a majority for new elections and with dissatisfaction over the current allocation of cabinet portfolios, there will be a "non-electoral reallocation of power."[31] The two premises and resultant conclusion seem to hold for the coalition crisis of April 2005. However, this model has one particular feature which means that it cannot explain the eventual outcome: it takes electoral performance as wholly exogenous, revealed to the actors by events outside the model. If our arguments about the UDC's desire to distance itself from the rest of the coalition are true, electoral performance is partially endogenous, and actors must set office-holding maximization against its consequences for future electoral appeal. Consequently, parties are pursuing a policy of constrained maximization.

This feature of the partial endogeneity of electoral performance in coalition renegotiation makes us reconsider the end-of-term effects commonly seen in Italian legislatures. As the end of a parliamentary term approaches, allocations of cabinet portfolios become more unstable. Lupia and Strøm note this when they mention that the worth of a cabinet portfolio declines toward the end of a term as the chances of making more policy under that portfolio decrease.[32] But cabinet lineups also become more unstable as parties find the value of such portfolios modified by the consequences for future electoral performance.

This strategy—of smaller parties putting greater distance between themselves and their larger coalition partners—is not new. Indeed, Mershon, in an analysis of coalition negotiation in the First Republic, comments that "the parties described as the DC's allies under coalition formulae usually won electoral credit for brief exits from coalition and banked on re-entering government, looking for additional credit."[33] If the UDC's behavior is rewarded by the electorate in April 2006, it may show that some of the reasons underlying coalition instability in the First Republic may still be present. If this is so, the longevity of the Berlusconi II government may be a result not just of the majoritarian electoral system and the new Italian party system, but of those novelties combined with the rather special features of a governing coalition headed by Silvio Berlusconi. No one else could hold together such a disparate alliance, and no one else could command the resources to underpin the center-right's election campaign.

Whether or not the coalition would do better in electoral terms under a different leader, if by some improbable chance such a leader could hold the coalition together—a question that finally began to emerge in open political debate in 2005—there was no agreement on who that might be and therefore no real alternative to Berlusconi. But what that suggested was not that the conventions of the institutional game as perceived by political actors or the mass public had changed, but simply that Berlusconi was still a unique type of actor with resources that no one else would be likely to command. It goes without saying that we should not expect such outcomes to be repeated unless FI can find a successor with similar resources to those enjoyed by the prime minister. Once Berlusconi has retired from the scene, we might expect the veto power of smaller parties to increase, along with the range of coalition-building possibilities and the instability of end games.

Notes

1. "This is how it's done in the most advanced democracies" (speech to the Senate, 26 April 2005). That such "advanced democracies" based on direct election of the prime minister do not exist in Europe was a minor inconvenience, and in any case no one had the temerity to point it out during the debate.
2. As Oreste Massari points out, a coalition in Italy is still a contract between its parties, not between a leader and the people. See O. Massari, "La crisi di governo e il bipolarismo difettoso," *Il Mulino*, no. 3 (2005): 442–450. In principle, indeed, this would remain so even with the reform of Part II of the Constitution passed by Parliament on 16 November 2005. The reform contained a principle widely described as *premierato forte* (a strong prime ministership), but it still allowed a parliamentary majority to discard a prime minister and install another, if it can agree on a replacement.
3. On the regional elections, see Salvatore Vassallo's chapter in this volume.
4. ANSA, "Governo: Ecco il testo della Direzione UDC approvato oggi," 15 April 2005.
5. C. Mershon, *The Costs of Coalition* (Stanford, CA: Stanford University Press, 2002), 66.
6. In this system, the president of the Council of Ministers (prime minister) counts for 5, a vice-president 4, a minister 3, a vice-minister 2, and an undersecretary 1. However, such scores are of little value when ministerial portfolios vary enormously in importance and power.
7. Speech to the Chamber, 26 April 2005 (http://www.governo.it/Presidente/Interventi/testo_int.asp?d = 25106).
8. "Questa nuova attenzione, questa concentrazione della nostra attività sui problemi del Sud, delle imprese, del potere di acquisto delle famiglie, *non ci fa mettere da parte gli altri impegni che abbiamo assunto nel 2001*" (This new attention, this concentration of our action on the problems of the South, of firms, of the purchasing power of families, *is not leading us to put aside the other commitments we made in 2001*) (speech to the Senate, 28 April 2005).
9. M. Sensini, "Finanziaria: Fondo famiglia torna ad 1,14mld," *Corriere della Sera*, 4 November 2005.
10. A. Cazzullo, "Finanziaria: Ultimatum dell'UDC a Tremonti," *Corriere della Sera*, 26 October 2005.
11. On the banking takeovers, see Marcello Messori's chapter in this volume.
12. I. Diamanti and E. Lello, "The Casa delle Libertà: A House of Cards?" *Modern Italy* 10, no. 1 (2005).
13. L. Ricolfi, *Dossier Italia: A che punto è il "Contratto con gli italiani"* (Bologna: Il Mulino, 2005).
14. CIRCaP, *Rapporto Circap sul governo in Italia*, 2005 (http://www.gips.unisi.it/circap).
15. According to the CIRCaP research, there was conflict on 4 out of 15 major measures in the Prodi government, but on 7 out of 17 under Berlusconi (ibid., 46 and 49).
16. Osservatorio Nord-ovest, "Rilevazione Maggio/Giugno 2005," 29 September 2005 (http://www.nordovest.org/). Participants were asked, "If at the next election in 2006 the center-right were to win, who would you prefer as president of the Council of Ministers, Berlusconi or Casini?" Of those who responded, 73.2 percent preferred Casini.

17. CIRCaP, *Rapporto*, 53.
18. R. Mannheimer, *Gli Italiani e la politica* (Milan: Bompiani, 2003), 80–81.
19. CIRCaP, *Rapporto*, 41.
20. F. Roncarolo, "Campaigning and Governing: An Analysis of Berlusconi's Rhetorical Leadership," *Modern Italy* 10, no. 1 (2005): 87.
21. Lest it should be supposed that this signals an end to *videocrazia*, Berlusconi has so far been bested in popularity contests by other media figures, most notably, former RAI news anchor Lilli Gruber, who polled twice as many personal votes as Berlusconi in the 2004 European Parliament elections.
22. See the analysis of the subjects of a series of editorials originally published in *Corriere della Sera* in the fourth year of the XIV Legislature in CIRCaP, *Rapporto*, 40.
23. This was the name of the joint list run by the CDU (Christian Democratic Union) and the CCD (Christian Democratic Center) before they fused as the UDC.
24. ANSA, "UE: Patto; Follini apre a Unione ma prevale lo scontro," 20 March 2005.
25. Marco Follini, speech to UDC National Congress, 2 August 2004.
26. Marco Follini, speech of 15 October 2005 (http://www.udc-italia.it).
27. Poll conducted by Lorien Consulting, week of 10–16 April 2005.
28. L. Fuccaro, "Il presidente della Camera: Adesso i cittadini decidano con serenità," *Corriere della Sera*, 18 November 2005.
29. Similarly, when Gianni De Michelis left the Nuovo PSI conference, thereby splitting the party, the party's ministers and undersecretaries remained in the rump of the party.
30. A. Lupia and K. Strøm, "Coalition Termination and the Strategic Timing of Legislative Elections," *American Political Science Review* 89, no. 3 (1995): 648–665.
31. Ibid.
32. Ibid., 656.
33. Mershon, *Costs of Coalition*, 76.

5

FROM RESOURCE TO CONSTRAINT? ITALY AND THE STABILITY AND GROWTH PACT

Vincent Della Sala

The areas of policy and politics that captured the notion that Italy was "saved by Europe" and "condemned to success" were budgetary politics and the state of Italy's public finances. During the dark days of the currency crisis of September 1992, few would have expected that by the end of the decade Italy's public finances would have managed to correct themselves to settle below the ceilings set by the Maastricht convergence criteria.[1] Justifiably, political, economic, and social leaders trumpeted Italy's entry into the euro economy as a great policy achievement and as a sign that its commitment to fiscal discipline could never be questioned again. Moreover, the Stability and Growth Pact (SGP) would guarantee that any relapse would be corrected by a healthy dose of EU medicine. This narrative of Italy's spendthrift ways being reformed by the discipline of Europe was seriously questioned in 2005 when the European Commission and Council initiated the excessive deficit procedure in response to Italy's violation of the terms of the SGP. Had the *vincolo esterno* (external constraint) that shaped Italian macro-economic policy in the 1990s lost its grip?[2] Were Italian policy-makers breaking free of European constraints, or were they simply adjusting to a more elastic framework for the control of public finances in the EU?

As we will see below, it became increasingly clear during the year that the Italian government was right to see more room for maneuver

---

Notes for this chapter begin on page 137.

in the EU macro-economic regime, but it had yet to build credibility as a fiscal disciplinarian in order to exploit fully the cracks in the SGP wall. The source of Italy's difficulties stemmed from political tensions within the governing majority as well as the structural problems of having to carry a heavy debt load. This reflected missed opportunities, not only by the center-right government (although with sluggish growth in Europe in recent years, it cannot be blamed entirely), but also due to the lack of structural reforms to spending and the economy that were not carried out in the second half of the 1990s. The SGP, which had been designed precisely to impose constraints on governments that would have liked to spend their way out of a sluggish economy, was an increasingly tight jacket for Italian policy-makers. Paradoxically, the more they complained about the SGP, the more difficult it became to regain credibility in international markets, thus making the jacket even tighter.

The first section of the chapter will provide a brief introduction to the SGP and the attempts to reform it in the last three years. It will demonstrate that the terms of the SGP were changed, but not in ways that were favorable to Italy. This will lead to the second section, which will examine the implementation of the excessive deficit procedure against Italy in July 2005. The final section of the chapter will analyze the steps Italy took to regain its credibility with the budget measures for 2006. The chapter will show that the *vincolo esterno*, which was a resource for the center-left governments in the 1990s, became increasingly viewed as a constraint by the center-right in 2005.

Italy and the Reform of the Stability and Growth Pact

There have been two contrasting pressures in European macro-economic policy-making, especially since steps were taken to create economic and monetary union. On the one hand, there has been a constant demand to have mechanisms for monetary policy subject to some form of political leadership, guided largely by member states. The French government of Lionel Jospin in the last part of the 1990s and the Schröder government in its early days with Oscar Lafontaine as minister of the economy were at the forefront of the push to create a European minister of the economy and to have a "political governance" of the economy. On the other hand, with few instruments to set fiscal policy at the supranational level, there were fears that European monetary union would create opportunities for free-riders to exploit the benefits of being within a single currency while abandoning the fiscal discipline that had been a requirement for entry. This led to the establishment of the SGP, which somewhat assuaged German worries that governments that had lacked fiscal discipline in the past, especially Italy, would be subject to clear criteria and mechanisms to monitor fiscal discipline. Moreover, the SGP was designed precisely to deal with those governments that might be tempted to temper the tight monetary policies of the European Central Bank (ECB) with a less rigorous approach to public finances.

The aim of the SGP, which emerged at the Amsterdam Council in 1997, was to ensure that member states would "undertake to comply with the medium-term budgetary objective of positions close to balance or in surplus."[3] It reaffirmed some of the key principles that had been part of the process for the creation of the single currency, namely, multi-lateral surveillance of member states' public finances and procedures to deal with excessive deficits. The question of multilateral surveillance combines both preventive measures and sanctions. The original terms of the SGP emphasized that states could not allow government deficits to breach the 3 percent of GDP threshold and that they were to submit regular stability and convergence programs to be monitored by the Commission. The latter had the power to issue "early warnings" if it felt that a member state's public finances were in danger of pushing beyond the 3 percent barrier. These warning signals were meant to have states face up to pressure not only from other members of the Eurozone but also from international financial markets. This was especially significant for those member states carrying large debt loads that might then be subject to higher borrowing costs, since financial markets could interpret the early warnings as a sign of lack of fiscal discipline and of increased risk. If states did not, or could not, heed the early warnings and did indeed break through the 3 percent barrier, they would be subject to the excessive deficit procedure. Not only would they be required to implement recommendations established by the Council, but they could also be subject to a precautionary deposit that could be converted to a fine if the excessive deficit was not corrected within two years.

There are many paradoxes that have characterized the short life of the SGP. It was supposedly an agreement that had as much widespread consensus as the convergence criteria. Despite countless statements of allegiance to the terms of the SGP, it had few ardent supporters outside of the ECB and the small "virtuous" member states such as the Netherlands and Austria. Governments such as those in France and Germany chafed under its restrictions on deficit financing. A second paradox was that the SGP was largely inspired by a desire to convince German businesses and public opinion that the surrendering of the German currency to the vagaries of a European currency would be countered by constraints on spendthrift governments, especially those in Italy. Yet while Italy would eventually run afoul of the SGP rules in 2005, it was the public finance problems of Germany and France that led to a crisis for the SGP in 2004.

Political leaders could rely on the political capital afforded by the ambitious objective of creating a single currency to help legitimize unpopular budgetary choices in the 1990s. However, their task became much more arduous when trying to gain support for continued fiscal discipline after entry, especially once growth levels began to stagnate at the start of the new century. The SGP was introduced partly to provide member states with an external pressure that could be used to help them overcome domestic political and institutional obstacles to sound money policies. The center-left government of Romano Prodi ran into problems in 1997 and especially in 1998, precisely because it had to contend with political forces within its coalition that were expressing fatigue with continued budgetary discipline.[4] The SGP was a resource for the center-left when it was in power as it helped keep together a difficult coalition. Moreover, with Prodi as president of the European Commission in 1999, there was an indirect link between the center-left parties of the Ulivo and the EU policies that Prodi was institutionally charged to defend and promote.

The election of the center-right government of Silvio Berlusconi in 2001 raised questions about Italy's position with respect to the SGP. There were three primary reasons to think that the new government might challenge the terms, if not the very basis, of the SGP. First, despite the free-market rhetoric of the House of Freedoms, its election promises of opening up construction sites across the peninsula to public works projects were certain to raise problems in terms of public finances. This was especially the case as the prime minister was also committed to introducing significant cuts to income tax rates.[5] The second, and related, factor was that the center-right coalition was hardly cohesive in its views on macro-economic policy as well as on Europe. The minister of the economy, Giulio Tremonti, sent out ambiguous signals about Italy's economic objectives and interests. He was careful always to express Italy's commitment to the SGP and to maintaining fiscal discipline. At the same time, he was seen as a modern-day Colbert—not entirely convinced of the power of markets and not entirely opposed to some forms of state intervention.

Tremonti was also the architect of the alliance between Forza Italia and the Lega Nord (LN). It is easy to dismiss as political posturing the LN's positions on Europe, which bordered on the hysterical at times. But its views on important economic questions could not be ignored so easily. For instance, its contention that the introduction of the euro would result in inflation and lack of growth would become a common government refrain after 2002. The position of the third major party in the governing coalition, the National Alliance (AN), also was ambiguous with respect to the SGP. On the one hand, its base of support in southern Italy and a more interventionist wing of the party tended to see the SGP as a constraint that weakened both the state and the political position of the party. On the other hand, AN's leader, Gianfranco Fini, had embarked on a strategy to bring the party into the mainstream of European conservative parties.[6]

Third, the policy and political tensions within the center-right government were exacerbated by the state of the country's public finances and economic fundamentals at the start of the new century. While the Berlusconi government tried to blame the country's economic challenges entirely on previous governments, it did inherit a number of problems that were to make the job of reaching the SGP thresholds more difficult. As Mark Hallerberg has noted, Italy's fiscal "discipline" in the mid-1990s was a reflection more of lower service charges on the debt due to lower interest rates and economic growth than a result of any tough decisions on the spending or revenue fronts.[7] Even with stability of interest rates brought about by entry into the euro economy in 1999, Italy's debt levels remained exceedingly high. They were expected to remain so in the absence of high rates of growth (something that not even the most optimistic forecasts called for) or unless governments sought austerity measures that went beyond what was called for in the SGP. Moreover, the fact that devaluation was no longer available as a policy instrument brought into relief the microeconomic challenges that Italy faced and that had not been addressed in the 1990s: low productivity levels, high labor costs, lack of R&D investment, costly and fragmented capital markets, and so forth.[8]

Despite the internal differences and the economic constraints on the Berlusconi government, its position in the summer of 2001 was that it was firmly committed to maintaining the terms of the SGP. The government's first update of the SGP, presented to the Commission in November 2001, was cautious about the future. It pointed out that the global economy had slowed down in the previous year and that political instability at the international level after the terrorist attacks on 11 September would mean a lowering of growth forecasts. However, this would not divert government policy, and a balanced budget would be achieved by 2003.[9]

These initial positive signals were difficult to sustain as they were based on GDP growth projections—2.3 percent in 2002, and 3.0 percent in 2003 and in 2004—that were never realized, since European economies, and especially that of Italy, were slow to respond to positive global trends. Growth was registered at only 0.4 percent in 2002, 0.3 percent in 2003, and 1.2 percent in 2004, significantly lower than the government's projected 1.9 percent.[10] Although in November 2003 the government did not foresee any problems in meeting the SGP's reference points, the stagnant economy would prove to be a test of the government's commitment to the SGP and to fiscal discipline. It continued to stand by the SGP, but signals were being sent out that some of its terms needed to be revisited.[11] At the Madrid ECOFIN meeting in June 2002, Italy would back the French proposal that the aim of reaching a balanced budget by 2004 be replaced by the objective of budgets that were "close to balance" for the 2004–2007 period. Italy did not feel that it was in any danger of running excessive deficits, but by 2002 it was clear that slower than expected economic growth would make it unlikely that Italy, along with Portugal, France, and Germany, was not going to have a balanced or surplus budget in 2004. Italy was glad to have an ally, in this case France, take the lead in discussions to change the wording.

Sluggish growth rates were not confined to Italy, and by 2002 and 2003, the French and Germans were facing problems in trying to meet their SGP commitments. When Italy assumed the presidency of the Council in July 2003, it was apparent that it would have to deal with a major confrontation between the Commission and the two largest economies in the EU over their repeated breaching of the 3 percent deficit barrier. The Commission had recommended that the excessive deficit procedure be applied to France and Germany to force them to take immediate action to respect the terms of the SGP. Italy's position was rather delicate in the looming confrontation between the Commission and the large member states. On the one hand, the SGP was not a straitjacket, but it did limit the room to maneuver in terms of the objective of decreasing taxes or of being able to use public spending to stimulate the economy. Thus, the government was happy to have the SGP being thrown into question. It also did not displease the government to have Prodi engaged in a political battle with powerful member states such as France and Germany. On the other hand, the government could not pursue a visible and aggressive campaign to change the terms of the SGP. Its large debt load meant that it had to continue to send signals to international financial markets that it remained wedded to fiscal discipline. Holding the presidency of the Council, Italy could not ignore the "virtuous" member states who were adamant that the terms of the SGP be respected and the excessive deficit procedure be applied.

In the end, Italy sided with the November 2003 ECOFIN decision to suspend the application of the SGP to Germany and France. While all the members of the Eurozone went to great lengths to claim that the

SGP was still the foundation of fiscal policy, its legitimacy had been seriously undermined. The central precept that basic macro-economic objectives and instruments were to be insulated from political calculations had been challenged. Moreover, that the two largest economies were able to use their weight to be exempted from sanctions created a split between the "virtuous" states and the laggards—a split that corresponded roughly to a division not only between small and large states but also between those states that had introduced structural reforms to their economies and those that had not. Italy found itself in the second group and could count as potential allies only other states that had trouble meeting the SGP criteria and were having problems liberalizing important parts of their economies. In addition, Italy had clearly sided with the member states in the challenge to the Commission's role as guardian of fiscal discipline in the Eurozone.

Despite the government's preference to reform the SGP, it was essential that the government continue to be seen as adhering to its terms. The loosening of the SGP meant that international financial markets would be paying even closer attention to the balance sheets of member states with public finances in fragile health. While Italy had not run afoul of the SGP rules, its policies had caused concern among the Commission and some of the other member states. What had drawn particular attention was the series of tax amnesties and ad hoc measures that were designed to raise additional revenues so that the 3 percent reference point would be respected. This helped fuel a growing suspicion that Italian authorities were engaging in creative accounting that respected the letter of the SGP but not the spirit. Clearly, Tremonti and the government hoped that the ad hoc measures would tide Italy over until the economy returned to sustained levels of growth in 2003 or 2004 at the latest.

Losing Credibility? Italy and the Excessive Deficit Procedure

The Italian government continued to insist that it would abide by the terms of the SGP, but the Commission did not seem convinced. By April 2004, it was ready to issue an early warning to Italy that it was in danger of running excessive deficits for 2004 and 2005. The Italian government's response was to attack on all fronts. Tremonti pointed out that member states representing 85 percent of GDP in the Eurozone were in danger of violating the terms of the SGP. He went on to state that the early warning mechanism was to be used in extraordinary situations, but it could hardly be applied to Italy now when so many member states seemed to be having trouble with public finances.[12] Tremonti emphasized that the SGP was not just about stability but also about growth, and if so many member states were in trouble, it was because the SGP was becoming a straitjacket for stagnating economies. Berlusconi argued that breaching the 3 percent barrier was not a major problem if it meant stimulating growth, and he remained confident that the early warning would not be applied to Italy, just as it had not been in the case of France and Germany a few months earlier.[13]

There were signs that the Italian case might be different. First, a possible violation of the SGP in 2004 was combined with exceptionally high public debt levels. As much as the government might have felt that it was the target of a political campaign, it had to be careful not to be seen as wanting to upset the basis of the SGP and as abandoning fiscal discipline. Italy's high level of debt meant that any sign of wavering would be interpreted as a return to the old ways of reckless public finances. It simply did not have the credibility in international markets that Germany, and even France, had; borrowing could become more expensive for Italy if there was an early warning and if this was ignored. The bond rating agencies such as Standard & Poor's and Moody's had made it clear that when assessing Italy's bond ratings, they were paying close attention to whether an early warning had been issued.[14] Bond markets were largely indifferent to Italy's budgetary politics, as reflected in relatively low bond prices, but there were signs that this was beginning to change in 2005.

A second, and related, sign was that Italy seemed to be going in a different direction from that required by the SGP. The Italian government in April 2004 was presenting plans to stimulate growth with cuts to income tax without any drastic and structural reforms of spending. Tremonti was fairly confident that Italy would find allies in Germany and France in its campaign to put the emphasis on growth rather than stability. His argument was that if there were a violation of the 3 percent barrier in 2004, it would be temporary and quickly reversed in 2005 as the economy returned to growth. There was no danger of excessive deficits because 2004 would prove to be an exception.

Tremonti never got to make his case to the July ECOFIN that was to take action on Italy. At a meeting on 11 May, he had promised that he would present a plan for the next ECOFIN on 5 July that would outline the measures Italy would take to avoid the early warning. However, tensions within the government in late June and early July led to his resignation and to the eventual appointment of Domenico Siniscalco, the most senior official in the Ministry of the Economy. It was Berlusconi himself who attended the 5 July ECOFIN to present the government's corrective measures. It was not an easy job as the prime minister was committed to introducing tax cuts that amounted to 6 billion euros. Corrective measures, totaling 7.5 billion euros, taken in July and the 2005–2008 economic plan were enough to satisfy Italy's European partners, so that no early warning was issued.[15] Moreover, there was even reason to surmise that Italy's interest in loosening the terms of the SGP was gaining ground: the Commission issued a communication on 3 September 2004 suggesting ways in which the SGP could be interpreted with greater flexibility and clarified with respect to stating medium-term objectives. The Commission seemed to be stating that the SGP could be improved, thus implying that, as Siniscalco argued, "the reform of the SGP is no longer a taboo subject."[16]

The Italian objective, then, at the end of 2004 was to change the terms of the SGP, and toward this goal the French and Germans were expected once again to take the lead. The danger was that the terms of the SGP might be changed but not in ways preferred by the Italian government, since different member states were looking to solve different problems without undermining the credibility of the SGP and the stability of the euro. At the 22–23 March 2005 European Council, Berlusconi presented a fairly optimistic picture of Italy's relationship with the Commission and of the state of Italy's public finances, promising more tax cuts in 2005 while staying under the 3 percent barrier. The Council did introduce changes to the SGP but not those that the Italian government had hoped for. The most important modifications were those found in section 2 ("Strengthening the Preventative Arm") of the ECOFIN report that was adopted by the Council. The new regime recognized the heterogeneity of the 25 economies and how they were not always at the same point in the economic cycle. The report also stated that there could be exceptional circumstances and relevant factors that could account for member states violating the 3 percent rule. These other relevant factors could include funds dedicated for international aid and development and policies that aim to meet the Lisbon agenda and to promote R&D.

The Council, however, did not adopt the Italian proposals for taking capital and infrastructure investments into account.[17] Perhaps more worrying for the government was that the report, while trying to provide greater flexibility for the SGP and to signal that growth was just as important as stability, went to great lengths to highlight the overall health of public finances, especially debt levels. Member states that introduced structural reforms to their economies that improved the long-term health of public finances through cost-savings and that brought down debt levels would be given more room to maneuver with respect to meeting the medium-term objectives of coming close to a balanced budget and the 3 percent reference point. The Council report charged the Commission to examine compliance with the SGP with respect to deficits and to focus increasingly on debt and sustainability. This did not augur well for Italy, whose high debt level seemed unable to drop below at least 106 percent of GDP. Indeed, in November the ECB announced that it would not accept sovereign debt (and therefore be the bank of last resort) for those states that had let their credit ratings slip.[18] It seemed that the reforms to the SGP met the demands of other member states, such as Germany and France, but not Italy.

Italy was immediately under the spotlight after the March Council for two reasons. First, although the discussion about changing the SGP had been going on for at least three years, and the SGP had suffered a serious blow with its suspension in the cases of France and Germany in November 2003, there was speculation that the latest modifications had undermined it. The Commission and some of the "virtuous" member states were determined to be especially vigilant and to send out signals that the changing of the rules did not mean any less of a commitment to fiscal discipline. Second, the Council report had also included a section titled "Statistical Governance," which called for reliable, timely, and credible fiscal statistics. This was partly a result of problems with Greece's data prior to that country's entry into the euro. But it also implicated Italy, since Eurostat was reviewing Italy's fiscal statistics for 2003 and 2004 with respect to reporting practices.[19]

There was a string of bad news on the financial and fiscal front in the first half of 2005, culminating in the Commission's recommendation that the excessive deficit procedure be applied to Italy. The Eurostat ruling did find that Italy's accounts for 2003 and 2004 had to be adjusted. The rulings meant that the deficit figure was revised upwards to 3.1 percent for both years, from 2.9 percent in 2003 and 3 percent in 2004. This minor adjustment meant that the projected deficit figures for 2005 (3.6 percent) and 2006 (4.6 percent) would result in violating the terms of the SGP for four consecutive years. It became hard for the government to counter the Commission claim that Italy's deficit problems were not due to exceptional circumstances and other relevant factors. The Commission report that recommended the excessive deficit procedure emphasized that Italy's slow rate of growth was not cyclical but structural, as it had lagged behind the rest of Europe since the beginning of the 1990s.[20] The Commission also pointed out that despite the structural weaknesses in the economy, Italian governments had consistently presented SGP updates with projected rates of growth in the 2.5 percent to 3 percent range—rates that the economy never came close to realizing. The Commission traced the roots of the problem to declining revenues because of tax cuts, which were added to increasing primary expenditures.[21] It argued: "The projected worsening of fiscal imbalances mainly reflects the fact that a structural budgetary correction necessary to replace the diminishing budgetary impact of temporary measures is not in place."[22] Even under the terms of the reformed SGP, Italy was in excessive deficit and measures would have to be taken.

Italy was going to be the test as to whether the new terms of the SGP still had enough teeth to compel states to reimpose fiscal discipline. Berlusconi and Economy Minister Siniscalco were able to negotiate a two-year grace period in which Italy would have to bring deficit levels below the 3 percent mark. Attempting to turn this to its advantage, the government heralded the deal with its European partners as a confirmation of its policies of seeking to have finances corrected by promoting growth and not simply through cuts in taxes. Siniscalco said the plan was "a diet, not starvation," because no corrective measures were requested for 2005 even though the deficit projected at the time was 3.6 percent of GDP.[23] The plan called for Italy to reduce its budget deficit by 0.8 percent in each of the 2006 and 2007 budgets, which would bring the deficit down to 3.0 percent of GDP (the projected deficit without corrective measures was 4.6 percent) and much closer to the SGP objectives. Even with the gradual adjustments, meeting the terms of the deal would require major fiscal measures involving spending cuts and revenue increases that would total around 20 billion euros for the successive budgets. Italy had gained an extra year that had been normally used in excessive deficit procedures as well as the possibility of getting an extension in 2007 if the 3 percent target was not reached because of lower than expected growth. This would be conceded only if both the Commission and ECOFIN were confident that the government had done everything possible to meet the terms of the deal.

A Budget Aimed at Credibility—and Re-election

The measures required to meet the European obligations as well as assure international financial markets would have been a challenge in the best of circumstances. However, it became apparent over the summer that the preparation of the 2006 budget would have to contend with a number of pressures that were hardly propitious for the prospects of establishing Italy's policy-making credentials in terms of fiscal discipline. First, despite the government's claims that it was not distracted by the fact that 2006 is an election year, the temptation to loosen the purse strings rather than impose fiscal rigor loomed large.[24]

Moreover, even Siniscalco, commenting on a warning from Standard & Poor's, said that Italy was paying the price for "political uncertainty" in the period leading to the elections.[25] Second, the electoral defeat for the center-right parties in the regional elections in April not only heightened fears about an electoral budget but exacerbated tensions between, and sometimes within, parties in the governing coalition. A government that seemed to lack direction and leadership and that had its sights firmly set on the electoral contest in 2006 was not the ideal vehicle to make tough decisions. Third, Siniscalco did not have the luxury to dedicate all of his energy and political capital to the budget preparation as he was swept up in the controversy surrounding the governor of the Bank of Italy, Antonio Fazio, and his role in overseeing takeover bids of Italian banks. The economy minister's task of trying to convince international markets and European partners that Italy was committed to economic liberalization and fiscal prudence could hardly have been made easier by reports of the governor's intervention (and probably also that of his wife) to support certain "friends."

Siniscalco eventually issued an ultimatum: either Fazio resigned or the government would have to find a new minister of the economy. The latter option is what materialized, and Giulio Tremonti returned on 22 September after more than a year's absence. He inherited a budget situation that was no less dire than when he left, with the added pressure that the European Union had initiated the excessive deficit procedure. At the end of September, Tremonti presented the budget, which included measures that totaled over 20 billion euros. It forecast that 16 billion euros would be necessary to ensure that the target deficit rate of 3.8 percent would be reached. This worked out to be about 5 billion euros more than initial estimates due to the fact that expected revenues from the sale of government-owned real estate did not materialize. The figure would be reached through a combination of tax increases and spending cuts. With respect to the former, revenues were increased largely by eliminating or changing provisions such as the amount that firms could claim as depreciation of assets. On the whole, taxpayers would not see any increases during the election campaign of 2006. The most notable of the 12.7 billion euros in spending cuts, which were spread widely, were those for government departments (6 billion euros). Also, transfers to regional, provincial, and local governments were cut by 3 billion euros. The government did not totally abandon its commitment to jump-starting the sluggish economy and set aside about 4 billion euros for this purpose. This would come primarily in the form of cutting social security costs for firms, as well as providing about 1.4 billion euros in transfers to families.

The budget was well received by the business community and by the European Commission. Predictably, trade unions were opposed, especially to cuts targeted for local governments and the ministries. Tremonti was satisfied that it was a budget that would not create any problems for Italy's credibility in international markets and with its European partners.[26] While the proposed budget did seem to strike a balance between meeting the targets set by the SGP procedures and the needs of a divided coalition heading into an electoral year, Tremonti may have been premature in his assessment about Italy's capacity to convince European and international actors about its ability to keep its finances under control. The government was forced on two occasions in the month of October to resort to supplementary measures that totaled over 10 billion euros. These were necessary to cover shortfalls in revenues in 2005 and ensure that the deficit for the fiscal year did not surpass the 4.7 percent figure established with the European partners.[27] Berlusconi, probably feeling frustrated by the need to remain at 4.7 percent for 2005, lashed out against the SGP while at the Hampton Court EU summit on the day of the government's announcement that it needed to find at least 4 billion euros. He stated that the economy was also sustained by deficit spending and that the SGP no longer had any sense when so many of its members, representing 75 percent of Eurozone GDP, had violated the 3 percent mark.[28] It would seem that Berlusconi did not see any problems in arguing for a return to policies that favored loose purse strings and public spending as ways to stimulate the economy. They may very well be solutions, but they would hardly dispel notions that Italy still had to prove its credentials in financial markets and with its European partners. Moreover, it did not help that Italian government ministers, and Berlusconi himself, continued to rail against the euro and the SGP.

Conclusion

There are several factors that help to explain Italy's difficulties in recent years. First, unlike the single-mindedness that characterized economic policy in the 1990s, the center-right governments sent mixed and often confusing messages. They never wavered in their rhetoric supporting fiscal discipline and the reference values of the SGP, but they often pursued policies that seemed to be going in a different direction and responding primarily to domestic political concerns. This was clearly the case with respect to pushing ahead with tax cuts even when Italy was perilously close to breaching the 3 percent barrier. These confusing messages contributed to another key factor. Italy's use of one-off measures (even before 1999) and creative financing rather than structural reforms did little to inspire confidence among the members of the Eurozone, the ECB, the Commission, and international financial markets.[29] Italy simply did not have room to maneuver because any wavering would be interpreted as a return to the old ways of the "sick man of Europe."

Also hurting Italy's credibility was the tendency for domestic politics to percolate to the European level. Problems within the center-right government corroded the credibility of Italy's commitment to the SGP. Even taking into account that they were meant to establish political and partisan points, statements made by the LN ministers about pulling Italy out of the single currency did not help to create allies for Italy within ECOFIN and the Eurozone. Berlusconi's accusations that it was the euro that was responsible for Italy's loss of competitiveness only confirmed the view that the Italian government was not addressing its fundamental economic weaknesses. Italy entered into the single currency because its partners were convinced that it was committed to its basic economic principles. But successive governments seemed to have succumbed to "Maastricht fatigue," lacking the political will or capital to continue on the path of reform. The reform of the electoral system at the end of the year also raised alarms about the ability of future governments to remain cohesive enough, especially in Parliament, to implement measures to meet the terms of the excessive deficit procedure and, after 2007, to continue to respect commitments in the SGP.

A third reason for the lack of success was that Italy's debt problem, and the lack of progress in reducing it, was an albatross that limited the government's options on a number of fronts. It could not come out and criticize the constraints imposed by the SGP for fear of alarming international financial markets and bond rating agencies. Unlike France and Germany, which had to negotiate their way out of problems related to deficit levels, Italy had to deal with two separate fronts. It could not push too much on changing the definition of the conditions for excessive deficit without risking more stringent conditions with respect to managing debt levels. In addition, there was the simple fact that servicing the debt continues to take up a sizable percentage of spending, thus crowding out other fiscal alternatives.

Gaining credibility as a committed and competent manager of public finances takes time, luck, and hard decisions, but the work does not stop there as it can be easily dissipated. The past year has seen, perhaps, what has been left of Italy's credibility after entry into the euro severely tested. Perhaps the excessive deficit procedures and the measures taken to respond to them will be a positive first step in re-establishing faith in Italy's role as a reliable partner in the Eurozone.

Notes

The author would like to thank Grant Amyot, Luca Verzichelli, and Erik Jones for their helpful comments.

1. T. Padoa-Schioppa, *La lunga via per l'euro* (Bologna: Il Mulino, 2004); F. Fauri, *L'Italia e l'integrazione economica europea, 1947–2000* (Bologna: Il Mulino, 2001); L. Spaventa and V. Chiorazzo, *Astuzia o virtù: Come accadde che l'Italia fu ammessa all'Unione monetaria* (Rome: Donzelli, 2000).
2. F. Giavazzi and M. Pagano, "The Advantage of Tying One's Hands," *European Economic Review*, no. 32 (1988): 1055–1082; K. Dyson and K. Featherstone, "Italy and EMU as a 'Vincolo Esterno': Empowering the Technocrats, Transforming the State," *South European Politics and Society* 1, no. 2 (1996): 279–299.
3. "Resolution of the European Council on the Stability and Growth Pact" (Amsterdam, 17 June 1997), Official Journal C 236, 2 August 1997.
4. Spaventa and Chiorazzo, *Astuzia o virtù*.
5. "Il Dpef conferma gli impegni europei," *Il Sole-24 Ore*, 17 July 2001, 3.
6. M. Donovan, "The Governance of the Center-Right Coalition," in *Italian Politics: Italy between Europeanization and Domestic Politics*, ed. S. Fabbrini and V. Della Sala (New York: Berghahn Books, 2004), 80–98.
7. M. Hallerberg, *Domestic Budgets in a United Europe* (Ithaca, NY: Cornell University Press, 2004).
8. OECD, *Policy Brief—Economic Survey of Italy, 2001* (Paris: OECD, 2002).
9. Ministero dell'Economia e delle Finanze, *Italy's Stability Program—November 2001 Update* (Rome, 2001), 10–11.
10. Ministero dell'Economia e delle Finanze, *Programma di Stabilità dell'Italia—Aggiornamento Novembre 2003* (Rome, 2003), 4; Commission of the European Communities, *Commission Staff Working Document—Technical Document Accompanying the Report on Italy Prepared in Accordance with Article 104(3) of the Treaty*, SEC (2005) 755, 7 June 2005.
11. "Accordi da rispettare," *Il Sole-24 Ore*, 7 December 2001, 6.
12. "L'Europa e i conti pubblici," *La Stampa*, 4 April 2004, 7.
13. "Lo scontro sui conti: A Bruxelles lumaconi e inadeguati," *Il Sole-24 Ore*, 8 April 2004, 4.
14. "Alla vigilia della riunione dei 25 ministri," *La Stampa*, 3 July 2004, 3.
15. Ministero dell'Economia e delle Finanze, *Documento di Programmazione Economico-Finanziaria, 2005–2008*, Rome, 29 July 2004.
16. "Il Ministro tedesco: 'Il dialogo non è così avanti,'" *La Stampa*, 22 November 2004, 2.
17. Council of the European Union, *European Council Brussels, 22 and 23 March 2005—Presidency Conclusions*, 7619/05, Annex II—"Improving the Implementation of the Stability and Growth Pact," 34.
18. G. Parker, "Eurozone Ministers Step Up Drive for Fiscal Discipline," *Financial Times*, 10 November 2005.
19. Eurostat was asked to review how Italy had reported receipts from securitization and from taxes raised mainly by banks on behalf of the state, as well as how debt for the financing of high-speed rail was classified. See Eurostat, *Euro-indicators*, press release, STAT/05/65, 23 May 2005.

20. Commission of the European Communities, *Report from the Commission—Italy: Report Prepared in Accordance with Article 104(3) of the Treaty*, SEC (2005), 750 final, 7 June 2005, 3–4.

21. The Commission's conclusions were in line with those of other international institutions' assessments of Italy. For instance, see International Monetary Fund, "Italy—2004 Article IV Consultation: Conclusions of the Mission," Washington, DC, IMF, 10 November 2004.

22. Commission of the European Communities, *Commission Staff Working Document—Technical Document Accompanying the Report on Italy Prepared in Accordance with Article 104(3) of the Treaty*, SEC (2005), 755, 7 June 2005, 9.

23. A. Michaels, "Italians Hail Budget Deal with Brussels," *Financial Times*, 30 June 2005.

24. A. Bonanni, "Ma una Finanziaria elettorale può fare saltare il risanamento," *La Repubblica*, 13 July 2005.

25. S. Rizzo, "Siniscalco: Paghiamo l'incertezza politica," *Corriere della Sera*, 9 August 2005.

26. D. Pesole, "La manovra si prepara al voto di fiducia," *Il Sole-24 Ore*, 30 September 2005.

27. M. Sensini, "Rischio buco di 4 miliardi: Spunta la manovra-ter," *Corriere della Sera*, 28 October 2005.

28. M. Galluzzo, "Berlusconi: L'euro ci frena, il Patto non ha più senso," *Corriere della Sera*, 28 October 2005.

29. Italian bond prices remained very close to those for Germany, roughly only 20 basis points higher. Berlusconi commented on this when news broke that the Commission was going to implement the excessive deficit procedure. There were signs that Berlusconi was more worried than he let on; he was the first Italian prime minister to meet with representatives of bond rating agencies. See M. Sensini, "E Siniscalco gioca con il premier la carta di Moody's," *Corriere della Sera*, 20 May 2005.

6

THE BANK TAKEOVER BIDS AND THE ROLE OF THE BANK OF ITALY

Marcello Messori

The vicissitudes of the banking system that characterized the whole of 2005 took a decisive turn during the last weeks of the year. The Bank of Italy (BdI) and part of the political and institutional elite became involved in a harmful defense of the "Italianness" of the banks, to the detriment of transparency and the proper functioning of the markets.

On 13 December, Giampiero Fiorani, former president (*amministratore delegato*) of the Banca Popolare Italiana (BPI)—formerly Banca Popolare di Lodi (BPL)—and the leading promoter of the intended takeover of the Banca Antonveneta (BAV), was arrested, and with him several of the Lodi group's managers. From Fiorani's depositions it becomes clear that members of the government and of Parliament had been involved in dubious financial operations of the BPI. On 19 December, on the eve of the cabinet meeting that would probably have asked for his removal, Antonio Fazio, the governor of the BdI, who was under investigation by the prosecutor's office and was also under scrutiny by the European Central Bank (ECB), resigned. On 22 December, the magistrates in Milan decided to release the 26 percent of BAV's shares held by BPI but already intended for the Dutch bank ABN AMRO, thus precipitating the acquisition of the BAV by the Dutch. On 23 December, after two years of barren discussions, Parliament approved the "savings law," in which substantial modifications of the nomination procedure and the term of office for the governor were introduced, as well as changes to the governance and supervision duties of the BdI.

Notes for this chapter begin on page 159.

That same day, the National Commission for Companies and the Stock Exchange (Commissione Nazionale per le Società e la Borsa, CONSOB), the stock exchange regulator, decided to require an increase in the price of the compulsory public tender offer (PTO; in Italian, *offerta pubblica di acquisto*, or *o.p.a.*) that Unipol had launched for the Banca Nazionale del Lavoro (BNL). On 28 December, the cooperatives that own Unipol, partners in the Holmo holding company, obtained the resignations of the two top managers of the insurance company, Giovanni Consorte e Ivano Sacchetti, then under investigation by the prosecutor's office. This meant the end of the PTO for BNL, a bid that was already deeply compromised by its financial fragility and its links with the failed takeover of the BAV.[1] Finally, on 29 December, Mario Draghi was appointed as the new governor of the BdI.

These facts show that the vicissitudes of the BAV and the BNL, which for a long time were distorted by a supposed defense of the "Italianness" of the banks, will have a strong influence on the future configuration of Italian financial markets. It is therefore interesting to examine them in some detail in the sections that follow. After a review of the processes of consolidation and ownership reorganization in the Italian banking system from the early 1990s on, I shall examine the supervisory stance of the BdI toward them. From this, it will become evident that in spite of changes in the rules, the system of regulation has remained excessively discretionary and intrusive with regard to the functioning of the market. The PTOs launched at the end of March 2005 by ABN AMRO and the Spanish Banco Bilbao Vizcaya Argentaria (BBVA) for, respectively, BAV and BNL failed in part because of the opaque rules of the game established by the BdI. The two European banks did not, however, submit to those rules and, at least in the case of the BAV, prevailed in the end. Fazio's reaction made clear the limitations of the BdI's governance structure and the lack of a proper regulatory framework. This has driven both the government and Parliament to introduce, belatedly, legislative changes. Despite several inconsistencies, these should improve the BdI's performance of its regulatory role. In the conclusion, I shall address whether this will restore the reputation of the BdI and improve the efficiency of the Italian financial market.

Central Bank Supervision and the Transformation of the Banking System

Between 1990 and 2004, there were 627 mergers, total acquisitions, or acquisitions of the majority of the capital (M&A) in the Italian banking system. As of the latter year, such operations had involved more than 55 percent of total banking activities and approximately 78 percent of the banks.[2] This was one of the most intense aggregation processes in the banking sector among the countries of the old European Union. If we take the number of M&As as a fraction of the average number of banks in the period from 1990 to 2003, we find that the rate for Italy was second only to those of two small countries, Belgium and Greece. As a result, by the end of 2004 the Italian system was composed of 82 banking groups, 67 independent banks, and a cluster of 435 cooperative credit banks, as opposed to 1,156 banks in 1990.[3] Moreover, between 1993 and 2001, the Italian state gave up the absolute majority stake it held—directly or indirectly—in seven of the most important Italian banking groups. It also gave up the minority holdings it had with another two of the bigger banking groups and its holdings (majority or minority) in four smaller financial institutions.[4] In the following years it liquidated its other, less important holdings. As a result, even though in 1992 the share of public ownership in Italian banks was around 75 percent and considerably exceeded the French (36 percent) and German (approximately 62 percent) levels, by 2004 the state's presence in the Italian banking system was almost nil.

This rapid evolution of the Italian banking system is the result of several factors. It is important to analyze here the multifaceted series of legislative reforms that removed many of the previous institutional obstacles that had prevented Italian banks from operating as market actors. From the second half of the 1980s on, Italy has: (1) applied, although belatedly, the two European directives on banking; (2) brought in anti-trust legislation that entrusted the protection of competition within the banking system to the BdI; and (3) prepared incentive schemes to promote both the process of aggregation in the sector and the transformation of a significant part of the banking system into public companies. In 1993, a great part of these legislative innovations were incorporated in the Consolidated Banking Act (Testo Unico Bancario, TUB), which confirmed the business character of the banks and their freedom to choose their organizational structures. It also marked the formal passage from a structural form of supervision to a prudential one.[5]

Unfortunately, the TUB and—above all—the implementing regulations have not produced a strong enough normative framework to limit the discretionary interventions of the BdI and to translate the new prudential form of supervision into a limited set of principles, defined ex ante, that would permit the verification ex post of the correlation between such principles and the independent behavior of the market actors. Thus, although the Consolidated Financial Sector Act (Testo Unico sulla Finanza, TUF) that followed in 1998 placed its emphasis on providing adequate information to the shareholders and the market, the supervisory authority must still today grant a discretionary authorization before the pre-established limits on ownership of the banks can be exceeded and must be informed before a bank can launch an PTO. Therefore, the banking consolidation of the 1990s and 2000s described above did not benefit from all of the potential changes allowed by the TUF. It followed a path where the traces of intrusion by the BdI—the construction of a small number of banking groups of a national scale that were able to act as poles of attraction, and the strengthening of a wider nucleus of banking groups or banks of medium and small-to-medium size with a mainly regional scope— were all too visible.[6]

The BdI's intervention became particularly heavy-handed as the process shifted its focus from the acquisition of smaller or specialized institutions by the bigger banks to mergers between the biggest banking groups. For instance, in March 1999, the BdI stopped the PTO voted by the board of directors of Unicredit for the Banca Commerciale Italiana and the PTO for the Banca di Roma proposed by the San Paolo IMI bank. The BdI argued that it had not been previously informed and added that it did not approve of hostile takeover bids, that is, those that had not previously been discussed with and approved by the management of the target company. Nevertheless, a few months later, the governor used a public speech to give his consent to an PTO that had not yet either been made public or approved by the target company.

In 2002, the scandalous management of the banking group Bipop Carire, that had for a long time escaped the surveillance of the supervisory authority, necessitated a rescue operation by one of its competitors. The BdI thwarted the signs of interest of a people's bank (*banca popolare*) of medium size and of other banking groups in order to reserve the attractive role of "white knight" for the Banca di Roma, which was thus transformed into Capitalia. In more recent years, Fazio had several times declared that the mergers between the larger groups were (at least for the time being) over and that it was now the turn of medium-sized banking groups and, in particular, of medium-sized people's banks.

It is not my purpose to prove here that in favoring medium-sized banks, the BdI went against trends in the European market and, therefore, has made it more difficult (as was the case with Unicredit) or even impossible (as was the case with Banca Intesa and San Paolo IMI) for Italy's larger banking groups, specialized in retail activities, to acquire leadership positions at a European level. The aim is simply to argue that this strategy, besides distorting the functioning of the market, created the conditions for the penetration of foreign banks in Italy. Since the middle of the last decade, the international banks that have specialized in corporate finance and in investment banking have taken advantage of the weakness of the national players and have benefited from the opportunities offered by the privatizations and the restructuring of several economic sectors, using them to conquer pre-eminent positions in the Italian market. On the other hand, until 2005 the great European banks—in general—had not built the capillary distribution channels for their corporate or retail activities in Italy; they had preferred to acquire relative majority or controlling ownership in a significant part of the larger banking groups or in some of the medium-sized banks. Such a situation, however, produced unstable equilibria, which the European banks used as a launching pad to acquire more important and more firmly entrenched positions as soon as they had the opportunity.

The Difficult PTOs of the European Banks

The above considerations are essential in order to explain how the launching of the PTOs on BAV and on BNL came about, why the reaction of the BdI followed a course that differed from the usual one, and why that course produced the perverse outcomes described in the introductory paragraphs of this chapter.[7]

Together with the French Crédit Agricole and the Spanish Banco Santander Central Hispano, by 2004 ABN AMRO and BBVA were the European banks with the strongest presence in the ownership structure of the largest Italian banking groups. Besides a relative majority in Capitalia, ABN AMRO owned the largest package of BAV shares (12.7 percent), to which we must add convertible bonds that amounted to about 8 percent of the capital. Moreover, it had agreed to form a controlling bloc (a "syndicate") with Deltaerre (a grouping of entrepreneurs and investors, mostly from the North-East, that included Emilio Gnutti), the Benetton family, and the insurance company Lloyd Adriatico. As for BBVA, it was the relative majority owner of BNL, with nearly 15 percent of the capital, and the leader of a syndicate that included (after the withdrawal of the Monte dei Paschi di Siena and the Banca Popolare di Vicenza) the Generali insurance company and a firm belonging to businessman Diego Della Valle.

Both ABN AMRO and BBVA had been exerting pressure on BdI for some time so that they could acquire a dominant position in these two Italian banks. Even though it was covered by the syndicate agreement until the middle of April 2005, ABN AMRO was worried by the tensions emerging with some members of the pact as a result of the limits imposed by the new president of BAV on the financing of related parties. Moreover, in spite of the opposition of the governor, ABN AMRO had not abandoned the idea of merging BAV and Capitalia, thus forming a new banking group that it would control with about 20 percent of the capital. BBVA also sought to increase its own package of BNL shares because it was worried by the pressure exerted on the bank's management by a group of minority stockholders (Stefano Ricucci, Danilo Coppola, Giuseppe Statuto, Vito Bonsignore, the brothers Ettore and Tiberio Lonati) headed by Francisco Caltagirone, who were mostly in the real estate business and were grouped in a rival syndicate (the "counterpact") with a bloc of shares almost as large as that of the controlling group. Moreover, BBVA feared the renewed acquisition efforts of the Monte dei Paschi di Siena.

The European Union authorities were not deaf to the aspirations of ABN AMRO and BBVA. In September 2004, the Dutch government, during its Council presidency, had in fact invited the heads of three great European banks (the same ABN AMRO, BNP Paribas, and Royal Bank of Scotland) to the Economic and Financial Affairs Council (ECOFIN) in order to discuss the issue of cross-border bank mergers and amalgamations. The document prepared as a basis for the meeting identified Italy as one of the countries that were less open to such fusions.[8] In the BAV case, matters were precipitated by the obscure schemes initiated by the BPL, in collaboration with some dissident members of the controlling syndicate (above all, Gnutti), and by the benign neglect with which the supervisory authority viewed these maneuvers. In the BNL case, the decisive impulse came instead from the vain attempt of the BdI to influence the movements of the counterpact without allowing for any increase in the shares held by BBVA. The failure of this strategy was signalized by the unsuccessful merger between BNL and Banco Popolare di Verona e Novara, which was due to the excessively high price asked by the real estate entrepreneurs for their shares.

Based on the information available at the end of 2005, the case of BAV is the clearest. On 30 March 2005, the board of directors of ABN AMRO, tired of following the BdI's advice to look for an impossible compromise with BPL, launched an PTO for BAV at a price of 25 euros per share. But BPL had already taken steps to ensure for itself a major role in the future ownership of the target bank. In fact, at the end of 2004, BPL had acquired a claim on 4.99 percent of BAV's shares by advancing a loan of equivalent value to the Benetton family's Edizione Holding. In mid-February 2005, it had obtained authorization from the BdI to buy up to 14.99 percent of BAV's capital. In addition, as an inquiry by CONSOB—initiated after submissions by ABN AMRO and closed in May 2005—revealed, since November 2004 BPL had granted financing facilities in the amount of approximately 1.1 billion euros to about 40 speculators. Among this group, some were Gnutti's partners in the Fingruppo and Hopa firms, some were Fiorani's friends, and the rest were real estate entrepreneurs involved in the BNL counterpact. They used the funds almost entirely to buy up 22.3 percent of BAV's shares, only to resell them—at the proper moment (and with considerable capital gains)—to BPL and Gnutti's firms.[9]

When in mid-April 2005 the agreement establishing the controlling syndicate expired and the date of the meeting of BAV shareholders drew near, most of the partners in Deltaerre and all those who benefited from the above-mentioned BPL financing—with the exception of the Lonati brothers, Coppola and Ricucci—relinquished their BAV shares to BPL itself and to two firms belonging to Gnutti (Fingruppo and GP Finanziaria). At the same time, Unipol had gathered together 3.7 percent of the capital of BAV. Thus, the shares held by the tandem Fiorani-Gnutti and their followers, by Ricucci's Magiste, by Coppola's firms, and by Unipol greatly exceeded the 50 percent threshold. This allowed the BPL to dominate BAV's shareholder meeting on 30 April, even though its possible allies were pursuing divergent strategies. For the BPL, the takeover of BAV had been, however, extremely expensive: an expenditure of nearly 2.13 billion euros. This worked out to an average purchase price for BAV's shares that was higher than the one offered in ABN AMRO's PTO (25.34 euros as opposed to 25 euros).[10] Furthermore, in a communication released in preparation for the meeting, the BPL announced its intention to launch a public exchange offer (PEO) for BAV.

As the apparent triumph of the BPL was sealed, the PEO of BBVA on BNL was making no progress. The Spanish bank had planned the launch for 29 March 2005—that is, the day before the launching of ABN AMRO's bid. BBVA's PEO offered one of its own shares for five of BNL's, thereby setting a price of 2.52 euros per BNL share. However, the authorization procedure followed by the BdI was so involved that the operation was allowed to start only on 22 June. In the meantime, Unipol had joined the game; it had acquired nearly 10 percent of BNL's capital, could count on roughly an additional 6 percent (held, among others, by BPI and the Banca Popolare dell'Emilia Romagna, BPER), and was undertaking negotiations with the counterpact of the real estate entrepreneurs to acquire their part.

By mid-July, immediately after the acquisition of a further 5 percent of BNL's capital (approved by the BdI) and shortly before the expiry of the PEO of BBVA, Unipol announced the following: (1) it had formed a pact with an international bank (Nomura), an Italian bank (Cassa di Risparmio di Genova, CARIGE), Gnutti's Hopa, and four cooperatives;

(2) it had acquired, together with its associates (with the exception of CARIGE) and other allies (among them, Credit Suisse First Boston, or CSFB, and the Banca Popolare di Vicenza), 19.5 percent of BNL's shares from the counterpact group at 2.70 euros; and (3) it had negotiated bilateral agreements with its others allies and with the BPI. Thus, Unipol controlled, directly or indirectly, a package corresponding to more than 41 percent of BNL's capital and was about to launch a compulsory PTO for the rest of the shares.[11]

The BAV Case: Pots without Covers

These initiatives of BPI and Unipol led to the failure of both ABN AMRO's PTO, in spite of an increase in the price to 26.50 euros and a postponement of the closing date, and BBVA's PEO. Nevertheless, the very fact that the two bids had taken place was a sign of positive change. Breaking with the eternal acquiescence of the Italian banks to the obscure discretionary decisions of the BdI, ABN AMRO and BBVA had used their strong European connections to force through two market operations that were to reveal the arbitrariness of the BdI's supervisory procedures and the fragility of the alliances that had been put together in the name of "Italianness." However, the two European banks did not stop there. They appealed to various tribunals, and, particularly in the case of ABN AMRO's complaint to CONSOB against the concerted action of the BPL and its partners and the Dutch bank's various charges presented to the judicial authorities, their appeals ended up by overturning the result of the game.

We have already mentioned that as the BAV shareholders' meeting scheduled for 30 April 2005 was approaching, BPL announced the launch of a "counter-PTO." This initiative was formalized 10 days later. It took the shape of an PEO valued at 26 euros and based on the exchange of BAV's shares for (1) a new issue of BPL's shares, (2) existing shares of Reti Bancarie Holding, which BPL controlled, (3) new five-year BPL bonds, and (4) a small cash payment to make up any difference in value. Several analysts believed such an PEO was no better than ABN AMRO's original PTO at 25 euros per share because it valued BPL's and Reti Bancarie's shares at prices about 16 percent and 12 percent, respectively, higher than their market prices. However, on 10 May, as BPL tried to persuade the analysts to revise their negative opinion, CONSOB endorsed ABN AMRO's complaint, thus recognizing that there was a concerted action between BPL, the two Gnutti firms, the Lonati brothers, and Coppola when they bought the shares held by the Deltaerre partners and by the group of speculators financed by

BPL itself. That action, since it led to the control of more than 40 percent of BAV's shares, and thus created a "dominant influence," was in violation of Article 112 of the TUF. The penalties for such a violation were the "sterilization" of the voting rights of the investors involved and the requirement that they launch a compulsory PTO payable in cash (at 24.47 euros)[12] or relinquish their package of BAV's shares. What is more, 15 days later CONSOB determined that BPL's original takeover bid was not an improvement on that of ABN AMRO and had, therefore, to be modified.

Together with its two subsequent findings that the concerted action had continued, CONSOB's decision of 10 May represented for BPL the classic snowball that grows into an avalanche. First of all, ABN AMRO then secured from the Padua district court the annulment of the decisions voted by BAV's shareholders at the meeting of 30 April and the nomination of a special trustee to manage the bank. Secondly, BPL and the other parties involved had to enter into a formal agreement in order to stave off the suspension of their voting rights, which the BdI had endorsed. Besides the provision that there was to be prior consultation before every extraordinary transaction, this agreement imposed on BPL the burden of launching the compulsory PTO (in addition to its original voluntary PEO) and forbade the other members, for their part, to sell their holdings in response to either of these bids. Finally, BPL was forced to put together a consortium in a great hurry to underwrite its launch of the compulsory PTO. This consortium included several foreign banks that received as collateral the BAV shares that BPL had acquired or could acquire in the future. What is more, BPL had to review the terms of the PEO and transform it into a public exchange and tender offer (PETO).

At the beginning of June, CONSOB approved only the prospectus for the compulsory PTO, reserving judgment on the new PETO. The price offered by ABN AMRO's PTO was, however, higher than that of the compulsory PTO, and BPL, now transformed into BPI,[13] was betting on the PETO and the accompanying share swap. BPI therefore spent the rest of the month trying to mask its financial fragility and to adapt the PETO to the requirements of the market while it awaited the authorization of both CONSOB and BdI. In particular, in reply to the relaunching of ABN AMRO's PTO of 26.50 euros, in mid-June BPI modified its own PETO so as to increase the cash component and raise the value of the bid price to 27.50 euros per BAV share. This represented an additional cost of approximately 600 million euros. Toward the end of the month, CONSOB approved the prospectus for the PETO, and before the middle of July, Governor Fazio also signed the authorization on behalf of BdI. The episode of the governor's signature and the accompanying nocturnal telephone kisses and congratulations between the members of the "concert" that followed (with the involvement of the prime minister) are by now sadly famous. I shall recall but two facts. The people in charge of the case at the supervision branch of the BdI were opposed to the authorization, based on three serious infractions committed by BPI: (1) its free and easy granting of credit in order to buy up indirectly BAV's shares (already censured by CONSOB), (2) its failure to fulfill the commitments undertaken with the BdI, and (3) its failure to adhere to the minimum asset thresholds required by the branch "for a certain period of time." The governor granted the authorization on the basis of some external opinions that were hurried, even if coming from respected authorities.

The authorization of the BdI for the takeover bids of the BPI, along with the subsequent negative ruling of the Regional Administrative Court (Tribunale Amministrativo Regionale, TAR) on a complaint by ABN AMRO about the timing of the authorization, seemed to mark the end of the game with the victory of the BPL and its allies. In the last 10 days of July, however, just before the next shareholders' meeting of BAV, CONSOB issued another two decisions stemming from collaborative work with the judicial authorities, as provided for by the new legislation on market abuse. These decisions included Ricucci's firm Magiste and two investment funds legally established in tax havens among the actors guilty of the concerted action that it had identified on 10 May. Also, they ruled that the trusts, which had bought BAV's shares at a slightly higher price than the other members of the "concert," were nothing but a front for BPI itself. Besides suspending the voting rights of these three entities, the new decisions of CONSOB forced BPI to readjust the price of the compulsory PTO and urged it to renegotiate the formal pact with its allies and to provide further information in the prospectuses.

However, the authorization to proceed with the takeover bids was blocked by a decision of the Milan prosecutor's office to seize the shares held by those involved in the "concerted action," which amounted to almost 50 percent of BAV's capital. The grounds for this decision were the violation of their commitments to the BdI and the presentation of false data, both to CONSOB and to the market, with regard to illegal operations. This action was upheld in the first days of August by the judge in charge of preliminary inquiries, who also decided to forbid Fiorani, Gnutti, and Ricucci from participating in any related activity for two months. In the meantime, the BAV shareholders' meeting had elected the board of directors proposed by ABN AMRO. Also, CONSOB had decided on a precautionary suspension of both the PETO and the compulsory PTO because of—among other reasons—the possibility of serious deficiencies in the information furnished, and because the shares given as collateral to the international consortium were now unavailable. Shortly after, even the BdI fell in line with CONSOB's position. Two months later, CONSOB and the BdI finally revoked their authorization for BPI's PETO and compulsory PTO. Before that decision and Fiorani's resignation, the board of directors of the BPI chose to sell the BAV shares it held to ABN AMRO at the price of 26.50 euros. However, the sale could take effect only once the seizure of the shares by Milan prosecutor's office was lifted, which happened on 22 December after the replacement of BPI's management.

The BNL Case: Lie Down with Dogs

In the middle of July 2005, Unipol and its allies held—de facto—an absolute majority of BNL shares, thanks (among other things) to the call and put contracts exchanged with the Deutsche Bank (DB) and to the BPER's readiness to vote with any controlling bloc.[14] What is more, other major shareholders of BNL had opted out of the contest between the Bologna insurance company and the Spanish BBVA. The previous month Monte dei Paschi di Siena had loaned (with a maturity date of February 2006) its shares in BNL to foreign banks, while Generali was on the sidelines, ready to sell its BNL shares to the highest bidder. Therefore, the PEO launched by BBVA failed, even though it offered a slightly higher value in exchange for each BNL share (2.72 euros at the closing of 22 July) than the compulsory PTO of Unipol and its allies (2.70 euros).

Unipol assumed the entire burden of financing the compulsory PTO in cash, and secured itself the possibility of holding an absolute majority of BNL's capital with several call contracts, open for the 30 days after the expiry of the bid at the PTO price, which it signed with virtually all of the pact members and its other allies. Formally, the PTO was for 59 percent of BNL's ordinary capital, but in reality it concerned less than 50 percent.[15] Unipol had then given put contracts that amounted to 16.40 percent of BNL's capital to some pact members and allies, with differentiated conditions. Besides the contracts with the DB, these put options were granted in particular to CARIGE, Hopa, and CSFB. Most probably, the beneficiaries of these options had required them as a sort of guarantee when Unipol asked them to buy BNL shares in order to reduce the financial burden of the PTO. However, these contracts weakened Unipol's asset ratios and made the entire operation more complex.

In the first days of August 2005, the complex authorization process for the compulsory PTO got under way. There were four authorities involved (BdI, CONSOB, the Institute for Supervision of Private and Public Interest Insurance, or ISVAP, and the Guarantor Authority for Competition and the Market, or AGCM). The new European guidelines on financial conglomerates had just been enacted into law in Italy two months before, and the implementing regulations had not yet been issued (this would happen only in the middle of the following November), nor were the current balance sheet data on which they were based available. As it turned out, a few days after Unipol's authorization request, BdI suspended the time limit for its own response in order to consult ISVAP on (1) the insurance components of the transaction (Unipol would gain control of a further 50 percent of BNL Life Insurance), (2) the compatibility between the acquisition of control of BNL and the predominantly insurance activities of the purchaser, and (3) the adequacy of Unipol's asset base for the operation.[16] Moreover, in mid-August, shortly before the deadline, Unipol submitted the prospectus for the compulsory PTO to CONSOB. CONSOB's first reaction was not a positive one. The prospectus did not refer to the two new put contracts signed between Unipol and DB during the first half of August, nor did it dispel doubts about a possible agreement with BPER, which was not included among Unipol's allies. Furthermore, as early as July, BBVA had alerted the magistrates to several obscure points of the pacts and agreements declared by Unipol, and CONSOB meant to go into the matter more deeply.

The authorization procedure for Unipol's compulsory PTO for BNL moved more quickly between the end of August and the first half of September. Even though it required addenda and explanations of many points and left open the possibility of further investigation of the contracts Unipol had negotiated, CONSOB authorized the publication of the modified prospectus on 31 August. Shortly after, ISVAP informed the BdI that Unipol's primary corporate object would not be changed by the aggregation of BNL's banking activities. Two later days the AGCM affirmed that the merger between Unipol and BNL would not substantially reduce competition in the relevant markets, and less than a week after that the BdI confirmed its approval in terms of competition in the banking sector. Finally, once it was convinced that the BPI could cover the call option it had granted Unipol for 1.6 percent of BNL's capital,[17] CONSOB dropped most of its objections. It simply postponed its final judgment on the price of the PTO, partly in response to BBVA's submissions. These authorizations seemed to be the prelude to an imminent positive judgment by ISVAP on the entire transaction and to the final authorization of the compulsory PTO by the BdI. However, as with the BPI-BAV case, in the Unipol-BNL case events supervened that were to turn the tide—the repeated modifications of the main features of the PTO by Unipol, which were perhaps prompted by the moral suasion of the BdI, and the negative judgment expressed by BNL's board of directors on 21 October 2005.

The criticisms of BNL's board were centered on three aspects: (1) the lack of financial backing for the PTO, due to the inadequate dimensions and asset base of the predator vis-à-vis the prey; (2) the overly optimistic expectations regarding the profitability and efficiency gains of the conglomerate, since it would come into being burdened by the debts contracted to pay for the PTO and stripped of some high value-added activities;[18] and (3) the inadequacy of the PTO price, which among other things was smaller than the updated value of the put options granted to some allies and pact members. The merits of these criticisms are not relevant for my argument. What is important is the resulting behavior of Unipol. Starting in mid-October, the Bologna insurance company canceled the put option granted to Gnutti's Hopa; transferred to related parties (cooperatives that are Unipol's shareholders and firms controlled by cooperatives) the obligation to cover the put option granted to CARIGE; introduced schemes of monetary compensation for the put and call options it had with DB; and offset the several put options it had granted with the acquisition of two options to sell to CSFB and to DB about 12 percent of BNL's capital at a price equivalent to little more than half of the PTO price.

The repeated modifications that Unipol made to the contents of the compulsory PTO, together with its second thoughts on selling minority interests in its subsidiary Aurora to a private equity fund (Clessidra) and to firms within the cooperative movement, resulted in the postponement of the supervisory bodies' authorizations, above all those of ISVAP and the BdI. ISVAP submitted its official opinion to the BdI at the end of November, instead of in mid-October. Despite giving a positive judgment on the operating plan and the financial coverage of the insurance section, it continued to collaborate with the BdI in the evaluation of the asset adequacy of the resulting financial conglomerate. For its part, as a result of the magistrates' initiatives against Unipol's management and BBVA's repeated charges that they had concluded secret pacts (in particular with DB and BPER), CONSOB re-examined the propriety of the compulsory PTO. This delayed even further the authorization of the BdI. On 23 December 2005, CONSOB discovered the existence of another, undeclared pact between Unipol and DB in which the BPI was also involved. It then raised the price of the compulsory PTO (to 2.755 euros per BNL share) to match the highest price paid for BNL shares in the transactions with DB.

The decision of CONSOB and the subsequent dismissal of the two most important managers of Unipol marked the ultimate failure of the attempt to take over BNL. Besides the modest increase in the cost of the bid and the need to postpone the various guaranteeing contracts, this decision led to the postponement to 2006 of the BdI's evaluation of the PTO. This delay, even assuming the BdI granted the authorization, would mean that the new provisions of the insurance code would come into play and thus a new general ex ante opinion from ISVAP would be needed.

The Governor's Actions

The vicissitudes of the BPI-BAV and Unipol-BNL cases, described in the previous paragraphs, have several points in common. First, the two groups that were organized to protect the "Italianness" of BAV and BNL were composed not of leading firms in the sector but of weak, nationally based groups: financial institutions of modest dimensions or dubious solidity, financiers who commanded little respect, and real estate speculators whose fortunes came from obscure activities.[19] Actually, the standard-bearers of the two pacts, BPI and Unipol, each had a declared capitalization that was two to three times less than those of their prey and incommensurably smaller than those of ABN AMRO and BBVA. Second, the weaknesses of the two groups led to actions that were against every rule of the market and sometimes even against the law. In one case, BPI offered financing and guaranteed capital gains to partners to buy up BAV's shares, used options (that were not announced to the market) in order to artificially swell its assets declared to the supervisory authorities with the pretended cession of minority shares of the firms under its control, and probably financed the subscribers to its own increases in capitalization. In the case of Unipol, there were options (some of which were communicated only after a delay) used to reduce the cost of the compulsory PTO, and some of these options were transferred and minority shares in subsidiaries were sold to related parties in order to artificially increase Unipol's assets. In both cases, this led to the construction of complex mechanisms to make these impossible takeovers feasible, even if this meant circumventing the market and violating every principle of transparency. Finally, the core group of actors who were involved in both cases were also those who engaged in the most reprehensible behavior.

It seems incredible that the BdI continued to support the two Italian takeovers in the face of such clear evidence, which was also available, thanks to the actions of CONSOB, to informed members of the public. This support created the unpleasant impression that BdI itself was one of the players, or even the coach of the two Italian groups, rather than the impartial referee of a match played according to the rules. What is worse, this impression is based on a series of questionable interventions by the BdI.

Just before the middle of February 2005, while the governor of the BdI pushed ABN AMRO to come to an agreement with the BPL, the latter asked the BdI for authorization to increase its share of BAV's capital to 14.99 percent. The request did not mention the existence of the creeping takeover—examined above—but it did refer to the desirability of counterbalancing the BAV "syndicate," dominated by its "foreign component." Instead of seeking to clarify those statements, in only three days the BdI granted its approval, seeming to encourage BPL's ambitions. Moreover, the BdI was not as prompt and efficient when it dealt with ABN AMRO's request, submitted at the time of its PTO of 25 euros per BAV share (30 March 2005). Worried that the waiting period before the PTO could be launched might extend beyond the expiry date of the syndicate agreement, ABN AMRO asked for authorization to exceed the threshold of 20 percent ownership of BAV by making purchases that followed the conditions set out in the PTO. Despite the promptings of the Dutch bank, the BdI gave a delaying answer only several days after the first request, and it granted permission almost at the same time as the approval of the PTO, at the end of the month of April.[20] In the meantime, the BAV syndicate's "pact" had expired, and BPL and its allies had concluded their purchases of BAV's shares.

Discriminatory delays in authorizations were also an important element in the Unipol-BNL case. As has already been pointed out, the actual launch of BBVA's PEO for BNL happened almost three months after it was decided on by the Spanish bank, as the BdI had slowed down the authorization procedure in order to obtain clarifications and introduce restrictions. In particular, the BdI had at first required BBVA to reach an absolute majority of BNL's capital for the PEO to take effect. It was only after doubts were expressed at the European level and after the Spanish bank asked for the threshold to be lowered to 30 percent that the BdI softened its position, reserving the right to verify ex post whether BBVA had obtained effective control of BNL. In the meantime, however, Unipol's plan to take over BNL had taken shape, in good measure thanks to the links it had formed with the members of the Roman bank's counterpact. Moreover, as the BBVA's PEO was entering its decisive stage, the BdI authorized Unipol to buy up to 14.99 percent of BNL's capital, which, as BBVA stressed in its submissions to magistrates at various levels, allowed Unipol to ensure the failure of the PEO launched by the Spanish bank without launching a "counter-PTO" and thus without risking a possible reply bid.[21]

The partisanship of the BdI, however, was most clearly evident in its appraisal of the statutory asset base of the BPL/BPI.[22] Even before the takeover of the BAV, many analysts believed that the very rapid growth of BPL through mergers and acquisitions, the resulting put options granted to its new partners, and the proportion of dubious credits required a significant capital increase. Nevertheless, in February 2005, the supervision branch of the BdI approved the complex scheme for augmenting its asset base presented by the BPL at the same time as the request to increase its own quota to 14.99 percent of BAV, without any closer investigation. At the beginning of April, to support its request to increase its share in BAV's capital to 29.99 percent, the BPL proposed in general outline a further reinforcement of its base. Three days latter, the BdI granted the authorization, setting as an explicit condition the "continuous" maintenance of the statutory asset base and suggesting gradual increases in the share of BAV's capital. However, less than a month later, the board of directors of the BPL decided on the PEO for BAV, and, in order to satisfy the requirements of prudential supervision, in the following weeks it approved a scheme to cede minority holdings in the firms it controlled, amounting to more than 1 billion euros, as well as the issuance of preferred shares, a capital increase of 1.5 billion euros, and a subordinated bond issue worth 600 million euros.[23]

The requirement to add a compulsory PTO in cash to the planned PEO and to improve the conditions of the latter at once made this plan to reinforce the bank's asset base, massive as it was, insufficient. The most serious problems, however, were with the sale of the minority holdings and the placement of the new BPI shares. From the second half of May to the beginning of July 2005, BPL signed various contracts with major international banks (DB and Dresdner Bank) and with companies to which it was related (Earchimede) in which it sold minority shareholdings in many of the firms it controlled and guaranteed a call option for itself. The problem was that those contracts, besides the fact that they often included extremely high commissions to be paid by the BPI, also granted put options to the buyers, and these were not communicated to the market. Thus, the proceeds of these potentially temporary sales could not be counted as part of the vendor's statutory asset base. Moreover, in the case of the transactions with related companies, the sales did not satisfy either minimal transparency requirements or minimum market standards (certainty on the transaction date and on the minority shares exchanged, for example). As for the increase in capitalization of the BPI carried out in July 2005, the placement was made through the distributive channels of BPL itself and without any guaranteeing consortium. The suspicion is that this placement, which was completely successful, was illicitly financed with loans advanced to the old shareholders of the BPI itself. Considering all of the above, it seems incongruous that in the middle of July, the governor of the BdI granted the authorization for the BPI's PTO, disregarding the advice of the supervision branch and ignoring the signals coming from CONSOB's investigation.[24]

The Difficult Path toward the New Legislation

Along with the picture of "amoral familism" that became apparent from the wiretaps published during the summer, one of the worst aspects of the banking scandals of 2005 was the damage to the reputation of the BdI, which had in the past been an effective antidote to the credibility deficit of the Italian political authorities and the inability of the government and the political system to intervene effectively. A symbolic example is the report made by Governor Fazio to the Interministerial Committee for Credit and Savings (CICR) on 26 August 2005. In that account the governor defended the correctness of his behavior on the basis of several bureaucratic considerations. The core of his reasoning can be synthesized in three arguments.

The first argument concerned the authorizations granted to BPL/BPI without requiring that it possess an adequate asset base in advance of its acquisitions. Following the reasoning of a passage of the preceding "Final Considerations,"[25] Fazio declared: "The acquisition of assets in advance would have repercussions ... on the shareholders, who would suffer from a decrease in the return on their capital." The second argument referred to the impact of the disciplinary procedures that the BdI had begun against the BPI as a result of the decisions of CONSOB. The governor held that these sanctions were directed against the management and therefore did not affect "the 'reliability' of the bank as a firm." The third argument had to do with the approval granted by BdI to BPL's PTOs. In spite of everything that had happened in the meantime, Fazio repeated that the PTOs did not jeopardize the "stability of the banking institution that was the target of the offer" and that the BPI showed "a considerable surplus relative to the minimum compulsory asset requirements" because of the capital increase of 1.5 billion euros.

None of the ministers in attendance pointed out to the governor that the first argument contradicted the supervisory style that the BdI had adopted up to that point; the second introduced an artificial distinction between the management and the bank; and the third was not accepted either by the heads of the supervision branch of the BdI or by market analysts. Moreover, none of the ministers noted that even in Fazio's reconstruction of events, the BdI always responded with a certain delay to the decisions of CONSOB and the magistrates, so much so that on several occasions it was constrained to review its own decisions. Finally, nobody raised the significant question that emerged from CONSOB's decisions: how was it possible that the BdI had not found anomalies in the methods used by the BPI to finance its allies and in the false sales of minority shares BPI used to augment its assets? Because of this passive approach, a fundamental aspect of the governor's defense—the excessively discretionary powers that the TUB and especially the related regulations gave to the BdI, even though they were inconsistent with the contents of the TUF—went unnoticed. This, together with the deficiencies in the governance of the BdI, had led to utterly autocratic behavior.

The result was a sad attempt by the Italian government to "pass the buck" to the ECB. Pointing to the fact that the term of the governor of the BdI was unlimited and arguing that the conditions laid down for dismissing a member of the European System of the Central Banks (ESCB) were not present, the Italian Council of Ministers did not decide upon any formal measure against Fazio, and trusted to the ECB to pronounce a moral judgment against him. The minister of the economy and finance, Siniscalco, simply prepared a draft of a proposed reform of the BdI to be submitted to the ECB. For its part, the ECB began informally to collect information on the behavior of Governor Fazio in connection with the banking takeovers. At the beginning of October 2005, the ECB gave its own opinion on two different versions of the draft reform of the BdI proposed by the Italian government. At the beginning of November 2005, the ECB finished its investigation of Fazio's activities. On the proposals for the reform of the BdI, the ECB agreed with the introduction of a term limit for the governor and urged the extension of this measure to the other members of the board, as well as the adoption of the principle of collegial decision-making instead of simple consultation. However, the conclusion of the ECB on Fazio's behavior in the matter of the bank takeovers was in line with the statements of several European Union commissioners: the governor had respected the letter of the Italian legislation, which allowed "a certain degree of discretionary action," but not the substance of the European Community principles whose purpose was to favor competition and banking integration in Europe.

Even though it was careful to respect national jurisdiction in the matter of banking supervision, the position taken by the ECB sent a clear message to the Italian political system concerning the urgent need to reform the governance of the BdI, to reduce the margin of discretion left by the TUB and its regulations, and to redraft the regulations governing the financial market.[26] The government's response, however, has been slow and partial. First, it did not act until the actions of the judiciary halted (definitively or de facto) the PTOs launched by BPI and Unipol and forced Governor Fazio to quit, bringing members of the government and the majority under suspicion of involvement in the illicit activities of the BPI. Then, it merely restructured the governance of the BdI and prepared a rough draft of new regulations for the financial markets. The most important opposition party, the Left Democrats (Democratici di sinistra, or DS), participated in this substantial abdication of the role of the political system: the problem was not so much their "rooting" for Unipol's takeover attempt as it was their promotion of fraudulent financiers to the role of standard-bearers of a "new model," in contrast to the old and fragile equilibria of Italian capitalism.[27] By misrepresenting them in this way, the DS certainly did nothing to enhance their credibility when it came to censuring the behavior of the governor and promoting the reform of the BdI—all the more so because long before the onset of the financial scandals, the DS had presented in Parliament a well-drafted bill that would have redrawn the regulations for the financial markets and reformed the nomination procedures, the term limits, and the responsibilities of the governor.

In the end, on 23 December 2005, the Italian Parliament approved the "savings law," of which Article 19 deals with the reform of the BdI. It provides that the appointment of the governor will no longer be entrusted to an unaccountable body, such as the Superior Council, but instead to the executive acting with the approval of the president of the Republic.[28] That same article, moreover, fixes the term of office of the governor and the other members of the board at six years, renewable only once. Since Fazio had resigned, there was no need for a transition period until the appointment of a new governor; however, such a period was necessary for the rest of the members of the board, among other things to avoid the simultaneous replacement of the entire membership. Finally, the decisions of the board are now collegial in character, with ties decided in favor of the position supported by the governor; they must be submitted in written form, making explicit the motivations.

As for the excessive discretion permitted by the TUB and the related regulations, the "savings law" simply provides that the supervisory rules shall be adapted to the new legislation. On the other hand, it makes safeguarding competition the responsibility of the AGCM, with the concomitant requirement that both bodies approve acquisitions and mergers in the banking sector that raise issues of stability or competition.[29]

Conclusions

The analysis presented in the preceding sections has shown that the actions of the BPI and Unipol did not result in competitive offers that improved on the PTOs from ABN AMRO and BBVA, but instead led to widespread violations of the rules of the market. What is more, those who cast themselves as defenders of the "Italianness" of the banks were in reality swindling speculators who certainly would not have been an effective alternative to the fragile elite of the Italian economy.[30] It is a matter of serious concern that Governor Fazio gave his support for a long time to such actions and to individuals of this sort, who were halted only because of the tenacity of the European banks involved, the initiatives of CONSOB, and the intervention of the magistrates. It is equally serious that several members of the government and of the majority coalition appear to have been involved in illicit transactions related to the attempted takeovers. The political system's abdication of its role was, moreover, worsened by the position taken by a segment of the largest opposition party, which mistook the violation of the rules of the market for the emergence of a new model of capitalism. As a result, politics lagged behind the judiciary, and it was only belatedly that Parliament was able to approve a partial and insufficient reform of the governance of the BdI and the banking regulations.

The new legislation, nevertheless, allowed the appointment of a new governor, Mario Draghi, who will have a limited-term appointment and will be restrained by a collegial form of management. The high international reputation and the organizational skills of the new governor lead us to hope that the BdI will be able to gradually recover its institutional role and introduce a style of supervision that is consistent with an open market and European integration. One thing that is certain is that the BdI is in a complex position, as is clearly demonstrated by the decision to resort, after many years, to an external rather than an internal appointee.

—Translated by Bethel Hernández

Notes

1. Up to 10 January 2006, when this text was being finalized, the BdI has not granted the authorization for the launch of the compulsory PTO for BNL by Unipol. At the present time, unless there is an unlikely positive outcome of the countermoves by Unipol, the story can be considered over. It only remains to be seen whether Banco Bilbao Vizcaya Argentaria will come back on the scene.
2. Cf. Banca d'Italia, *Relazione annuale* (Rome, 2005).
3. Cf. Banca d'Italia, *Relazione annuale* (Rome, 1991); Banca d'Italia, *Relazione annuale* (Rome, 2005).
4. Cf. M. Messori, "Consolidation, Ownership Structure and Efficiency in the Italian Banking System," *BNL Quarterly Review* 55, no. 221 (2002): 189–191.
5. Cf. R. Costi, *L'ordinamento bancario* (Bologna, 2001).
6. Cf. R. Costi and M. Messori, *Per lo sviluppo: Un capitalismo senza rendite e con capitale* (Bologna, 2005).
7. The analysis undertaken in this chapter is based on published materials: the offer documents of the potential buyers, the successive press releases of those same buyers, the releases of the firms targeted by the bids, and the decisions of the official bodies involved. It is also based on several reconstructions of the facts of the takeover bids for the BAV and the BNL. Cf. V. Malagutti and M. Onado, "Andava a piedi da Lodi a Lugano: Storia della scalata alla Banca Antonveneta," *Mercati concorrenza regole* 7, no. 2 (2005); F. Massaro and M. Panerai, *I furbetti del quartierino* (Milan: Milano Finanza, 2005); G. Oddo and G. Pons, *L'intrigo: Banche e risparmiatori nell'era di Fazio* (Milan: Feltrinelli, 2005); G. Turani, *I quattro delle opa selvage* (Milan: Sperling & Kupfer, 2005); V. Borrelli, *Banca padrona* (Milano: Rizzoli, 2005). I also consulted the following newspapers: *Il Sole-24 Ore, Corriere della Sera, la Repubblica,* and *Financial Times.*
8. The so-called pact of the *sciacchetrà*, sealed in January 2005 between the prime minister and the governor of the BdI to defend the "Italianness" of the banks and made public by an insider, confirmed the worries of the European authorities. In fact, a few weeks later European Commissioner Charlie McCreevy sent an unusual open letter to warn Governor Fazio not to place obstacles in the way of the "free movement" of financial services within the Single Market.
9. We should note the tight ownership links between the BPL and Gnutti's firms. For instance, BPL is one of the major shareholders of Hopa, while the firm that controls Hopa (Fingruppo) has a significant share of the BPL. However, Hopa, a firm in which the Italian investors involved in the takeover bid for BNL also have shares, was not directly involved in the acquisition of BAV shares.
10. Refer to the prospectus published on 2 May by the BPL in conformity with CONSOB regulations.
11. Note that Unipol had also signed call and put contracts with the Deutsche Bank (London branch) for about 5 percent of BNL's capital. If we include in the calculation the shares held by the BPER (about 4 percent, bought between May and July 2005), which was formally not a member of the pact, after the middle of July 2005 Unipol's group controlled about 51 percent of BNL's shares.
12. In accordance with Article 106 of the TUF, the price of a compulsory open takeover bid is the arithmetic mean of: (1) the weighted average price of the ordinary shares of the firm, which is the object of the PTO during the year preceding the announcement to the market of the PTO; and (2) the highest price paid, during the same period, by one of the parties that is required to launch the PTO.

13. The new name of Banca Popolare Italiana was decided upon by the assembly of 2 June 2005. In the text, the acronym BPI is used whenever reference is made to events that happened after the name change.

14. Cf. above, in the second section of this chapter and note 11. A call contract gives the option to buy a certain asset at a fixed price and at a specific date in the future (European call) or before a pre-established future date (American call); a put contract grants the option to sell an asset at a specific price and at a specific date (European put) or before a specified future date (American put) (cf., for example, R. A. Brealey and S. C. Myers, *Principles of Corporate Finance* [New York: McGraw-Hill, 1991]). In this particular case, the following obtained: (1) an American call in favor of Unipol, open until 30 days after the expiry of the PTO, and a European put in favor of the DB, to be exercised three years from the date of the agreement, on a package of shares that amounted to 2.16 percent of the common stock of BNL; and (2) European call and put options in favor of, respectively, Unipol and the DB, to be exercised three years from the signature of the agreement, on a package of shares that amounted to 2.83 percent of the common stock of BNL. A little before the middle of August, the call and put contracts described above were complemented by two put contracts in favor of Unipol aimed at covering, respectively, the risk that the DB would not have enough shares to cover its commitments under (2) and the risk that Unipol would have more BNL shares than foreseen. The economic meaning of these agreements will be clarified shortly in the text.

15. Recall that Unipol controlled, directly or indirectly, slightly more than 41 percent of BNL's capital and that the pact members and its other allies were forbidden to accept the compulsory PTO. Unipol committed itself to release sufficient shares to the market so as to maintain BNL's listing on the exchange, even if the result of the compulsory PTO led to a residual PTO.

16. According to the legislation then in force, the opinion of ISVAP did not have a binding character for the launch of the PTO. ISVAP could intervene only ex post, by ordering the cession of any stockholdings that gave total or partial control in non-insurance firms and that jeopardized the stability of the insurance company that held them. The question of the compatibility between the takeover on the BNL and the corporate object of Unipol was, moreover, relevant. In the event of a negative reply by the ISVAP or an intervention of the judiciary, Unipol's shareholders would have had the right to redeem their shares from the firm, which would have significantly increased the financial burden of the transaction.

17. The problem was that an equity swap had been arranged with the DB for that quota.

18. In the pacts and other agreements signed with Nomura, CSFB, and the DB, Unipol had in fact agreed to cede to those banks important service activities in the sectors of investment banking, managed savings, private banking, and consumer credit.

19. The international banks that were involved in different ways in the two groups (for instance, the DB and CSFB) were pursuing short-term objectives (maximization of their revenues from services and contractual agreements) or strategies aimed at acquiring shares of the Italian market in specific sectors.

20. The reason given by the BdI—to prevent the possibility that by exceeding the threshold of 20 percent of BAV's capital, ABN AMRO could use its share of convertible bonds to surpass the 30 percent threshold before the approval of

the PTO—seems paradoxical, given the behavior of the BPL and its allies. The paradox becomes deeper if we consider that at the approach of the end of the "pact" and, as usual, within three days, the BdI granted the BPL approval to increase its share to 29.9 percent of BAV without asking what the reason for such a request could be when an PTO was in the process of being authorized.

21. It is interesting to note that by increasing its share of BNL's capital to 14.99 percent and by continuing its negotiations with the members of the counter-pact, Unipol was in a position to go beyond 30 percent of BNL's capital. If the BdI had acted as it did with ABN AMRO, it should have postponed the authorization that the Bologna insurance company had asked for. What is more, as opposed to ABN AMRO, Unipol had not decided on any PTO for BNL.

22. The statutory asset base is defined by: (1) the addition of the basic assets and the supplementary assets, whose total cannot, however, exceed the basic assets; and (2) the subtraction from that sum of the shares, hybrid asset instruments, and subordinate assets held in other banks or financial firms. Cf. Banca d'Italia, *Relazione annuale* (Rome, 2005), appendix.

23. Preference shares are the shares issued by a firm (in this case a bank) that receive a remuneration at market rates and share in the risks of the banking activity.

24. On the other hand, partly because of the "corrections" the ISVAP made to the assets of the resulting financial conglomerate (almost 900 million euros), the BdI did not approve the PTO launched by Unipol for BNL, on the grounds of failure to meet the asset requirements. In fact, the maximum expenditure required by the intended PTO was valued at 4.2 billion euros. To that amount were added expenses already incurred by Unipol in order to acquire 14.89 percent of BNL's capital (approximately 1.2 billion euros) and the possible cost of the put options granted to several of its allies (approximately 1 billion). To cover this 6.4 billion euro cost, in mid-September 2005 Unipol had launched an increase in capitalization roughly equivalent to its assets (nearly 2.6 billion euros), offering it as an option to the old shareholders. Moreover, Unipol undertook to give up minority shares worth 800 million euros in companies it controlled, and to issue subordinate loans and other financial instruments with a maximum value of 1.4 million euros. Finally, Unipol declared it had 200 million euros of its own resources available. Given the valuation of the BNL, those figures were absolutely insufficient to bring the assets of the new conglomerate to the average values for the Italian insurance and banking sectors. They were even less so if the new European laws on conglomerates were applied. What is more, the plan to augment the asset base would not have avoided a degree of financial leverage so great that it would have hindered the functioning of the new conglomerate and, in particular, the growth of the BNL. Many analysts agreed that the new merged company would have suffered from a debt level too high for the insurance sector and stated that it would need to increase its assets by a further 1 billion euros.

25. A. Fazio, "Considerazioni Finali," in Banca d'Italia, *Relazione annuale*, 31 May 2005, 28–29. Note that on page 27, the governor had given an implicit endorsement of the Unipol project, which had not been made public yet, by affirming that "in the ownership structure of the major European banks it is important that insurance companies be present."

26. The European Commission, which in mid-December started the "infraction procedure" against Italy with reference to the banking takeovers, reinforced the signals coming from the ECB. The charges referred to the possible restrictions

introduced by the Italian banking supervision authorities to the freedom of movement of capital among the member states.

27. O. Carabini, *Il Sole-24 Ore*, 5 August 2005. In this interview, given by Massimo D'Alema after the three decisions of CONSOB on the fraudulent means used by the duo Fiorani-Gnutti and their allies in buying up BAV's shares, the chairman of the DS asked: "And what is it about Gnutti that's not all right?" Also, forgetting that only a few days earlier Unipol had been forced to launch a compulsory PTO because of the complex net of agreements it has signed with various allies (Gnutti and Fiorani included), he declared: "The two groups are different. In the case of BNL there is only Unipol, supported by foreign banks." D'Alema expressed similar views even in interviews given at the beginning of January 2006.

28. The law provides for the Superior Council to express its opinion on the nominee; however, it does not provide for Parliament to give its view. A working group of Astrid, coordinated by Luigi Spaventa, presented a proposal for the reform of the BdI that eliminated the Superior Council and provided for a binding opinion by a special parliamentary committee on the appointment of the governor (cf. Astrid, "La Banca d'Italia e l'assetto della vigilanza bancaria: Proposte di riforma," *Astrid-Rassegna*, no. 20 [2005]). That proposal would have had the further advantage of reducing the supposed conflict of interest, due to the fact that some of those regulated have formal ownership of the regulator. It should be stressed that on this matter the new law proposes gradual solutions.

29. In the Astrid proposal mentioned above more radical changes to the TUB are introduced, and the need to obtain dual approval by the AGCM and the BdI is eliminated through the introduction of sequential decisions. Moreover, in the same proposal, other areas of overlap between the different authorities are eliminated. Instead, the new legislation establishes forms of coordination between the BdI, the other authorities, and a newly created commission with undefined functions.

30. The hypothesis that the takeover bids for BAV and BNL were the prelude to an attempt to replace the personnel of the Italian economic elite is not a completely futile one. The main characters in the two banking takeovers (Gnutti, Fiorani, and Consorte) in fact had links—directly or indirectly—with the group that tried to take over one of the holiest shrines of the frozen Italian economic power structure: RCS (the media conglomerate Rizzoli-Corriere della Sera).

7

THE REFERENDUM ON ARTIFICIAL INSEMINATION

Chiara Martini

On 12 and 13 June 2005, the citizens of Italy were called to the polls to vote on law no. 40 of 19 February 2004, which for the first time in Italy established regulations on medically assisted reproduction (MAR). This law, even if it arrived later in Italy than in other European countries, was not suddenly "born." Its adoption came about after a long and tormented debate that concluded with the approval of a text supported by a majority that crossed the boundary between the two political coalitions, which included almost the whole of the center-right and the majority of the Margherita. The four referendum questions, proposed by representatives of the left and supported by the Radical movement, aimed to introduce modifications to the law, which, stated simply, would allow research on surplus embryos for therapeutic purposes, genetic diagnosis pre-implantation, and the use of heterologous fertilization (i.e., donated sperm). All of these procedures are forbidden by law no. 40.

Italians answered the referendum questions by abstaining in huge numbers: 74.1 percent of the electorate did not vote, making it one of the lowest turnouts in Italian history. Since the required quorum of a 50 percent turnout was not reached, none of the proposed amendments to the law was adopted (cf. appendix, tables 9a–9d). The outcome of the referendum literally stunned many politicians, electoral analysts, and political scientists, who did not expect such a low rate of participation. One might be tempted not to see anything new in these results, given the growing

---

aversion among Italian voters for the referendum procedure. However, the entire episode of the law on artificial insemination is particularly significant for at least three reasons. First, it opened a public debate on issues that have become central to all Western democracies—those that are called "ethically sensitive" since they concern life and death, the family, and sexuality. At the same time, the bitter and harsh tones in which this discussion was conducted brought to light the weakness of Italian democracy in its search for a shared ethos on subjects of such a delicate nature. Finally, it raised again the topic of the relationship between secular culture and Catholic culture, and its complex connection with the development of bipolarism in the Italian political system.

In an attempt to offer an interpretation of all of these events, this chapter will analyze some aspects of them. First of all, it will go over the crucial steps that led to the approval of law no. 40. Next, it will examine the principal motives for the opposition to the law expressed by one part of the country, which led it to take the issue directly to the electorate, concentrating attention on the themes of the referendum campaign and on the positions taken by the political parties and groups in civil society. In the third part, there will be an analysis of the outcome of the referendum, suggesting possible interpretations. In conclusion, we shall try to indicate what effects the episode of law no. 40 has had on Italian politics and what the prospects are for the future.

The Previous Regulation of Medically Assisted Reproduction and the Debate up until Law No. 40

The progress of research on human reproduction and the spread, even in Italy, of MAR techniques, was not followed by a timely legislative action to regulate this field. Before law no. 40, Italy's system made up for a lack of legal regulation with a series of administrative measures that established limits and conditions for artificial insemination.

The administrative controls were certainly not particularly exhaustive, as they proved to be fragmentary and offered solutions only to the most urgent issues. The 1 March 1985 circular of the health minister, known as the Degan Circular, established the principal limitations on artificial insemination, allowing only married couples who were not separated to request medical treatment for reproductive pathologies and allowing only for "homologous" fertilization (that is, using gametes of the couple). These rules applied only to facilities belonging to the national health service or contracted to it and not to private clinics, where the use of heterologous insemination (using the genetic material of a donor) is widely practiced.

At the same time, the governments that alternated over the years, often pressed by parliamentary motions, set up technical working groups to study and research the scientific, ethical, and legal aspects of reproductive biotechnology and genetic engineering. As long ago as 1990, the National Committee for Bioethics was created, and numerous other expert ministerial committees were subsequently formed with the specific mandate to prepare a document to serve as the foundation for a law on the subject. The fate of the materials they prepared was always the same. As one regular participant in the committees noted, the studies were assigned to "a drawer in the minister's desk, to which the key had been lost."[1] This public partial regulation was then complemented by the codes of conduct of the professionals involved. The total freedom left to private clinics did not mean, in fact, a total absence of rules in this sector. The private sector, over time, adopted rules of self-regulation via the norms contained in the medical ethics code approved by the National Federation of Colleges of Physicians, which closed the door to the spread of the more controversial practices.[2]

This rapid excursus shows that it certainly cannot be said that law no. 40 put an end to the "reproductive Wild West" that is so often spoken of. Rather, law no. 40 filled a "legislative gap" on the subject, introducing norms that, even though they have significant lacunae, provide a coherent regulatory framework. In this way, Italy came into line with the other countries of the European Union, the last of the 15 to do so, 20 years after Sweden passed the first law on the subject. The reasons for such a noticeable delay in legislating on the subject are still not clear: even with the inevitable difficulty of giving legal form to "ethically sensitive" issues, an inability and a lack of will to legislate have characterized what has been called the "Italian way" on the issue of artificial insemination.[3]

For a long time, the absence of rules was certainly not the result of a conscious choice between those who believe legislative intervention is necessary on this subject and those who think that legislation would infringe on an area that ought to be left to the free decisions of individuals. A public discussion of the matter never took place; the Degan Circular represented an option for partial regulation. In this way, the choice was avoided, and the debate (and conflict) that opened up with the advent of reproductive technology was defused. The conditions for parliamentary action appeared only in the course of the 13th Legislature, with the wave of anxiety created in public opinion by the first striking success of efforts at animal cloning,[4] and also with pressure generated by growing European sensitivity on these issues.[5]

When the debate opened in this Parliament, controlled by a center-left majority, on how and to what degree law-makers should regulate this subject, the difficulty of finding a middle ground became imme-diately obvious: right from the beginning the Catholics within both political coalitions and the Northern League voiced their total and intransigent opposition to access to reproductive technology for non-married couples and to donor insemination. In this situation, the left-wing parties in the governing coalition, in an attempt to overcome the split within the Ulivo, counted on support from the secular members of the center-right, particularly those from Forza Italia (FI).[6]

The next step was the drafting of a consolidated text, which (for the first time in Italian parliamentary history) passed the commit-tee stage and reached the floor of Parliament; this was the so-called Bolognesi text, from the name of its *rapporteur*, a Left Democrat (DS) member of Parliament. But the expectation that it would elicit the degree of consensus necessary to lead to convergence on a common position, supported by a "secular" majority crossing the line between the two coalitions, was dashed: at the beginning of the debate on the floor, the deputies rejected the possibility of donor insemination. On the one hand, the vote held by secret ballot confirmed the "no" vote announced by the Partito Popolare Italiano (PPI), Alleanza Nazionale (AN), the Centro Cristiano-Democratico (CCD), the Lega Nord (LN), the Cristiano-Sociali (a Catholic group that joined the DS), and the Unione Democratici per l'Europa (UDEUR). On the other hand, it was evidence of the "betrayal" of FI. The text itself passed a third reading in the Chamber but not in the Senate.

At the beginning of the 14th Legislature, this time with a center-right majority in power, Parliament tried again. On 18 February 2002, the Chamber of Deputies approved the text that was to become law no. 40. It addressed all the key points of the debate: the aim of MAR, which techniques are permitted, how and when they may be used, and the so-called status of the embryo. First of all, artificial insemina-tion was defined as a remedy allowed exclusively "in order to further the solution of reproductive problems derived from human sterility or infertility." This limitation in effect does not allow for the use of MAR to prevent the transmission of genetic illnesses through pre-implanta-tion diagnosis. Secondly, the text speaks of a right to access only to the technique of "homologous" fertilization, and only for "couples consist-ing of adults of the opposite sex, married or cohabiting, of a potentially fertile age, both living." Therefore, the law prohibits donor insemina-tion, as well as post mortem insemination. Thirdly, the law contains a series of provisions for the protection of the human embryo, starting from the declaration of principle that the law "ensures the rights of all persons concerned, including those who have been conceived." Any form of experimentation on embryos or eugenic selection is prohibited, as is the production of embryos solely for research; however, clinical and experimental research is allowed on the condition that its purpose is exclusively therapeutic and diagnostic and is aimed at protecting human health and assisting the development of the embryos. Lastly, crioconservation (that is, the freezing of embryos) and the destruction of embryos, except for those terminations of pregnancy permitted by law no. 194 (the abortion law), are prohibited. MAR techniques may not create more embryos than needed for a single implantation at one time, and in any case not more than three.

The final approval of this text was an extenuating process that took place in a climate of bitter polemics, but what is most striking is the lack of a constructive (and desirable) dialectic, which can be attributed to the rigidity of the positions of the participants. This can be illustrated by what happened during the Senate's consideration of the bill. At first, the representatives of the government majority demonstrated an openness and willingness to discuss the text;[7] however, they then closed off the possibility of accepting any counterproposals to modify the more controversial aspects of the measure, even though the amendments had been frequently requested by a large number of highly qualified health workers and scholars who were heard during the discussion. In the face of this hardening of the majority's position, a cohesive minority group took shape, led by the DS together with a "secular" component of the center-right, who continued to the bitter end in their attempts to find common ground on modifications to the text.[8] The hope of a compromise was frustrated on the one hand by the center-right's political decision to "fast-track" the law (i.e., require a vote on the bill without amendments) and on the other hand by the belief of the majority of the Margherita that any modification of the text would mean the continuation of an unregulated reproductive "Wild West." The Church hierarchy also entered the fray in support of the law, which it considered the only acceptable compromise. In their repeated interventions, Church officials appealed to the consciences of Catholic legislators to follow the values and fundamental principles of the teachings of the Church. Even Pope John Paul II publicly intervened, urging the Senate to approve the law quickly.[9]

Law no. 40 was passed by Parliament, giving rise to two "transversal" groups that crossed the boundary between the two coalitions. From a political point of view, this division re-created the old cleavage between Catholic and secular forces. In fact, almost all the representatives of the center-right voted "yes," as well as the Margherita, while the DS, Socialisti Democratici Italiani (SDI), Greens, Rifondazione Comunista (RC), and Partito dei Comunisti Italiani (PdCI) voted "no."

The Referendum Questions and the Campaign

Putting aside the principled and ideological motives that inspired the major elements of law no. 40, the new rules on artificial insemination have sparked some doubts in light of a comparison with the ways that other countries have dealt with the matter. In contrast with other countries, the Italian law takes an extremely restrictive approach with peculiar results: as one observer has cogently remarked, "in various European countries this or that is prohibited but none of them prohibits all the things that Italy does."[10] The preference for a "prohibitionist" framework with regard to bioethics is often tied to cultural concepts related to fear of the impact of technology on human reproduction. It stems from the idea that the use of this technology has an explosive potential that could have very dangerous results, and thus the subject should be approached very cautiously. Because of their fear of possible unwelcome consequences, those who hold these beliefs favor a precautionary principle through the implementation of "reassuring" regulations that impose a series of rules and limits.[11]

To return to the case of Italy, a similar attitude helps to explain, at least in part, the choices with regard to both method and content in law no. 40. On the one hand, there was a predominant conviction that legislative intervention was absolutely necessary and could no longer be put off, or in any case it was the lesser evil compared to having absolutely no rules at all. This also explains the resistance of the Senate to requests to make even one correction to the text passed by the Chamber—they feared that reopening the debate could possibly have put at risk the majority backing for the law, a majority that was in any case fragile. On the other hand, the law uses the instrument of absolute and peremptory prohibitions. Many of these were acceptable and, in fact, broadly accepted. Others were excessive, and on these one might have expected a further consideration, given the diversity of opinions on the subject and the approach taken in the legislation of most neighboring countries.

By proceeding in this manner, the majority that passed law no. 40 ended up by imposing an exclusive and excluding logic. It is exclusive in that it is based on a particular point of view on a subject where the positions differ strongly, not only as a result of cultural and religious divisions, but also because of varying scientific opinions. From this point of view, law no. 40 cannot be defined as a "Catholic law," in that its content does not completely overlap with the Church's official doctrine on the subject,[12] but at the same time it takes as its starting point the equality of the embryo with those already born. This reflects only one limited part of the positions of religion, science, and philosophy on the matter. It is also excluding because it has the effect of delegitimizing all of the positions that fall outside of the one that is legally imposed. In this way, however, it risks increasing and perpetuating the very conflicts whose prevention is one of the principal functions of law.[13]

The end of the parliamentary debate did not close the question of artificial insemination. On the contrary, the day after the approval of the law, five requests for a referendum on its repeal were put forward. One omnibus question, proposed by the Radicals and RC, asked for the repeal of the entire law, while the four other questions involved its partial repeal. Organized by representatives of the DS,[14] these four questions aimed to correct certain significant points of the law, specifically those that had been most controversial in the scientific, political, and parliamentary debates. All of the questions passed the examination by the Constitutional Court, with the exception of the total repeal, which was judged as inadmissible since it deprived the system of "constitutionally necessary" regulations.[15] On all of the other questions, however, the referendum campaign began. It promised to be bitterly fought, with possibly very divisive effects on the country, and thus generated uncertainty and concern. It is not accidental that following the decision that the four questions were admissible, the political debate at first centered on whether Parliament should amend the articles whose repeal had been requested before the referendum took place. In the Senate, various bills were submitted by representatives of the majority and of the center-left in an ultimate attempt at mediation, but these limited initiatives, not adequately underpinned by a shared political will, were destined to failure.

Citizens were thus called to state their opinions on extremely specific questions, such as the admissibility of genetic diagnosis pre-implantation, the limits of stem-cell research, and, indirectly, the status of the embryo. The first question in the referendum aimed to eliminate the prohibition of the experimental use of surplus embryos for therapeutic purposes. The intention was to allow scientific research on illnesses that at the moment are incurable. The second question dealt with the limit on the number of embryos that could be implanted in a woman. In order to avoid the production of surplus embryos, the law requires that no more than three embryos be created in vitro and that they be implanted all at one time, whatever the possibility of success. The referendum's proponents called for the elimination of these limitations, arguing that they could damage the woman's health, given that she would risk being exposed to repeated ovarian stimulation because under these regulations there would be a lower probability that each implant would succeed. If this question had been approved, it would also have permitted three other procedures prohibited by the law: pre-implantation diagnosis, embryonic selection, and the freezing of embryos. The aim was therefore to extend to couples carrying genetic disorders (as well as those that are sterile) the right to resort to artificial insemination. The third question deleted from the law the reference to the "rights of the conceived." This proposal technically would not have any effect, but it would have great symbolic value because of its implications for the question of establishing the beginning of the life of a "human being." Finally, the fourth question proposed to eliminate the prohibition on techniques of donor insemination, as well as the associated penalties.

The positions of the political forces on the referendum questions were not far from the positions they had taken in Parliament, but this time the parties' decisions were overtaken by another factor that was going to be decisive: the Church mobilized in favor of abstention in the referendum. This course was suggested by Camillo Ruini, the president of the Conference of Italian Bishops (CEI), and adopted by the leaders and representatives of almost all the Catholic movements and associations, who founded the "Science and Life for the Support of Law No. 40"[16] committee. The signatories of its manifesto expressed a "double no": first, on the content of the referendum questions, which would have subverted a law that they considered "not perfect" but "that ensures that every child has the guarantee of a life and the protection of a real family"; second, on the improper use of the institution of the referendum on the subject of artificial insemination.

Faced with this abstentionist position, only parties of the left voiced their "yes" to the four questions. On the other side, the center-right coalition positioned itself alongside the abstentionist movement, with the exception of a fringe group inside the FI party and the leader of AN, Gianfranco Fini. The Margherita officially chose the line of "freedom of conscience," but the principal representatives of the Catholic section of the party and its leader, Francesco Rutelli, declared their intention not to go to the polls.

The call for abstention as a means of defending the law caught the supporters of the referendum off guard and shifted the theme of the debate to the slogan "on life one does not vote." The formulation of the referendum questions raised matters that on the one hand were very specific, requiring precise scientific knowledge, and on the other were complex issues with major moral implications. As such, it was difficult to respond with a simple "yes" or "no," as is standard for a repeal referendum. Voters were asked to consider the following: Is it reasonable for an embryo to enjoy greater protection than a fetus in a system where one is allowed to terminate a pregnancy, but no medical interference with embryos is permitted? What is the appropriate balance between two rights that both deserve protection—the physical and mental health of women on one side, and the right to life of those who have been conceived on the other? Is it suitable in every case to forbid the use of donor insemination on the basis of an exclusively biological model of parenthood?

In fact, the promoters of the referendum, belonging or close to the DS, were at first wary of taking the referendum route before deciding to bet on the possibility of involving public opinion in a "pragmatic" discussion. Their objective was to achieve what they had failed to obtain in Parliament—not to throw out the law, as the Radicals proposed in their question, but rather to correct the points they considered critical.[17] Yet in the end, the referendum campaign marginalized the debate on the substance of the individual problems. It was dominated by other key protagonists, whose impact was all the greater because the campaign was concentrated in the month and a half preceding the vote. The regional elections were now over, and the media focused their spotlight on the referendum.

The first problem is represented by the great question that stood out in the background of law no. 40—the topic of the embryo and its status, found in the third referendum question. Without a doubt this was the most complex issue with the strongest social and emotional impact, but it was also the most "slippery," since it allowed the debate to slide into the terrain of ideology. On the substance of this question, all positions—philosophical, cultural, and religious—were legitimately expressed, a demonstration, if any were needed, of how broad the range of opinions is, even in Italy. Meanwhile, the debate leading up to the referendum became a confrontation between two simplified, extreme theories: the affirmation of the personhood of the embryo, which required the defense of the law with all its prohibitions and limitations, and the argument that it is acceptable to perform experiments on and manipulate embryos.

There was no lack of moderate positions, such as that of Giuliano Amato, who proposed to find a common ground in the acknowledgment of the "human dignity" of the embryo.[18] But these positions were overshadowed by the predominant trend toward the radicalization of the conflict. This was symbolized by the leading speakers at the closing rallies of the referendum campaign:[19] representing one side was Marco Pannella, the leader of the Radicals, who had organized the rejected referendum proposal to repeal law no. 40 altogether, and representing the other side was Giuliano Ferrara, the editor of *Il Foglio*, who was the best-known supporter of "Operation Theocon," which contributed to George W. Bush's victory in the last American election.

One could say that in fact only one of the two conceptions of the referendum initiative prevailed in the end, that of the Radicals, which had been initially sidelined by the Constitutional Court. It crowded out the "reformist" position based on the four partial questions, which failed in its objective of channeling the discussion along the lines of amending the law point by point. The centrality that the embryo argument took on created an imbalance between the positions in the debate. Faced with an argument of principle such as the value of life, used by the abstentionists, the promoters of the referendum were not able to shift the focus of the discussion to the concrete topics that the people would be voting on.

During the discussions that followed, it proved impossible to limit the debate to the letter of the law because the questions revived bioethical and religious dilemmas, one of which was the role of science and its social effects. Many times, in the columns of the *Corriere della Sera*, Ernesto Galli Della Loggia urged his readers not to evade the fundamental question of the ethical limits to the application of the techniques and discoveries of scientific research (in the field of reproduction, in the first place).[20] He asked them to distinguish between that which can be objectively established by science, which only experts can determine, and that which is morally and ethically acceptable, which all citizens of Italy had the responsibility of deciding. This led to a discussion of the relationship between science and ethics and of the equally important connection between science and religion. The parties and their leaders all seemed to avoid these themes and failed to offer any guidance on this issue by suggesting an ethical vision of science or a set of standards of behavior that could serve a society undergoing enormous change. A large part of the Italian scientific community, however, mobilized publicly. Although they were divided, most scientists supported the pro-referendum camp in the name of the freedom of research and out of opposition to old and new anti-scientific prohibitions.[21]

During the course of the referendum campaign, the polemic over the Church hierarchy's appeal for abstention was like a constant noise in the background. The bishops, considering it the most effective way to defend the law that they had already "supported" in Parliament, introduced the notion of abstention even before the discussion of the various options began and the authors of the law had weighed in. Many criticisms were directed at the propaganda campaign for abstention: its legal legitimacy was not in question, although the issue has been debated at length by influential scholars. But the supporters of the referendum viewed the abstention campaign as a crafty expedient, a politically unethical technical contrivance that would make opening up a debate on the merits of the questions even more difficult. They argued that it was a symptom of the weakness of the ethical arguments advanced to support abstention. The fact that the invitation to abstain came from the Church gave some the opportunity to deplore the Church's increasing involvement in temporal matters and to defend the autonomy of the state and civil society in the face of this trend. Others, in more measured tones, pointed out that it raised the issue of what constitutes a secular democracy and what role the dialogue between political actors and religious authorities should have.[22]

The referendum, then, raised many themes that engaged the public in a debate that was certainly not useless, once we discount the multiplier effect of the polemical intensity that is part of every electoral campaign. But, given the multiplicity and heterogeneity of the questions, the reasons behind the "yes" and "no" positions on the partial repeal of the law got lost in the excess of arguments.

The Results of the Referendum

As we have already mentioned, on 12 and 13 June, the voter turnout was 25.9 percent, the lowest in Italian repeal referendum history alongside that in the 2003 referendum on Article 18 of the Statute of Workers' Rights (25.7 percent). It was clear enough to all that it would be impossible to achieve the quorum of 50 percent, but no one had expected such a high level of abstention. To the promoters of the referendum, a turnout that was less than the quorum but around 40 percent would have been useful as a demonstration of strength, since at that figure they would have been able to delegitimate parts of the law, if not to repeal them. This did not occur. Therefore, the "yes" side's victory was useless, even though it won about 88 percent of the votes cast on the first three questions and 78.2 percent on the question on donor insemination.

Since there were numerous themes raised in the campaign, once the polls closed commentators offered diverse interpretations of the mood of Italian society as revealed by the vote, depending on the vantage point from which it was viewed. Some spoke of a critical or negative attitude toward scientific research, or of a revolt against the party elites. Some advanced the hypothesis of a new alliance between secular conservative tendencies and integralist leanings within the Catholic camp. Rather than starting from these reconstructions, however, it may be more prudent to limit our analysis to the facts, using the available data and concentrating our attention only on certain aspects.

A reading of the referendum results (see the appendix, tables 9a–9d, for the summary data) shows, first of all, the geographical differentiation of the vote. We can see, in particular, a clear disjunction between the Northern and Central regions, on the one hand, and the South, on the other: the voters in the former were roughly twice as likely to come out to the polls as the latter. In any case, in no region or province was the quorum met, though the highest turnout was registered in the regions with the strongest bond linking the electorate to the left-wing parties. At this point it is more difficult to analyze the vote according to other categories. A study conducted by the SWG polling firm using data collected before the referendum suggested that gender was not a significant variable: women did not show up as predominant among those who voted in the referendum. The age of the voter seemed to have a greater influence, with those over 55 more likely to abstain. The level of education had even more impact: secondary and post-secondary graduates accounted for almost 50 percent of the voters, but only 38 percent of the abstainers.[23]

More than anything, though, the analysts emphasized the large number of non-voters, which was higher than all expectations and open to various interpretations. If we consider Italian society as a whole, the 75 percent abstention rate is a sign of widespread disen-chantment, disinterest, or even what the sociologist Giuseppe De Rita has called referendum-induced "political/media stress."[24] It is clear that there are varying types of abstention: behind the "silence" of two-thirds of Italians there were distinct states of mind, differing moti-vations, and various types of indifference. There is always a certain amount of non-voting due to disinterest or inertia, but its extent this time was a reflection of the disfavor into which the institution of the referendum has fallen. Those who abstained to make a point about the political system could easily be confused with disinterested voters. But there were also those who did not vote for reasons that stemmed specifically from the subject matter of the referendum.

On this last point we can refer to the research done by the Cattaneo Institute, which elaborated a model to predict the results of the referen-dum vote that proved to be extremely accurate. The experts at the Insti-tute, using their own data, estimated that the rate of turnout would be 27.4 percent, very close to the actual figure. To reach this result, they hypothesized that all of the voters would follow the suggestions of the leaders of their reference groups, political or ecclesiastical, with some variation according to the clarity with which the latter expressed their positions. Thus, the more unequivocal the message, the more the vot-ers would be united in following it. Vice versa, the voters who received contradictory suggestions or whose leaders took no official position (for example, voters whose parties chose the "freedom of conscience" stance) would be evenly divided between abstention and voting.[25] This predictive model, whose validity is confirmed by its great accuracy in estimating geographical voting differences, offers a starting point for some further reflections on its substantive findings.

The choices that Italians made in the referendum were greatly affected both by the actions of the parties, which often crossed the boundary between the two coalitions, and by those of the Church. According to the Cattaneo Institute's comparison of the expectations of their model with the actual results, "neither of the two coalitions of elites (pro- and anti-referendum) managed to encroach significantly on the constituency of the other,"[26] considering that in any case it was more difficult to mobilize Italians to go to the polls than to convince them to abstain from voting. This rules out the more extreme interpretations of the vote: the failure of the referendum was not a symptom of the eclipse of politics itself, since the activity of the political forces had a decisive influence on the orientation of the citizens. If anything, it points to an error in political judgment committed by the leaders of the groups that promoted the referendum, who probably underestimated the moods and tendencies present in society and thus supported an initiative that was destined to fail. On the other hand, the outcome of the referendum cannot be read as the victory of an ethical and political position of exclusively Catholic origin, a clerical revanche on secular Italy, even less as the reflection of a country divided by a deep split between Catholic and secular camps. Indeed, all the initial evaluations of the analysts highlight the fact that each of the two halves of the electorate—those that abstained and those that voted—cut across the two camps, containing both Catholic and secular voters.

The fact that the expressed positions of the voters were greatly influenced by the positions of the organizations that they used as reference points confirms the difficulty and the sense of inadequacy that was generated by questions that were too complicated and abstract, and over which it seemed that opposing extremes were fighting on very uncertain terrain. For Italians disoriented by the referendum, whose ethical and scientific aspects they were unable to come to terms with, the words of the leaders to whom they felt closest gave them a point of reference for their voting decision.[27] From this perspective, the results of the vote were a defeat for the referendum strategy as a means of amending a law that many considered unsatisfactory. It thus demonstrated—to use the words of Ilvo Diamanti—that for subjects of such a delicate and complex nature, "we cannot entrust direct democracy with the task of substituting for representative democracy."[28]

These observations force us to ask whether we can consider the referendum vote as a judgment on the part of Italians vis-à-vis the content of law no. 40. Technically, the victory of the abstentionist camp has no effect on the law that was submitted to referendum; it is not equivalent to a confirmation of the law (which would have happened with a winning "no" vote) and in any case cannot prevent Parliament from subsequently modifying it in any way whatever. In its ambiguity, abstention obviously does not give any certainty as to the opinion of the country.

Nevertheless, some opinion polls offer starting points for further thoughts. In the months preceding the referendum vote, a relative majority of Italians declared, according to some surveys, that they were in favor of some modifications to the law.[29] When asked to answer detailed questions, such as those that would be asked in the future referendum, they demonstrated a similar propensity. A report titled "Biotechnology and Public Opinion in Italy," prepared by Observa in collaboration with the National Committee on Biotechnology in the autumn of 2004, stated that 68 percent of Italians believed it was "morally acceptable" to use human embryonic stem cells for research, and 76 percent considered this research "useful."[30] Finally, research carried out by ISPO confirmed this position: after the referendum, 46 percent of those surveyed said they were in favor of limited modifications to law no. 40, 16 percent were in favor of radical modifications, and 26 percent believed it should not be changed at all. This means, in the first place, that in Italy there is a large majority (62 percent) that is in favor of revisiting law no. 40 with a view to improving it, a balance of opinion that probably existed even before the referendum. In the second place, the opinions of Italians are varied but not polarized. Therefore, an intermediate position ("partial modifications") prevails over more rigid ones ("radical modifications" or "no change").[31]

In light of this data, Italy does not seem to be a nation polarized on the issue of artificial insemination. The clashes of radically opposed positions in Parliament or in the referendum debates do not seem to reflect public opinion. Instead, the picture that emerges is that of a nation searching for a balanced solution. In this sense, it can be said that abstention from voting in the referendum—occasioned by a mixture of detachment and discomfort—rather than indicating a defense of the law, was an attempt to return the discussion to Parliament, so that it might reach an agreement on a set of regulations that could attract a reasonably broad consensus.

The Political Implications

It is true that the referendum vote cannot be read as a partisan political vote, in the narrow sense. It is difficult, for example, to place it alongside that of the regional elections that were held only slightly earlier, which altered the political geography of the country, with the center-left sweeping 12 out of 14 regions. It is just as true, however, that the entire MAR episode sheds light on two different trends within the opposing political coalitions.

Above all, this issue can be used as a litmus test to discern whether the center-right coalition is evolving from a meeting ground for conservative political forces, with a strong internal liberal component, into a clerical-moderate or Catholic-conservative grouping. The moment that symbolizes the start of this sort of "genetic mutation" dates from the previous legislature and coincides with the defeat of the Bolognesi text, which was the result of the position adopted by FI against the opinion of the secular members in its ranks. From that moment, the center-right has tried to present a united front on reproductive issues and, more generally, in the area of "ethically sensitive" questions. This is what happened with law no. 40 and the referendum on it, which were a partial success for this operation. That the politics of the center-right has passed a turning point is confirmed in particular by the role of the Union of Christian Democrats and Center Democrats (UDC), which not coincidentally began to assert itself more within the coalition after the referendum vote. The day after the referendum, the speaker of the Chamber, Pierferdinando Casini, said that if his coalition wanted to win elections again, "it must take on board the lessons of the referendum and respond to the demand for values that today only the Church seems able to offer."[32] The temptation for the center-right to refashion its identity in this direction stems, then, from an obvious calculation of electoral advantage: it reckons that it could aim to get more electoral support among that swath of uncertain voters who do not identify a priori with one of the contending coalitions, but who may respond to an appeal to values. In the imminent electoral contest, the center-right could use the theme of values strategically with respect to other topics, starting with economic issues, on which they will have to defend their record as a government to the country. This might allow them to shift the center of the debate from the political and programmatic plane to that of ideology and values.

For the center-left, on the other hand, the issues are different, although connected to those of the center-right. The different positions adopted by the two principal partners in the coalition, the Margherita and the DS, both in Parliament and in the referendum campaign, created the image of a divided rather than a pluralistic coalition. This in fact set back the original project of the Ulivo to ally the Catholic reformist movement with its secular and socialist counterpart. Beyond the contingent circumstances of the referendum, this experience symbolized the still imperfect fusion between the two political souls of the coalition. This point is reinforced by each party's interpretation of the outcome of the referendum and of the position of the other. Within the Margherita, which did not give the electorate an indication of how it should vote, many theorized that there should be internal pluralism on the theme of bioethics, and there were warnings that uniformity on these matters brings with it a risk of falling back on ideological positions. This attitude was based on, first, an "internal" consideration, that is, that to adopt any position would in itself have created a division within the party, and, second, an "external" consideration, that is, the belief that the "freedom of conscience" approach would allow the party to speak to a broader electorate.

The DS, on the other hand, chose to offer themselves as a small experimental laboratory to test the interaction of the same dynamics represented within the coalition. In this sense, the successful attempt to create a synthesis between the diverse currents of thought in the party, despite the referendum defeat, counts as a sign of maturity. As a result, the DS suggested going beyond the "freedom of conscience" approach and, with a view to a future government, constructing a shared position with their allies, which could then take a prominent place in the development of the center-left's program. This is a crucial point at issue, both political and cultural, that is anything but irrelevant from the perspective of the construction of a Democratic Party that would see the two political partners united in a single entity. Despite the "moderate" position that Rutelli assumed in the debate, it should be noted that one of the three matters that he clearly put to the DS as conditions for concretizing this idea was "the need to cultivate a deeper democratic pluralism in the new organizational forms of politics ... which cannot fall under the sway of a hegemonic pattern of thought or a *single* political orientation (whether, for example, secular or confessional)."[33] In this context, the recent decision of the committee drafting the program of the Unione to commit the coalition to resolving two ethically sensitive issues, civil unions for same-sex couples and posthumous organ donation,[34] may allow us to measure its ability to find a common solution to the problem.

Conclusions

A few weeks after the polls closed, a newspaper ran an article with the eye-catching title, "No More Artificial Insemination," to point out the danger that the debate over law no. 40 would peter out. In effect, there are several factors which suggest that the issue will be taken off the political agenda, at least in the short term. As far as a parliamentary initiative is concerned, it is clear that the center-right is not prepared to modify the law, which they believe could be adjusted and corrected only at the end of the mandated three-year trial period. On the other hand, for the center-left to take up the issue again, it not only has to win the next election but also must manage to formulate a common position. In any case, neither of the platforms of the two coalitions mentions law no. 40. It is instead more likely that it could return to the political agenda after the Constitutional Court issues its expected ruling on the legitimacy of the article that prohibits pre-implantation genetic diagnosis.

Nevertheless, dismissing the referendum would clearly be an error, especially if one aims to understand Italian society or give an accurate account of it. Among the serious risks it faces is that ethical issues may be reduced to a new terrain for political competition—a risk that is present in other major democracies, as George W. Bush's United States, on the one hand, and in part Rodríguez Zapatero's Spain, on the other, demonstrate. This may lead to an "ethical bipolarism" in which the opposing coalitions radicalize the conflict on ethically sensitive subjects. In this way, laws on extremely delicate topics that involve the essential values of the community would be subject to amendment with each shift in the parliamentary majority.[35] The entire MAR episode offers several instances in which politicians were tempted to act in this way. And yet the outcome of the referendum, beyond the surprise at the rate of voter participation, should lead to reflection on the need to safeguard a pluralism of ethical points of view through the search—which must be above all political—for a mediation that respects each one of them, both in the debate on these issues and in the laws that regulate them. The referendum was a signal that civil society cannot be understood through the prism of the historical division between Catholic and secular forces and that issues related to the use of biotechnology cannot be approached by employing the same concepts and the same cultural framework that furnished the weapons for the battle for civil rights in the 1970s.

The issue is delicate, and at the same time it seems more urgent if we look beyond the narrow confines of Italy. In 1978, when the Italian abortion referendum was being conducted, the first test-tube baby, Louise Brown, was born. Almost 25 years later, while in Italy the first law on the subject was being passed, news was coming in from other parts of our globalized planet about the latest research delving into "the book of life." Universities, governments, and businesses from such countries as the US and Great Britain, and even China and South Korea, are investing resources in stem-cell research and therapeutic cloning. For some time already it has seemed likely that biomedical research will be one of the fields where international competition will be intense. Preparing to confront this phenomenon and understanding how to control it has no doubt been valuable, but what is needed is a commitment to continue down this road. The referendum questions on law no. 40, which served to raise public awareness on issues that are relevant for our times, highlight many challenges on which Italy, too, will soon have to reflect once again.

— *Translated by Cora Stern*

Notes

1. C. Flamigni, *La procreazione assistita* (Bologna: Il Mulino, 2002), 118.
2. Many countries, including the United States, still rely on professional stan-dards of ethics as a way of regulating reproductive technology. See the infor-mation collected by the International Federation of Fertility Societies (IFFS) in its report "IFFS Surveillance 04" (http://www.iffs-reproduction.org).
3. This expression is used by P. Zatti, "Verso un diritto per la bioetica: Risorse e limiti del discorso giuridico," *Rivista di diritto civile*, no. 1 (1995): 45.
4. As C. Valentini notes in her book, *La fecondazione proibita* (Milan: Feltrinelli, 2004), 117–118.
5. On 4 April 1997, the convention of the Council of Europe on human rights and biomedicine was approved in Oviedo. While it does not directly address the issue of artificial insemination, it does stress the need for clear rules on the subject.
6. For a fuller discussion, please consult C. Martini, "Il dibattito parlamen-tare sulla Pma nella XIII e XIV legislatura," in *La ricerca e la coscienza: La procreazione assistita fra legge e referendum*, ed. G. Tonini (Rome: Edizioni Riformiste, 2005).
7. At the beginning of the Senate debate, the mover of the bill for the government majority, Senator Flavio Tredese (FI), said: "The law as it is now cannot be applied. It contains some absurdities. We have to correct it, otherwise we will find ourselves with useless rules" (*Corriere della Sera*, 18 September 2002).
8. The five critical points on which the opposition asked the government to negotiate and on which it focused its amendments are listed in the "minority report" presented by DS Senator Giorgio Tonini.
9. O. La Rocca, *La Repubblica*, 23 May 2003.
10. Tonini, *La ricerca e la coscienza*, 97. For a brief but complete overview of European legislation, cf. V. Franco, *Bioetica e procreazione assistita* (Rome: Donzelli, 2005), 118–121.
11. This is the position that Mary Warnock calls the "slippery slope" in *Fare bam-bini: Esiste un diritto di avere figli?* (Turin: Einaudi, 2004), 46.
12. For Catholics, the guiding principles are formulated in *Donum Vitae*, the instruction issued on 22 February 1987 by the Congregation for the Doctrine

of the Faith: protection of life from the moment of conception, condemnation of any form of procreation other than natural sexual intercourse by married couples, and prohibition of any medical procedure involving a human embryo that is not strictly necessary for the health of the embryo itself.

13. See the reflections of S. Rodotà, based in part on the experience in other countries, in *Tecnologie e diritti* (Bologna: Il Mulino, 1995), 147ff.
14. The Radicals subsequently also supported these questions.
15. The Constitutional Court ruled on the questions in its decisions of 28 January 2005, nos. 45-49, available at www.cortecostituzionale.it.
16. The manifesto of the committee and the list of signatories are published in *Avvenire*, 20 February 2005.
17. See the interview with the secretary of the DS, Piero Fassino, in *La Stampa*, 9 May 2005.
18. *Corriere della Sera*, 11 April 2005.
19. C. De Gregorio, *La Repubblica*, 21 May 2005.
20. *Corriere della Sera*, 6 October 2004.
21. Ar.M., *Il Sole-24 Ore*, 18 May 2005.
22. See the reflections of G. E. Rusconi on this point in "La legge sulla fecondazione: Un'occasione mancata di democrazia laica," *Il Mulino*, no. 2 (2005): 221–228.
23. The surveys were carried out in the period November 2004–June 2005. The results are contained in SWG's report, "Il referendum sulla fecondazione assistita" (July 2005).
24. *Corriere della Sera*, 13 June 2005.
25. The model used by the Cattaneo Institute was based on the results of the last general election, combined with two other variables measuring the effects of the positions of the various parties and that of the Church. The prediction was based only on the pool of potential voters obtained by calculating the typical turnout for a referendum. The number of Catholics among each party's voters was used to estimate the influence of the Church. The results of the study are discussed by S. Vassallo in "La 'missione impossibile' di un referendum," *Il Mulino*, no. 5 (2005): 931–935.
26. Ibid., 934.
27. What Salvatore Vassallo calls the "most reliable cognitive short-cut" (cf. ibid., 933).
28. *Il Sole-24 Ore*, 16 June 2005.
29. According to the surveys conducted by SWG, for instance, the percentage who said during the campaign that they were in favor of changes to the law oscillated between 48 percent and 53 percent.
30. M. Bartolini and F. Cerati, *Il Sole-24 Ore*, 15 March 2005.
31. ISPO, "Le questioni eticamente sensibili: Le opinioni degli italiani" (research report, October 2005).
32. Interview with M. Calabresi, *La Repubblica*, 16 June 2005.
33. *Europa*, 28 October 2005.
34. M. Guerzoni, *Corriere della Sera*, 6 December 2005.
35. See on this point the reflections of A. Barbera and S. Ceccanti, "Un principio di maggioranza mitigato contro il rischio di un bipolarismo etico," *Il Riformista*, 20 August 2005.

8

THE ITALIAN CHURCH IN THE YEAR OF THE PAPAL SUCCESSION

Alberto Melloni

Arturo Carlo Jemolo wrote *Church and State during the Last Hundred Years* in 1948. Jemolo, an insightful scholar of a relationship that has been scrutinized from all angles, continually updated his "long-seller," publishing fresh editions at various points. It was even reprinted after his death. By this time, historiographical knowledge of the single segments of that experience had increased in significant ways. Yet there is one reason in particular that explains this book's resistance to both the progress of time and advances in research and illustrates why it still deserves our attention today. Jemolo had intuited the broad chronological dimension that was and still remains indispensable in order to understand the relationship between church and state in Italy. If we did not precisely place the phenomena on a wide parabola, we would, in fact, risk confusing episodes with tendencies, outcomes with processes—and, in the end, become prisoners (if I may pun on the subtitle of the newspaper *Osservatore Romano*) of a "political and religious daily" life in which the ephemeral becomes memorable, and vice versa.

Ever more so today, we need to proceed with caution in evaluating the aspects of the life of the Catholic Church that significantly influenced the course of Italian politics during 2005. The list of memorabilia should be sorted according to less spontaneous criteria than those that normally govern the daily news. Above all, we should at least attempt to reposition the processes in motion in a broader framework, which,

---

Notes for this chapter begin on page 198.

for good or ill, usually has the effect of making what may have seemed "decisive" at the start somewhat less important.

Our first task, therefore, is to evaluate critically the commonly available information concerning the events surrounding the relationship between the state and the Church in Italy during the two six-month periods of 2005. Too often it has been supposed that the papal succession in April and the referendum on law no. 40 in June necessarily constitute the decisive events and turning points of that relationship. It is taken for granted that it is precisely in those experiences that the Church changed its way of acting on the public stage, that thanks to the new pope's anti-relativistic verve and the easy success given by the electoral mechanisms of the referendum, the Church decided (to use a soccer metaphor) to enter the political arena with a sliding tackle, without worrying too much about fouling the right leg of the partisan spectrum, and with even less regard for the left. Each of these popular theses has, obviously, some foundation. Nevertheless, a more profound examination is necessary, taking into account the lines of development that the Italian Church has followed throughout 2005. In this chapter, then, I will first consider the phase of the papal succession and then the Church's attitude toward the referendum in June. In addition, I will analyze the significance of the intense activity of the Conference of Italian Bishops (Conferenza Episcopale Italiana, CEI), the statements and the appointments resulting from the summit of the same conference in the first months of the new pontificate, and the question of the plurality of viewpoints within the Italian Church.

The Death of John Paul II and the Papal Succession

There is no doubt that the papal succession—marked by another smarting defeat of the contingent of Italian cardinals, unable to find among themselves a man worthy of ascending to Peter's throne—was, starting from the build-up to the conclave, an important event for Italian politics as well. In fact, during the weeks of the Pope's deteriorating health, it did not pass without notice that problematic characteristics of Catholicism—and of Italian Catholicism, in particular—were coming to light.

On the one hand, the way in which the Church and the press synchronized themselves in following the final phase of the Pope's long illness was indicative. The papal court's decision to secrete itself and to hide the seriousness of John Paul II's illness was not as such something that was imposed on the media or on the Church. Nonetheless, the question of who was making the decisions for the Pope in those final days and in those final hours was not raised, not even when the last two dozen appointments were announced, without fear of scandal, on 1–2 April, when the Pope was already in the throes of death. At the same time, however, the Pope's suffering, especially in his last heart-rending, mute appearances at the window of the Apostolic Palace, was not the least bit filtered, neither for the mass media nor on the pastoral level. From the open-camera car that brought the Pope back from the Gemelli Hospital to the Palace, to the search for the feeding tube in the photographs of Easter devotions, the television and photograph industries dwelt piti-lessly on the most excruciating details, almost like a "reality show."

Conversely, the response from the diocese of Rome and the local churches followed the most routine lines. There were some more or less solemn liturgical intercessions, but a certain stiffness took hold that reached its apex during the last night of Pope Karol Wojtyla's life, when no one managed to celebrate the mass before a packed St. Peter's Square. In comparison, Cardinal Luigi Traglia had been able to say that mass for John XXIII in 1963. The loving and morbid atten-tion surrounding the Pope's illness provided visual confirmation, once again, that the unity of the Church during Wojtyla's era did not come from a profound communion, sacramental in structure and shared among the parts of the Church. Rather, it confirmed that the unity came from the fact that all of these parts—without recognizing each other, or even in order to *avoid* recognizing each other—turned to the Pope as the holder of a new primacy of communication. There-fore, from the media's point of view, they accepted and suggested the journalistic simplification in which the death throes of a man, ill and beloved like John Paul II, were represented by focusing the camera on him, as if the last and only Catholic was dying.

On the other hand, the organization of the mourning for the death of John Paul II demonstrated an intensity of participation, both quan-titatively and qualitatively, that was of great significance. The Poles came, as did pilgrims mobilized by movements that owed him so much, and the curious poured forth from every part of the world, all to pay homage to the mortal remains of the Pope of the Jubilee. In addition, a significant number of everyday Catholics rushed to pay their respects. These Catholics frequent the parish and attend Sunday mass, but they are not as numerous or as manipulable at election time as some politicians believe. In any event, they still represent today one of the collectivities most ingrained in the fabric of the country—one that is more likely to organize itself than to be organized.

In this mystical-media framework, a conclave took shape that had some original elements. The deafening media noise around the vacant Holy See was in fact an over-amplified rustling that replaced a col-lective discussion of the state of the Church, like those particularly vibrant and fruitful conversations that took place in other similar circumstances during the twentieth century. The "press silence" imposed on the cardinals, which had no grounds in the apostolic constitution *Universi dominici gregis* that John Paul II published in 1996 to regulate the election of his successor, was a fragile innovation. The press and the television stations did not attempt to penetrate this silence with any of the stratagems typical of these circumstances, which usually sharpen journalistic ingenuity because of the very lack of communication. Hypnotized by the enormous crowd that came to Rome, the media refused to reflect on the meaning of this affection for the dying Pope, on the hypocrisy and tame lies flying around the media circus, on the difficulties and the hesitations that punctuated this phase, nor on the fact that no one could account for a grief that overflowed far beyond the boundaries of Catholicism.

A mystical atmosphere even conditioned the interest in the proceedings of the imminent conclave. In April, the floods of discussions and conversations surrounding the preparation for the conclave were sprinkled with some allusions to the prospect of the return, after a quarter of a century, of an Italian papacy. The candidacy of Cardinal Dionigi Tettamanzi seemed to many observers a realistic hypothesis, and it would have meant (as a hypothesis, without considering the outcome) the recognition of the rediscovered pastoral credibility of the largest episcopate in the world. In opposition to Tettamanzi, there was talk of a possible candidacy from Cardinal Camillo Ruini, who, as the newspapers reported, would make a very clear political mark on the peninsula, or—symbolizing a more international political vocation—that of the secretary of state, Angelo Sodano (theoretically penalized by age, which, in the end, did not constitute a problem), whose political vision was broader and more universal. In reality, there does not even seem to have been a conflict between the Italians as there was in the second conclave of 1978, which benefited Wojtyla. And perhaps (admitting for the sake of argument that the fragments of an anonymous diary that Lucio Brunelli used on TG2 television and that then appeared in *Limes* are authentic) they did not even line up behind the candidacy of Martini, though this seemed or seems plausible to some.

Whatever the case, the Italians at the conclave did not have any weight, whether because of the illusory expectation of a chance that never arose, or in order to avoid too sharp a conflict. Not even the packages of votes that they are supposed to have moved did so autonomously. Rather, they followed the general movements of the college, which (according to the diary Brunelli made public) hesitated on the name of Joseph Ratzinger on the morning of 19 April—a hesitation that was potentially fatal for his chances—and then, after a few hours, broke through the threshold of a qualified majority, electing the Bavarian cardinal to succeed the Polish Pope.

Now with the conclave concluded so rapidly, has a new era begun? Time will tell. But in narrative terms, the portrait of Benedict XVI has been sketched: he is a man who has expressed everything he believes, in the categories of the end of the Wojtylian pontificate, in a large library of works and acts of doctrinal government. Crowd presence, communicative ability, the power to intervene in public debate, and verbal activism are measured in vain because not one of these parameters seems to be relevant to a Pope who is, above all, a theologian and a non-Italian. While the news media have a strongly retrospective viewpoint on his papacy, Pope Ratzinger is looking for his own way. He celebrates mass without emphasis, prays without the presence of television cameras, speaks little, does not travel, avoids contact with the masses, and, above all, holds his decisions in abeyance. By the end of 2005, he has made hardly any decisions, and those he has made are hardly indicative. For example, he shortened the synod, nominated an American bishop to the ex-Holy Office, wrote something for an encyclical originally announced for the fortieth anniversary of the close of the Vatican II Council—and then put it off until 2006. But he has not put his hand to anything else. While we wait for the "great papal surprise," which some of the defeated cardinals continue to talk about, we can only make the most of some remarks (the denunciation of the tyranny of relativism and of the hypocrisy of tolerance in secular states), scrutinize the audiences given (to Oriana Fallaci and Hans Küng), decipher the political relationships (like the one with the speaker of the Senate, Marcello Pera, which consecrated him as the interlocutor of that part of the lay ecclesial movement, Communion and Liberation [CL] that is active in the Casa delle Libertà), and analyze the silences (like the one over the fortieth anniversary of the Vatican II Council).

One of the most serious problems during the final phase of Wojtlya's pontificate was the internal antagonism within the papal court, and it has not been resolved. The secretary of state, who was most committed to stemming the autonomous activities of the papal apartment and John Paul II's most intimate circle, not only has been reconfirmed but has been reappointed without any qualifications and therefore, at least in theory, for a five-year term, or until his 80th year. The heads of the departments of the Curia have been reconfirmed, *donec aliter provideatur* (until other provisions are made), which leaves open the possibility of a turnover in the Roman Curia. If this turnover were carried out according to the canonical norms regarding age limits, it could redraw the map of power in the Church's government.

If, therefore, anything relevant happened to the Italian political scene in April, we should not look for it in the succession to the pontificate, the consequences of which will become clear in time and stretch well beyond the narrow confines of the peninsula. Rather, we should see it in the fact that the representation of the Church has been crystallized in a simplified form that is laden with possible effects, and that the CEI, as a result of this further extension of the period of "foreign" papacy, will remain the organ designated to decode Italian politics for the Pope, and vice versa.

The Referendum

Two months after the papal succession, the Church once again became a major participant in political debate, with its commitment to the campaign on the referendum on law no. 40/2004 and with the success it achieved.[1] Though the CEI claims to have been "forced" to take up the referendum challenge, it had also constructed it when it galvanized Catholic politicians to ensure that the passage of law no. 40 in the Senate would take place under the banner of *nihil innovetur* (nothing should be changed). And the referendum challenge was significant. It should be analyzed alongside the papal election proceedings, certainly not in a strict comparison, but for the very different ways in which it was analyzed both in the news media and within the Church itself. The success of the masses of non-voters in blocking the abrogation of the law on artificial insemination had the force of a fact that was eloquent testimony in and of itself. Cardinal Ruini, knowing that abstention had reached comparable levels in the failed referendum votes of the past decade, was the first to deny exclusive credit for that mass of votes. At first, he even found himself in the extremely difficult position of having to "defend" the abortion law, insofar as he gave assurances on live television that the Church was not going to use this easy victory to launch a far more alarming attack on law no. 190. Then, in the space of just a few months, he raised the question again in different terms.

In any event, more than a few people believed, whether with enthusiasm or regret, that in the referendum result they were seeing a kind of epic event. They saw it, in turn, as the comeback victory after the lost referenda on divorce and abortion; the beginning of a neo-centrist recovery; the refoundation of a Catholic activism unburdened by Christian Democratic mediation; the embryo of a clerical-conservatism that flavored the American "theo-cons" with a papal sauce; an assault on the principle of secularism; the end to the separation of church and state, prompted by Ruini's hatred of Romano Prodi; the predominance throughout the entire Church of a new obsession with politics; or the triumph of the newspaper *Avvenire*—a David against the news media Goliaths, *Corriere della Sera* and *La Repubblica*—and the dawning of a new counter-reformation that is setting out to reconquer control over the human body.

In this clash of interpretations, a more internal facet of the make-up of the Italian Catholic Church lies in the background. Though it may be true that there was no internal conflict among the bishops over how to deal with law no. 40 (even if it is well known, for example, that Monsignor Carlo Caffarra did not consider the law strong enough and that Cardinal Tarcisio Bertone in fact broke up the diocesan hospital team who were treating infertility within the limits of law no. 40), nor was there any conspicuous dissent from the instructions of the president of the CEI on the referendum campaign, it is also true that this took place in an atmosphere in which dialogue was limited, both between bishops and within the Church as a whole. Even the position of a dean of the most conservative Catholic philosophy, such as Giovanni Reale, editor of the Pope's writings, was made the object of extensive condemnation in the newspaper *Avvenire* when he reached conclusions different from those of the CEI president. Reale was not even afforded the opportunity of a plea bargain. The action of the electoral committee Science and Life was ancillary to the political line dictated by the bishops in January. This way of operating recalls the Civic Committees that Luigi Gedda constructed in order to condition the Christian Democrats. Instead of showing the significant shades of difference that existed among the promoters as among the defenders of law no. 40, these organs lumped them all together, so as to hold up to public scorn within the Church almost all Catholics who hinted at risks, negative consequences, or problems resulting from abstention (almost all, because there was evidently an indulgence for the president of the Republic, Carlo Azeglio Ciampi, and his wife).

In this way, abstention, a clearly legitimate position, which just as clearly does not involve taking a bold ethical-political stand, became a dividing line. It was used not so much to distinguish the good from the bad or to stimulate an analysis of how it is possible to make decisions on scientific questions or to reveal the differences between approaches or the ethical consequences of various religious traditions. Rather, it served to trigger an internal dialectic within the parties and the coalitions. Betraying a fairly naive vision of the Church, politicians were more worried about not losing the electoral booty that the CEI president would be able to procure for them by indicating to the bishops to indicate to the parish priests to indicate to the laity how they should vote.

The Unknown Side of the CEI

The media's superficial treatment of the year's events should, then, be looked at with caution—not because it reflects the minor episodes, but because the bright light it radiates can cast a shadow on the slower and longer processes, which need a wider temporal context in order to be understood. In fact, although its agenda is still to be determined, the National Ecclesial Congress in Verona in the autumn of 2006 is already in view. Thus, it is ever more necessary to keep in mind the ordinary action of the Conference of Italian Bishops, which held its general assembly in Rome on 18–22 April, and reassembled in Assisi on 14–17 November. This action is carried out on various levels and is rarely considered, although it combines rhetorical exercises and indications of more profound tendencies.

On one level, there are the interventions oriented more toward the internal life of the Catholic Church that come from the presidency of the Conference or from its commissions. Such interventions often fall into the silence of the grave, but they are indicative of a level of interest and of complex expectations, and as such merit our attention. Let us turn now to look at the most important ones that took place in the course of 2005.

First of all, the year opened with a document on Jewish-Christian dialogue, dated 17 January. It was signed by the president of the Commission for Ecumenism and Inter-religious Dialogue, who was then Monsignor Vicenzo Paglia, bishop of Terni-Narni-Amelia and ecclesiastical assistant of the community of Sant'Egido, and by Rav Giuseppe Laras, then the chief rabbi of Milan. This strongly worded document, which reaffirmed the sense of mutual sensitivity and a common reading of the scriptures, was published precisely when the virulent discussion exploded between the accusers and defenders of Pius XII's action during the Shoa, prompting suspicions of broader aims related to the issues raised by Pope Pacelli's actions.[2]

On 25 January, the membership of the preparatory committee for the 4th National Congress, to be held in Verona in September 2006, was finalized.[3] Cardinal Dionigi Tettamanzi was named as the chair of the committee; he was the leading speaker at the 44th Social Week of Italian Catholics in Bologna (7–10 October), where he courageously broke with the policy of indulgence toward Berlusconi's government that the CEI had pursued until that point. The organizing committee of this "estates general" of Italian Catholicism plays a decisive role. Tettamanzi has three vice-chairmen (Luciano Monari, Francesco Lambiasi, and Cataldo Naro) and the secretary general, Monsignor Giuseppe Betori. In the *giunta* (executive committee), names of note included Paola Bignardi, the president of Italian Catholic Action (ACI), and Luigi Alici, who would become her successor a short time later. In addition, other well-known figures include Adriano Roccucci, from the community of Sant'Egidio, sociologist Luca Diotallevi, and theologian Franco Giulio Brambilla. The president of the CEI, for his part, nominated, among others, the president of the Christian Associations of Italian Workers (ACLI), Luigi Bobba; the rector of the Catholic University of the Sacred Heart, Lorenzo Ornaghi; the director of *Civiltà Cattolica*, Father Giampaolo Salvini; the Bolognese economist Stefano Zamagni; and the editor of *Avvenire*, Dino Boffo.

On 31 January, the Permanent Council of the CEI approved the statute of the new Missio Foundation, which, following the model of the other European episcopal conferences, concentrates and directs resources intended for the support of missionary work. As a strategic fulcrum of the international policy of the Italian Church (if only considering the weight that the cardinals from missionary countries have in the conclave), the new foundation constitutes an institutional venue that reduces the weight of the presidency of the CEI and brings different figures together in dialogue in order to define the orientation and methods of its aid to the Third World.

On 19 March, the Commission for Social Problems and Work, Justice and Peace published a document titled "The Rural World and the Italian Church," 30 years after a similar text was published by the CEI at the end of the pontificate of Paul VI. It is an analysis that brings together, if a little extrinsically, rural values and ecological sensitivity ("each farmer, faithful to the land ... feels himself a guardian of creation, with a responsibility to defend and improve it"), and offers suggestions for parochial life in these areas that are no longer the place of origin or the destination of young clergy. The note makes an appeal to politicians, asking them to promote the survival of rural communities, "especially in hilly and mountainous areas."

On 29 April, a document titled "Marriages between Catholics and Muslims in Italy" was published after a lengthy series of discussions among Catholic regional organizations, groups of experts, and agencies. It is a document that is harsh in tone and (alone in Europe) aligned with the theses of the Pontifical Council for the Ministry to Migrants, which suggested, in 2004, a policy of discouraging mixed marriages: "Marriage between Catholics and non-Christian migrants should be advised against, though with varying firmness, according to the religion of each person, excepting special cases, in accordance with the norms of the *codex iuris canonici* (CIC) and of the *codex canonum orientalis ecclesiae* (CCOE)." The CEI considers the juridical and canonical problems stemming from *disparitas cultus*, or the spouses' membership in different religions, in great detail (at the end, there is a form to fill out). However, it does not consider the dimension of recip-rocal love in the same detail, although its existence is not ruled out. In any case, given the civil implications of religious marriage and of its eventual annulment in a situation of *disparitas cultus*, the explicit suggestion is to consider the matter with extreme caution. This is not without significance for politics more generally.[4]

On 10 April, the referendum climate was already being felt in a message issued for the day of fund-raising for the Catholic Univer-sity of the Sacred Heart. Three years after the CEI had intervened to cut short Sergio Zaninelli's rectorship (perhaps because he was guilty of not bowing sufficiently to the claim of CL to hegemonize the university) and had promoted the rise of the political scientist Lorenzo Ornaghi, the Conference announced its support for the uni-versity "particularly in the crucial area of genetic, cellular, and clinical research, knowing that the Catholic University of the Sacred Heart is deeply aware that science must never omit consideration of ethical and spiritual concerns. For this reason, the Italian Church invites the university of Italian Catholics to instill in its different components a responsibility for the fate of humankind, in a multi-disciplinary exchange that is capable of demonstrating how each truly significant scientific advancement attracts the contributions of many other fields of knowledge."[5] It is a message, then, dripping with themes from the referendum propaganda but also containing allusions to the initia-tive of Don Pietro Verzé, founder of the San Raffaele medical empire. Verzé had flanked his scientific laboratories with a private university and a philosophy course given first by Massimo Cacciari and then by Ernesto Galli della Loggia.

On 15 May, the Episcopal Commission for the Doctrine of the Faith published its note titled "The First Announcement of the Gospel," an instrument geared toward evangelization that reflects how both the significance of the Christian message and its most critical points are viewed from within the episcopate. Soon after, on 30 May, the outline drawn up for the Congress in Verona was approved. This kind of docu-ment offers more precise indications on the Congress's general theme ("Witnesses of the Risen Christ, Hope of the World") and follows the model of the first letter of Peter. The biblical reference introduces variations on the five themes of debate (personal relationships, work and holidays, the fragility of creation, tradition, citizenship[6]) for the assembly, now scheduled to take place on 16–20 October 2006.

During the course of the abovementioned CEI assembly in Assisi, the document on the preparation of presbyters and on seminaries was approved. It attempts to introduce an idea of community life into the seminary (the propaedeutic community, the rules of communal life), in reaction to the impression of a hegemony over vocations exercised by the movements, which could aggregate their own seminarians on a national scale and intimidate the dioceses.[7]

The acts that we have briefly reviewed are not without political import, if only because they demonstrate that the most pressing concern of the bishops—or at least of the majority of them—when they meet is not in the first instance the changing Italian political scene but rather the problems of Christian life as it is actually lived. These CEI proceedings often are not classifiable along simple partisan lines. They bear witness to a pastoral attention that exists in the organization of the Conference and whose major political significance is precisely that it is distinct from the political agenda. The latter, however, is never absent from the meetings of the Permanent Council nor from Ruini's inaugural addresses.

Inaugural Addresses and Appointments

One original characteristic of the CEI, compared to other national episcopal conferences, concerns the method of work of the presidency (*consiglio di presidenza*): the vice-presidents of the Conference (the highest elective office, as the CEI is the only conference in the world presided over by a bishop selected by the Pope), are members along with the chairs of the commissions that produced the abovementioned documents. The presidency begins its work with an address by Cardinal Ruini and then most often is reduced to—at least as far as its work is made known to the public—a defense of the controversial political passages that, by now, the news media expect in Ruini's inaugural addresses and that make the rest of his speech seem like padding.

This explains why an episcopal conference that is much more politicized than the others ends up appearing at a loss when very important themes appear on the political horizon. Take, for example, the constitutional reform introducing devolution, which potentially exposes Italy to the risk of a marked division (for instance, should the referendum on the reform highlight the difference between some northern regions and the rest of the country), but no less exposes the Holy See to instability, which was precisely what the presence of Article 7 in the Constitution was supposed to avoid.

The inaugural addresses, in fact, can develop only immediate political themes, as a brief investigation of their language and their structure demonstrates. A careful analysis of Ruini's inaugural addresses—one that would include their lexicon, implicit sources, rhetorical expression, accessibility to the media, and selection or omission of themes—is still wanting. But a cursory reading reveals that no current political topic, no matter how small, is ever overlooked. From an appreciation of the solution of the crisis of Fiat to a constitutional challenge to the possible law on fiscal and contractual privileges for common-law couples, from the iron and steel industry to public works, from taxation to wiretapping—Cardinal Ruini's ability to evoke resonance from the political chords of journalism is such that the proceedings of the ecclesiastical government, the pastoral work of the bishops, the internal dialectic, and finally the background of appointments and internal elections never receive media attention as part of the representation, or self-representation, of the Church.

In 2005, the elections and new appointments within the CEI, for example, were particularly significant and gain increasing importance because, with the papal succession and the passage of time, the leadership of the CEI is destined to be reconstituted, either because any changes will alter the make-up of the organization, or because any confirmations will make it more stable than it appears today. Besides the appointments for the Verona assembly (which we can read as an indication of the favored and less-favored areas of the Church, hardly balanced by the appointments at the level of the regional conferences) the CEI in fact filled, for the next five years, the chairmanships of its own working commissions and of the Council for Economic Affairs.[8] In addition, it elected two new vice-presidents in the persons of Monsignor Luciano Monari, Archbishop of Piacenza, and Monsignor Giuseppe Chiaretti, Archbishop of Perugia.

While in the past the vice-presidency was given to cardinal archbishops, now two personalities who possess a marked spiritual quality and who have been bishops for a decade fill the position. Monari comes from the clergy of Reggio Emilia, where Cardinal Ruini also served. His background as a biblical scholar and spiritual guide has always kept him far away from the political and anthropological arenas that are more familiar to his older confrère. Chiaretti comes from the Rieti clergy and was formerly bishop of San Benedetto del Tronto before his appointment to Perugia. He is one of the Italian bishops with the best preparation in ecumenical subjects and belongs to the plenary of the Pontifical Council for Christian Unity. Neither of these two was chosen as an antagonist for Cardinal Ruini, as far as the centrality of politics in the mission of the CEI is concerned. Objectively, however, a spiritual and pastoral profile such as theirs has become increasingly necessary for a presidency that for years had a not always welcomed counterweight in Cardinal Martini, who in any case effectively "covered" interests and areas of activity that were otherwise ignored. Ruini's presidency also benefited from the intensity of faith stimulated by the charismatic figure of Wojtyla that kept in balance the several political and cultural "levels" of the Conference's activity, which are as many in number as they are monotonic in outcome.[9] Neither of these two new vice-presidents voiced any doubts during the campaign for tactical abstention from voting in the referendum. Yet at the same time, neither is the kind of bishop who is willing to accept developments in the political arena in order to be able to satisfy goals in the pastoral sphere.

The manner in which the new make-up of the presidency will face the delicate political season ahead is still to unfold. The return to a proportional electoral system for the 2006 general election could suggest the introduction of an ethical dividing line (rights of the embryo, same-sex unions, and, above all, euthanasia) that would keep the hierarchy even more in the center of the debate, if it chooses to pick out candidates who are ready to become spokesmen for those causes, at least in principle or in a purely instrumental way. Conversely, it could allow for the return to a leadership that opts for rewarding those Catholics who bring to politics a desire to heal divisions, leaving them to find the necessary ways and means.

Freedom of Speech

Alongside the climate of the new pontificate, the continuing emphasis placed on the referendum victory, and the new power balance within the CEI, the quality of the dialogue within the Church itself also plays a crucial role in redefining the relationship between church and state. The central political issues belong, by definition, to that area of action on which Catholic doctrine can shed some light, but which as such is the subject of general debate leading to conclusions that are fallible, questionable, and provisional with respect to the ultimate goals of justice and peace. The Church in its wisdom meant to underline this aspect by forbidding the clergy to take on active political roles. And the history of republican Italy has shown that the Catholic Church most successfully contributed to the democratic life of the country when it was able to educate men with great intellectual stature and a deep sense of public morality who bore testimony to the fruitful results that could be achieved by a practice of dialogue and freedom of thought born from Church experience that was pursued within the Church as well, and even against the line that it itself indicated.

These kinds of men appeared in the most varied incarnations: Alcide De Gasperi was quite different from Giuseppe Dossetti, as was Aldo

Moro from Beniamino Andreatta. The problem that we find now facing the Church, and thus also indirectly facing politics, is that today that type of training is very limited in the actual practice of the Catholic experience. Similarly limited is the horizon of thought concerning the most wide-ranging issues of social life (Alici highlighted some in the report just cited). These issues simply cannot be reduced to an ethical-moral questionnaire with set answers, which gives zealots and opportunists higher scores than the liberal-minded and the scrupulous.

Some lay organizations—for example, CL, whose leading group formed between the late 1960s and the end of Montini's pontificate and has been left since 22 February 2005 without the charismatic leadership of its founder, Don Luigi Giussani—are also quite visible in the political sphere. Nevertheless, these movements make up but a small fraction of a large Catholic community. Franco G. Brambilla has correctly noted that despite its shrinking numbers, the Church still totals today 7 or 8 million people who regularly attend Sunday mass in Italy's thousands of parishes. It also includes priests who do not aspire to become bishops and militants who do not pursue political positions or contracts in the name of the "visibility of the faith." Some opportunities for discussion have also arisen, stemming from unpleasant events such as the European Parliament's veto of the appointment of Rocco Buttiglione to the Commission of the European Union, or the heckling of Cardinal Ruini by a small group of troublemakers in Siena. In the first case—a possibly malicious parliamentary trap, but one that was certainly elementary in comparison with what happens at the confirmation hearings of the US Congress—Buttiglione's defenders cried persecution. They did not pay much attention, however, to the issue of the relationship between individual rights and the moral opinions of decision-makers, which will certainly come up again. In the second case, Church spokesmen castigated the lack of respect shown to the cardinal. However, they did not question the correctness of the CEI president's accepting an honor offered by an old political hand and by an institution unable to guarantee the winner of its "Liberal of the Year" award an undisturbed ceremony.

Above all, it would be appropriate to examine the faith's ability to humanize this life on earth and those who live it. But in the Catholicism of today, as Enzo Bianchi wrote in a serious and bitter tone on 30 November in *La Stampa*, the inclination toward dialogue is increasingly less widespread. Some bishops may even be pleased about this, if they confuse silence with obedience, passivity with humility, and indifference with docility. And even some politicians may delude themselves that this will make electoral negotiations with the Church easier, as they may think that once the president of the CEI, or a movement that illegitimately claims its support, has been persuaded, everything will be resolved. In reality, precisely the opposite is true. In this bitter silence, barely broken by a few discontented murmurs that are immediately extinguished by press statements, neither Christian nor civic virtue can grow.

Concluding Considerations

While a broader perspective on the new pontificate and its effects on political debate will naturally come only with the passing of time, the elements quickly touched upon in this chapter point out in any case that the relationship between Catholicism and Italian politics must be examined taking into account the linguistic simplification (common to, but just as perilous in, Italian public discourse) that speaks of "the Church" in a rather loose way. In fact, when we say "the Church," we are talking about something of such large and complex dimensions that it is impossible to confine it within the categories of everyday politics. A community that surpasses a billion faithful is represented in Italy not only by great events and by the media's presentation of it (necessary or mercenary, as the case may be), but by many Catholics, very different from each other on the spiritual plane as well as on the political and electoral level. There is no denying that between a neo-catechumenal and a Lefebvrian Lepantist[10] stands an impassable political division, whatever the parish priest, the bishop, or the CEI says.

In sum, we can say that especially after the fateful year 1989, the orientations of Catholics are as diverse as those of the country and do not automatically follow a chain of command leading from the CEI president down to the parishioner of the suburban church. And if it occasionally seems like this happens, it is not due to the strength of the hierarchy but for the opposite reason: the territorial rootedness of the "everyday Catholics" is, in fact, so deep that it transmits a sort of political shudder from the ground up, which the Church absorbs so quickly that whoever is not watching closely would think that the Church had moved votes, when in actual fact they shifted it or even split it apart. Because the Church did not create *doroteismo* (Dorotheism),[11] Christians for socialism, Christians for the "no," the Catholicism of the Lega à la Pivetti of a few years ago, and not even, in this past year, the boycott of the artificial insemination vote—as much as it may warm the hearts of those who believe they have set up a milestone in the history of the Church itself to think so. All of these processes have been the fruit of a complex, two-way dialectic that either has been subject to or has exploited the choices of others and does not constitute proof of temporal power. In a time when politicians seem uncertain of their own reasons and have lost their innocence, there is a widespread idea that in order not to run any risks, it is wise to get or request ecclesiastical support—or conversely, to position oneself in opposition with some attention-seeking statements. But this has little to do with the Church—in the proper and broad sense.

Is it then a question that concerns Ruini (referred to now by his last name like a politician, both by his devoted followers and by his Sienese hecklers)? There are many distinctions to be made here as well. The CEI is very new; it originated during the Vatican Council II, endowing Italy with an institution that other countries had known for decades. Out of respect for the Pope, the primate of Italy, it was decided that the Conference of Italian Bishops, however, would not elect its own president but rather would have him named by the Pope. And Paul VI, in order to make this senate of bishops work, made it his business to appoint presidents who were ready to implement his political intentions (Urbani, Poma, Ballestrero), and secretaries general who would broaden its political horizon (the most important of whom was Bartoletti, who was given the task of organizing the referendum on divorce). With Wojtyla, things changed a little. After the parenthesis of Poletti (the first cardinal vicar also to become the president of the CEI), Monsignor Ruini became secretary general of the CEI in 1986, and then vicar of Rome and cardinal president in 1991. The Polish Pope had in Ruini not only a collaborator, but someone capable of explaining Italian politics to him, and of acting in that forum in the name of the Pope more than in the name of the bishops.

Nevertheless, the power of this "dictating the line," as Giuseppe De Rita correctly observes in *La Repubblica,* does not come from the cardinal, but from those who receive these ideas as amulets around which they dance the dance of obsequiousness (or toward which, as happened more recently, they address catcalls and whistles), even at the risk of praising principles they have not lived by or of contesting someone who is about to disappear from the scene. From this perspective, therefore, there is nothing less fruitful than accusing the Concordat, which devolution, as mentioned above, is threatening with dark clouds. Instead, what should be avoided—at least, for anyone who sincerely takes Christianity and the life of faith to heart—is the temptation to participate in the game of electoral flirtation/negotiation/ blackmail with the Italian Church, for this could only push the Church to act as a lobbyist. And even if it were a lobby for ethical causes, it is not good in a democracy for the Church to be reduced to a lobby. The Church, in fact, has the power that comes from maintaining the balance between principles and life, laws and acts of faith, tradition and fresh ideas. Certainly, there are circumstances in which it cannot recognize constraints and, when the world remains silent, must forcefully bear its own witness. But there are other circumstances in which all the points of view are already in play. In these cases, the Church should bear witness to the simple beauty of Christian life, lived as the fullness of humanity, and in so doing cause peace to grow in the City.

— *Translated by Sheila Das*

Notes

1. On the contents of law no. 40/2004, which limited artificial insemination, and on the referendum to abrogate parts of it, see Chiara Martini's chapter in this volume.
2. If the episcopal document did not get all the attention it deserved, the *querelle* on Pius XII (centering on the orders the Holy Office gave on the future of the French Jewish children who had survived the Shoa in Catholic institutions, which were cited in a review) was the occasion that sparked a violent and profound antagonism between the CEI's newspaper and the paper that had published the first report of the document in question, *Corriere della Sera*. The exchange of verbal blows was so harsh that *Avvenire* (never followed by the *Osservatore Romano*) went so far as to advise Catholics not to read the other newspaper. The *Corriere* in the meantime had announced to its readers its support for the "yes" side in the referenda on artificial insemination, which had now been called, and promised to give readers both sides of the issue. This historiographical episode had still other implications of political interest, specifically when, in the middle of January, the original document of the 1946 decision of the Holy Office was made public by Andrea Tornielli, a former journalist from *Il Sabato*, who had been working for many years at *Il Giornale* as a Vaticanist. Perhaps with a bit of naiveté (Tornielli and a collaborator of his did not understand that the interpolated clause "it is another thing if the parents were to come" referred only to unbaptized babies), someone decided to make an exception to the rules of access to the papers of the Secretariat of State.
3. Cardinal Ruini, in fact, was to complete his term as president of the CEI in February 2006, and at that moment (that is, before the election of a 78-year-old Pope) the fact that this deadline coincided with the age limit for active service in the episcopate, set by canon 411, could have led to the assumption that the Conference of Verona would be presided over by a new president of the CEI. (On 14 February 2006, Benedict XVI confirmed Cardinal Ruini as president of the CEI *donec aliter provideatur* [translator's note].)
4. It is noteworthy, I believe, that the question of the entry of Turkey into the European Union (the Turkey of the throne of St. Andrew, the Turkey of the secularism of Atatürk, the Turkey of prudent re-Islamization) is not a subject of debate: on 25

January, the Permanent Council declared that it was in favor of enlargement, stating that "regarding the path of the European Union, the bishops underlined how the recent signing of the constitutional treaty commits the present 25 countries to its consequential ratification and to its concrete implementation specifically with respect to shared democratic principles, the full respect for religious freedom among them, toward which we hope may also converge those countries, like Turkey, which have received approval for the start of negotiations on entry." The line expressed by the CEI, therefore, is sharply different from the one Ratzinger supported as a cardinal. And it is unclear, even now, whether or not he has kept to the same line after succeeding to the Church's highest office.

5. The message is available on the CEI's Web site at www.chiesacattolica.it/pls/cci_new/bd_edit_doc.edit_documento?p_id = 10457.

6. On this theme, the most political, the outline goes on at length on the problem of citizenship, "in which the dimension of people's civil and social belonging is expressed." The questions for debate follow: What does Christian hope bring to the duty of citizenship? How can civic duty, while reflecting its social and political specificity, be a form of Christian testimony? How can we prevent interest in the big questions that confront citizens in our times from being reduced to a question of ideological battle lines, and instead stimulate forms of meaningful involvement? How can the social doctrine of the Church become a fertile point of reference? Both texts are available on the CEI's Web site (http://www.chiesacattolica.it).

7. This session also published a message to the nation on the fortieth anniversary of Vatican Council II and Monsignor Betori's reflection on the trajectory from the National Congress of the Church in Palermo in 1995 to the upcoming one in Verona.

8. At the end of spring, the chairmen of the episcopal commissions were elected: Bruno Forte (Chieti-Vasto) for the doctrine of the faith, the announcement, and the catechism; Felice Di Molfetta (Cerignola) for liturgy; Francesco Montenegro (auxiliary of Messina) for charitable services and health; Benvenuto Italo Castellani (Lucca) for the clergy and the consecrated life; Paolo Rabitti (Ferrara) for the laity; Giuseppe Anfossi (Aosta) for the family and life; Luigi Bressan (Trento) for evangelization of the peoples and cooperation between churches; Vincenzo Paglia (Terni) for ecumenism and dialogue; Diego Coletti (Livorno) for Catholic education, schools, and universities; Arrigo Miglio (Ivrea) for social problems and work, justice, and peace; Cataldo Naro (Monreale) for culture and social communication; and Lino Bortolo Belotti (auxiliary of Bergamo) for migration. The bishops of Susa, Savona, and San Benedetto del Tronto and the auxiliary bishop of Milan were also elected members of the Council for Economic Affairs.

9. In December, the CEI held a summing-up conference of the Committee for the Cultural Project, during which the new president of the ACI, Luigi Alici, gave an important report on "the crisis of anthropology and the infinity of the person," finishing with a plea for a "free coming together" of Catholics in politics around major ethical and moral issues.

10. The neo-catechumenal movement began in the shantytowns of Madrid in 1964, inspired by John XXIII's words "Christ is present among the poor"; Archbishop Lefebvre rejected the innovations of the Vatican II Council; the Lepanto League is an organization of conservative Catholics (translator's note).

11. The *dorotei* were for many years the dominant centrist faction in the Christian Democratic Party (translator's note).

9

THE GOVERNMENT'S EDUCATIONAL REFORMS: BLUNTED ARROWS, WRONG TARGETS?

Giancarlo Gasperoni

In 2005, the educational policies promoted by the center-right, and in particular by the minister of education, universities, and research, Letizia Moratti, saw several significant developments. No doubt they will be the last chapters of the reforms in this sector passed by the 14th Legislature.

During the year, the government issued four of the six legislative decrees implementing law no. 53 of 28 March 2003 on the comprehensive reorganization of the educational system; two decrees on nursery and primary schools and on monitoring the system's performance had already been issued in 2004. Of particular importance is the decree reforming the "second cycle," approved in its final form by the cabinet on 14 October (after a long process in which more than a dozen drafts were produced under intense time pressure), just three days before the deadline set by the law. This could be the only successful attempt in the history of the Republic to redesign higher secondary education. The reform of the school system had been delayed (Minister Moratti stated in her "programmatic declaration" at the beginning of the legislature that she wanted to "begin the 2002–2003 school year under the new system"),[1] due to disagreements within the majority, financial constraints that dictated changes at "zero cost," and lack of support from the schools, the unions, and, in particular, the local authorities. On the same day, the government issued another decree regulating

---

the recruitment of teachers that, at least formally, raised their level of qualification by requiring that in future all teachers—even in nursery schools—would have to have completed a university program of at least five years. In the university system, a reform of academic programs introduced by the preceding center-left government had almost been phased in. Parliament approved a law in October—again as a result of a hasty process—that introduced significant changes in the method of recruitment of university faculty and their working conditions.

In this chapter we shall outline and discuss these measures. First, however, we shall briefly describe some features of the educational system and some recent developments, in order to place these reforms in context.

The Development and Current Problems of the Italian Educational System

In the 2004–2005 school year, over 2.6 million students were enrolled in higher secondary schools. Although current demographic trends have significantly reduced the number of school-age adolescents (there were, for example, less than 600,000 nineteen-year-olds in 2004, compared to over 950,000 in the mid-1980s), this has had a relatively small impact on student numbers because of the notable increase in the rate of participation in higher secondary school programs. In recent years, the school-attendance rate of the fifteen-to-eighteen-year-old group has been over 80 percent, a level never previously attained (although lower than that in other European countries).[2] In the short interval between the 1999–2000 and 2003–2004 school years, the participation rate jumped by almost 6 percent, an increase due only in part to the raising of the school-leaving age,[3] while regional differences in participation were reduced.

Other tendencies also point to an increased desire on the part of the younger generation to improve their qualifications. The percentage graduating with a higher secondary school diploma has increased, and the percentage who go on to a university degree has also risen compared to a decade ago (fig. 1). Moreover, a growing proportion of higher secondary school students choose to frequent the *licei* (whose programs are designed to lead to university studies) rather than the schools with a well-defined occupational character (the technical and professional institutes), which nevertheless still attract the majority.

These "improvements" in the school system have been accompanied, however, by several problems, some long-standing and others just emerging. The former include social inequalities, especially those related to family background, which still have a major influence on young people's opportunities to continue their education and on the

FIGURE 1 *Students graduating from upper secondary school as a percentage of all 19-year-olds, and students entering university as a percentage of students graduating from upper secondary school, 1980–2004*

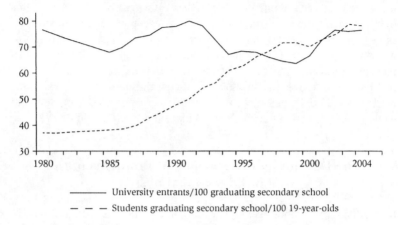

——————— University entrants/100 graduating secondary school

– – – – Students graduating secondary school/100 19-year-olds

Source: Calculated from Comitato Nazionale per la Valutazione del Sistema Universitario, Sesto rapporto sullo stato del sistema universitario: Sintesi (Rome: 2005), table 2.

likelihood that they will leave school before the legal age, have a poor attendance record, or drop out later. In addition, the "quantitative" expansion of education we have described has not meant a corresponding "qualitative" improvement. For several decades, various international studies of students' levels of knowledge and ability have regularly highlighted the weaknesses of Italy's higher secondary schools in comparison both with similar schools in other countries and with the lower levels of the Italian educational system.

The findings of the Programme for International Student Assessment (PISA), an international research project sponsored by the Organisation for Economic Co-operation and Development (OECD), present a picture of Italy's educational achievement that is far from reassuring.[4] The ability of Italian fifteen-year-olds—in reading comprehension, science, and especially mathematics—is significantly below the average for the OECD countries.[5] Moreover, the PISA findings highlight—as similar studies had done in previous decades—a notable and worrying geographical differentiation: students in the Northern regions are superior in ability to the OECD average, while in the South the results are extremely poor.[6] In keeping with a now consolidated tradition, the Ministry of Education, Universities, and Research (MIUR) does not publicize the results of these international tests or stimulate debate on the Italian situation. On the contrary, there are grounds for suspecting that PISA is downplayed in favor of the National Educational Evaluation Service.[7]

An emerging problem stems from the number of foreign students in Italian schools. In the school year 2004–2005, over 360,000 students did not have Italian citizenship, amounting to 4.2 percent of the student population.[8] For almost a decade, the number of foreign students has been increasing by at least 20 percent a year. These numbers—the result of immigration—are destined to grow and have a major effect on the operation of the school system. The children of immigrants have serious difficulties, not only with respect to scholastic attainment (they have little experience of the Italian school system and have the additional hurdles of learning a new language and mastering unfamiliar content),[9] but also in participating in the socialization and integration that also take place at school. The presence of students of non-Italian background in a class is clearly a challenge for educators, since it increases the social heterogeneity of the students (in terms of religious practices, dietary habits, clothing, relations between genders, etc.) and tends to detract from the effectiveness of the instruction given to all students. Both the schools and the teachers must take on the task of cultural intermediation for non-Italian students who come from different cultural traditions.

In addition, the foreign students are not a homogeneous reality within the Italian school system. In the first place, they are not evenly distributed geographically: the non-Italian students are concentrated in the North (they make up 7.4 percent of the student body in the North-East and 6.8 percent in the North-West, but less than 1 percent in the South and the islands) and especially in certain regions (8.4 percent in Emilia-Romagna), provinces (about 10 percent in Mantua, Reggio Emilia, and Piacenza), and cities (11.6 percent in Milan; over 8 percent in Reggio Emilia, Alessandria, Bologna, Cremona, Turin, Modena, Brescia, Rimini, and Prato; nearly 20 percent in some smaller communes).[10] Moreover, their national backgrounds are quite varied: while five countries account for more than half of all foreign students, the fact that these are Albania, Morocco, Romania, China, and Serbia-Montenegro demonstrates the diversity of their cultural origins.

The distribution of foreign students by grade is particularly noteworthy. At present, the non-Italians are concentrated in the lower grades (5.4 percent of the total in primary schools, 4.8 percent in lower secondary schools, 4.6 percent in nursery schools); as they grow up, however, their share of upper secondary school enrollment (now at 2.3 percent) will increase. As noted above, the choice of upper secondary school results in a clear social differentiation, with the upper classes preferring the *licei* and the lower classes the technical and vocational institutes. The increase in the number of non-Italian students could consolidate this segregation and indeed accentuate it, by giving it a further cultural characterization. If the foreign students continue to choose their educational programs as they do now, they will tend to concentrate in the vocational institutes (and, to a lesser extent, the technical schools)—that is, the schools that will give them lower-level qualifications.

In the Italian university system, we can perceive some basic trends that are common to higher education throughout the world: "massification," or the increasingly standardized instruction of large numbers of students, due to the democratization of access to post-secondary institutions; the increasing importance of knowledge for economic development; internationalization; and attempts to introduce forms of competition.[11] These trends have given rise to often contradictory demands that are difficult to reconcile, such as, for example, admitting large numbers of students while maintaining standards of excellence, fostering "high" culture while furnishing workers for the labor market, or allowing students and researchers to gain international experience while discouraging the most talented of them from emigrating. As in other European countries, however, the Italian university system is having difficulty adapting to these trends because it labors under serious constraints, including the conservative tendencies of the academic profession (which has the universities' governing bodies firmly under its control) and the state's inability to increase its funding for universities (based in part on its unwillingness to raise tuition fees).

At the university level, both the pattern of student demand and the courses offered have changed significantly as a result of the reform of degree programs mandated by ministerial decree no. 509/1999 ("Regulation Containing Norms on the Teaching Autonomy of the Universities"). This measure came as part of the policy of increasing the autonomy of the individual universities that was initiated in the late 1980s. The former degree programs lasted four or five years, and the establishment of new programs was subject to strict control by the Ministry. Starting for the most part from the 2001–2002 academic year, they were replaced by a new model, called the "3 + 2," which consisted of a first level of three-year degree programs and a second level of two-year specialized programs. The reform was intended to allow the universities to decide autonomously the requirements for each program, to facilitate transfers by students, to reduce the drop-out rate and the times to complete the degrees, and to make the courses more relevant to the job market.

The "3 + 2" led to a rapid and only partly controlled increase in the number of programs offered: in the 2000–2001 academic year, under the previous regulations, there were 2,260 degree programs (and many hundreds of university diploma programs), but by 2003–2004 there were over 3,000 three-year programs and over 1,200 specialized programs.[12] The reform undoubtedly induced a greater number of young (and not so young) people to go to university (see fig. 1); the numbers then apparently stabilized at around 350,000 students entering first year and 1.8 million total enrollment each year. The first students who have studied under the new regulations are graduating only now, so it is still too early to draw reliable conclusions as to whether they have succeeded in reducing times to completion, cutting the drop-out rate, etc. The first signs are promising, but we cannot yet call the initiatives a success.[13] Moreover, the new regulations have been the subject of many criticisms—especially from professors—for their harmful effects on the "weight" or cultural "quality" of instruction, their introduction of a market-like logic (internships, competition between degree programs), and the increased administrative burden they have caused (evaluation of practical experience for degree credit, subdivision of courses into "modules").[14]

The New "Second Cycle": Unanswered Questions and Structural Tensions

The reorganization of the cycles of instruction in the school system was launched by law no. 53/2003 ("Delegation of Power to the Government to Establish General Norms for Education and Essential Performance Standards in Education and Vocational Training"). Although the content of the reform was in large part left to the government to decide (by means of legislative decrees),[15] the text of the law itself set some major guidelines.

The delegating law divides the educational system into (1) a nursery school level of three years, (2) a "first cycle" (five years of primary school and three years of lower secondary school), and (3) a "second cycle" (which is split into two tracks—education and vocational training).[16] It asserts the "right to education and training for at least 12 years or, in any case, until a qualification has been obtained by the age of 18."[17] This is a reformulation and reinforcement of the requirement to obtain an education that had already been established by several measures in the previous legislature. Law no. 9/1999 and its implementing regulations had increased the length of compulsory education to nine years, starting with the 1999–2000 school year, while law no. 144/1999 gradually introduced the "requirement to attend educational or training programs until the student's eighteenth birthday."

The new legislation differs from the previous provisions in that it uses the expression *diritto-dovere* (right and duty) to obtain an education and—much more importantly—it permits students to satisfy this requirement outside of the school system itself.

On the strictly "scholastic" side, the reform reduces the number of streams and programs at the upper secondary level and redesigns them. It organizes them in only eight types of five-year *licei* (some of which are divided into more than one stream): classical, linguistic, scientific, social-scientific, musical-choreographic, artistic, economic, and technological. From one point of view, this is just a change of terminology, since there is a great deal of continuity between the current types of school and the new ones, which have now been dignified with the *liceo* label. The vocational institutes are not included here, as their programs are transferred to the second track.

The basic thrust of the reform tends to move education out of the schools proper. The new framework envisages educational activity taking place in many venues, including businesses, and tries to rehabilitate vocational training. The regions will have to organize programs (not based in the schools) that will lead to vocational "qualifications" and "diplomas," lasting at least three and four years, respectively. Among the distinguishing features of the reform there is also the "alternation between school and work," in which periods of classroom instruction alternate with periods of work experience. These programs will be managed by the educational institutions within the framework of agreements entered into with businesses, associations, and public and private agencies (legislative decree no. 77/2005). Furthermore, the *diritto-dovere* to obtain an education can be satisfied even by a three-year apprenticeship contract (legislative decree no. 276/2003, art. 48), which not only exonerates a young person from any other educational obligation, but also gives him or her a vocational qualification.

The center-left and the unions attacked the reorganization of the second cycle on the grounds that it subordinated education to the needs of the labor market and was "classist" because it forced students to choose one of the two tracks as early as age 13. Indeed, the contention that the two tracks are of "equal worth" (as the law states) seems indefensible: the second track is bound to attract mainly students from the lower classes and/or those who have performed poorly in primary school, while providing a poorer cultural background and less highly skilled job opportunities.[18] This situation is only marginally ameliorated by the possibilities offered by the law to transfer from one track to the other.

Some opponents of the reform saw another sign of a reinforcement of the mechanism of selection in the part of the decree (art. 5) that seems to furnish a pretext for preventing students who have not obtained a diploma from a classical *liceo* from entering university (an interpretation that the Ministry promptly rejected). Nevertheless, the new regulations seem to restrict the opportunities for those who have chosen a vocational education to proceed to the university level. On the one hand, the fact that the regions must establish vocational training programs lasting "at least" four years seems to imply that they may also establish programs lasting, for instance, five years, similar to those that they already offer now. On the other hand, however, legislative decree no. 226/2005 stipulates (art. 15, sec. 6) that those who complete these programs—even, it seems, if they last five years—can enter university only "after attending a special one-year course." This stipulation is additional to what is required now.

Another distinctive feature of the reform originally was to have placed a greater emphasis on the teaching of English. However, the time allotted to it in the schedules of the *licei* has been reduced (unless the students decide to study English in the periods allocated for a second foreign language). Moreover, the reform provides that in the fifth year another subject should be taught in English. Yet this is impracticable, given the teachers' lack of proficiency in languages and the absence of funding for the plan.

The most questionable aspect of the reorganization of the second cycle is the role of the local authorities. According to Title V of the Constitution (as amended in 2001), the national Parliament retains exclusive legislative power only over "general principles of education" and shares the rest of the educational field with the regions. The regions, however, have exclusive power over vocational education and training. The fear that concurrent power over education could lead to conflicts was proven justified when the government challenged Emilia-Romagna's regional law no. 12 of 30 June 2003, governing various aspects of "access to knowledge," on the grounds that it encroached on the powers of the national Parliament. At the beginning of 2005, the Constitutional Court declared that all of the constitutional arguments raised by the government were unfounded (judgment no. 34, 26 January 2005).[19]

Analogous points of conflict are inherent in the Moratti reform, as can be seen from the history of legislative decree no. 226/2005. This decree limits itself to defining a few "essential standards" that the regions should respect in the development of vocational education and training. Among other things, given that the new legislation requires them to offer only three- and four-year courses, each region will have to decide what to do with the existing five-year professional institutes (in which more 500,000 students are enrolled) and introductory vocational training courses (in which more than 200,000 are enrolled), and, in general, whether simply to meet the "essential standards" or to come up with a wider range of offerings. It is easy to predict that the second track will take on a different shape in the different regions, in terms of its contents, its form, the access to university that it offers, and the composition, pay, and conditions of employment of its teaching staff.

In September, the draft of the legislative decree reforming the second cycle had received non-binding negative opinions from the National-Regional Conference,[20] the Union of Italian Provinces (UPI), the National Association of Italian Communes (ANCI), and the National Council of Public Education. These opinions were motivated by the belief that the reform could not be implemented, especially with respect to vocational training, which they argued had not been funded. The regions were able to persuade the MIUR not to mount any experimental trials of the new regulations before they officially came into effect. In order to implement the reform, schools will have to decide which streams to offer and how to coordinate among themselves, especially in managing the "campuses" that will bring together the *licei* and the vocational educational/training programs. These are decisions that require time because they must be approved by provincial conferences and regional planning bodies. Plus, the process of redesigning the vocational education and training courses will be even more protracted.

The decree on the second cycle was accompanied, as has been stated, by that on the recruitment and initial training of teachers. As set out in law no. 53/2003, the following requirements for intending school teachers (including nursery and primary school teachers, who until now did not need a degree) have been introduced. They must be admitted to special university programs with limited enrollment, obtain a five-year *laurea magistrale*,[21] pass a qualifying examination (*abilitazione*), register with an accrediting body, and complete a "practicum" (*applicazione*) of one year in a school. After this they will finally be able to enter competitive examinations for teaching positions, open only to those who meet these requirements. This curriculum will have a strong regional basis, inasmuch as the number of places available in the university programs will be determined primarily by the need for teachers in the regions where these programs will be offered, and the future teachers will be required to register in a particular region before undertaking their practicum.

The reform, nevertheless, regulates access to the teaching profession only for "state schools." The new system of recruitment, thus, does not cover private schools or the vocational education and training programs. For the latter, legislative decree no. 226/2005 (art. 29) requires the regions to appoint people who are "in possession of the *abilitazione*" (and who have thus not necessarily done the year of *applicazione*, much less won a competition by examination) or "experts with documented experience of at least five years." Outside of the *liceo* system, therefore, there will be little guarantee of the professional qualifications of the teachers and of the quality of teaching. Not only this, but it is reasonable to expect that the current regular teachers in the vocational institutes will view their new position as a loss of status and will naturally resist it.

The new system sets out to lower the average age of teachers when they are hired as permanent staff. The path of entry into the teaching career, however, remains a long one: five years of university education (plus any additional time taken to complete the degree), one year of *applicazione*, and a waiting period of up to three years for the examination. Moreover, granted that the new method of recruitment guarantees that the teachers will be better prepared, the fact remains that only half of the permanent positions will be filled by the competitive examinations. The other half will, as is the case now, be reserved for those who are on the permanent waiting lists, which will constitute the only means of access to permanent jobs for the current contract and sessional teachers. Already now there are warning signs of friction between teachers without permanent positions who have carried on for years with annual contracts and younger teachers who have graduated from the new, specialized secondary education programs, who are indeed equipped with a specific preparation, though not with any teaching experience, and are ranked ahead of the former on the waiting lists. The new regime will heighten these conflicts.

On this front, the Ministry has taken steps in the last few years to reduce both the numbers of the "historic" non-permanent group and the resulting delays in filling the teaching staff at the beginning of every school year. In October, the government approved a three-year plan to give permanent status to 65,000 teachers (35,000 had already been hired)—thereby following a standard practice around election time[22]—without, however, any consideration of the implications of the reorganization of the school system for the distribution and role of higher secondary teachers, especially in the vocational institutes. Thus, the problem of managing the inevitable structural tensions has been left to the future on this point as well.

University Faculty

On 25 October 2005, the Chamber of Deputies approved a government bill—passed by the Senate in September and originally presented (in February 2004) by Moratti—that introduced significant changes in the recruitment process for university faculty. Public interest became aroused not so much by the measures themselves but rather by the media's coverage of a few negative reactions. These took the form both of articles and letters in the press, often written by university professors (who took advantage of their privileged access to the mass media), and, especially in the autumn, of demonstrations by students and university staff, periodic interruptions of teaching, and occupations of university buildings. The law[23] has several objectives that are distinct from one another: (1) the elimination of the position of "researcher" (roughly analogous to the rank of assistant professor in North America); (2) the reform of the so-called legal status of professors; and (3) the modification of recruitment procedures for university professors.

The new law "eliminates" the position of researcher, in that it sets a final date for posting appointments to the position. After that deadline (which is rather far away, September 2013) the position will in effect cease to exist. The research and teaching now carried out by the researchers will be covered by means of "limited-term private law contracts," which—posted and administered directly by the individual universities—"may have a maximum duration of three years and can be renewed for a total duration of six years." Thus, the position of university researcher will be replaced by that of contract faculty member. These new contract faculty will receive compensation "in relation to that of the current confirmed researchers" but also according to "general criteria established by a decree of the minister." The contract faculty will not enjoy the security of a permanent position and will have, in the best-case scenario, "only" six years at their disposal to win a permanent appointment.[24]

The reform was criticized by the current researchers, who are grandparented into a residual category (*ruolo ad esaurimento*),[25] by those who wished to apply for the position (who foresee a future of employment without permanent status), and by the trade unions. According to the critics, young scholars who have completed a doctorate or a medical specialization will face a longer wait than they do now before establishing themselves stably in an academic career—and might even find the idea of emigration more appealing, thus swelling the "brain drain" that the reform is intended to stem. The opinion of the Conference of Rectors of Italian Universities (CRUI) was also decidedly negative, and this view was shared by the National University Council (CUN) (representing the various academic disciplines) and the National Committee of the Conferences of Deans of Faculties. They were prepared to support the transformation of the position of researcher into a third level of the professoriate, and were concerned about the effects on young scholars of limiting the opportunities to establish themselves in a career, as well as the consequences for the quality of research and teaching and the increased costs entailed by the need to offer competitive contracts.

According to supporters of the reform, the criticisms of the elimination of the position of researcher reflect the resistance of the Italian academic culture to the notion of competition.[26] They argue that the permanent contracts awarded to Italian researchers are not found in other university systems, where it is widely recognized that a scholar needs to give evidence of productivity and competence over a period of many years and that those who do not measure up should leave the profession. However, new researchers already must go through a procedure of confirmation after the first three years of service; thus, the new arrangement is not, from this point of view, radically innovative. The fact that the confirmation decision is almost always positive, on the other hand, proves the propensity of the academic class not to dismiss mediocre scholars—a tendency that the new law probably will not diminish. Still, the current system of recruitment has not in fact facilitated young scholars in beginning a university career (see below).

The fact remains that the increasingly unstable conditions for young scholars, brought about by the new law, are unlikely to be effectively outweighed by better salaries. The government made another seemingly curious proposal: it envisaged bringing forward the researchers' confirmation to one year (as opposed to three) after their initial appointment, in order to improve the pay of junior researchers, with the objective, according to the minister, of "keeping the best young scholars in our universities." While improving junior researchers' pay is laudable, to achieve this goal by weakening the confirmation procedure (one of the few occasions when faculty are evaluated by the university) makes less credible the government's announced commitment to criteria of competitiveness and to rewarding merit.[27] Even CRUI, often accused of fighting only to maintain corporate privileges, opposed the measure.

The new law also regulates, as stated above, the "legal status" of professors and introduces changes of various types in their conditions of work.[28] In its intentions, the law introduces a system of incentives aimed at rewarding the ablest professors. For example, it states that professors may be paid an "additional salary ... with respect to their additional commitment to research, teaching, or administrative duties to which they have been specifically assigned, or with respect to the results they have achieved, according to the criteria and procedures defined by ministerial decree." Nevertheless, this option of differentiating conditions of employment is only "possible" and is subject to the "availability of funds."

Before examining the modifications introduced to the recruitment procedures for university professors, we must briefly outline the pre-existing appointment process. Until 1998, associate and full professors were recruited by means of national competitions, which occurred biennially. In fact, because of the conflicts and laborious negotiations within the assessment committees, which were controlled by the "barons" of the various academic disciplines, the competitions lasted for many years, postponing the posting of the next competitions and raising the number of hopefuls, which in turn slowed down the work even more. Moreover, appeals to the courts by unsuccessful candidates blocked the appointment of the winning candidates, which caused even more delays.

To eliminate these obstacles (and to bestow greater autonomy on the universities), in 1998 the national competitions were replaced by "comparative evaluations" carried out by individual universities. Each assessment committee was required (until 2000) to declare three candidates *idonei* (suitable) for the position; subsequently, this number was reduced to two and then (since 2005) to only one. The work of the committees became noticeably faster. Nevertheless, the highly decentralized nature of the recruitment process gave internal candidates a considerable advantage in the comparative evaluation process. Numerous other factors helped account for their relative advantage: the teaching staff employed in the faculty concerned lobbied for career advancement; that faculty designated one member of the assessment committee (who therefore represented their interests); the university had a significant economic incentive to "hope" that a scholar who was already on their staff would be declared *idoneo*.[29] Such recruitment mechanisms have functioned more as a means of career advancement for insiders (who usually continue to perform the same duties as before, but at a higher cost) than as a way of bringing in new talent, or even just faculty with experience elsewhere. In fact, the overwhelming majority of the professorial positions advertised under the latest regime have been won by candidates who already worked at the same university. Moreover, the average age of newly appointed researchers over the last few years (38 in 2001, 44 in 2002, 39 in 2003)[30] suggests that this is anything but a way of recruiting "young" scholars.

The new law provides that competitions for positions as associate and full professors will be advertised every year directly by the MIUR, according to the requirements indicated by the universities and the funding provided in the budget (in this way the government controls in advance the number of positions that are advertised). There will be single national committees for all the positions at each rank in each discipline. The justification for this reform is that it will reduce favoritism, weaken corporate privileges, and introduce more meritocratic criteria.

However, nothing in the text of the law—particularly with regard to the composition of the assessment committees—leads one to think that the problems that plagued the national competitions before 1998 will be attenuated. If anything, the new procedures will strengthen the powers of co-option of the "barons" (who will not have to abide by the decision of the individual faculty that advertises the position, as they do now),[31] will limit the autonomy of the individual universities (without introducing elements of competition), and will be neither more nor less meritocratic than the procedures that existed until 1998. The law abolishes the current recruitment system with immediate effect, so that the new places can be advertised only after the government issues an implementing decree, which it could easily neglect to do in the usual confusion at the end of the legislature. Finally, it is completely reasonable to expect that the funds allocated by the universities to consolidate their permanent faculty complement will be expended, for a longer or shorter period, to recruit researchers—that is, to swell the ranks of this "residual" category.[32] With respect to the meritocratic criteria that the national competitions are supposed to promote, it moreover seems incongruous that some positions are reserved for individuals whose only merit is to have accumulated a certain number of years of seniority.

The governing bodies of the universities accuse the new law of "loading all of the additional financial burdens onto the universities ...: the stipends for the extra tasks taken on by the teaching staff, which must be paid out of university funds; the financing ... of an adequate number of positions for associate and full professors ...; coverage of future appointments of *idonei* and of appointments of professors from abroad; increased costs resulting from the types of contracts it envisages, particularly for 'young' faculty" (motion of CRUI, 13 October 2005). And all of this is to take place against the background of budget proposals that reduce notably the funding for universities.[33]

The expansion of the universities' autonomy, which began more than 15 years ago, sought to promote competition among universities (and thus achieve differentiation within the university system) and to weaken the bureaucratic control of the Ministry. This period of autonomy has not achieved the hoped-for results, in part because of the conservatism of the academic class, which is engaged in managing resources according to its own corporative criteria, and in part because the changes that were undertaken were inadequate. The reforms did not introduce financial mechanisms that rewarded quality in research and teaching, nor did they find a way to restructure the governance of the university system in such a way as to limit the power of the professors.[34] Some mechanisms of evaluation—the National Committee for the Evaluation of the University System, the Steering Committee for the Evaluation of Research, and evaluation units set up in individual universities—have been organized, but their effect on the distribution of funds remains limited, just as "earmarked revenues" (flowing from agreements with external bodies, contracts, sales of services, projects of significant national interest financed by the MIUR, etc.) are of limited importance among the sources of funding for the university system.[35]

Conclusion

Although the reform of the second cycle has been passed into law, its effective implementation has remained in a state of suspension. As stated above, following the decisions made in September by the National-Regional Conference (which is gaining in significance as a privileged venue for coordinating educational policy), the new regime will not begin to come into effect before the 2007–2008 school year. By then, either there will be a center-left government that is inclined to suspend the reform, or, if the center-right is re-elected in the coming election, a different minister. (The urgency that the government displayed in its efforts to pass the reforms discussed here can also be put down to the need to embellish the minister's "calling card," in view of her expected candidacy for mayor of Milan for the Casa delle Libertà,[36] which was mooted from May on and made official in December.)

In any case, whether it is actually possible to implement the new second cycle will depend on the ability of the schools and administrations to adapt to the reformed system and on that of the local authorities to institute the vocational education and training track. They will have no funding allocated for the purpose (on the contrary, they will probably have fewer resources than in the past), and they will have to deal with conflicts within their jurisdictions between political forces and economic interests, and among the teaching staff as well. Moreover, we can reasonably expect that the system will be geographically differentiated; indeed, differences have already appeared in the pilot projects undertaken in some regions following the framework agreement signed in June 2003 by the MIUR, the Ministry of Labor and Social Policy, and the local authorities. The innovations in the university sector will also require collaboration between the .Ministry and the universities, both to negotiate the implementing decrees (assuming that the government wants to negotiate) and to ensure that the systems for evaluating research and teaching, which everyone is calling for, work as they should.

Within the center-left, some are promising to suspend the reform, if they form the government, while others repeat the call "not to erase everything," if only in order not to lose any more time in the extenuating process of formulating new policies.[37] In any case, the reforms approved at the end of the legislature have several important features in common. To begin with, their implementation will be at "zero cost" to the national government; indeed, they shift to other bodies not only the associated costs (the regions and the other local authorities for the training component of the second cycle, and the individual universities for the legal status of the faculty and, in part, the running of the national competitions), but also the management of the social conflicts that will be sparked by the changes and the responsibility for the weakest sectors of education that will need the most support (vocational education and training). To these we can add the opposition of major organizations representing the institutions involved (the National-Regional Conference, UPI, ANCI, and CRUI), which has highlighted the government's tendency not to pay attention to other views.

The reforms that have been set in motion do not contribute to the solution of crucial questions, such as the improvement of the quality of instruction, the development of research, and the restructuring of university governance. Therefore, they appear to be, in large part, only superficial. They are intended to show that the government has faced up to some issues, that it has taken action, and that it has introduced tangible changes. But these will probably have little impact on the most important problems.

— *Translated by Anna Edwards*

Notes

1. On her programmatic declaration and initial actions as minister, see G. Capano, "A Manager in Education," in *Italian Politics: The Return of Berlusconi*, ed. P. Bellucci and M. Bull (New York: Berghahn, 2002), 203–222.
2. OECD, *Education at a Glance: OECD Indicators 2005* (Paris, OECD), indicators A1, A2, and C2 (http://www.sourceoecd.org/education/9264011900).
3. A. Micali, ed., "La scuola in cifre 2005" (Rome: Ministry of Education, Universities and Research, General Directorate for Research and Planning, 2005). The participation rate is an overestimate, as the numerator includes students of all ages, including those older than the norm for higher secondary school.
4. PISA is a program that involves the assessment every three years of the level of educational attainment of fifteen-year-olds in the school systems of several dozen countries (http://www.pisa.oecd.org).

5. OECD, *Knowledge and Skills for Life: First Results from PISA 2000* (Paris: OECD, 2001); *Reading for Change: Performance and Engagement across Countries* (Paris: OECD, 2002); *Literacy Skills for the World of Tomorrow: Further Results from PISA 2000* (Paris: OECD, 2003); *Learning for Tomorrow's World: First Results from PISA 2003* (Paris: OECD, 2004); *Problem Solving for Tomorrow's World: First Measures of Cross-Curricular Competencies from PISA 2003* (Paris: OECD, 2004) (http://www.pisa.oecd.org).

6. A Martini, "Il rendimento scolastico italiano: Valori nazionali e differenze regionali," *Il Mulino*, no. 3 (2005): 473–483; M. Foresti and A. Pennisi, "Fare i conti con la scuola," 24 October 2005 (http://www.lavoce.info).

7. The National Educational Evaluation Service is located in the Istituto Nazionale di Valutazione del Sistema Educativo di Istruzione e di Formazione (INVALSI), the current incarnation of an agency created in 1979 and reorganized in November 2004. Since the 2002–2003 academic year, INVALSI has collected data on pupils' levels of achievement, largely on a voluntary basis. Starting in the 2005–2006 school year, primary schools will be required to participate, and this obligation will be extended to other schools as provided by law no. 53/2003 (cited above), which requires "periodic and systematic monitoring of the knowledge and ability of the students and of the overall quality of instruction" (Article 3).

8. These figures are an underestimate, above all because they are based on a survey that did not include information on a small number of schools or those foreign students whose national origin was unknown. Moreover, the figures do not include those students who held Italian citizenship but one or both of whose parents were foreigners (MIUR, "Alunni con cittadinanza non italiana. Scuole statali e non statali: Anno scolastico 2004/05" (Rome, 2005).

9. MIUR, "Indagine sugli esiti degli alunni con cittadinanza non italiana: Anno scolastico 2003–2004" (Rome, 2005).

10. MIUR, "Alunni con cittadinanza non italiana"; Eurydice, *L'integrazione scolastica dei bambini immigrati in Europa* (Brussels: European Commission, 2004).

11. A. Wooldridge, "The Brains Business: A Survey of Higher Education," *The Economist*, 10 September 2005.

12. To this number we should add about 180 "single-level" specialized degree programs, five years in length, that have been established in some sectors of medicine and pharmacy (in conformity with European rules) and of architecture. See Comitato Nazionale per la Valutazione del Sistema Universitario (CNVSU), *Sesto rapporto sullo stato del sistema universitario: Sintesi* (Rome, 2005) (http://www.cnvsu.it), and A. Micali and M. Scalisi, eds., *L'università in cifre 2005* (Rome: MIUR, 2005).

13. CNVSU, *Sesto rapporto*, part 1.

14. For an example of "cultural" resistance to the reform, see G. L. Beccaria, ed., *Tre più due uguale zero: La riforma dell'università da Berlinguer alla Moratti* (Milan: Garzanti, 2004). In recent years the Ministry has, however, felt the need to limit the proliferation of programs, setting some minimum requirements (for instance, with respect to the student-faculty ratio) for the establishment and continuance of programs and introducing some changes in the programs for the specialized degree (now called *laurea magistrale*, which could be translated as "master's degree"; see ministerial decree no. 270, 22 October 2004). The inordinate growth in the number of programs can also be attributed to the geographical proliferation of universities: Italy now has over 80 universities, and university courses are offered in over 200 communes.

15. To implement the law, the government issued six legislative decrees, dealing with, respectively, the reform—now already under way—of nursery schools and the first cycle, that is, primary schools and lower secondary schools (decree no. 59, 19 February 2004); the reorganization of INVALSI (decree no. 286, 19 November 2004); the right and duty to attend school (decree no. 76, 15 April 2005); cooperative work-school programs (decree no. 77, 15 April 2005); the reform of the second cycle (decree no. 226, 17 October 2005); and the recruitment of teachers and their initial training (decree no. 227, 17 October 2005).

16. This appears to be a reversal of the basic scheme of the "reorganization of the cycles" introduced by the preceding government, whose launch was "suspended" by Silvio Berlusconi's government shortly after it took office in 2001. This plan would have reduced the total length of primary and secondary education to 12 years, by combining primary and lower secondary school into a single "primary" cycle of 7 years. This reform, steered through by Luigi Berlinguer and Tullio De Mauro, ministers of education in the period 1996–2001, aimed to let students complete school one year earlier. The Moratti reform, which keeps the total length of schooling at 13 years, tries to accomplish the same goal by allowing parents to start their children in nursery school or primary school if their third or sixth birthday, respectively, falls on or before the following 30 April. This provision was hotly debated: opposition was more due to the concern that children should not leave the home too early than to other serious considerations, such as the greater range of ages in each class that could have resulted and the pedagogical difficulties that this would have created. The government abandoned the idea of counting "attendance at nursery school for the three years ... as a possible credit toward at least one year of compulsory schooling." This proposal—contained in the minister's July 2001 "programmatic declarations"—would have permitted students to complete school earlier. Beyond this, the reform of primary education—which included, among other things, new flexible timetables, individualized programs of study, the introduction of tutors, and the updating of methods of evaluation—led to certain difficulties in the schools, if only because a considerable number of innovations were introduced simultaneously (starting in September 2004) in nine different grades.

17. In fact, therefore, compulsory schooling may last only 11 years, as a child may still be enrolled in the first year of primary school as late as the eve of his or her seventh birthday.

18. A. Schizzerotto, "Le false promesse dell'alternanza scuola lavoro," 11 March 2003 (http://www.lavoce.info).

19. At the beginning of 2004, the Court had ruled in favor of Emilia-Romagna in its challenge to the 2002 budget law, which contained some provisions concerning the regulation of regular teaching complements that encroached on regional powers.

20. The complete name is Conferenza Permanente per i Rapporti tra lo Stato, le Regioni e le Province Autonome di Trento e Bolzano (Standing Conference on Relations between the State, the Regions, and the Autonomous Provinces of Trento and Bolzano).

21. See note 14 above.

22. G. Scaminaci, "Elezioni e assunzioni," *Il Sole-24 Ore Scuola*, 3–16 June 2005, 6. We can view in the same context the signature in September of the collective agreement for the school sector (which had expired over 20 months before), with a monthly increase of 130 euros for the teachers and 100 euros

for the technical and administrative personnel. The salary increases affected, in total, more than a million workers. It has been calculated that there are 127,000 teachers without permanent appointments (to whom we can add more than 70,000 non-teaching personnel), whose acquisition of permanent status could be facilitated by the anticipated retirement of many thousands of teachers in the next few years.

23. Law no. 230 of 4 November 2005, "New Provisions Concerning University Faculty and Delegation of Power to the Government to Reorganize the Recruitment Process for University Professors."

24. Contract teaching staff, without permanent positions, have been central figures in the university system for some time. Since the end of the 1990s, their numbers have risen considerably so that there are now more than 25,000, that is, one-third of the entire university teaching staff (Micali and Scalisi, *L'università in cifre 2005*, 18–19).

25. While the current researchers would remain in their jobs as members of the residual category (*ruolo ad esaurimento*) of researchers, they feared that their career advancement might be blocked because their positions as researchers would disappear if they were appointed to a higher rank, while at the same time there might be fewer contractual improvements in the future for a shrinking category.

26. R. Perotti, "Università, mancano ancora incentivi e concorrenza," 9 December 2004 (http://www.lavoce.info); "The Italian University System: Rules vs. Incentives," in *Annual Report on Monitoring Italy 2002* (Rome: Istituto di Studi e Analisi Economica, 2002) (http://www.isae.it/report_Monitoring_Italy.htm).

27. T. Jappelli, "Un provvedimento incoerente," 7 February 2005 (http://www.lavoce.info). The proposal was then implemented only with respect to the timing of the salary increase, without modifying the duration of the trial period (decree law no. 7 of 31 January 2005, art. 1; law no. 43 of 31 March 2005).

28. For example, university professors must undertake "350 hours a year of teaching, of which 120 must be classroom instruction." This is the only explicit quantification of a professor's duties in the university, and it is quite generous. Nevertheless, it represents an increase in the teaching load, which permits the university system to offer without additional costs the increased number of programs that have been set up in the past few years as a result of the "3 + 2" reform.

29. D. Rizzi, "Università: il processo decisionale dei concorsi," 5 November 2002 (http://www.lavoce.info); D. Rizzi and P. Silvestri, "Mercato, concorrenza e regole nel sistema universitario," *Mercato, Concorrenza, Regole*, no. 1 (2001), and "I docenti," *Università Obiettivo Valutazione 2—Documenti*, no. 1–2 (2003): 93–155.

30. Figure 1.4.4 in Micali and Scalisi, *L'università in cifre 2005*.

31. The debate around the reform allows us to distinguish between two academic roles that exercise power: first, those who govern the university institutions (such as rectors, deans of faculties, and directors of departments) and who strongly opposed the reform, and, second, those who control, by unofficial means, the academic disciplines and whose power of co-option was reduced by the comparative evaluations of 1998. Other concessions to these "barons" in the law are (1) the choice of the pool of potential national committee members by election (instead of by lot, as in the original bill), and (2) the exceptional provision that "in the first two annual competitions at the full professor level, the maximum number of candidates who can be declared suitable [*idonei*] relative to the requirements indicated by the universities [is] increased by 100 percent of these same requirements."

32. F. Donzelli, "Università, la riforma del Gattopardo," 24 October 2005 (http://www.lavoce.info).

33. The text of the motion was included in a paid advertisement that was published by CRUI on 19 October in some daily papers. The National Committee of the Conferences of Deans of Faculties went so far as to appeal to the president of the Republic not to sign the law.

34. P. P. Giglioli, "On (Not) Coping with Mass Higher Education: The Italian Experience," in *Transition to Mass Higher Education Systems: International Comparisons and Perspectives* (Haifa: S. Neaman Press, 2006); G. Capano, *La politica universitaria* (Bologna: Il Mulino, 1998).

35. In 2004, "earmarked revenues" from the MIUR and from other sources accounted for 4.1 percent and 8.2 percent, respectively, of the total revenue of the universities. The largest part of their income (59.8 percent) comes from the "original funding account" administered by the MIUR. Its distribution among the individual universities does not depend in any way on the quality of the research done, and depends only in a quite limited way on the student/faculty ratio (CNVSU, *Sesto rapporto*).

36. A. Figà Talamanca, "Che c'entra l'università col sindaco di Milano," *Il Riformista*, 18 October 2005, 7.

37. See, for instance, the interview with Andrea Ranieri, the head of schools policy for the Left Democrats, in *Il Manifesto*, 7 October 2005.

10

MORTAL RISKS? THE PROBLEM OF ITALY'S INTERNATIONAL COMPETITIVENESS

Grant Amyot and Francesco Marangoni

In 2005, the flagging competitiveness of the Italian economy, which had preoccupied journalistic and academic commentators for the past two or three years,[1] was brought forcefully to the attention of public and politicians by the sudden upsurge of Third World competition, especially from China. With the ending of the Multifiber Agreement on 1 January, Chinese clothing and textile products were allowed free entry into the European Union, and Italy, with its large number of firms in this sector, was especially vulnerable.

Chinese production costs for shoes, for instance, were one-sixth of Italian costs; and with the opening of the world market, Chinese prices were reduced from their previous already low levels. In the first four months of 2005, exports of T-shirts from China to the EU increased by 187 percent over the same period in 2004, while prices fell by 36 percent; the story for other products such as women's underwear, boots, shoes, and trousers was similar.[2] Over the whole year, total Chinese exports to Italy rose by 19.5 percent, bringing Italy's bilateral trade deficit to 9.5 billion euros.[3]

Some 200,000 jobs in the Italian textile and clothing industry were considered at risk, and the Northern League (Lega Nord, LN) was quick to take advantage of the alarm with the demagogic demand that Italy impose tariffs on Chinese imports, well knowing that as a member of the European Union, Italy cannot do so. In June, the EU negotiated a temporary

---

agreement with China that allowed it to limit the importation of 12 products until the end of 2007, but this transitional measure can only postpone the inevitable adjustments that European producers will have to make.

But the problems for Italy's international competitiveness were not limited to the challenge from the Far East. The comparative data on its competitive capacity, relative to those for many other European countries, painted a grim picture: in 2005, Italy repeated its disastrous result of the previous year when it slipped to forty-seventh in the rankings of the World Economic Forum's *Global Competitiveness Report*,[4] the second-to-last position among the EU countries. This was seen as further evidence of Italy's structural inability to respond promptly to crises, while most of the European states, especially the northern ones, were able to do so successfully.

In this chapter we cannot do full justice to the economic and political origins of this problem. In what follows we shall concentrate on the most important developments related to Italy's competitiveness as it became a more and more central theme of discussion during the course of 2005. First, we shall trace the debate on the issue as it evolved over the year. Then we shall describe the measures adopted by the government to address the problem over the medium to long period and analyze the reactions of the major interest groups. Finally, we shall suggest an initial interpretation of the attempts by the "Italian system" to regain lost ground in the international market.

The Debate on Competitiveness: Diagnoses and Prescriptions

The threat posed by low-cost Chinese competition was in fact only the most evident symptom of the malaise from which Italy's economy has been suffering. Its growth rate over the past 12 years has been the lowest in the European Union (see table 1), which has itself experienced slow growth compared to both the US and its major Asian competitors. According to the Organisation for Economic Co-operation and Development (OECD), in 2002 and 2003, Italy's growth was at a rate of only 0.4 percent.[5] A principal reason for this stagnation is that Italy's share of world merchandise exports fell from 4.8 percent in 1996 to 3.8 percent in 2004, when Italy's merchandise trade showed a deficit for the first time since the dark days of 1992.[6]

The immediate causes of this fall in competitiveness are also not difficult to identify. Since 2000, labor productivity growth has actually been negative, so that unit labor costs have risen significantly (by 23 percent relative to major competitors).[7] Germany, by contrast, has seen a significant fall in unit labor costs and a major export boom since the introduction of the euro in 1999 (see table 2).

Part of the explanation for Italy's faltering performance is its concentration in more mature product markets, including clothing, textiles, and leather goods, where competition is more intense and demand less dynamic, and on slower-growing markets, such as the EU.[8] Yet another significant factor, of course, is that since adopting the euro, Italy no longer has the weapon of competitive devaluation with which to offset rising relative costs—hence the calls by some representatives of the LN for Italy to withdraw from the European Economic and Monetary Union (EMU). In truth, entry into the EMU has brought in its train many significant advantages, among them lower interest rates, lower inflation, greater fiscal discipline, and a national system of bargaining that has delivered wage moderation. If in spite of these significant gains the Italian economy is still losing ground, it is not clear that the exchange rate of the euro—though it did rise through 2003 and 2004 before declining slightly in 2005—is to blame.

Beyond these immediate explanations, diagnoses of the structural problems facing the Italian economy have been numerous. The minister of the economy, Giulio Tremonti, himself published a much discussed short book in December 2005.[9] In it, he focused attention on the Chinese threat and the inability of Europe to meet such unfair,

TABLE 1 *Average GDP growth rates in the major EU Members, 1991–2003 (percent)*

Italy	1.4
France	1.7
Germany	1.5
Spain	2.6
UK	2.3
EU-15	1.9

Source: A. Ricci, *Dopo il liberismo* (Rome: Fazi, 2004), 174.

TABLE 2 *Exports (goods and services) as a share of GDP, 1998 and 2003 (percent)*

	1998	2003
Italy	27.0	26.6
Germany	29.6	37.5

Source: Calculated from OECD national accounts data.

low-wage competition without taking vigorous measures to defend itself.[10] Pointing the finger at China and placing the onus of responding on the European Union, however, seem like an exculpatory plea by the man who was responsible for Italy's economic policy for most of the past five years and an attempt to build a bridge to the LN, Tremonti's partner in the "axis of the North" within the coalition.

For the majority of Italian economists and business leaders, Tremonti's pamphlet is focused more on the headline-catching surge in Asian competition than the deeper, long-term competitive weaknesses of the Italian economy. Their "consensus" view of these weaknesses is well summed up in a Confindustria document of March 2005, which lists five priority areas for action to improve competitiveness: (1) promotion of research and development; (2) administrative simplification; (3) liberalization of markets and promotion of competition, especially in sectors such as energy, financial services, and the professions; (4) investments in infrastructure, especially transportation; and (5) development of the South.[11] Rather than shift responsibility to the EU, Confindustria points out how Italy is lagging in fulfilling the European Union's Lisbon strategy for growth.[12] Similar priorities emerge from, for instance, the OECD economic survey of Italy,[13] which, in a wider-ranging overview, adds recommendations for upgrading workers' education and training, increasing labor force participation, ensuring the soundness of public finances, and reforming corporate governance.

These proposals point to long-standing problems of the Italian economy; for instance, it has the lowest investment in research and development of the G7 countries. Although the adaptability of "Third Italy"[14] firms has been a major strength in the past, these small enterprises are not able to undertake basic, long-term industrial research. Italy's weakness in research also explains its failure to develop a strong high-tech sector at a time when low-wage competition will inevitably cost jobs in the traditional industrial branches. Moreover, the delays of Italian bureaucracy impose considerable costs on business. And lack of competition in electricity, for instance, means Italy had the most expensive industrial electricity in the EU-15 (50 percent above the European average cost in 2002),[15] and similarly in other sectors business costs are increased by restrictive practices. The weaknesses and bottlenecks of the Italian transportation system are well known, as is the fact that the South harbors large untapped resources—human and material—that could contribute significantly to the country's growth.

However, many commentators have argued that beyond the failures of the state in these and other areas, the foundering competitiveness of the Italian economy is due to the private sector itself. While the state made serious errors in industrial policy in the past—for example, with massive and misguided aid to the chemical sector in the 1970s—it is not taking leadership in industrial policy in the present. In the absence of initiative from the state, the firms themselves have been the authors of industrial policy; it is they that have failed to improve productivity, engage in research and development, and recognize the need to shift the structure of industry from traditional to high-tech fields. In this context, the structure of corporate governance, rightly stressed in the OECD survey, is a problem, and not simply because it does not protect the interests of small shareholders.

The typical "Chinese box" system allows individuals or families to control large empires with quite small amounts of capital, using a series of holding companies, each with a controlling interest in the next. The companies, then, are not answerable to the shareholders at large, nor is the controlling family or group subject to supervision by lending banks, as in the German *Hausbank* system. While Mediobanca under Enrico Cuccia performed this role at times in the past, today the banks are not in a position to do so. Left to themselves, the controlling families such as the Agnellis and Pirellis have been driven neither by the search for short-term profit, as in the much-criticized "Anglo-Saxon" variety of capitalism, nor by a longer-term plan for rational industrial development, as in the "Rhenish" variety. Instead, they have engaged in diversification and financial operations, overstretching their resources and accumulating indebtedness in the process.[16] Such operations helped bring Fiat to the brink of bankruptcy, from which it is only now drawing back at the end of 2005. Often the major groups have preferred to invest in safe utilities that can yield large profits from a protected domestic market: Marco Tronchetti Provera of Pirelli has acquired Telecom, the Benetton family controls Autostrade S.p.A., etc. Silvio Berlusconi's own Mediaset television stations, which he and his family have tenaciously kept under their ownership and control, are another example of a business serving a protected domestic market.

This diversification has limited the major groups' ability to expand in their own fields and invest in research and development. The dominant families have put more emphasis on extending and securing their financial control than on industrial development, and even the newcomers to the "good salon" of Italian capitalism, such as the Benetton family, seem to have adopted the same habits. As Marcello Messori documents in this volume, the banking sector is also affected by the problem of weak structures of governance, which allow managers or controlling shareholders the freedom to engage in imprudent speculation. At the other end of the spectrum, in the industrial districts family control of small and medium enterprises limits their ability to grow and to raise capital.

By and large, the response of the state to the abovementioned problems, both those subject to its direct intervention and those stemming from the nature of private capital, has been slow. The issue was indeed raised during the 2001 election campaign, when the center-right accused the governments of the Ulivo of having reduced the country's ability to compete in the global marketplace. The word "competitiveness" was used five times by Silvio Berlusconi in his speech in the confidence debate in the Senate (18 June 2001) in connection with various promises of action (on information systems, administrative reorganization, the removal of structural imbalances in the economy, and taxation policy). International observers such as the OECD typically give the Berlusconi government credit for some policies adopted in the following years, in particular, two major measures: reforming the pension system to increase control over the budget and reduce future government expenditures, and liberalizing the labor market with the so-called Biagi law of 2003, allowing various forms of non-permanent contracts—limited-term, apprenticeship, etc.—as well as giving greater scope to employment agencies as intermediaries.[17] But the Italian labor market already allowed considerably more flexibility than, for instance, the German, and the slowness of employers to take advantage of all the possibilities offered by the new law suggests that it was not the boost that the economy needed.

Even the new employment it has created has not been an unequivocal benefit: while it has helped bring down unemployment to the lowest level in 12 years, it has also contributed to the fall in labor productivity.[18] On the issue of corporate governance, the Berlusconi government's law on savings, finally passed at the end of 2005 after four readings by the two houses of Parliament and nearly 700 days after its introduction, contains only weak provisions for the protection of small shareholders, and none to limit the controlling influence of small groups and families over large companies.

These policies were perhaps less than could have been expected from a government openly committed to a neo-liberal interpretation of free-market principles, and in any case they were not enough to forestall the problems mentioned at the outset of this chapter, which put the theme of competitiveness forcefully back on the cabinet's agenda in the spring of 2005.

The Government's Response: The "Competitiveness Package" of March 2005 and Its Legislative Progress

In response to the outcry over economic stagnation and foreign competition in 2005, the Berlusconi government did decide in March to launch a "competitiveness package." This consisted of a decree law containing the most urgent measures, and a government bill (*disegno di legge*) encompassing the other issues.[19] In reality, the government had a considerable amount of difficulty in formulating the provisions contained in the package. In February, Vice-Minister Adolfo Urso, who had been given the task of preparing the laws and carrying out extenuating consultations with the social partners (business and labor), had already had to deal with protests from the unions, who attacked the method adopted by the government even before addressing the contents of the package.[20] And the business associations had reservations concerning the "10 points" on which the package was based. Urso several times called for a "unity of intention" on the part of the social partners in the name of the country's interests, but the discussion nevertheless delayed the measures' progress, disrupting the timetable envisaged by the prime minister's office.

From the political point of view, the major obstacles that the competitiveness package encountered in its preparation were created by pressures and divisions within the majority and the cabinet itself.[21] An open rupture occurred on the question of the imposition of tariffs on Chinese products, a measure on which the LN was insistent but which Vice-Minister Urso and the government rejected. The conflict was so evident that on 11 March, when the competitiveness package was approved by the cabinet, the LN's ministers voted against Article 1 of the decree law, on counterfeit products, "threatening a battle" on the floor of Parliament.[22] In fact, the entire parliamentary debate of the "Action Plan for Economic, Social, and Territorial Development"[23] was not the easiest. The decree law was approved on 12 May,[24] three days before its expiry, but was criticized at the moment of its presentation in Parliament by the speaker of the Senate, Marcello Pera, for its lack of coherence.[25] Subsequently, it was modified by a large number of amendments (of which about 50 were presented by members of the government).[26] Finally, the decree was modified during its first reading in the Senate by a maxi-amendment presented by the government,[27] which the cabinet made a question of confidence, and then was altered again during its second reading in the Chamber.[28] The most substantially important change was the elimination of the entire criminal law part of the reform of the bankruptcy laws, which had led to a great deal of disquiet within the majority.

Decree law no. 35 was thus passed by Parliament (becoming law no. 80 of 2005) with contents quite different from the text approved by the cabinet in mid-March.[29] Even if it retained its cardinal points, it ended up taking on the appearance of an omnibus decree, or, as some suggested, a mini-*Finanziaria* (budget bill), containing provisions only indirectly related to competitiveness, such as the deductibility of certain charitable donations or simpler procedures for the sale of cars and motorcycles. Among its principal measures were anti-counterfeiting rules, which increased the penalties for producing, selling, or knowingly buying counterfeit merchandise; deductions from the Regional Tax on Business Activities (IRAP) for hiring new workers in less developed regions; streamlining of the rules for setting up a business; introduction of the rule that silence on the part of the administration is consent to a business's request; and reform of the bankruptcy law. The law also provided funds for infrastructure and research and development, including digital technology; subsidies and incentives for agriculture and tourism; and other minor incentives for industry. The amount of new money allocated was limited; for instance, the 1.8 billion euros for research was to come from an existing revolving fund.[30]

Two major issues that had been under discussion were not addressed: direct anti-dumping measures against China and a major reform of the professions. On the former, the LN had pressed vociferously for tariffs, which, as noted above, Italy has no power to impose under the Treaty on European Union. Even the associations of industrialists in the shoe and fashion sectors called national tariffs "illusory and anti-historical," and urged that only measures permitted by EU rules be taken.[31] The reform of the professions, on the other hand, was perceived as a grave threat by many self-employed professionals (e.g., notaries and pharmacists) who enjoyed monopoly privileges over the provision of certain services; these groups are among the strongest supporters of Forza Italia (FI) and Alleanza Nazionale (AN), the two largest governing parties, and hence the discussion of this very sensitive topic was postponed.

All in all, the government's response to the problem of competitiveness was judged as rather late and insufficient,[32] although it did respond in part to the industrialists' requests on research, reduction of bureaucracy, and infrastructure. The president of Confindustria, Luca Cordero di Montezemolo, asserted that it was "only a first step" and went on to repeat the long-stated demands of his association, including more infrastructure spending and a reduction of payroll taxes. While anti-dumping measures had their place, he said, making Italian enterprises more competitive was the best defense against foreign competition.[33] His subsequent statements revealed a growing impatience with the pace of the government's action, and on 10 April at Legnano he called for the dissolution of Parliament and a general election, if the conditions for an effective government did not materialize, even if this meant that the competitiveness measures would not be passed.[34] The industrialists had come a long way from their close alignment with Berlusconi and the Casa delle Libertà at their 2001 Parma congress, and the serious economic situation and the government's perceived inaction were the main reasons. Montezemolo has criticized the government on numerous other counts, from immigration to its program of "federal" constitutional reforms. At the same time, he has spoken out often in favor of the method of concertation with the unions and abandoned the campaign to weaken the protection against individual dismissal furnished by Article 18 of the Statute of Workers' Rights. This is a radical shift from the stance of Antonio D'Amato's Confindustria in 2000–2004, when it encouraged Berlusconi to take neo-liberal initiatives.

As for the unions' positions, we have already noted their initial opposition to the "method" adopted by the government. They also accused it of never having seriously considered other paths more consonant with policies of social justice and regional development, which were indicated in the EU's Lisbon strategy and also formalized in an agreement between the union confederations and Confindustria.[35] Even the initial tentative approval by Confcommercio,[36] the shopkeepers' lobby, who were most worried about the data on the influx of Chinese products, was not followed by any strong support during the year.

Conclusion: Different Visions of the Italian Economy

The recent positions of Confindustria are consonant with the evolution of Italian capitalism within the framework of the "European social model," derived from the Rhenish model of "coordinated market capitalism."[37] Italian business has reaped major benefits from this approach. In labor relations, the July accord of 1993 was the culmination of 20 years of attempts to accommodate the new strength of the unions in a regularized system that would allow firms to control costs and governments to prevent inflation. Previous attempts, such as the "EUR line" adopted by the unions in 1978, had failed, but the emergency situation of 1992–1993 provided the occasion that many of the actors had been waiting for. The method of concertation with the "social partners" was then fruitfully extended to the reform of the pension system and to broader policies for employment and growth.

At the same time, however, in the face of competitive pressures, Confindustria has advanced its proposals for reforms to eliminate some of Italy's competitive disadvantages. The Berlusconi government, while moving to partly satisfy some of industry's requests, does not share the same vision for the economy. It has abandoned neo-corporatist practices—for instance, in its pension reforms—and, particularly with the approach of elections, has shown greater interest in protection of threatened sectors and pockets of privilege in the economy. Its Euroskeptical tendencies, unlike those of the British Conservatives, are defensive rather than genuinely based on free-market principles.

In fact, as the *Economist* has noted with regret,[38] Italy lacks a truly free-market political force. On the surface, this is ironic, given that the government is led by the country's richest man, who heads its third-largest private business conglomerate. Yet Silvio Berlusconi himself has never been a charter member of the "good salon" of Italian capitalism, and as noted above, his corporate success depends on political support, which was necessary to secure Mediaset's access to frequencies and permission to operate on a national scale. Furthermore, his companies now hold a near monopoly on national private television, while technical, linguistic, and cultural barriers also shield them from direct foreign competition. Hence, Berlusconi does not share the concerns of other large firms that must compete in international markets. Furthermore, support for FI and its allies is strongest among the self-employed,[39] who are the most likely to be affected by the liberalization of trade and services. And the LN, finally, is ready to outflank its coalition partners with populist demands for protection. While Berlusconi's program of tax cuts and his labor market reforms suggest a commitment to a neo-liberal policy direction, they have in fact done more for smaller business and the upper middle classes.

In this context, it is not surprising that some major business leaders see the center-left as more likely to take the issue of competitiveness seriously. They also share with the center-left a commitment to the method of concertation with the trade unions. The Prodi government of 1996–1998 was responsible for achieving entry into the EMU in the first wave, making some unpopular decisions in order to achieve the Maastricht criteria. This was seen as a necessary goal by business, and a center-left government was able to reach it while maintaining relative social harmony. The experience gave business a modest confidence in the center-left's ability to govern. In the present economic situation, the tasks before the government are of a different order. In the 1990s, the objective was to secure a favorable macro-economic climate through entry into the EMU, which would resolve the long-standing issues of inflation, high interest rates, and large government deficits. Now, while respecting the 3 percent deficit limit of the Stability and Growth Pact remains a struggle, the real problems are on the supply side—product mix, productivity, human capital, infrastructure, and corporate governance.[40] Tackling them will require a different, more targeted, and more difficult type of intervention by the government, and here the center-left may be subject to cross-pressures from its own constituencies. The strong opposition to the high-speed rail line (TAV/TGV) between Turin and Lyons from environmentalists and local activists in the Val di Susa demonstrates that infrastructural improvements, for instance, are not simply a matter of finding the money to finance them. And while the center-left is likely to tackle the issue of corporate governance and the protection of small shareholders more seriously, the enthusiasm of the business community for far-reaching measures in this field is limited, given the control structures of the major firms. But since it is more firmly pro-European than the center-right, the center-left is not likely to resort to blaming the EU or the euro for Italy's problems, nor is it as likely to seek to downplay them for electoral purposes.

In sum, economists and business leaders, though with different emphases, by and large share a common core diagnosis of the causes of Italy's competitiveness problem, and also a fair degree of agreement on the possible remedies. Some of the roots of the problem require long-term solutions, and many are not necessarily responsive to public policy, depending more on the ability of the private sector to take up the challenges of the new globalized economy. The center-right government does not fully share this diagnosis, partly out of electoral concerns, and many of its exponents instead seek to blame outside forces, the EU, or China. Its action on the competitiveness agenda has therefore been, in the opinion of many critics, too little and too late. However paradoxical it may seem, at the end of the 14th Legislature, the center-left appears to be in closer sympathy with the overall agenda of business, which also hopes that a revival of concertation may also yield further progress on labor costs. The 2006 election may then open the door for a new and more robust set of policies to boost Italian competitiveness.

Notes

While this chapter is the result of a sharing of ideas between the two authors, the first and last sections were drafted by Grant Amyot, the middle section by Francesco Marangoni.

1. Most emblematic for its title is G. Turani, *Perché abbiamo il peggior capitalismo del mondo* (Milan: Sperling & Kupfer, 2004). For a selection, see also L. Gallino, *La scomparsa dell'Italia industriale* (Turin: Einaudi, 2003); M. Mucchetti, *Licenziare i padroni?* expanded edition (Milan: Feltrinelli, 2004); and A. Ricci, *Dopo il liberismo* (Rome: Fazi, 2004).
2. *La Repubblica*, 10 June 2005. The EU reported increases of 1748 percent for imports of leather boots and 674 percent for trousers in the first three months of the year.
3. ISTAT, Comunicato stampa, "Commercio con l'estero (extra Ue) Dicembre 2005," 26 January 2006.
4. The data can be consulted at http://www.weforum.org.
5. OECD, *Economic Surveys*, no. 7 (November 2005).
6. According to ISTAT data (released in February 2005), the trade balance for 2004 was in deficit by 393 million euros, compared to a surplus of 1,618 million euros in 2003.

7. OECD, *Economic Surveys*, no. 7 (November 2005). Note that inflationary wage pressure is not seen as a major problem (29).

8. Ibid., 24–25.

9. G. Tremonti, *Rischi fatali* (Milan: Mondadori, 2005).

10. Tremonti repeated these ideas on several occasions, for instance, when he presented the 2006 budget maneuver to the Senate. "Italy's low growth rate in Europe," he said, "was not influenced by the attacks of 11 September 2001, but rather by the effects on the economic system of the adoption of the euro and of Chinese competition." The minister also reiterated what he believed were Europe's responsibilities in this situation: "We have common problems, and therefore we must put forward common solutions. In Europe, economic policy is either European or it doesn't exist ... It is no longer the time for guarantees and promises, for protection of established positions and good feelings. It is the time for commitment and for assuming obligations. We cannot use solutions that were good for the past. We need solutions that will be good for the future." Among the solutions the minister indicated: "[W]e must decide to issue European public debt instruments to finance the reconversion of industry; moreover, we must attract foreign capital to the Eurozone and transfer the major burden of taxation from people to things." But first of all, continued Tremonti, Europe must look to support its own economy: "I believe it is fundamental that Europe stop applying its rules unilaterally. We are the only region of the world that manufactures and imposes rules on its own producers, while it imports goods from outside without any regulatory controls. There is no parity of standards."

11. Confindustria, "Un nuovo impegno per la crescita e l'occupazione in Europa e in Italia: Le proposte di Confindustria" (Brussels, 2 March 2005), 5ff.

12. Ibid., 15.

13. OECD, *Economic Surveys*, no. 7 (November 2005).

14. This is the widely used term coined in the late 1970s by the sociologist Arnaldo Bagnasco. See A. Bagnasco, *Tre Italie: La problematica territoriale dello sviluppo italiano* (Bologna: Il Mulino, 1977).

15. Confindustria, "Un nuovo impegno," 21.

16. This is the central thesis of Mucchetti, *Licenziare i padroni?*

17. On these measures, see D. Natali and M. Rhodes, "The Berlusconi Pension Reform and the Emerging 'Double Cleavage' in Distributive Politics," in *Italian Politics: Quo Vadis?* ed. C. Guarnieri and J. Newell (New York: Berghahn, 2005), 172–189; and L. Baccaro and M. Simoni, "The Referendum on Article 18 and Labor Market Flexibility," in *Italian Politics: Italy between Europeanization and Domestic Politics*, ed. S. Fabbrini and V. Della Sala, (New York: Berghahn, 2004), 166–183.

18. OECD, *Economic Surveys*, no. 7 (2005): 34–36.

19. See *La Repubblica*, 11 March 2005.

20. At the first meeting between the government and the social partners on 1 March, the unions demanded a postponement of the launching of the package, initially planned for the 4 March cabinet meeting, complaining that they had only two days to study its text (see *Il Sole-24 Ore*, 2 March 2005).

21. As in the case, for instance, of the conflict between the minister of the economy and finance, Domenico Siniscalco, and the minister of productive activities, Antonio Marzano, on the division of responsibilities between them and on the management of the fund for firms in crisis. Other issues that gave rise to lengthy

struggles within the majority were the liberalization of the electricity market and the proposed reform of the professions (see *Corriere della Sera*, 3 March 2005).

22. *Corriere della Sera*, 12 March 2005. At this time, Tremonti was still outside the cabinet, having been replaced as minister of the economy the previous year by Domenico Siniscalco, a less political "technical" minister. Tremonti was not to return to this post until September 2005.

23. This is the title of the dossier prepared by the government on the introduction of the two laws (http://www.governo.it/GovernoInforma/Dossier/sviluppo_piano/index.html).

24. The cabinet may pass decree laws on urgent matters, but they must be "converted" into regular laws by Parliament within 90 days or lose their validity.

25. *Il Sole-24 Ore*, 18 March 2005.

26. Ibid., 10 April 2005.

27. A document of some 70 pages, which basically included the amendments proposed by the majority in the Budget Committee (*Corriere della Sera*, 4 May 2005).

28. One of the amendments approved, on hiring by the National Commission for Companies and the Stock Exchange (CONSOB), which had been signed by Daniela Santanché of AN, had received a negative recommendation from the government.

29. The number of words went from roughly 15,000 to over 105,000.

30. The bill was approved by the Chamber of Deputies on 5 July 2005, but was still being debated by Parliament on 9 February 2006, 335 days after it was proposed by the cabinet.

31. *La Repubblica*, 4 March 2005.

32. R. Faini, *Il Sole-24 Ore*, 12 March 2005; E. Cisnetto, *Il Foglio*, 11 March 2005; R. Bagnoli, *Corriere della Sera*, 11 March 2005; E. Livini, *La Repubblica*, 13 March 2005.

33. *La Repubblica*, 19 March 2005.

34. *La Repubblica*, 11 April 2005. At the assembly of industrialists at Legnano, Montezemolo said: "I am not saying it to favor one or the other political camp, I am saying it because our primary interest is that the country is governed with the economy and enterprises at the center of the decisions. We are expecting an immediate and strong signal in this direction ... [Italy] needs a government that is determined to face at once the questions we have before us: the economy which for too long has not been growing and the need to create general conditions that help enterprises to be more competitive."

35. "For Development, Employment, and the Competitiveness of the Economic System: Common Policy Priorities for Research, Training, Infrastructure, and the South," signed 19 June 2003.

36. "In the Right Direction" was the title of a Confcommercio press release during the formulation of the package (3 March 2005).

37. To use Hall and Soskice's term. See P. Hall and D. Soskice, eds., *Varieties of Capitalism* (Oxford: Oxford University Press, 2001).

38. "Addio, Dolce Vita: A Survey of Italy," *Economist*, 26 November 2005, 4 and 13.

39. See, for example, the poll reported in ITANES, *Perché ha vinto il centro-destra* (Bologna: Il Mulino, 2001), 66, table 4.4, which found that 56.3 percent of the self-employed respondents voted for the center-right in 2001, as opposed to 44.5 percent of all employed respondents.

40. While Communist Refoundation is calling for more equitable taxation and income redistribution, no commentators are suggesting that lack of domestic demand is the most serious problem.

DOCUMENTARY APPENDIX

Compiled by Debora Mantovani

The following appendix provides a background of demographic, economic, political, and social information relevant to the main events of 2005 discussed in the volume.

The appendix is divided into two sections. The first (tables A1 to A14) includes data regarding resident population subdivided by sex and age (table A1); population changes—births, deaths, and marriages (table A2); foreign resident population in total and relative to the whole population, as well as number of residence permits issued, subdivided by region and reason issued (tables A3 and A4). Some of the principal indicators of the state of the Italian economy and of public finances are also given: gross domestic product, size of the public debt, and public-sector borrowing (tables A5 and A6). Tables A7, A8, and A9 compare the Italian situation with that of other European Union countries, focusing on natural and migratory changes in the population and on some indicators of education and rates of unemployment by sex. Tables A10, A11, and A12 contain essential information on Italy's labor force: resident population subdivided by employment status, sector of activity, and employment category (table A10); unemployment rates by geographical area, age group, and sex (table A11); and unemployment rates by geographical area, age group, and educational qualifications (table A12). Focusing on educational qualifications, table A13 compares the percentage distribution of the resident population by educational qualifications, age group, and sex in 1991, 2001, and 2004. Finally, table A14 shows trends in crimes reported to the authorities in 1991, 2001, 2002, and 2004.

Translated by Laura Kopp

The second section reports the results of the elections held in 2005. In the course of several rounds between April and November, municipal elections called to the polls the voters of 18 provincial capitals, while provincial elections called to the polls voters in 10 provinces: Viterbo and Caserta on 3 and 4 April, and the 8 provinces of Sardinia on 8 and 9 May. In addition, in April, the voters of ordinary autonomous regions, excepting only Molise, were called to cast ballots in regional elections. On 12 and 13 June, the referendum on the modification of law no. 40/2004 on medically assisted reproduction took place. Finally, in October 2005, the first primaries were held to select the leader of the center-left coalition, the Unione. On this occasion, more than 4 million voters went to the polls throughout Italy. Tables B1a, B1b, B2, and B3 give the results of the municipal elections, including voter turnout, votes cast for party lists, and the election of mayors in each provincial capital. Tables B4a, B4b, B5, and B6 provide the same information for the provincial elections. Tables B7a, B7b, and B8 report information for the regional elections. Tables B9a, B9b, B9c, and B9d summarize the results of the referendum, while the results of the primaries of the Unione are reported in table B10.

A: BACKGROUND DATA

TABLE A1. *Resident Population by Age Group and Sex, as of 1 January (percentages)*

Age	0–14	15–24	25–44	45–64	65 +	Total	(N)
Males and Females							
1981	21.7	15.4	26.9	22.5	13.5	100	(57,140,355)
1991	16.3	15.8	29.1	24.0	14.8	100	(57,746,163)
2001[a]	14.2	11.2	30.7	25.2	18.7	100	(56,995,744)
2003	14.2	10.8	30.7	25.3	19.0	100	(57,321,070)
2004	14.1	10.6	30.8	25.2	19.2	100	(57,888,245)
Males							
1981	22.8	16.0	27.7	22.0	11.5	100	(27,900,645)
1991	17.2	16.6	30.1	23.8	12.3	100	(28,072,498)
2001[a]	15.1	11.8	31.7	25.5	15.9	100	(27,586,982)
2003	15.1	11.4	31.9	25.5	16.2	100	(27,766,223)
2004	15.0	11.2	32.0	25.5	16.4	100	(28,068,608)
Females							
1981	20.7	14.7	26.2	22.9	15.5	100	(29,239,710)
1991	15.4	15.0	28.3	24.1	17.2	100	(29,673,665)
2001[a]	13.4	10.6	29.7	25.0	21.3	100	(29,408,762)
2003	13.4	10.2	29.6	25.0	21.7	100	(29,554,847)
2004	13.4	10.0	29.7	25.0	21.9	100	(29,819,637)

[a]Figures refer to 21 October 2001, date of the 14th general census.

Sources: ISTAT, *Popolazione e movimento anagrafico dei comuni* (Rome, 2001); our compilation is based on the 14th general census data on the ISTAT Web site: http://dawinci.istat.it; http://www.demo.istat.it.

TABLE A2. *Live Births, Deaths, and Marriages among the*
Resident Population

| | | BIRTHS | |
Year	Total	Rate of change (1981 = 100)	Natural childbirth (% of total live births)
1981	621,805	100.0	4.2
1991	562,787	90.5	6.7
2001	531,880	85.5	11.1
2002	535,538	86.1	12.3
2003[a]	539,503	86.8	13.6
2004[a]	548,244	88.2	14.9

| | | DEATHS | |
Year	Total	Rate of change (1981 = 100)	Natural balance (live births – deaths)
1981	542,204	100.0	+ 79,601
1991	553,833	102.1	+ 8,954
2001	556,892	102.7	−25,012
2002	560,390	103.4	−24,852
2003[a]	585,259	107.9	−45,756
2004[a]	543,162	100.2	+ 5,082

| | | MARRIAGES | | |
Year	Total	Index (1981 = 100)	Religious	% Religious (of total marriages)
1981	313,736	100.0	272,326	86.8
1991	312,061	99.5	257,555	82.5
2001	264,026	84.2	192,558	70.7
2002	270,013	86.1	192,006	70.5
2003[a]	257,503	82.1	183,678	67.4
2004[a]	250,764	79.9	172,600	63.4

[a] Provisional data according to civil registry records.

Source: ISTAT, *Annuario statistico italiano 2005* (Rome, 2005).

TABLE A3. *Total Resident and Foreign Population as of 31 December 2004,* *by Region*

Region	Resident Population	Foreign Population	Foreign (% of total resident population)
Valle D'Aosta	122,868	4,258	3.5
Piedmont	4,330,172	208,538	4.8
Lombardy	9,393,092	594,279	6.3
Trentino-Alto Adige	974,613	49,608	5.1
Veneto	4,699,950	287,732	6.1
Friuli-Venezia Giulia	1,204,718	58,915	4.9
Liguria	1,592,309	65,994	4.1
Emilia-Romagna	4,151,369	257,161	6.2
Tuscany	3,598,269	193,608	5.4
Umbria	858,938	53,470	6.2
Marche	1,518,780	81,890	5.4
Lazio	5,269,972	247,847	4.7
Abruzzo	1,299,272	38,582	3.0
Molise	321,953	3,790	1.2
Campania	5,788,986	85,773	1.5
Puglia	4,068,167	47,943	1.2
Basilicata	596,546	5,923	1.0
Calabria	2,009,268	31,195	1.6
Sicily	5,013,081	69,679	1.4
Sardinia	1,650,052	15,972	1.0
Italy	58,462,375	2,402,157	4.1

Source: Compiled from ISTAT data.

TABLE A4. Foreign Population Holding Residence Permits as of 1 January 2004, Reason for Issuing Permit, and 2003–2004 Percentage Variation in Residence Permits Issued, by Region

Region	Residence Permits 2004	Reason for Issuing Residence Permit (percentages)										2004 vs. 2003 % variation
		Work	Family	Religion	Chosen residence	Study	Tourism	Asylum	Asylum sought	Other	Total	
Valle d'Aosta	3,681	61.0	31.2	0.5	4.1	1.4	0.5	0.1	–	1.2	100	+28.3
Piedmont	171,497	68.1	25.7	0.5	2.0	1.3	0.8	0.2	0.3	1.0	100	+58.9
Lombardy	512,632	69.4	24.3	0.3	3.0	1.2	0.3	0.2	0.2	1.0	100	+47.8
Trentino-Alto A.	44,006	63.3	27.7	0.4	4.8	1.5	0.3	0.3	0.2	1.5	100	+15.5
Veneto	225,994	68.1	26.6	0.3	1.3	1.5	0.3	0.2	0.3	1.3	100	+47.2
Friuli-V. Giulia	61,522	55.6	33.5	0.2	3.3	3.3	0.5	0.5	0.9	2.1	100	+25.5
Liguria	58,336	63.6	24.5	0.9	7.1	1.9	0.3	0.2	0.1	1.4	100	+65.0
Emilia-Romagna	218,573	68.4	26.2	0.3	1.3	1.9	0.4	0.2	0.2	1.0	100	+47.9
Tuscany	174,997	65.0	24.7	0.9	3.8	3.3	0.6	0.2	0.2	1.4	100	+57.5
Umbria	44,696	63.8	25.9	1.7	3.2	3.6	0.6	0.2	0.1	0.8	100	+49.3
Marche	65,419	60.6	31.1	0.6	2.6	2.1	0.5	0.3	0.2	1.9	100	+38.9
Lazio	333,533	64.1	17.1	12.6	2.7	1.4	0.3	0.6	0.3	0.8	100	+39.8
Abruzzo	33,037	58.9	33.7	1.1	1.1	1.8	1.2	0.3	0.2	1.7	100	+55.7
Molise	3,500	51.7	32.2	2.5	3.1	1.9	3.5	0.1	0.1	5.0	100	+46.1
Campania	114,360	74.6	20.9	1.0	1.4	0.7	0.3	0.2	0.1	1.0	100	+97.0
Puglia	42,608	60.3	26.8	1.1	1.6	2.5	0.8	0.6	2.5	3.8	100	+36.7
Basilicata	5,649	65.3	25.5	1.0	1.0	0.9	1.8	0.8	0.2	3.5	100	+62.6
Calabria	33,051	64.8	18.7	1.3	1.0	1.1	0.5	1.1	8.7	2.8	100	+89.1
Sicily	65,331	62.9	28.6	1.3	2.2	1.1	0.6	0.3	1.6	1.5	100	+31.4
Sardinia	15,145	50.0	31.6	1.2	12.5	1.6	1.2	0.1	0.3	1.7	100	+29.4
Italy	2,227,567	66.4	24.5	2.4	2.6	1.7	0.4	0.3	0.5	1.2	100	+48.2

Source: Compiled from ISTAT data.

TABLE A5. *Gross Domestic Product (at market prices) and Consumer Price Index (totals in millions of euros)*

	GROSS DOMESTIC PRODUCT				
Year	Value at current prices	% Change from prev. year	Value at 1995 prices	% Change from prev. year	% Change of CPI from previous year
1992	783,774	+ 5.3	885,284	+ 0.8	+ 5.2
1993	807,362	+ 3.0	877,460	-0.9	+ 4.5
1994	853,911	+ 5.8	896,830	+ 2.2	+ 4.0
1995	923,052	+ 8.1	923,052	+ 2.9	+ 5.2
1996	982,443	+ 6.4	933,142	+ 1.1	+ 4.0
1997	1,026,285	+ 4.5	952,050	+ 2.0	+ 2.0
1998	1,073,019	+ 4.6	969,130	+ 1.8	+ 2.0
1999	1,107,994	+ 3.3	985,253	+ 1.7	+ 1.7
2000	1,166,548	+ 5.3	1,015,077	+ 3.0	+ 2.5
2001	1,218,535	+ 4.5	1,032,985	+ 1.8	+ 2.8
2002	1,260,598	+ 3.5	1,036,945	+ 0.4	+ 2.5
2003	1,300,929	+ 3.2	1,039,581	+ 0.3	+ 2.6
2004	1,351,328	+ 3.9	1,052,308	+ 1.2	+ 2.1

Source: ISTAT, *Annuario statistico italiano 2005* (Rome, 2005).

TABLE A6. *Public Debt and Public Sector Deficit (millions of euros)*

	PUBLIC DEBT			PUBLIC SECTOR DEFICIT		
Year	Absolute value	% Var. from prev. year	% of GDP	Absolute value	% Var. from prev. year	% of GDP
1992	843,891	+ 12.8	107.7	74,191	-0.3	9.5
1993	954,691	+ 13.1	118.2	75,877	+ 2.3	9.4
1994	1,061,802	+ 11.2	124.3	79,370	+ 4.6	9.3
1995	1,142,788	+ 7.6	123.8	70,081	-11.7	7.6
1996	1,205,392	+ 5.5	122.7	69,746	-0.5	7.1
1997	1,233,683	+ 2.3	120.2	27,723	-60.3	2.7
1998	1,248,469	+ 1.2	116.4	30,198	+ 8.9	2.8
1999	1,280,554	+ 2.6	115.6	19,125	-36.7	1.7
2000[a]	1,298,670	+ 1.4	111.3	21,359a	+ 11.7	1.8
2001	1,350,948	+ 4.0	110.9	35,963	+ 68.4	3.0
2002	1,364,880	+ 1.0	108.3	32,656	-9.2	2.6
2003	1,386,884	+ 1.6	106.6	37,792	+ 15.7	2.9
2004	1,429,256	+ 3.1	105.8	40,877	+ 8.2	3.0

[a] The figure for 2000 does not include revenue from the sale of UMTS licenses (13,815 million euros); in national accounts, the revenue from these sales is recorded as a reduction in expenditures.

Source: Bank of Italy, *Relazione annuale sul 2004* (Rome, 2005).

TABLE A7. *Population Density and Change in European Countries in 2003 (figures in thousands, except density)*

Country	Density (inhabitants per km²)	Births	Deaths	Natural increase	Net migration[a]	Net change	Population at year end
Austria	96.8	76.9	77.2	-0.3	+38.2	+37.9	8,140.1
Belgium	340.0	112.0	107.0	+5.0	+35.6	+40.6	10,396.4
Denmark	125.1	64.7	57.6	+7.1	+7.0	+14.1	5,397.6
Finland	15.4	56.6	49.0	+7.6	+5.8	+13.4	5,219.7
France	108.4	760.3	549.6	+210.7	+55.0	+265.7	59,900.7
Germany	231.2	706.7	853.9	-147.2	+142.2	-5.0	82,531.7
Greece	83.5	104.4	105.5	-1.1	+35.8	+34.7	11,041.1
Ireland	56.9	61.5	28.8	+32.7	+31.3	+64.0	4,027.7
Italy	191.2	544.1	586.5	-42.4	+609.6	+567.2	57,888.2
Luxembourg	174.0	5.3	4.1	+1.2	+2.2	+3.3	451.6
Netherlands	390.7	200.3	141.9	+58.4	+7.0	+65.4	16,258.0
Portugal	113.0	112.5	108.8	+3.7	+63.5	+67.2	10,474.7
Spain	83.1	439.9	383.7	+56.2	+738.5	+794.7	42,345.3
Sweden	19.9	99.2	93.0	+6.2	+28.7	+34.9	8,975.7
UK	246.1	695.5	611.8	+83.7	+260.5	+344.2	59,673.1
EU (15 countries)	117.1	4,035.4	3,745.0	+290.4	+2,052.1	+2,342.5	382,721.4
Cyprus	78.1	8.1	5.2	+2.9	+12.4	+15.3	730.4
Czech Republic	129.4	93.7	111.3	-17.6	+25.8	-8.2	10,211.5
Estonia	29.9	13.2	18.2	-5.0	+0.0	-5.0	1,351.0
Hungary	108.9	94.6	135.8	-41.2	+15.5	-25.7	10,116.7
Latvia	36.0	21.0	32.4	-11.4	-0.9	-12.3	2,319.2
Lithuania	52.9	30.6	41.0	-10.4	-6.3	-16.7	3,445.9
Malta	1,261.4	3.9	3.1	+0.8	+1.8	+2.6	399.9
Poland	122.2	351.1	365.2	-14.1	-13.8	-27.9	38,190.6
Slovakia	109.7	51.7	52.2	-0.5	+1.4	+0.9	5,380.1
Slovenia	98.4	17.3	19.5	-2.2	+3.6	+1.4	1,996.4
EU (25 countries)	114.5	4,720.6	4,528.9	191.7	2,091.5	2,283.2	456,863.1

[a] Includes post-census corrections and the regularization of registry records regarding events other than births, deaths, or migration.

Source: ISTAT, *Annuario statistico italiano 2005* (Rome, 2005).

Table A8. *Education Indicators for Selected Countries (2001–2002 academic year)*

Country	Public spending on education as % of GDP[a]		Schooling expectation (in years)[b]	School enrollment rate (ages 15–19)[c]	Rates of attainment[d]	
	Total (including indivisible expenses)	Post-sec. education spending only			Higher secondary education	Post-secondary education
European Union						
Austria	5.8	1.2	16.0	77	—	18.0
Belgium	6.4	1.4	19.4	92	79	—
Denmark	7.1	1.8	18.0	82	—	—
Finland	5.8	1.7	19.4	85	—	45.4
France	6.0	1.1	16.6	87	—	24.8
Germany	5.3	1.0	17.1	89	93	19.2
Greece	4.1	1.1	16.3	83	85	—
Ireland	4.5	1.3	16.5	82	77	31.1
Italy	5.3	0.9	16.7	72	82	22.7
Luxembourg	3.6	—	14.4	75	68	—
Netherlands	4.9	1.3	17.2	87	—	—
Portugal	5.9	1.1	17.0	71	—	—
Spain	4.9	1.2	17.3	80	68	33.5
Sweden	6.5	1.7	20.1	86	72	32.7
UK	5.5	1.1	20.4	77	—	35.9
Other OECD Countries						
Australia	6.0	1.5	21.1	83	—	45.4
Canada	6.1	2.5	—	—	—	—
Japan	4.6	1.1	—	—	92	33.8
United States	7.3	2.7	16.8	75	73	—

[a] The indicator represents public spending on education for all levels of education as a percentage of GDP, taking into account as financing sources direct public spending on schools and all government subsidies to families.

[b] Schooling expectation figures represent the expected average number of years of schooling for a 5-year-old in the course of his or her lifetime.

[c] The school enrollment rate (ages 15–19) is the number of 15- to 19-year-olds enrolled at all levels of education expressed as a percentage of the total population in that age range.

[d] The rate of attainment represents the number of students who at their first attempt obtain a higher secondary education diploma or post-secondary education degree, as a percentage of the total population in the same age range seeking the qualification.

Source: ISTAT, *Annuario statistico italiano 2005* (Rome, 2005).

TABLE A9. *Unemployment Rates by Sex in the 25 EU Countries for 2003, 2004, and 2005 (ages 15 and over)*

	Rate of Unemployment[a]								
	Males			Females			Total		
	2003	2004	2005	2003	2004	2005	2003	2004	2005
Austria	4.0	4.4	4.8	4.7	5.3	5.6	4.3	4.8	5.2
Belgium	7.6	7.1	7.6[b]	8.4	8.9	9.4[b]	8.0	7.9	8.4[b]
Cyprus	3.9	4.1	4.8	5.2	6.5	7.6	4.5	5.2	6.1
Czech Republic	6.2	7.1	6.5	9.9	9.9	9.8	7.8	8.3	8.0
Denmark	5.3	5.1	4.2[b]	5.9	5.7	5.7[b]	5.6	5.4	4.9[b]
Estonia	10.5	10.4	9.0[b]	9.9	8.0	6.0[b]	10.2	9.2	7.5[b]
Finland	9.2	8.7	8.2[b]	8.9	8.9	8.4[b]	9.0	8.8	8.3[b]
France	8.6	8.7	8.7[b]	10.5	10.5	10.4[b]	9.5	9.6	9.5[b]
Germany	8.2	8.7	8.8[b]	10.1	10.5	10.1[b]	9.0	9.5	9.4[b]
Greece	6.2	6.6	—	15.0	16.2	—	9.7	10.5	—
Hungary	6.0	5.9	6.8[b]	5.5	6.1	7.4[b]	5.8	6.0	7.1[b]
Ireland	4.9	4.9	4.6	4.2	4.0	3.9	4.6	4.5	4.3
Italy	6.5	6.4	—	11.3	10.5	—	8.4	8.0	—
Latvia	10.1	9.4	9.4[b]	10.6	10.1	8.7[b]	10.4	9.8	9.1[b]
Lithuania	12.3	10.5	8.0	13.1	11.2	8.4	12.7	10.9	8.2
Luxembourg	3.0	3.3	3.8[b]	4.7	6.8	7.5[b]	3.7	4.8	5.3[b]
Malta	6.8	7.1	7.1[b]	10.7	9.0	9.7[b]	8.0	7.7	7.9[b]
Netherlands	3.5	4.3	4.5[b]	3.9	4.8	5.0[b]	3.7	4.6	4.7[b]
Poland	18.6	18.0	16.8[b]	20.0	19.8	19.1[b]	19.2	18.8	17.9[b]
Portugal	5.4	5.9	6.4[b]	7.2	7.6	8.3[b]	6.3	6.7	7.3[b]
Slovakia	17.2	17.3	15.7[b]	17.8	19.3	17.4[b]	17.5	18.2	16.5[b]
Slovenia	6.0	5.6	5.4[b]	7.0	6.4	6.2[b]	6.5	6.0	5.8[b]
Spain	8.4	8.1	7.0[b]	16.0	15	12.2[b]	11.5	11.0	9.2[b]
Sweden	6.0	6.5	6.4[b]	5.2	6.1	6.3[b]	5.6	6.3	6.3[b]
UK	5.5	5.0	5.0[b]	4.3	4.2	4.2[b]	4.9	4.7	4.6[b]
EU (25 countries)	8.1	8.1	7.8[b]	10.2	10.2	9.7[b]	9.0	9.0	8.7[b]
EU (15 countries)	7.0	7.1	7.0[b]	9.2	9.3	8.8[b]	8.0	8.1	7.8[b]

[a] The unemployment rate is the number of persons unemployed expressed as a percentage of the total labor force (the total of employed and unemployed persons). The unemployed comprise persons between the ages of 15 and 74 who (a) were without work during the week in which the survey took place; (b) were willing to undertake paid employment (as employees or as self-employed) in the two weeks after the survey; (c) had taken specific steps toward finding paid employment (as employees or as self-employed) in the four weeks prior to (and including) the survey week; or (d) had found employment that was due to start within the following three months.

[b] Provisional figures.

Source: Compiled from data provided on the Eurostat Web site: http://epp.eurostat .cec.eu.int/portal/page?_pageid = 1996,39140985&_dad = portal&_schema = portal &screen = detailref&language = en&product = sdi_ed&root = sdi_ed/sdi_ed/sdi_ed_ emp/sdi_ed1431.

TABLE A10. *Labor Force by Employment Status and Sex, and Employed Population by Sector of Activity, Employment Category, and Sex for the Years 2001, 2002, 2003, and 2004 (percentages)*

	2001		2002		2003		2004	
	M	F	M	F	M	F	M	F
Labor force by employment status								
Employed	92.6	87.0	93.1	87.8	93.2	88.4	93.6	89.5
Unemployed	3.4	3.7	3.2	3.6	3.1	3.5	6.4	10.5
Seeking first job[a]	3.3	4.9	3.0	4.6	3.0	4.2	—	—
Other[a]	0.7	4.4	0.7	4.0	0.7	3.9	—	—
Total labor force	100	100	100	100	100	100	100	100
(N in thousands)	(14,521)	(9,261)	(14,609)	(9,383)	(14,685)	(9,465)	(14,546)	(9,818)
Employed population by sector of activity								
Agriculture	5.2	3.9	5.0	4.2	5.0	3.9	5.0	3.5
Industry	38.1	18.9	38.3	20.1	38.5	19.9	38.9	17.9
Other activities	56.7	77.2	56.7	75.7	56.5	76.2	56.1	78.6
Total employed	100	100	100	100	100	100	100	100
(N in thousands)	(13,268)	(8,337)	(13,392)	(8,521)	(13,544)	(8,697)	(13,622)	(8,783)
Employed population by employment category								
Entrepreneurs	3.2	1.4	3.6	1.6	3.7	1.7	2.3	0.9
Self-employed professionals	6.0	3.3	5.9	3.4	5.9	3.4	6.0	3.4
Other self-employed	18.2	9.8	17.7	9.4	17.5	9.3	19.9	10.6
Partners in cooperatives	1.2	1.0	0.9	0.9	0.9	0.9	0.3	0.3
Family workers[b]	3.1	6.0	3.0	5.9	3.0	5.8	1.8	3.7
Temp. non-employee collaborators[c]	—	—	—	—	—	—	1.2	2.6
Temp. hires[c]	—	—	—	—	—	—	0.3	0.7
Senior managers	2.0	0.8	1.9	0.9	1.9	0.9	3.0	1.5
Middle managers	5.0	4.7	4.8	4.6	4.7	4.5	4.9	5.0
White-collar employees	24.2	44.0	24.7	44.5	24.9	45.1	21.5	41.0
Blue-collar employees	36.3	27.9	36.6	27.7	36.8	27.4	37.5	28.9
Apprentices	0.8	0.8	0.8	0.9	0.7	0.8	1.2	1.3
Home workers	—	0.3	—	0.2	—	0.2	—	0.2
Total employed	100	100	100	100	100	100	100	100
(N in thousands)	(13,455)	(8,060)	(13,593)	(8,236)	(13,622)	(8,783)	(13,622)	(8,783)

[a] This category was dropped from the ISTAT 2004 average labor force survey.
[b] Working with another family member who is self-employed.
[c] For the years prior to 2004, ISTAT labor force surveys did not include this category.
Sources: ISTAT, *Annuario statistico italiano 2005* (Rome, 2005); ISTAT, *Forze di lavoro, media 2004* (Rome, 2006).

TABLE A11. *Unemployment Rates by Geographical Area, Age Group (15 and older), and Sex for 2004 (percentages)*

Age group and sex	Northwest	Northeast	Center	South	Italy
Males	*3.4*	*2.5*	*4.9*	*11.9*	*6.4*
15–24	13.0	7.9	17.5	32.8	20.6
25–34	3.7	2.9	6.4	16.6	8.3
35–44	1.9	1.9	2.7	8.1	4.1
45–54	1.9	1.5	3.1	5.5	3.3
55–64	3.1	1.9	3.5	6.3	4.1
65 and older	1.7	0.4	2.4	1.6	1.6
Females	*6.1*	*5.7*	*8.7*	*20.5*	*10.5*
15–24	15.3	13.9	25.9	44.6	27.2
25–34	6.8	6.8	10.7	27.2	13.2
35–44	4.7	4.5	7.1	16.5	8.2
45–54	4.4	3.5	5.0	8.5	5.4
55–64	3.5	2.9	2.8	6.2	4.0
65 and older	1.0	4.8	—	4.9	2.4
Total	*4.5*	*3.9*	*6.5*	*15.0*	*8.0*
15–24	13.6	8.8	22.4	49.1	27.1
15–24	14.1	10.6	21.4	37.6	23.5
25–34	5.1	4.7	8.3	20.7	10.4
35–44	3.1	3.1	4.6	11.1	5.8
45–54	2.9	2.3	3.9	6.5	4.1
55–64	3.3	2.2	3.3	6.3	4.1
65 and older	1.6	1.3	1.8	2.4	1.7

Source: ISTAT, *Forze di lavoro, media 2004* (Rome, 2006).

TABLE A12. *Unemployment Rates by Geographical Area, Age Group, and Educational Qualification for 2004 (percentages)*

Age group and educational qualification	Northwest	Northeast	Center	South	Italy
15–24	*14.1*	*10.3*	*21.4*	*37.6*	*23.5*
Primary school diploma	24.3	24.8	14.1	41.6	34.1
Middle school diploma	15.7	13.3	23.4	36.1	25.3
Vocational qualification	11.3	7.3	19.1	35.7	14.6
High school diploma	12.8	8.9	19.9	38.7	22.8
University degree	19.1	22.7	37.3	47.5	31.2
25–34	*5.1*	*4.7*	*8.3*	*20.7*	*10.4*
Primary school diploma	20.0	11.4	11.4	28.1	23.0
Middle school diploma	6.3	5.4	8.0	20.9	11.4
Vocational qualification	3.1	3.3	6.4	20.3	5.7
High school diploma	3.7	3.3	7.7	18.0	8.8
University degree	5.6	7.3	11.1	25.8	12.6
35 and older	*3.0*	*2.6*	*4.1*	*8.6*	*4.8*
Primary school diploma	4.6	4.0	6.2	13.4	8.2
Middle school diploma	3.8	3.0	5.2	10.9	6.1
Vocational qualification	3.6	2.3	5.2	8.7	4.3
High school diploma	2.4	2.3	3.1	6.0	3.6
University degree	0.9	1.3	2.0	2.4	1.7

Source: ISTAT, *Forze di lavoro, media 2004* (Rome, 2006).

TABLE A13. *Resident Population (ages 15 and over) by Educational Qualification, Age Group, and Sex for 1991, 2001, and 2004*

Education level	1991					2001					2004				
	15–19	20–44	45–64	65+	Total	15–19	20–44	45–64	65+	Total	15–19	20–44	45–64	65+	Total
Males and Females															
PhD, univ. degree or diploma	—	6.1	4.0	2.4	4.2	—	9.5	8.3	3.3	7.2	—	11.8	9.3	3.5	8.6
High school diploma or voc. qualification	11.0	34.7	11.6	5.6	20.5	13.4	46.1	22.4	7.9	29.1	15.2	48.3	27.0	9.5	31.4
Middle school diploma	79.3	40.4	20.3	10.7	33.4	82.0	38.0	28.8	13.0	32.8	82.8	34.9	29.7	13.6	31.5
Primary school diploma or no qualif.	9.7	18.8	64.1	81.3	41.9	4.6	6.4	40.5	75.8	30.9	2.0	5.0	34.0	73.4	28.5
Total	100.0	100.0	100.0	100.0	100.0	100.0	100.0	100.0	100.0	100.0	100.0	100.0	100.0	100.0	100.0
(N in thousands)	(5,041)	(21,025)	(13,746)	(8,700)	(48,512)	(3,040)	(21,317)	(14,407)	(10,320)	(49,084)	(2,892)	(20,989)	(14,522)	(10,935)	(49,338)
Males															
PhD, univ. degree or diploma	—	6.3	5.5	4.3	5.1	—	8.8	9.5	5.0	7.7	—	10.3	10.1	5.5	8.7
High school diploma or voc. qualification	8.9	33.7	13.3	6.7	21.0	12.2	44.5	25.0	9.7	30.2	13.2	46.5	29.7	11.7	32.7
Middle school diploma	80.3	43.8	23.5	12.8	37.4	83.0	40.9	31.5	16.0	36.4	84.2	38.3	32.5	17.0	35.3
Primary school diploma or no qualif.	10.8	16.2	57.7	76.2	36.5	4.8	5.8	34.0	69.3	25.7	2.6	4.9	27.7	65.8	23.3
Total	100.0	100.0	100.0	100.0	100.0	100.0	100.0	100.0	100.0	100.0	100.0	100.0	100.0	100.0	100.0
(N in thousands)	(2,566)	(10,564)	(6,652)	(3,529)	(23,311)	(1,557)	(10,747)	(7,075)	(4,253)	(23,632)	(1,483)	(10,562)	(7,113)	(4,564)	(23,722)
Females															
PhD, univ. degree or diploma	—	5.9	2.7	1.1	3.4	—	10.1	7.1	2.1	6.7	—	13.3	8.5	2.2	8.4
High school diploma or voc. qualification	13.1	35.8	10.0	4.9	20.0	14.7	48.1	19.8	6.6	28.1	17.3	50.1	24.3	8.0	30.3
Middle school diploma	78.3	36.8	17.2	9.3	29.7	80.9	34.9	26.2	11.0	29.4	81.3	31.5	27.0	11.2	27.9
Primary school diploma or no qualif.	8.6	21.5	70.1	84.7	46.9	4.4	6.9	46.9	80.3	35.8	1.4	5.1	40.2	78.6	33.4
Total	100.0	100.0	100.0	100.0	100.0	100.0	100.0	100.0	100.0	100.0	100.0	100.0	100.0	100.0	100.0
(N in thousands)	(2,475)	(10,461)	(7,094)	(5,171)	(25,201)	(1,483)	(10,570)	(7,332)	(6,067)	(25,452)	(1,409)	(10,428)	(7,409)	(6,371)	(25,616)

Sources: ISTAT, *13° Censimento generale della popolazione 1991* (Rome, 1995); ISTAT, *Forze di lavoro, media 2001* (Rome, 2002); ISTAT, *Forze di lavoro, media 2004* (Rome, 2006).

TABLE A14. Crimes Reported to Judicial Authorities by Police Forces (by type of crime)^a

Type of Crime	Total				CRIMES REPORTED Of which perpetrator unknown		
	1991	2002	2003	2004^b	1991	2002	2003
Massacre	13	8	7	24	0	0	0
Homicide	1,916	639	712	714	1,352	260	318
Infanticide	22	5	7	6	8	1	1
Manslaughter	46	47	46	47	5	7	7
Attempted homicide	2,197	1,555	1,470	1,425	1,063	346	306
Accidental negligent homicide	2,684	1,856	1,606	2,160	269	217	152
Serious injury	19,748	28,699	30,644	51,823	3,729	6,321	6,329
Sexual violence	733	2,543	2,744	3,734	175	418	458
Simple and aggravated theft	1,702,073	1,305,245	1,328,350	1,466,582	1,610,846	1,248,295	1,273,585
Robbery	39,206	40,006	41,747	46,265	33,477	31,357	32,947
Extortion	2,851	3,628	3,751	5,413	1,240	779	808
Kidnapping	822	1,260	1,166	1,239	372	369	312
Criminal association	817	1,037	1,007	1,390	11	0	0
Mafia association	201	178	206	138	5	0	0
Arson	10,277	9,957	11,086	12,331	9,211	8,960	9,999
Attempted bombing and/or arson attack	2,600	1,262	1,448	458	2,426	1,189	1,366
Fraud	34,545	54,328	187,858	66,294	11,658	22,802	163,427
Smuggling	32,901	1,512	1,653	—	2,144	94	196
Production, trade, etc., of drugs	40,421	37,965	37,288	30,053	2,582	2,042	1,646
Exploiting and abetting prostitution	2,123	3,174	2,461	1,374	97	204	255
Other crimes	751,538	736,646	801,630	726,246	478,378	293,739	348,097
Total	2,647,734	2,231,550	2,456,887	2,417,716	2,159,048	1,617,401	1,840,209

^a Figures represent crimes as reported to judicial authorities by state police, carabinieri, and financial police. They do not include crimes reported to judicial authorities by others (other public officials or private citizens). The figures cannot be compared, therefore, with those for reported crimes for which the judicial authorities have begun criminal proceedings.

^b The data for 2004 are not strictly comparable to those for previous years, for two reasons: (1) they include crimes reported by all police forces, and (2) some offenses have been redefined.

Sources: ISTAT, Annuario statistico italiano 2005 (Rome, 2005), and http://giustiziaincifre.istat.it/Nemesis/jsp/IndiceTavole .jsp?id = 4A|18A&it = 2004|1|0|3|001|001|0|0.

B: ELECTION RESULTS

Municipal Elections, 2005

TABLE B1a. *Voter Turnout at the Municipal Elections of 2005 (first ballot, provincial capitals)*

City	Voters registered	Actual voters (% of registered)	Actual voters	Valid ballots (% of voters)	Blank ballots (% of voters)	Invalid or contested ballots (% of voters)	Valid ballots	Votes cast for mayor alone (% of valid ballots)
3 and 4 April 2005								
Lodi	34,848	78.0	27,179	96.7	1.4	1.9	26,290	19.5
Mantua	40,139	75.2	30,175	96.7	1.3	2.0	29,168	17.5
Pavia	61,668	77.5	47,788	94.7	1.8	3.5	45,261	10.6
Venice	233,316	72.0	168,087	96.1	1.4	2.5	161,465	22.3
Macerata	35,825	76.1	27,279	95.5	1.9	2.6	26,049	9.6
Chieti	48,014	81.0	38,879	96.2	1.3	2.5	37,383	7.7
Andria	77,070	82.1	63,268	95.9	1.7	2.4	60,674	5.2
Taranto	178,852	77.3	138,294	95.0	2.1	2.9	131,338	6.8
Vibo Valentia	29,180	78.6	22,921	96.7	1.2	2.1	22,159	2.1
8 and 9 May 2005								
Aosta	29,267	73.6	21,554	95.8	1.2	3.1	20,643	3.1
Bolzano[a]	79,028	73.7	58,278	95.6	1.9	2.5	55,707	7.8
Trento	89,180	70.2	62,578	95.7	1.8	2.6	59,868	7.2
Sassari	109,247	76.1	83,153	95.2	1.5	3.3	79,154	8.1
Nuoro	32,465	77.8	25,272	96.6	0.7	2.7	24,421	6.3
Iglesias	24,485	77.6	19,011	96.4	0.9	2.7	18,322	8.0
15 and 16 May 2005								
Catania	271,146	75.1	203,761	92.7	2.2	5.1	188,851	6.5
Enna	27,496	75.0	20,634	97.2	0.2	2.6	20,061	1.8
6 November 2005								
Bolzano[a]	78,849	75.3	59,379	97.0	1.4	1.6	57,582	8.5
27 and 28 November 2005								
Messina	204,608	78.2	159,976	92.2	1.7	6.1	147,519	4.1
Total	1,684,683	75.8	1,277,466	94.9	1.7	3.5	1,211,915	9.2

[a] The Bolzano municipal election was held on 8 and 9 May 2005 and was followed by a run-off vote on 22 May 2005. The winning mayor was not, however, able to form a *giunta* (executive committee). The voters of Bolzano were therefore again called to the polls on 6 November 2005.

Sources: Adapted from data provided by the Ministry of the Interior, Central Election Service. Other results extrapolated from the following Web sites: Catania election (http://www.comune.catania.it); Aosta election (http://www.regione.vda.it); Trento election (http://www.regione.taa.it); Bolzano election (http://www.comune.bolzano.it); Messina election (http://www.regione.sicilia.it).

TABLE B1b. *Voter Turnout at the Municipal Elections of 2005 (second ballot, provincial capitals)*

City	Voters registered	Actual voters (% of reg- istered)	Actual voters	Valid ballots (% of voters)	Blank ballots (% of voters)	Invalid or contested ballots (% of voters)	Diff. in voters (% of reg. voters) between 1st & 2nd ballots	Diff. in valid votes (% of reg. voters) between 1st & 2nd ballots
17 April 2005								
Mantua	40,139	63.1	25,336	97.6	1.1	1.3	-12.0	-11.1
Pavia	61,668	64.1	39,542	97.9	0.6	1.4	-13.4	-10.6
Venice	233,316	55.7	129,885	98.0	0.6	1.4	-16.4	-14.6
Chieti	48,014	66.3	31,835	97.6	0.9	1.6	-14.7	-13.2
Andria	77,070	72.3	55,714	98.4	0.4	1.1	-9.8	-7.6
22 and 23 May 2005								
Bolzano	79,028	66.2	52,289	98.0	0.5	1.5	-7.6	-5.7
Iglesias	24,485	69.2	16,953	98.7	0.4	0.9	-8.4	-6.5
11 December 2005								
Messina	204,608	59.3	121,306	97.9	0.6	1.6	-18.9	-14.1
Total	768,328	61.5	472,860	98.0	0.6	1.4	-14.7	-12.0

Sources: Compiled from data provided by the Ministry of the Interior, Central Election Service. Data for the Bolzano election were extrapolated from the City of Bolzano Web site (http://www.comune.bolzano.it); data for the Messina election were extrapolated from the Regione Sicilia Web site (http://www.regione.sicilia.it).

TABLE B2. *Municipal Elections of 2005, Votes for Party Lists (percentages)*

City	No. mayoral candidates	No. lists	Other c-l parties[a]	Rifond. comunista	Fed. verdi[b]	Italia dei valori[c]	Comunisti italiani	DS[d]	SDI[e]	La Margh.[f]	UDEUR	UDC	Nuovo PSI[g]	FI	AN	Lega Nord	Other c-r parties[h]	Other lists[i]	Total
3 and 4 April 2005																			
Vercelli	5	19	8.1	6.9	4.6	1.0	1.1	11.5	3.6	5.7	1.0	3.3	2.2	33.3	6.9	4.4	5.3	1.1	100
Lodi	3	13	8.4	4.1	2.5	1.6	2.5	15.4	3.2	15.4	—	4.3	—	22.2	5.0	13.6	—	1.8	100
Mantua	7	14	—	8.0	2.2	2.1	3.0	41.3	—	—	—	2.9	—	17.3	7.9	6.3	5.5	3.5	100
Pavia	7	17	11.6	3.8	2.0	1.0	1.6	20.5	3.9	—	—	2.5	1.0	24.0	8.9	6.8	—	12.4	100
Venice	11	24	3.6	6.8	3.9	2.0	2.1	21.1	1.3	13.4	1.4	3.2	—	20.5	6.5	3.7	—	10.5	100
Macerata	4	16	9.2	6.3	—	1.5	5.2	16.2	3.4	15.0	1.8	7.1	—	9.3	12.4	0.6	1.0	11.0	100
Chieti	8	18	7.5	4.6	—	—	—	14.0	3.2	12.0	3.9	4.3	—	12.0	9.4	—	3.5	23.5	100
Andria	4	19	10.9	4.6	4.1	2.1	1.3	14.0	—	11.5	1.0	7.3	1.8	12.7	9.4	—	17.4	4.0	100
Taranto	7	24	4.7	2.2	0.5	0.2	1.7	15.8	3.1	4.4	1.5	16.4	—	10.8	9.7	—	22.0	7.0	100
Vibo Valentia	4	14	10.4	3.3	4.9	—	—	12.4	5.3	19.5	9.0	10.8	2.0	8.5	11.4	—	2.5	—	100
8 and 9 May 2005																			
Aosta	5	14	44.2	3.3	6.9	—	—	11.2	—	2.2	—	—	—	6.8	2.1	—	—	23.3	100
Bolzano	7	19	2.0	3.2	5.6	0.9	1.7	8.2	0.9	12.2	—	1.4	—	9.9	20.0	1.4	10.2	22.4	100
Bolzano (Nov.)	7	22	23.9	3.0	4.3	0.9	1.0	9.2	1.5	7.2	—	1.0	0.3	10.1	17.7	1.0	15.3	3.6	100
Trento	9	17	40.8	5.7	4.1	2.1	1.4	17.7	—	—	—	3.8	—	11.6	4.0	5.2	—	3.6	100
Sassari	5	20	13.9	2.4	—	—	—	15.7	3.5	13.1	8.4	5.1	0.9	14.8	6.5	—	10.9	4.8	100
Nuoro	4	13	3.4	5.6	3.1	—	3.1	16.0	11.3	20.7	5.7	5.8	—	—	—	—	9.0	16.3	100
Iglesias	5	17	11.3	2.7	—	—	3.2	12.7	—	6.4	3.3	—	1.2	7.6	1.5	—	47.9	2.2	100
15 and 16 May 2005																			
Catania	7	32	20.8	1.2	0.5	0.9	1.6	5.5	1.4	6.4	2.7	4.1	0.6	16.2	7.7	—	28.5	1.9	100
Enna	6	14	6.8	1.9	—	0.5	0.2	24.3	2.7	22.5	—	12.3	1.1	13.8	10.6	—	1.9	1.4	100
27 and 28 November 2005																			
Messina	5	40	14.4	1.7	1.3	—	0.5	4.3	2.8	9.5	3.1	4.4	—	8.7	8.0	—	34.5	6.8	100

a The heading "Other center-left parties" includes all of the (minor and civic) lists affiliated with the center-left alliance, and also those affiliated with this alliance in the run-off round. In Aosta, the Union Valdotaine list got 25.5 percent of votes. In Bolzano, in the November election, the Südtiroler Volkspartei party got 21.8 percent of votes.

b In Nuoro, Fed. verdi-Aut. soc.; in Messina, Fed. verdi-Per la pace No ponte.

c In Enna, Italia dei valori-Fed. verdi.

d In Mantua, Uniti nell'Ulivo; in Trento, Trento democratica per l'Ulivo.

e In Lodi, SDI-Others; in Pavia, SDI-Repubblicani europei; in Sassari and Nuoro, SDI-Soc. uniti; in Enna, SDI-UDEUR.

f In Nuoro, Margherita-Civic list.

g In Vibo Valentia, Nuovo PSI-Partito lib.; in Iglesias, Fortza Paris-Nuovo PSI; in Enna, Nuovo PSI-Noi siciliani.

h The heading "Other center-right parties" includes all the (minor and civic) lists affiliated with the center-right alliance, and also those affiliated with this alliance in the run-off round.

i The heading "Other lists" includes all those lists not affiliated with any alliance. It includes, besides civic lists, lists of parties with a presence throughout the country, such as the Fiamma tricolore and Alternativa sociale. In Aosta, the Aosta viva Louvin list got 16.5 percent of the votes.

Sources: Compiled from data provided by the Ministry of the Interior, Central Election Service. Data for the Bolzano election were extrapolated from the City of Bolzano Web site (http://www.comune.bolzano.it); data for the Messina election were extrapolated from the Regione Sicilia Web site (http://www.regione.sicilia.it).

TABLE B3. Election of Mayors in Provincial Capitals in 2005 *(with run-offs)*

City	Mayoral candidate[a]	1st round (%)	Run-off round (%)	1st round votes	Run-off round votes	Parties and supporting civic lists at both voting rounds[b]	1st round votes for supp. lists	% votes for supp. lists at 1st round	Votes for cand. alone[c]
Lodi	**Guerini Lorenzo**	54.1		14,219		Uniti nell'Ulivo, PdCI, Fed. verdi, Italia dei valori	11,221	53.0	2,998
	Rossi Mauro	44.1		11,600		FI, LN, AN, UDC	9,565	45.2	2,035
	Invernizzi Gianmario	1.8		471		Alternativa sociale	378	1.8	93
	Total	100		26,290		Total	21,164	100	5,126
Mantua	**Brioni Fiorenza**	46.2	54.5	13,478	13,475	Uniti nell'Ulivo, PdCI, Fed. verdi, Italia dei valori	11,707	48.7	1,771
	Vassalle Roberto	37.2	45.5	10,853	11,250	FI, LN, AN, UDC, Obiettivo Mantova (Con te per Mantova, Civic list)	8,461	35.2	2,392
	Gaddi Matteo	9.0		2,621		RC	1,936	8.0	685
	Conte Sergio	2.7		782		Con te per Mantova	635	2.6	147
	Cliegi Sergio	2.2		641		Forum	619	2.6	22
	Saggiani Giorgio	1.9		546		Civic list	506	2.1	40
	Azzali Aldo	0.8		247		Alternativa sociale	200	0.8	47
	Total	100	100	29,168	24,725	Total	24,064	100	5,104
Pavia	**Capitelli Piera**	45.1	54.5	20,391	21,126	DS, Per Pavia, SDI-Repubblicani eur., RC, Fed. verdi, PdCI, Italia dei valori	17,903	44.2	2,488
	Rondini Giorgio	41.9	45.5	18,979	17,602	FI, AN, Lega Nord, UDC	17,106	42.3	1,873
	Veltri Elio	6.0		2,717		Cantiere per Pavia	2,570	6.4	147
	Adenti Francesco	3.4		1,553		Città per l'uomo	1,426	3.5	127
	Rona Giammatteo	1.4		625		Comitato per Pavia, Alternativa sociale	488	1.2	137
	Amiti Costantino	1.3		576		Partito pensionati	575	1.4	1
	Magenta B. Giancarlo	0.9		420		Nuovo PSI	397	1.0	23
	Total	100	100	45,261	38,728	Total	40,465	100	4,796

Venice

	%	Votes	%	Votes
Cacciari Massimo	23.2	37,488	50.5	64,315
Casson Felice	37.7	60,837	49.5	62,974
Campa Cesare	20.3	32,726		
Speranzon Raffaele	6.2	10,021		
Salvadori Augusto	4.3	6,905		
Mozzonetto Alberto	3.3	5,419		
Crovato Maurizio	2.6	4,268		
Ripa di Meana Carlo	1.0	1,619		
Salvagno Vittorio	0.9	1,424		
Pighin Giampaolo	0.3	494		
D'Elia Francesco Mario	0.2	264		
Total	100	161,465	100	127,289

	Votes	%	
Margherita, UDEUR	18,639	14.8	18,849
DS, RC, Fed. verdi, Socialdemocrazia, PdCI, Italia dei valori, SDI	51,220	40.8	9,617
FI, UDC	29,692	23.7	3,034
AN, Più donne	8,490	6.7	1,531
Lista Salvadori, Progetto Nord-est	5,141	4.1	1,764
LN, Venezia e Mestre	4,955	4.0	464
Uno di noi	3,579	2.9	689
Lista verde civica, Movimento lavoratori, Lista consumatori	1,550	1.2	69
Socialisti laici liberali	1,461	1.2	-37
Progetto autonomia	465	0.4	29
Mov. auton. Venezia-Mestre	225	0.2	39
Total	125,417	100	36,048

Macerata

	%	Votes	%	Votes
Meschini Giorgio	59.4	15,464	64.3	19,968
Meriggi Giovanni	27.1	7,070		
Menghi Anna	9.1	2,360		
Antolini Arrigo	4.4	1,155		
Total	100	26,049		

	Votes	%	
DS, Margherita, Città viva, RC, PdCI, SDI, Repubblicani eur-Others, UDEUR, Italia dei valori	13,802	58.6	1,662
AN, FI, UDC, Lista Meriggi, LN	7,178	30.4	-108
Comitato A. Menghi	1,779	7.6	581
Uniti per Macerata	801	3.4	354
Total	23,560	100	2,489

Chieti

	%	Votes	%	Votes
Ricci Francesco	46.4	17,331	64.3	19,968
Rispoli Enrico	25.3	9,460	35.7	11,089
Buracchio Emanuele	11.0	4,104		
Di Felice Raffaele	10.3	3,868		
Angeloni Giustino	3.0	1,133		
Rocci Antonio	1.9	716		
Giardinelli Vito A.	1.9	698		
Vero Annamaria Lucia	0.2	73		
Total	100	37,383	100	31,057

	Votes	%	
DS, Margherita, Città domani, RC, SDI, Italia dei valori	14,946	43.3	2,385
FI, AN, Democrazia cristiana	8,605	24.9	855
Lista Chieti	4,533	13.1	-429
UDC, UDEUR, Città libera, Patto Chieti	3,866	11.2	2
Alternativa sociale	870	2.5	263
Progetto Chieti	692	2.0	24
Chieti futura	953	2.8	-255
Sogno italiano	58	0.2	15
Total	34,523	100	2,860

TABLE B3. Election of Mayors in Provincial Capitals in 2005 (with run-offs) (cont.)

City	Mayoral candidate[a]	1st round (%)	Run-off round (%)	1st round votes	Run-off round votes	Parties and supporting civic lists at both voting rounds[b]	1st round votes for supp. lists	% votes for supp. lists at 1st round	Votes for cand. alone[c]
Andria	Zaccaro Vincenzo	41.9	52.0	25,452	28,484	DS, Margherita, Con Zaccaro, RC, Recupero e sviluppo, UDEUR	24,165	42.0	1,287
	Fucci Benedetto	47.9	48.0	29,072	26,343	FI, AN, Tutti per Andria, UDC, Patto per Andria, Popolari per Puglia, Andria, Dem. Popolare (Nuovo PSI)	27,163	47.2	1,909
	Piccolo Francesco	8.1		4,896		Fed. verdi, Sinistra attiva, PdCI, Socialdemocrazia	5,193	9.0	-297
	Zingaro Riccardo	2.1		1,254		Nuovo PSI	1,024	1.8	230
	Total	100	100	60,674	54,827	Total	57,545	100	3,129
Taranto	Di Bello Rossana	57.9		76,046		UDC, Con Di Bello, FI, AN, Forum, Rosa, Progetto sud, Taranto sana, Mov. idea soc.	72,094	58.9	3,952
	Vico Ludovico	34.5		45,324		DS, Lista Florido, Margherita, SDI, RC, PdCI, UDEUR, Fed. Verdi, Italia dei valori	41,683	34.0	3,641
	Condemi Filippo	6.2		8,103		Lista Condemi, Mov. pop.	7,065	5.8	1,038
	Masi Arturo	0.6		815		Alternativa sociale	751	0.6	64
	La Gioia Giovanni	0.6		789		Lista Taranto	643	0.5	146
	Quaranta Giuseppe	0.1		172		Sud libero	94	0.1	78
	Alfano Alfonso	0.1		139		Mov. dis. prec. merid.	106	0.1	33
	Total	100		131,388		Total	122,436	100	8,952
Vibo Valentia	Sammarco Francesco	65.1		14,432		Margherita, DS, UDEUR, Socialismo è libertà, SDI, Fed. Verdi, RC, Social-democrazia, Progetto Calabrie	14,054	64.8	378
	Grillo Martino	32.4		7,174		AN, UDC, FI, DC	7,199	33.2	-25
	Carchedi Francesco	2.5		553		Nuovo PSI-Partito lib.	440	2.0	113
	Total	100		22,159		Total	21,693	100	466

	%	Votes	%	Votes		Votes	%	
Aosta								
Grimod Guido	57.4	11,846			Union Valdotaine, Gauche Vald-DS, Stella alpina Vallée D'Aoste, Fed. Autonomiste, Margherita	11,518	57.6	328
Louvin Roberto	33.1	6,833			Aosta viva Louvin, Fed. Verdi, Alé, Vallée-UDEUR-Unità socialista, RC, Uniti	6,569	32.8	264
Vierin Ettore	6.6	1,361			FI	1,361	6.8	–
Aloisi Domenico	2.4	491			AN, Centro-destra per Aosta	450	2.2	41
Borluzzi Giancarlo	0.5	112			Alternativa sociale	112	0.6	–
Total	100	20,643			Total	20,010	100	633
Bolzano[d] (May)								
Benussi Giovanni	42.3	23,520	50.0	25,619	AN, FI, LN, Lista Benussi, Unitalia, DC	21,283	41.5	2,237
Salghetti Drioli Giovanni	34.8	19,400	50.0	25,612	DS, Margherita, RC, Italia dei valori, Fed. verdi, UDC, SDI, Projekt Bozen (SVP)	17,707	34.5	1,693
Pichler Rolle Elmar	16.7	9,327			SVP	9,109	17.7	218
Zanella Cristina	2.1	1,161			Alternativa-Enrosadira-Alternative	1,095	2.1	66
Carlini Carlo	1.7	954			PdCI	898	1.7	56
Trevisan Donatella	1.2	688			Antiproibizionisti	665	1.3	23
Klotz Eva	1.2	657			Union für Südtirol	628	1.2	29
Total	100	55,707	100	51,231	Total	51,385	100	4,322
Bolzano[d] (November)								
Spagnolli Luigi	50.3	28,992			Südtiroler Volkspartei, DS, Margherita, Verdi, RC, Projekt Bozen, SDI, UDC, Italia dei valori, Ladins	26,890	51.1	2,102
Benussi Giovanni	45.2	26,032			AN, FI, Lista Benussi, Democrazia cristiana per le autonomie, Unitalia, LN, Nuovo PSI	23,376	44.4	2,656
Trevisan Donatella	1.4	798			Nautilus cittadinanza attiva Bozen aktiv	761	1.4	37
Delli Zotti Viviana	1.4	781			Al centro con Cigolla	746	1.4	35
Munerato Luciano	1.0	570			PdCI	531	1.0	39
Bonsignore Alex	0.5	290			Partito per tutti	279	0.5	11
Marangoni Patrizia	0.2	119			Südtiroler VolksBewegung	118	0.2	1
Total	100	57,582			Total	52,701	100	4,881

TABLE B3. Election of Mayors in Provincial Capitals in 2005 (with run-offs) (cont.)

City	Mayoral candidate[a]	1st round (%)	Run-off round (%)	1st round votes	Run-off round votes	Parties and supporting civic lists at both voting rounds[b]	1st round votes for supp. lists	% votes for supp. lists at 1st round	Votes for cand. alone[c]
Trento	Pacher Alberto	64.3		38,514		Civica per il governo del Trentino, Trento democratica per l'Ulivo, Fed. verdi e democratici, Socialisti e democratici per Trento, Partito autonomista Trentino tirolese, Centro pop. autonomista per Trento, Leali al Trentino, PdCI	35,498	63.9	3,016
	Zampiccoli Ettore	11.1		6,642		FI	6,442	11.6	200
	Divina Sergio	6.5		3,890		LN, Civica autonomista Port'Aquila	3,428	6.2	462
	Coppola Lucia	5.7		3,410		RC	3,172	5.7	238
	Coradello Antonio	3.9		2,366		AN	2,195	3.9	171
	Tarolli Flavio Maria	3.7		2,195		Unione di centro	2,135	3.8	60
	Firmani Bruno	2.0		1,202		Italia dei valori	1,169	2.1	33
	Taverna Claudia	1.7		1,013		Lista Taverna	933	1.7	80
	De Paoli Claudio	1.1		636		Su la testa Trento	599	1.1	37
	Total	100		59,868		Total	55,571	100	4,297
Sassari	Ganau Gianfranco	58.1		46,000		DS, Margherita, UDEUR, Progetto Sardegna, PS d'Azione, SDI-Soc. uniti, Autonomia socialista, RC	41,430	56.9	4,570
	Milla Sergio	36.4		28,830		FI, AN, UDC, Sardegna sveglia, Riformatori sardi, Rinascita sassarese, Forza Paris, UDS-Others, Nuovo PSI	27,802	38.2	1,028
	Piana Salvatore	3.3		2,579		Uniti per Sassari	2,354	3.2	225
	Mele Massimo	1.3		996		Lista Angioy	552	0.8	444
	Satta Giovanni Maria	0.9		749		Sardigna Natzione	621	0.9	128
	Total	100		79,154		Total	72,759	100	6,395

Nuoro

Demuru Zidda Mario	56.5	13,805			69.0	-1,987
Margherita-Civic, DS, SDI-Soc. uniti, UDEUR, RC, PS d'Azione, Fed. verdi-Aut. soc., PdCI				15,792		
Tupponi Giuseppe	21.6	5,266		3,318	14.5	1,948
Città in comune						
Capelli Roberto	16.5	4,034		3,387	14.8	647
UDC, Per Nuoro, Forza Paris						
Soddu Leonardo	5.4	1,316		397	1.7	919
Lista tecnica						
Total	100	24,421		22,894	100	1,527

Iglesias

Carta Pierluigi	55.5	7,491	9,285	6,130	36.4	1,361
DS, Progetto Sardegna, Margherita, PdCI, RC, Giovani per la città						
Steri Giulio	44.5	6,165	7,440	7,226	42.8	-1,061
Centro popolare, FI, Riformatori sardi, Dem. catt. sardi, Rinascita progresso, AN, Fortza Paris-Nuovo PSI (Lista per Iglesias, Lista Fogu)						
Paolo Fogu	25.5	4,666		3,503	20.8	1,163
Lista per Iglesias, Lista Fogu, UDEUR, PS d'Azione						
Total	100	18,322	16,725	16,859	100	1,463

Catania

Scapagnini Umberto	52.1	98,557		100,822	57.0	-2,265
FI, AN, UDC, Nuovo PSI-PLI, Forza Catania, Nuova Sicilia, Noi, Mov. per l'autonomia, Fam. la. solid., UGS, Patto Sicilia, Giovane alleanza, Ama Catania, In centro dem.						
Bianco Enzo	45.7	86,252		72,328	41.0	13,924
DS, Margherita, PdCI, SDI, UDEUR, RC, Fed. verdi, Con Bianco, Lista del Popolo, Italia dei valori, Vivere la città, Margherita						
Attaguile Angelo	0.7	1,298		1,223	0.7	75
DC						
Fiumefreddo Antonino	0.6	1,192		848	0.5	344
Lista Fiumefreddo						
Montalto Giuseppe	0.4	667		649	0.4	18
Alternativa sociale						
Zappalà Alessandra	0.4	666		494	0.3	172
Lista consumatori						
Zaccà Francesco	0.1	219		214	0.1	5
PRI						
Total	100	188,851		176,578	100	12,273

TABLE B3. Election of Mayors in Provincial Capitals in 2005 (with run-offs) (cont.)

City	Mayoral candidate[a]	1st round (%)	Run-off round (%)	1st round votes	Run-off round votes	Parties and supporting civic lists at both voting rounds[b]	1st round votes for supp. lists	% votes for supp. lists at 1st round	Votes for cand. alone[c]
Enna	Agnello Gaspare	56.3		11,279		DS, Margherita, PdCI, RC, SDI-UDEUR, Italia dei valori-Fed. Verdi, Sinistra democratica	11,618	59.0	-339
	Palermo Giovanni	23.5		4,717		FI, UDC, Solidarietà	5,530	28.0	-813
	Ferrari Dante	16.1		3,234		AN	2,080	10.6	1,154
	Lombardo Paolo	1.6		330		Nuovo PSI-Noi siciliani	220	1.1	110
	Cannarozzo Giuseppe	1.3		266		Dem. cristiani-Popolari europei	154	0.8	112
	Gloria Giuseppe	1.2		235		Partito naz. dem.	101	0.5	134
	Total	100		20,061		Total	19,703	100	358
Messina	Genovese Francantonio	45.7	54.6	67,466	64,760	Margherita, Genovese sindaco, DS, Con Francantonio per Messina, UDEUR, SDI, Vince Messina con Antonio Saitta, RC, Fed. verdi, Ricostruire insieme Messina, PdCI, Nuova presenza Giorgio La Pira	53,255	37.6	14,211
	Ragno Luigi	46.0	45.4	67,833	53,939	FI, AN, UDC-DL per Messina con d'Alia, UDC, Nuova Sicilia, La città per l'uomo, Ragno sindaco, Azzurri per Messina, PRI, Alleanza per Messina, UDC Messina nel cuore, Area AN destra sociale, Alleanza giovani, Alleanza rosa, Casa delle Libertà, Alleanza tricolore, Alleanza futura, Patto per la Sicilia, DC per le autonomie, Fieramente messinesi, CDU per Messina	78,694	55.6	-10,861

Romeo Nunzio	7.4	10.853		9,002	6.4	1,851
Mov. per l'autonomia, Sos, Riscatto Messina Mpa, Ama Messina Mpa, Alleanza siciliana						
Clementi Filippo	0.5	732		272	0.2	460
Alternativa sociale						
Alastra Vincenzo	0.4	635		270	0.2	365
Fiamma tricolore						
Total	100	147.519	118.699	141.493	100	6.026

[a] The winning candidate is in bold type.

[b] Lists that supported the candidate only in the run-off are given in parentheses.

[c] The votes for the candidate alone have been calculated as the difference between the number of votes obtained by the candidate at the first round (these comprised both votes cast for the mayoral candidate alone and those cast for the lists supporting the candidate, provided that votes for the supporting list were not accompanied by votes in favor of a mayoral candidate other than that supported by the list) and the number of votes cast for the lists supporting that candidate at the first round.

[d] The Bolzano municipal election was held on 8 and 9 May 2005, and was followed by a run-off vote on 22 May 2005. The winning mayor was not, however, able to form a *giunta* (executive committee); therefore, the voters of Bolzano were again called to the polls on 6 November 2005.

Source: Compiled from data provided by the Ministry of the Interior, Central Election Service.

Provincial Elections, 2005

TABLE B4a. *Voter Turnout at Provincial Elections (first round)*

Province	Voters registered	Actual voters (% of registered)	Actual voters	Valid ballots (% of voters)	Blank ballots (% of voters)	Invalid or contested ballots (% of voters)	Valid ballots	Votes cast for president alone (% of valid ballots)
3 and 4 April 2005								
Viterbo	251,506	79.8	200,810	93.7	3.0	3.3	188,098	5.6
Caserta	720,660	75.6	544,672	91.7	4.5	3.8	499,552	2.8
8 and 9 May 2005								
Cagliari	476,468	62.9	299,754	92.8	2.8	4.4	278,159	15.1
Carbonia-Iglesias	119,168	67.8	80,838	94.1	2.7	3.2	76,098	6.0
Medio Campidano	92,551	72.4	67,004	89.6	4.2	6.2	60,005	2.7
Nuoro	145,837	70.7	103,035	93.7	3.0	3.3	96,569	5.2
Ogliastra	52,457	72.7	38,145	95.6	1.7	2.7	36,465	3.8
Olbia-Tempio	121,792	73.7	89,725	95.2	0.0	4.8	85,453	4.3
Oristano	152,506	68.7	104,793	94.6	2.5	2.9	99,139	3.1
Sassari	294,153	72.5	213,268	92.4	4.2	3.3	197,120	8.0
Total	2,427,098	71.8	1,742,044	92.8	3.4	3.8	1,616,658	6.3

Sources: Compiled from data provided by the Ministry of the Interior, Central Election Service. The data for the province of Viterbo were drawn from the prefecture of Viterbo Web site (http://www.utgviterbo.it/Elezioni_Referendum/el2005/el2005.htm).

TABLE B4b. *Voter Turnout at Provincial Elections (second round)*

Province	Voters registered	Actual voters (% of registered)	Actual voters	Valid ballots (% of voters)	Blank ballots (% of voters)	Invalid or contested ballots (% of voters)	Diff. in voters (% of reg. voters) between 1st & 2nd ballots	Diff. in valid votes (% of reg. voters) between 1st & 2nd ballots
17 and 18 April 2005								
Viterbo	251,506	65.8	165,418	97.2	0.9	1.9	−14.0	−10.9
22 and 23 May 2005								
Olbia-Tempio	121,792	62.3	75,895	98.4	0.6	1.0	−11.4	−8.8
Total	373,298	64.6	241,313	97.6	0.8	1.6	−13.2	−10.2

Source: Compiled from data provided by the Ministry of the Interior, Central Election Service.

TABLE B5. *Provincial Elections of 3 and 4 April 2005 and 8 and 9 May 2005, Votes for Party Lists (percentages)*

Province	No. candidates	No. lists	Other c-l parties[a]	Rifond. com-unista	Fed. verdi[b]	Italia dei valori[c]	Com-unisti italiani	DS	SDI[d]	La Margh.	UDEUR	UDC	Nuovo PSI	FI	AN	Other c-r parties[e]	Other lists[f]	Total
Viterbo	5	14	–	6.2	2.0	–	2.8	19.5	4.4	9.3	–	9.4	2.5	19.8	17.7	1.4	5.0	100
Caserta	5	25	4.5	3.8	3.3	1.2	1.8	12.4	5.3	11.8	7.8	9.4	3.2	15.6	11.1	6.6	2.2	100
Cagliari	7	22	8.5	5.8	1.4	2.5	2.8	14.7	3.9	9.6	3.5	9.0	–	11.2	8.0	14.9	4.2	100
Carbonia-Iglesias	5	19	7.7	6.3	–	1.7	2.6	17.8	6.5	9.2	3.0	17.3	1.2	8.6	4.4	8.0	5.7	100
Medio Campidano	6	19	9.7	6.1	0.9	2.2	3.4	23.3	4.4	11.5	5.9	4.6	2.3	6.0	7.8	3.8	8.1	100
Nuoro	5	15	16.1	6.5	–	–	4.6	17.7	9.5	14.1	–	7.0	–	4.5	5.4	11.3	3.3	100
Ogliastra	3	15	9.7	4.5	–	–	3.1	15.7	8.2	14.1	5.4	6.7	3.0	10.3	3.6	9.7	6.0	100
Olbia-Tempio	5	15	12.0	–	–	–	–	13.8	–	12.6	7.8	10.4	2.5	15.4	10.4	8.4	6.7	100
Oristano	4	16	11.4	4.7	0.4	–	–	12.3	4.6	11.4	0.0	9.9	1.0	7.6	8.4	25.9	2.4	100
Sassari	5	23	13.4	5.1	1.1	1.0	1.6	13.2	5.4	10.8	9.3	4.0	0.6	12.7	7.8	7.7	6.3	100

[a] The heading "Other center-left parties" includes all the (minor and civic) lists affiliated with the center-left alliance at the first round, as well as those that affiliated at the second round.

[b] In Viterbo, Fed. verdi-Others; in Nuoro, Fed. verdi-Aut. soc.

[c] In Caserta, Italia dei valori-Lista consumatori.

[d] In Viterbo, SDI-UDEUR-Others; in Cagliari, Carbonia-Iglesias, Medio Campidano, Nuoro, Ogliastra, Oristano, and Sassari, SDI-Soc. uniti.

[e] The heading "Other center-right parties" includes all the (minor and civic) lists affiliated with the center-right alliance at the first round, as well as those that affiliated at the second round.

[f] The heading "Other lists" includes all those lists not affiliated with any alliance. It includes, besides the civic lists, the lists of parties with a presence throughout the country, such as Alternativa sociale and the Repubblicani europei, unless they were allied with one or the other of the two main alliances.

Sources: Compiled from data provided by the Ministry of the Interior, Central Election Service. The data for the province of Viterbo were drawn from the prefecture of Viterbo Web site (http://www.utgviterbo.it/Elezioni_Referendum/el2005/el2005.htm).

TABLE B6. *Election of Provincial Presidents*

3 and 4 April 2005 (with runoff round 17 and 18 April)

Province	Presidential candidate[a]	1st round (%)	Run-off round (%)	1st round votes	Run-off round votes	Parties and supporting civic lists at both voting rounds[b]	1st round votes for supp. lists	1st round votes for supp. lists (%)	Votes for cand. alone
Viterbo	Mazzoli Alessandro	36.1	52.3	67,899	84,145	DS, Margherita, SDI-UDEUR-Others, PdCI (RC, Fed. Verdi-Others)	64,054	36.0	3,845
	Battistoni Francesco	49.7	47.7	93,519	76,618	FI, AN, UDC, Nuovo PSI, PRI, Il Trifoglio	90,202	50.8	3,317
	Battisti Bengasi	9.1		16,973		RC, Fed. Verdi-Others	14,598	8.2	2,375
	Gigli Ugo	3.3		6,254		Tuscia	5,606	3.2	648
	Barboni Angelo	1.8		3,453		Alternativa sociale	3,185	1.8	268
	Total	100	100	188,098	160,763	Total	177,645	100	10,453
Caserta	De Franciscis Alessandro	52.3		261,095		DS, Margherita, UDEUR, SDI, RC, Fed. verdi,Per De Franciscis, PdCI, Italia dei valori-Lista consumatori, Democristiani, PRI, Repubblicani europei	252,230	51.9	8,865
	Cosentino Nicola	45.6		227,644		FI, AN, UDC, Nuovo PSI, Democrazia cristiana, Partito liberale-Others, Mov. idea soc. Rauti, Mov. pro pensionati, Consumatori	222,935	45.9	4,709
	Di Benedetto Giuseppe	1.1		5,674		Alternativa sociale	5,476	1.2	198
	Tavoletta Vincenzo	0.8		3,903		Partito soc. lib. auton.	3,883	0.8	20
	Cirillo Giuseppe	0.2		1,236		Preservativi gratis	1,109	0.2	127
	Total	100		499,552		Total	485,633	100	13,919

8 and 9 May 2005 (with runoff round 22 and 23 May)

Cagliari		%	Votes		Votes	%	
	Milia Graziano Ernesto	51.8	143,992	DS, Margherita, RC, PS d'Azione, SDI-Soc. uniti, Progetto Sardegna, UDEUR, PdCI, Italia dei valori, Fed. verdi, Ambientalisti	124,403	52.7	19,589
	Delogu Mariano	44.2	122,936	FI, Riformatori sardi, UDC, AN, Fortza Paris, PRI UDS PN	101,946	43.2	20,990
	Pirina Matteo	1.0	2,891	A.c.p.	2,710	1.1	181
	Angioni Raffaele	0.8	2,217	Sardigna natzione	2,034	0.9	183
	Pitzurra Elisabetta	0.8	2,209	IRS	1,900	0.8	309
	Massa Irene	0.7	2,035	Progetto donna	1,516	0.6	519
	Pisano Antonio	0.7	1,879	N.a.t.	1,646	0.7	233
	Total	100	278,159	Total	236,155	100	42,004
Carbonia-Iglesias	Gaviano Pierfranco	54.8	41,733	DS, Margherita, SDI-Soc. uniti, RC, PS d'Azione, Progetto Sardegna, UDEUR, PdCI, Italia dei valori	39,224	54.9	2,509
	Macciò A. Pietro Mauro	39.5	30,026	UDC, FI, Riformatori sardi, AN, Nuovo PSI, Fortza Paris, PRI	28,239	39.5	1,787
	Masciarelli Alessandro	4.3	3,301	UDS prog. nazional.	3,069	4.3	232
	Sedda Giovannino	0.9	701	IRS	653	0.9	48
	Cossu Sergio Gabriele	0.5	337	Sardigna natzione	318	0.4	19
	Total	100	76,098	Total	71,503	100	4,595
Medio Campidano	Tocco Fulvio	67.2	40,332	DS, Margherita, RC, UDEUR, Progetto Sardegna, PS d'Azione, SDI-Soc. uniti, PdCI, Italia dei valori, Fed. verdi	39,287	67.4	1,045
	Atzori Francesco	24.3	14,593	AN, FI, UDC, Riformatori sardi, Nuovo PSI	14,327	24.5	266
	Spiga Giuseppe	2.7	1,600	N.a.t.	1,537	2.6	63

TABLE B6. *Election of Provincial Presidents (cont.)*

Province	Presidential candidate[a]	1st round (%)	Run-off round (%)	1st round votes	Run-off round votes	Parties and supporting civic lists at both voting rounds[b]	1st round votes for supp. lists	1st round votes for supp. lists (%)	Votes for cand. alone
	Cosentino Nicola	45.6		227,644		FI, AN, UDC, Nuovo PSI, Democrazia	222,935	45.9	4,709
	Agabbio Angelo Giuseppe	2.4		1,461		Nuovi prov. Medio Campidano	1,412	2.4	49
	Aresti Silvio	1.9		1,148		Autonomia socialista	965	1.7	183
	Sedda Francesco	1.5		871		IRS	831	1.4	40
	Total	100		60,005		Total	58,359	100	1,646
Nuoro	Deriu Roberto	60.6		58,488		DS, Margherita, SDI-Soc. uniti, Progetto Sardegna, PS d'Azione, PdCI, Fed. verdi-Aut. soc.	56,746	62.0	1,742
	Ladu Silvestro	29.0		27,975		Fortza Paris, UDC, AN, FI, Riformatori sardi	25,784	28.2	2,191
	Rubanu Pietrina	6.9		6,687		RC	5,983	6.5	704
	Cumpostu Sebastiano	2.1		2,054		Sardigna natzione	1,826	2.0	228
	Soro Pasqualina	1.4		1,365		IRS	1,235	1.3	130
	Total	100		96,569		Total	91,574	100	4,995
Ogliastra	Carta Pier Luigi	60.0		21,897		DS, Margherita, SDI-Soc. uniti, PS d'Azione, UDEUR, RC, Progetto Sardegna, PdCI	21,282	60.6	615
	Murru Attilio	34.0		12,380		FI, UDC, UDS. prog. nazional., Fortza Paris, AN, Nuovo PSI	11,703	33.4	677
	Deidda Sergio	6.0		2,188		Mov. pop. tutela ambiente	2,089	6.0	99
	Total	100		36,465		Total	35,074	100	1,391
Olbia-Tempio	Murrighile A. Pietrina	46.8	51.9	40,039	38,757	DS, Margherita, Gallura unita, UDEUR, PS d'Azione	37,812	46.3	2,227

	Candidate	%	Votes	Run-off %	Run-off votes	Supporting lists	Votes	%	
	Fideli Livio Salvatore	46.4	39,684	48.1	35,936	FI, UDC, AN, Riformatori sardi, Fortza Paris, Nuovo PSI, PRI	38,489	47.1	1,195
	Marongiu Gian Mario	4.4	3,739			Mov. pop. tutela ambiente	3,623	4.4	116
	Pala Giovanni Luigi	1.4	1,158			IRS	1,093	1.3	65
	Careddu Domenico	1.0	833			Sardigna natzione	771	0.9	62
	Total	100	85,453	100	74,693	Total	81,788	100	3,665
Oristano	**Onida Pasquale**	52.6	52,021			Fortza Paris, UDC, AN, FI, UDS prog. nazional, Riformatori sardi, Nuovo PSI	50,767	52.9	1,254
	Cadoni Silvano	44.9	44,644			DS, Margherita, PS d'Azione, RC, SDI-Soc. uniti, Insieme, Fed. verdi	43,079	44.8	1,565
	Sanna Francesco	1.8	1,819			IRS	1,678	1.7	141
	Muroni Marcello	0.7	655			Sardigna natzione	589	0.6	66
	Total	100	99,139			Total	96,113	100	3,026
Sassari	**Giudici Alessandra**	60.7	119,693			DS, Margherita, UDEUR, PS d'Azione, Progetto Sardegna, SDI-Soc. uniti, RC, PdCI, Autonomia socialista, Fed. verdi, Italia dei valori	110,596	61.0	9,097
	Poddighe Stefano	32.6	64,252			FI, AN, UDC, Civic list, Fortza Paris, Riformatori sardi, Rinascita sassarese, Nuovo PSI, Part. pensionati	59,447	32.7	4,805
	Sale Gavino	4.3	8,384			IRS	6,758	3.7	1,626
	Pinna Giovanni Agostino	1.2	2,402			Democrazia cristiana	2,296	1.3	106
	Marras G. Pietro Agostino	1.2	2,389			Sardigna natzione	2,293	1.3	96
	Total	100	197,120			Total	181,390	100	15,730

a The winning candidate is in bold type.

b Lists that supported the candidate only in the run-off are given in parentheses.

Source: Compiled from data provided by the Ministry of the Interior, Central Election Service. The data for the province of Viterbo were drawn from the prefecture of Viterbo Web site (http://www.utgviterbo.it/Elezioni_Referendum/el2005/el2005.htm).

Regional Elections, 2005

TABLE B7a. *Voter Turnout at the Regional Elections of 3 and 4 April 2005*

Region	Voters registered	Actual voters (% of registered)	Actual voters	Valid ballots (% of voters)	Blank ballots (% of voters)	Invalid or contested ballots (% of voters)	Valid ballots	Votes cast for president alone (% of valid ballots)
Piedmont	3,651,876	71.4	2,607,115	93.1	1.7	5.2	2,428,014	15.7
Lombardy	7,638,813	73.0	5,573,402	94.8	1.5	3.7	5,285,975	17.2
Liguria	1,406,865	69.6	979,780	95.5	1.1	3.4	935,281	13.0
Veneto	3,913,421	72.4	2,834,868	95.3	1.5	3.2	2,700,742	14.7
Emilia-Romagna	3,441,210	76.7	2,638,414	95.8	1.4	2.9	2,527,559	9.7
Tuscany	3,022,354	71.4	2,156,460	95.8	1.5	1.2	2,066,096	12.6
Marche	1,287,323	71.5	919,925	94.1	2.4	3.6	865,503	8.7
Umbria	716,367	74.2	531,512	95.3	1.4	3.3	506,437	9.4
Lazio	4,609,125	72.6	3,347,956	96.0	1.1	3.0	3,213,036	13.9
Abruzzo	1,203,608	68.7	826,510	94.8	1.9	3.3	783,504	6.4
Campania	4,867,313	67.7	3,293,673	93.5	2.9	3.6	3,078,322	6.6
Puglia	3,518,164	70.5	2,480,064	94.3	—	—	2,338,391	8.5
Calabria	1,845,431	64.4	1,188,237	94.6	2.1	3.3	1,124,526	3.1
Basilicata[a]	554,266	67.2	372,338	94.9	1.4	3.7	353,464	2.6
Total[b]	41,676,136	71.4	29,750,254	94.8	1.7	3.4	28,206,850	12.0

[a] Basilicata voters went to the polls on 17 and 18 April 2005.
[b] Percentages for blank and invalid or contested ballots exclude the figures for Puglia. Detailed data were unavailable for the region.

Sources: Compiled from data provided by the Ministry of the Interior, Central Election Service.

TABLE B7b. Regional Elections of 3 and 4 April 2005, Votes for Party Lists (percentages)

Region	No. pres. candi-dates	No. lists	Other c-l parties[a]	Rifond. comunista	Fed. verdi	Italia dei valori[b]	Com-unisti italiani	DS	SDI[c]	La Mar-gherita	UDEUR[d]	Uniti nell' Ulivo	PRI	UDC	Nuovo PSI[e]	Demo-crazia cristiana	FI	AN	Lega Nord	Alterna-tiva sociale	Mov. soc. idea	Other c-r parties[f]	Other lists[g]	Total
Piedmont	4	20	3.2	6.4	2.8	1.5	2.6	20.1	2.4	10.4	0.5	—	—	4.6	—	0.7	22.4	9.5	8.5	0.7	—	3.7	—	100
Lombardy	4	16	2.6	5.7	2.9	1.4	2.4	—	—	—	—	27.1	—	3.8	0.8	—	26.0	8.7	15.8	1.2	—	0.3	1.3	100
Liguria	3	20	5.6	6.6	2.0	1.3	2.7	—	—	—	0.9	34.3	—	3.3	—	—	19.7	7.1	4.7	0.7	—	11.1	—	100
Veneto	4	16	6.5	3.5	3.0	1.3	1.5	—	—	—	0.3	24.3	—	6.4	1.4	—	22.7	8.1	14.7	0.9	—	—	5.4	100
Emilia-Romagna	4	13	—	5.7	3.0	1.4	3.4	—	—	—	0.3	48.2	—	3.9	0.8	—	18.2	8.9	4.8	0.7	—	—	0.7	100
Tuscany	5	11	—	8.2	2.8	0.9	4.3	—	—	—	—	48.8	—	3.6	—	—	17.2	10.9	1.2	0.8	—	—	1.3	100
Marche	4	15	0.7	6.3	3.3	1.4	4.0	—	—	—	1.8	40.1	—	7.2	—	1.4	18.0	12.9	0.9	1.3	—	—	0.7	100
Umbria	4	10	—	9.2	2.3	—	5.3	—	—	—	1.2	45.4	—	4.8	1.4	—	15.8	13.7	—	0.9	—	—	—	100
Lazio	3	24	7.8	5.9	2.6	1.0	2.3	—	—	—	1.7	27.1	—	7.8	1.1	—	15.4	16.9	—	1.2	0.5	8.6	0.1	100
Abruzzo	3	17	0.3	4.9	2.0	2.4	2.9	18.6	5.2	16.8	4.7	—	—	8.4	—	2.8	16.0	11.2	—	0.9	0.7	2.2	—	100
Campania	4	21	3.8	4.1	3.5	2.3	2.7	15.3	5.4	16.0	10.3	—	0.9	6.7	2.9	1.9	11.9	10.6	—	1.2	0.1	0.4	—	100
Puglia	4	20	5.0	5.1	1.6	1.8	2.3	16.6	4.0	9.7	3.3	—	—	7.8	2.2	0.3	17.8	12.1	—	0.4	0.5	9.1	0.4	100
Calabria	4	17	10.2	5.1	—	—	—	15.4	6.8	14.5	8.7	—	—	10.4	5.4	—	10.0	9.9	—	0.6	0.4	2.5	0.1	100
Basilicata[h]	5	14	1.7	4.7	5.6	2.7	4.1	—	—	—	11.1	38.9	—	7.9	2.2	—	12.7	6.5	—	0.7	—	0.9	0.3	100
Total	55	234	3.3	5.6	2.3	1.4	2.6	6.1	1.6	4.7	2.5	21.9	0.1	5.8	1.3	0.4	18.7	10.6	5.6	0.9	0.1	2.7	1.8	100

a Minor and civic lists affiliated with the center-left alliance.
b In Campania, Italia dei valori-Lista consumatori.
c In Puglia, SDI-Unità soc.; in Calabria, SDI-Others.
d In Puglia, UDEUR-RI.
e In Veneto, Nuovo PSI-Others; in Puglia, Nuovo PSI-PRI.
f Minor and civic lists affiliated with the center-right alliance.
g All lists not affiliated with any alliance.
h Basilicata voters went to the polls on 17 and 18 April 2005.

Sources: Compiled from data provided by the Ministry of the Interior, Central Election Service.

TABLE B8. Election of Regional Presidents, 3 and 4 April 2005

Region	Presidential candidate[a]	Votes (%)	Votes	Parties and supporting civic lists	Votes for supp. lists	Votes for supp. lists (%)	Votes for cand. alone
Piedmont	Bresso Mercedes	50.8	1,234,354	DS, Margherita, RC, Insieme per Bresso, Fed. verdi, PdCI, SDI, Italia dei valori, UDEUR, Pensionati Europa	1,022,273	50.1	212,081
	Ghigo Enzo	47.2	1,143,993	FI, AN, LN, UDC, Ambienta-lista, Lista consumatori, Socialisti liberali, Partito pensionati	994,727	48.6	149,266
	Ellena Lodovico	1.0	24,650	Alternativa sociale	14,131	0.7	10,519
	Rotondi Gianfranco	1.0	25,017	Democrazia cristiana	14,204	0.6	10,813
	Total	100	2,428,014	Total	2,045,335	100	382,679
Lombardy	Formigoni Roberto	53.8	2,846,926	FI, AN, UDC, LN, Nuovo PSI, Polo laico	2,424,317	55.4	422,609
	Sarfatti Riccardo	43.2	2,282,424	Uniti nell'Ulivo, PdCI, Fed. verdi, RC, Italia dei valori, Partito pensionati	1,843,744	42.1	438,680
	Invernizzi Gianmario	2.7	142,689	Alternativa sociale-Others	101,177	2.3	41,512
	Marsili Marco	0.3	13,936	Liberaldemocratici	3,800	0.2	5,136
	Total	100	5,285,975	Total	4,373,038	100	907,937
Liguria	Burlando Claudio	52.6	492,352	Uniti nell'Ulivo, RC, Gente della Liguria, PdCI, Fed. verdi, Italia dei valori, UDEUR, Partito pensionati, Consumatori, Patto	434,403	53.4	57,949
	Biasotti Sandro Mario	46.6	435,601	FI, Lista Sandro Biasotti, AN, LN, UDC, Castellaneta, Socialisti liberali, Pensionati-Animalisti, Lista consumatori	374,119	45.9	61,482
	Riccobaldi Angelo	0.8	7,328	Alternativa sociale	5,401	0.7	1,927
	Total	100	935,281	Total	813,923	100	121,358
Veneto	Galan Giancarlo	50.6	1,365,698	FI, LN, AN, UDC, Nuovo PSI-Others	1,225,878	53.3	138,820
	Carrara Massimo	42.3	1,144,358	Uniti nell'Ulivo, Per il Veneto, RC, Fed. verdi, PdCI, Italia dei valori, Liga fronte Veneto, Lista consumatori, UDEUR	933,579	40.4	213,779
	Panto Giorgio	6.0	162,037	Progetto Nord-Est	125,417	5.4	36,620
	Bussinello Roberto	1.1	28,649	Alternativa sociale	23,426	0.9	8,223
	Total	100	2,700,742	Total	2,303,360	100	397,442

Region	Candidate	Votes	%	Coalition / Lists	Votes	%	Votes
Emilia-Romagna	**Errani Vasco**						
	Monaco Carlo	1585714	62.7	Uniti nell'Ulivo, RC, PdCI, Fed. verdi, Italia dei valori, UDEUR	1,414,872	62.0	170,842
	Barbieri Bruno	889231	35.2	FI, AN, LN, UDC, Nuovo PSI	835,326	36.6	53,905
	Correggiari Gianni	27220	1.1	Lista consumatori	15,656	0.7	11,564
		25394	1.0	Alternativa sociale	15,022	0.7	10,372
	Total	2527,559	100	Total	2,280,876	100	246,683
Tuscany	**Martini Claudio**						
	Antichi Alessandro	1,185,264	57.4	Uniti nell'Ulivo, PdCI, Fed. verdi, Italia dei valori	1,024,129	56.8	161,135
	Ciabatti Luca	678,254	32.8	FI, AN, UDC, LN	595,924	32.9	82,330
	Macelloni Renzo	151,657	7.3	RC	148,051	8.2	3,606
	Gozzoli Marzio	30,068	1.5	Socialisti e laici	23,377	1.3	6,691
		20,853	1.0	Alternativa sociale	14,646	0.8	6,207
	Total	2,066,096	100	Total	1,806,127	100	259,969
Marche	**Spacca Gian Mario**						
	Massi Francesco	499,793	57.7	Uniti nell'Ulivo, RC, PdCI, Fed. verdi, UDEUR, Italia dei valori, Liste civiche Marche	454,970	57.6	44,823
	Tiraboschi A. Maria	333,635	38.6	FI, AN, UDC, LN	308,416	39.0	25,219
	Rosini Vincenzo	19,802	2.3	DC, Soc.-PRI-PLI-PSDI-Others	15,967	2.1	3,835
		12,273	1.4	Alternativa sociale, No euro	10,433	1.3	1,840
	Total	865,503	100	Total	789,786	100	75,717
Umbria	**Lorenzetti Maria Rita**						
	Lafranco Pietro	319,109	63.0	Uniti nell'Ulivo, RC, PdCI, Fed. verdi, UDEUR	291,120	63.4	27,989
	Ramadori Marcello	170,357	33.6	FI, AN, UDC	157,220	34.3	13,137
	Romagnoli Luca	9,561	1.9	Nuovo PSI	6,681	1.4	2,880
		7,410	1.5	Alternativa sociale	3,979	0.9	3,431
	Total	506,437	100	Total	459,000	100	47,437
Lazio	**Marazzo Pietro**	1,628,486	50.7	Uniti nell'Ulivo, Civic list Marrazzo, RC, Fed. verdi, PdCI, UDEUR, Italia dei valori, Consumatori uniti, Forza Roma, Avanti Lazio	1,340,661	48.4	287,825
	Storace Francesco	1,522,198	47.4	AN, FI, UDC, Lista Storace, Nuovo PSI, Il Trifoglio, Mov. soc. idea, Partito liberale-PRI, Partito pensionati, Lista consumatori, Costituente democratica	1,389,830	50.3	132,368
	Mussolini Alessandra	62,352	1.9	Alternativa sociale, Lista quadrifoglio	34,134	1.3	28,218
	Total	3,213,036	100	Total	2,764,625	100	448,411

TABLE B8. *Election of Regional Presidents, 3 and 4 April 2005 (cont.)*

Region	Presidential candidate[a]	Votes (%)	Votes	Parties and supporting civic lists	Votes for supp. lists	Votes for supp. lists (%)	Votes for cand. alone
Abruzzo	Del Turco Ottaviano	58.1	455,307	DS, Margherita, SDI, RC, UDEUR, PdCI, Italia dei valori, Fed. verdi, Socialdemocrazia	424,466	57.8	30,841
	Pace Giovanni	40.6	317,976	FI, AN, UDC, Moderati riformisti, Democrazia cristiana, Rep. soc. lib., Mov. soc. idea	302,353	41.3	15,623
	Bosi Fabrizio	1.3	10,221	Alternativa sociale	5,343	0.9	3,878
	Total	100	783,504	Total	733,162	100	50,342
Campania	Bassolino Antonio	61.6	1,896,664	Margherita, DS, UDEUR, SDI, RC, Fed. verdi, PdCI, Italia dei valori-Lista consumatori, Repubblicani, Democrazia federalista, Rep. europei, Governo civico	1,822,712	63.4	73,952
	Bocchino Italo	34.4	1,057,523	FI, AN, UDC, Nuovo PSI, PRI, Partito pensionati, Mov. soc. idea	963,191	33.5	94,332
	Rotondi Gianfranco	2.1	64,483	Democrazia cristiana	55,223	1.9	9,260
	Mussolini Alessandra	1.9	59,652	Alternativa sociale	33,562	1.2	26,090
	Total	100	3,078,322	Total	2,874,688	100	203,634
Puglia	Vendola Nichi	49.8	1,165,536	DS, Margherita, Lista primavera, RC, PdCI, Fed. verdi, Lista Di Pietro, SDI-Unità soc., UDEUR-RI, Partito pensionati, DC uniti, PSDI-Soc. aut.-Rep. europei	1,064,410	49.8	101,126
	Fitto Raffaele	49.3	1,151,405	FI, AN, UDC, Nuovo PSI-PRI, Mov. soc. idea, Puglia prima di tutto	1,059,869	49.5	91,536
	Galassi Gianfelice	0.5	10,973	Alternativa sociale	9,307	0.4	1,666
	Scalabrini Laura	0.4	10,477	Democrazia cristiana	6,741	0.3	3,736
	Total	100	2,338,391	Total	2,140,327	100	198,064
Calabria	Loiero Agazio	59.0	662,722	DS, Margherita, UDEUR, SDI-Others, RC, Progetto Calabrie, Uniti per la Calabria, Rep. europei-Others, Lista consumatori	662,137	60.7	585
	Abramo Sergio	39.7	446,634	UDC, FI, AN, Nuovo PSI, Con Abramo, Mov. soc. idea	419,211	38.6	27,423

Aloi Fortunato	1.1	12,577	Alternativa sociale	7,184	0.6	5,393
Bilello Giuseppe	0.2	2,593	Dem crist ecologisti	816	0.1	1,777
Total	100	1124526	Total	1,089,348	100	35,178
Basilicata[b]						
De Filippo Vito	**67.0**	**236,814**	Uniti nell'Ulivo, UDEUR, Fed. verdi, RC, PdCI, Italia dei valori, Patto	236,948	68.8	-134
Latronico Cosimo	28.8	101,843	FI, UDC, AN, Federazione di centro	96,408	28.0	5,435
Torrio Margherita	2.5	8,783	Nuovo PSI	7,711	2.2	1,072
Fiore Roberto	1.0	3,578	Alternativa sociale	2,259	0.7	1,319
Mancuso Angela Rosa	0.7	2,446	Unità popolare	938	0.3	1,508
Total	100	353,464	Total	344,264	100	9,200

[a] The winning candidate is in bold type.
[b] Basilicata voters went to the polls on 17 and 18 April 2005.
Source: Compiled from data provided by the Ministry of the Interior, Central Election Service.

Referendum of 12 and 13 June 2005

TABLE B9a. *Referendum of 12 and 13 June 2005, No. 1: Restrictions on Clinical and Experimental Research on Embryos*

Region	Voters registered	Actual voters	Voters (% of registered)	Valid ballots	Valid ballots (% of voters)	Votes in favor	Votes in favor (%)	Votes against	Votes against (%)	Invalid ballots	Of which blank
Valle d'Aosta	100,402	26,591	26.5	25,391	95.5	22,691	89.4	2,700	10.6	1,200	899
Piedmont	3,524,793	1,062,340	30.1	1,022,349	96.2	898,366	87.9	123,983	12.1	39,991	27,595
Lombardy	7,435,867	1,988,982	26.7	1,926,144	96.8	1,692,340	87.9	233,804	12.1	62,838	44,787
Liguria	1,341,470	457,159	34.1	443,469	97.0	408,068	92.0	35,401	8.0	13,690	9,738
Trentino-Alto Adige	752,416	156,004	20.7	150,149	96.2	126,142	84.0	24,007	16.0	5,855	4,524
Friuli-Venezia Giulia	983,782	297,506	30.2	287,826	96.7	251,356	87.3	36,470	12.7	9,680	6,940
Veneto	3,710,153	943,756	25.4	910,567	96.5	783,956	86.1	126,611	13.9	33,189	24,842
Emilia-Romagna	3,348,058	1,392,557	41.6	1,352,594	97.1	1,243,677	91.9	108,917	8.1	39,963	30,116
Tuscany	2,939,982	1,169,101	39.8	1,135,710	97.1	1,054,382	92.8	81,328	7.2	33,391	24,771
Marche	1,219,342	327,229	26.8	312,010	95.3	276,359	88.6	35,651	11.4	15,219	11,618
Umbria	690,981	205,658	29.8	197,447	96.0	177,888	90.1	19,559	9.9	8,211	5,605
Lazio	4,390,682	1,381,653	31.5	1,343,378	97.2	1,219,387	90.8	123,991	9.2	38,275	25,349
Abruzzo	1,058,069	245,674	23.2	231,789	94.3	203,954	88.0	27,835	12.0	13,885	10,912
Molise	264,592	47,677	18.0	44,383	93.1	38,487	86.7	5,896	13.3	3,294	2,382
Campania	4,551,112	712,708	15.7	680,860	95.5	605,168	88.9	75,692	11.1	31,848	21,922
Puglia	3,266,781	501,710	15.4	480,067	95.7	422,614	88.0	57,453	12.0	21,643	15,108
Calabria	1,593,533	202,566	12.7	190,319	94.0	169,065	88.8	21,254	11.2	12,247	8,472
Basilicata	482,296	76,995	16.0	72,425	94.1	64,071	88.5	8,354	11.5	4,570	3,091
Sicily	4,034,721	636,108	15.8	599,886	94.3	511,764	85.3	88,122	14.7	36,222	21,802
Sardinia	1,377,713	374,162	27.2	357,278	95.5	320,542	89.7	36,736	10.3	16,884	13,142
Total	47,066,745	12,206,136	25.9	11,764,041	96.4	10,490,277	89.2	1,273,764	10.8	442,095	313,615

Source: Compiled from data provided by the Ministry of the Interior, Central Election Service.

TABLE B9b. Referendum of 12 and 13 June 2005, No. 2: Restrictions on Access to Artificial Insemination

Region	Voters registered	Actual voters	Voters (% of registered)	Valid ballots	Valid ballots (% of voters)	Votes in favor	Votes in favor (%)	Votes against	Votes against (%)	Invalid ballots	Of which blank
Valle d'Aosta	100,402	26,587	26.5	25,313	95.2	22,728	89.8	2,585	10.2	1,274	983
Piedmont	3,524,793	1,062,241	30.1	1,020,110	96.0	902,188	88.4	117,922	11.6	42,131	29,757
Lombardy	7,435,867	1,988,759	26.7	1,922,853	96.7	1,701,173	88.5	221,680	11.5	65,906	48,255
Liguria	1,341,470	457,123	34.1	442,983	96.9	410,135	92.6	32,848	7.4	14,140	10,297
Trentino-Alto Adige	752,416	155,985	20.7	150,019	96.2	130,942	87.3	19,077	12.7	5,966	4,644
Friuli-Venezia Giulia	983,782	297,442	30.2	287,240	96.6	252,477	87.9	34,763	12.1	10,202	7,495
Veneto	3,710,153	943,323	25.4	908,645	96.3	788,342	86.8	120,303	13.2	34,678	26,866
Emilia-Romagna	3,348,058	1,392,424	41.6	1,350,552	97.0	1,248,437	92.4	102,115	7.6	41,872	32,209
Tuscany	2,939,982	1,169,058	39.8	1,133,729	97.0	1,059,084	93.4	74,645	6.6	35,329	26,780
Marche	1,219,342	327,414	26.9	311,192	95.0	276,962	89.0	34,230	11.0	16,222	12,383
Umbria	690,981	205,614	29.8	197,026	95.8	178,553	90.6	18,473	9.4	8,588	6,002
Lazio	4,390,682	1,381,622	31.5	1,342,564	97.2	1,231,449	91.7	111,115	8.3	39,058	26,654
Abruzzo	1,058,069	245,338	23.2	231,265	94.3	205,051	88.7	26,214	11.3	14,073	11,410
Molise	264,592	47,680	18.0	44,222	92.7	38,430	86.9	5,792	13.1	3,458	2,541
Campania	4,551,112	712,726	15.7	679,795	95.4	609,239	89.6	70,556	10.4	32,931	23,259
Puglia	3,266,781	501,632	15.4	478,729	95.4	424,051	88.6	54,678	11.4	22,903	16,411
Calabria	1,593,533	202,595	12.7	189,822	93.7	169,674	89.4	20,148	10.6	12,773	8,909
Basilicata	482,296	76,979	16.0	72,181	93.8	64,186	88.9	7,995	11.1	4,798	3,313
Sicily	4,034,721	636,090	15.8	598,769	94.1	517,398	86.4	81,371	13.6	37,321	23,186
Sardinia	1,377,713	374,137	27.2	357,000	95.4	324,149	90.8	32,851	9.2	17,137	13,603
Total	47,066,745	12,204,769	25.9	11,744,009	96.2	10,554,648	89.9	1,189,361	10.1	460,760	334,957

Source: Compiled from data provided by the Ministry of the Interior, Central Election Service.

TABLE B9c. *Referendum of 12 and 13 June 2005, No. 3: Provisions Regarding Purpose of Artificial Insemination, Rights of Those Involved, and Access Restrictions*

Region	Voters registered	Actual voters	Voters (% of registered)	Valid ballots	Valid ballots (% of voters)	Votes in favor	Votes in favor (%)	Votes against	Votes against (%)	Invalid ballots	Of which blank
Valle d'Aosta	100,402	26,577	26.5	25,219	94.9	22,336	88.6	2,883	11.4	1,358	1,059
Piedmont	3,524,793	1,061,988	30.1	1,017,293	95.8	886,634	87.2	130,659	12.8	44,695	31,788
Lombardy	7,435,867	1,988,141	26.7	1,918,360	96.5	1,671,192	87.1	247,168	12.9	69,781	51,603
Liguria	1,341,470	457,013	34.1	434,731	95.1	398,808	91.7	35,923	8.3	22,282	10,944
Trentino-Alto Adige	752,416	155,960	20.7	149,444	95.8	127,979	85.6	21,465	14.4	6,516	5,203
Friuli-Venezia Giulia	983,782	297,323	30.2	286,462	96.3	249,089	87.0	37,373	13.0	10,861	8,124
Veneto	3,710,153	943,142	25.4	905,770	96.0	771,981	85.2	133,789	14.8	37,372	29,097
Emilia-Romagna	3,348,058	1,392,267	41.6	1,347,805	96.8	1,234,989	91.6	112,816	8.4	44,462	34,436
Tuscany	2,939,982	1,168,765	39.8	1,131,442	96.8	1,047,405	92.6	84,037	7.4	37,323	28,616
Marche	1,219,342	327,346	26.8	310,377	94.8	273,030	88.0	37,347	12.0	16,969	13,076
Umbria	690,981	205,573	29.8	196,640	95.7	176,250	89.6	20,390	10.4	8,933	6,325
Lazio	4,390,682	1,381,358	31.5	1,339,907	97.0	1,216,751	90.8	123,156	9.2	41,451	28,496
Abruzzo	1,058,069	245,623	23.2	230,869	94.0	202,327	87.6	28,542	12.4	14,754	12,184
Molise	264,592	47,671	18.0	44,157	92.6	37,928	85.9	6,229	14.1	3,514	2,606
Campania	4,551,112	712,666	15.7	677,797	95.1	599,589	88.5	78,208	11.5	34,869	24,469
Puglia	3,266,781	501,580	15.4	477,568	95.2	417,395	87.4	60,173	12.6	24,012	17,414
Calabria	1,593,533	202,547	12.7	189,272	93.4	167,328	88.4	21,944	11.6	13,275	9,495
Basilicata	482,296	76,967	16.0	71,995	93.5	63,439	88.1	8,556	11.9	4,972	3,502
Sicily	4,034,721	635,948	15.8	597,466	93.9	509,117	85.2	88,349	14.8	38,482	24,143
Sardinia	1,377,713	374,050	27.2	356,220	95.2	321,293	90.2	34,927	9.8	17,830	14,135
Total	47,066,745	12,202,505	25.9	11,708,794	96.0	10,394,860	88.8	1,313,934	11.2	493,771	356,715

Source: Compiled from data provided by the Ministry of the Interior, Central Election Service.

TABLE B9d. *Referendum of 12 and 13 June 2005, No. 4: Prohibition of Donor Insemination*

Region	Voters registered	Actual voters	Voters (% of registered)	Valid ballots	Valid ballots (% of voters)	Votes in favor	Votes in favor (%)	Votes against	Votes against (%)	Invalid ballots	Of which blank
Valle d'Aosta	100,402	26,561	26.5	25,156	94.7	19,274	76.6	5,882	23.4	1,405	1,090
Piedmont	3,524,793	1,061,355	30.1	1,016,212	95.7	771,485	75.9	244,727	24.1	45,143	31,712
Lombardy	7,435,867	1,986,141	26.7	1,913,540	96.3	1,447,965	75.7	465,575	24.3	72,601	53,352
Liguria	1,341,470	456,682	34.0	440,517	96.5	359,689	81.7	80,828	18.3	16,165	11,845
Trentino-Alto Adige	752,416	155,848	20.7	149,289	95.8	110,043	73.7	39,246	26.3	6,559	5,102
Friuli-Venezia Giulia	983,782	297,062	30.2	285,793	96.2	212,255	74.3	73,538	25.7	11,269	8,416
Veneto	3,710,153	942,383	25.4	904,449	96.0	660,866	73.1	243,583	26.9	37,934	28,931
Emilia-Romagna	3,348,058	1,391,375	41.6	1,344,697	96.6	1,114,061	82.8	230,636	17.2	46,678	36,097
Tuscany	2,939,982	1,167,800	39.7	1,127,069	96.5	942,673	83.6	184,396	16.4	40,731	31,011
Marche	1,219,342	327,105	26.8	309,694	94.7	240,806	77.8	68,888	22.2	17,411	13,332
Umbria	690,981	205,397	29.7	196,022	95.4	156,054	79.6	39,968	20.4	9,375	6,594
Lazio	4,390,682	1,380,489	31.4	1,337,921	96.9	1,078,559	80.6	259,362	19.4	42,568	29,079
Abruzzo	1,058,069	245,089	23.2	230,404	94.0	178,569	77.5	51,835	22.5	14,685	12,038
Molise	264,592	47,645	18.0	44,115	92.6	33,339	75.6	10,776	24.4	3,530	2,587
Campania	4,551,112	712,334	15.7	676,917	95.0	526,248	77.7	150,669	22.3	35,417	24,797
Puglia	3,266,781	501,367	15.3	476,271	95.0	353,366	74.2	122,905	25.8	25,096	18,130
Calabria	1,593,533	202,477	12.7	188,700	93.2	146,997	77.9	41,703	22.1	13,777	9,644
Basilicata	482,296	76,940	16.0	71,891	93.4	55,580	77.3	16,311	22.7	5,049	3,450
Sicily	4,034,721	635,486	15.8	596,794	93.9	440,304	73.8	156,490	26.2	38,692	23,992
Sardinia	1,377,713	373,836	27.1	355,986	95.2	290,960	81.7	65,026	18.3	17,850	13,965
Total	47,066,745	12,193,372	25.9	11,691,437	95.9	9,139,093	78.2	2,552,344	21.8	501,935	365,164

Source: Compiled from data provided by the Ministry of the Interior, Central Election Service.

Unione Primaries

TABLE B10. *Unione Primary Elections of 16 October 2005*

Region	Fausto Bertinotti	Antonio Di Pietro	Ivan Scalfarotto	Simona Panzino	Alfonso Pecoraro Scanio	Romano Prodi	Clemente Mastella	Total valid votes	Blank ballots (% of total votes)
Valle d'Aosta	14.2	3.7	0.6	0.6	4.8	73.9	2.3	4,846	0.3
Piedmont	15.9	3.8	0.7	0.5	2.2	76.0	0.9	258,953	0.3
Lombardy	16.2	4.0	0.9	0.5	1.8	75.8	0.7	578,046	0.3
Liguria	16.4	2.7	0.7	0.4	1.6	77.3	0.9	141,149	0.4
Trentino-Alto Adige	13.2	4.2	0.8	0.6	2.7	78.1	0.5	40,332	0.4
Friuli-Venezia Giulia	14.6	3.3	1.2	0.7	1.7	77.3	1.2	76,294	0.6
Veneto	12.4	3.9	0.9	0.6	2.0	79.4	0.8	266,779	0.3
Emilia-Romagna	9.4	1.9	0.5	0.4	1.2	86.2	0.5	625,084	0.5
Tuscany	15.8	1.8	0.5	0.3	1.5	79.6	0.6	479,777	0.5
Marche	14.2	2.7	0.5	0.6	2.1	78.6	1.5	133,331	0.4
Umbria	17.5	2.0	0.4	0.4	1.3	77.4	1.0	101,405	0.5
Lazio	17.3	2.9	0.7	0.6	2.5	71.1	5.0	434,335	0.2
Abruzzo	17.0	5.3	0.5	0.4	1.9	68.7	6.1	98,937	0.6
Molise	15.5	12.7	0.4	0.4	1.6	60.2	9.2	24,881	0.6
Campania	14.3	4.2	0.5	0.3	5.0	54.4	21.3	332,316	0.4
Puglia	17.2	3.6	0.5	0.3	2.7	66.0	9.7	193,549	0.4
Calabria	14.5	2.8	0.2	0.5	5.1	58.6	18.3	121,326	0.4
Basilicata	11.5	5.1	0.4	0.4	6.5	56.9	19.1	51,773	0.4
Sicily	15.4	5.8	0.4	0.5	2.5	66.1	9.3	194,181	0.3
Sardinia	17.0	3.6	0.4	0.4	1.3	72.2	5.1	116,618	0.2
Total	14.7	3.3	0.6	0.5	2.2	74.1	4.6	4,273,832	0.4

Source: Compiled from data provided by the Unione Web site (http://www.unioneweb.it).

ABOUT THE EDITORS AND CONTRIBUTORS

Grant Amyot is a Professor in the Department of Political Studies at Queen's University, Kingston, Canada, where he teaches comparative politics.

Marco Clementi is a Researcher in the Faculty of Political Science at the University of Pavia, where he teaches international relations.

Vincent Della Sala is an Associate Professor in the Faculty of Sociology of the University of Trento, where he teaches international politics and institutions.

Giancarlo Gasperoni is an Associate Professor in the Faculty of Letters and Philosophy of the University of Bologna, where he teaches methods of social research, political sociology, and public opinion and polling.

Chris Hanretty is a graduate student in European Politics and Society at Oxford University.

David Hine is an Official Student (Fellow) of Christ Church, Oxford, and Director of the Centre for the Study of Democratic Government in the Department of Politics and International Relations, University of Oxford.

Jonathan Hopkin is an Associate Professor in the Department of Government of the London School of Economics, where he teaches comparative politics.

Francesco Marangoni is a doctoral student in Comparative and European Politics at the University of Siena. His major research interests include the legislative performance of Italian governments.

Chiara Martini is a doctoral student in Public Economic Law at the University of Rome I (La Sapienza). She edits the constitutional developments section of the *European Review of Public Law*.

Alberto Melloni is a Professor in the Faculty of Education Studies at the University of Modena and Reggio Emilia, where he teaches contemporary history and the teaching of history.

Marcello Messori is a Professor in the Faculty of Economics of the University of Rome II (Tor Vergata), where he teaches the economics of financial and currency markets, the economics of information, and the theory of banking.

Salvatore Vassallo is *professore straordinario* in the Roberto Ruffilli Faculty of Political Science at the University of Bologna (Forlì campus), where he teaches political science and comparative politics.

Luca Verzichelli is an Associate Professor in the Faculty of Political Science at the University of Siena, where he teaches about the Italian political system.